THE HARPERCOLLINS
DICTIONARY OF
PHILOSOPHY

Other *HarperCollins* dictionaries

HarperCollins Dictionary of Art Terms and Techniques
HarperCollins Dictionary of Astronomy & Space Science
HarperCollins Dictionary of Biology
HarperCollins Dictionary of Computer Terms
HarperCollins Dictionary of Economics
HarperCollins Dictionary of Electronics
HarperCollins Dictionary of English Usage
HarperCollins Dictionary of Environmental Science
HarperCollins Dictionary of Mathematics
HarperCollins Dictionary of Music
HarperCollins Dictionary of Sociology
HarperCollins Dictionary of Statistics

THE
HARPERCOLLINS
DICTIONARY OF
PHILOSOPHY

SECOND EDITION

Peter A. Angeles

Series Editor, Eugene Ehrlich

HarperPerennial
A Division of HarperCollins*Publishers*

FIRST HARPERPERENNIAL EDITION

ISBN 0-06-271564-X
ISBN 0-06-461026-8 (pbk.)

92 93 94 95 96 ◆/RRD 5 4 3 2 1

In Love and Gratitude to my Wife
Darlene Elaine Angeles
who has seen this new, revised edition through to its
completion with loving care and concern and who is
the source of my inspiration, strength, and motivation
for all my writing projects and life plans.

All my love goes out to her for her gentleness, love,
and commitment. I could not have done any of my
recent work without her—without her intelligence,
presence, camaraderie, and enthusiastic support.

ACKNOWLEDGMENTS

My children, Beth, Jane, Adam, Michael, and Dina, in their unselfish, loving way were patient, kind, gentle, and helpful in giving their father the time, care, and privacy to work.

I want also to thank the staff at the Sedona Public Library for their help, friendliness, and services.

My thanks especially to my wife, Darlene, who has contributed in every way to making this edition a reality. Without her vital, cheerful spirit and enthusiastic support, this project would not have been completed. I am grateful for her total dedication to me and to my work.

PREFACE

The second edition of this dictionary presents informal and understandable definitions for important philosophic terms. Emphasis is on terms most commonly covered in beginning philosophy courses: epistemology, metaphysics, ethics, aesthetics, logic, and the philosophies of religion and politics. A new feature has been added: biographical entries of more than one hundred major philosophers.

The book is intended as an at-hand reference for students, laypersons, and teachers. It can be used as a supplement to texts and philosophy readings; it can also be consulted for philosophy's own enjoyment and enlightenment. Small capitals are used for cross-references.

A

Abelard, Peter (1079–1142) French medieval dialectician, logician, theologian; born near Nantes; lived in Brittany, where he was a monk at the Abbey of St. Denis; taught at Paris. (He is remembered popularly for his love affair with the beautiful and talented Héloïse.) His principal works include *On the Divine Unity and Trinity*, which was denounced and burned at the Eccesiastical Council at Soissons in 1121; and *Sic et Non*, on dialectic, debate, and apologetics.

absolute (from Latin, *absolutus; ab,* from, away + *solvere,* loosen, free) **1.** free from limitations, qualification, or restrictions (absolute being, absolute beauty, absolute good, absolute authority). **2.** independent and not relative (absolute space, absolute time). **3.** free from variability, change, error (That is the absolute truth.) **4.** certain and true without reservation (Matter is physical.) **5.** not arbitrary or relative but (a) as in aesthetics, objectively real and applicable; (Proportionality, symmetry, harmony, consistency, suggestibility, economy of attention, unity in variety, and richness of imagination are a few of the absolute standards by which a work of art is judged.); or (b) as in ethics, completely and universally binding ("It is an absolute duty.") **6.** in metaphysics, *absolute* is used with concepts such as completeness, totality, all-inclusiveness, perfection, independence, objective reality; that which is underived, unconditioned, uncaused, unchanging, unwavering, pure, positive, simple, universal.

absolute, the 1. the ultimate, underlying reality, world ground, or cosmic principle that is the origin of existence and all its activity, unity, and variety (see entries under LOGOS). **2.** that being which depends on nothing else for its existence and activity, but (a) upon which all other things depend for their existence and activity and (b) to which they can ultimately be reduced. See NECESSARY BEING (THEOLOGY). **3.** the all-inclusive, perfectly interrelated organic and thinking whole (reality, being) that is in the process of actualizing and fulfilling all finite, transient existence. See entries under IDEALISM, ABSOLUTE. **4.** reality (being, substance) as it is in itself in contrast to its appearance to us. See entries under NOUMENON.

The absolute in all the above senses is regarded as ONE, perfect, eternal, uncaused, complete, all-embracing, infinite—actualized thought (spirit, ego) engaging in the multifarious activities of a finite and imperfect universe. The concept of *the absolute* is found in varieties of IDEALISM. *The absolute* is not directly given to us in the world of phenomena or appearances and is often believed to be unknowable in any complete sense.

absolutism 1. the view that truth (value, reality) is objectively real, final, and eternal. **2.** the belief that there is only one unchanging and correct objective explanation of reality. Contrast with entries under RELATIVISM and SUBJECTIVISM. **3.** in political theory, the demand for unquestioning allegiance to a ruler or ruling class.

abstraction (from Latin, *ab(s),* from, away + *trahere,* draw, hence "draw away from") **1.** that which is regarded apart from reference to any particular object or event and which represents symbolically, conceptually, or imaginatively something not directly or concretely perceivable in experience. Examples: the abstraction (abstract concept) of redness, justice, humanity. **2.** the end product of a process (of abstracting) by which a quality, a relation, or some feature of a whole (class) is separated as an idea from that whole. **3.** in traditional logic, the universal derived from an examination of what is common to a number of particular things. Abstraction is also the *process* of deriving a universal. Example: Deriving the universal *human* from an examination of particular instances of women and men.

abstractionism see HYPOSTATIZATION, REIFICATION/REISM.

absurd (from Latin, *absurdus,* harsh-sounding) **1.** contrary to reason, to the rules of logic, to what is obvious to common sense and to the truth. **2.** in existentialist philosophies, *absurd* refers to life's meaninglessness, inconsistency, and lack of structure. **3.** nonsense, that which does not make sense or have meaning, and hence is not understandable. An example of an absurd statement is, "The time colored itself ready, and slept always awake." See CATEGORY MISTAKE.

accident (from Latin, *accidere,* happen; from *ad,* down, to + *cadere,* fall) **1.** an event that occurs without intention, foresight, necessity, or expectation, and need not have occurred at all. **2.** that which interferes with (or assists in) a process without itself being necessary or integral to that process.

accidental attribute sometimes also referred to as *accidental property, characteristic, quality,* or *predicate.* **1.** an attribute not definitely excluded by the essence of a thing that may or may not be possessed by that thing during its existence. Example: Having measles is an accidental attribute that may or may not be possessed by an individual. **2.** a quality (characteristic, feature, property) of a thing that (a) is not essential to the true nature of the thing, (b) is not needed by the thing in order to be what it is, and (c) cannot be inferred from the essential nature of that thing. Example: the redness of an apple. **3.** an incidental quality of a thing that is not essential or necessary for its inclusion as a member of a particular class. Example: Having black skin is an accidental attribute that cannot be used to include or exclude a person from membership in the class *Homo sapiens.* **4.** the characteristic of a thing that can be removed or abstracted away without altering the essential and necessary defining characteristics of the thing. Example: Hearing is an important but accidental attribute to humanness. **5.** a quality that is not self-sufficient but needs a persistent something or ground (a substance, an existent, matter) in order to exist. Examples: the spatial dimension of extension; a relation; order; position.

Compare with entries under ATTRIBUTE, QUALITY, PREDICATE, PROPERTY.

accidentalism 1. the theory that some or all events do not have to happen as they do. **2.** the theory that all events are caused, but (a) some cannot be predicted, and (b) some are inherently unpredictable. Compare with CASUALISM, TYCHISM. Occasionally used incorrectly as a synonym for INDETERMINISM. Opposite to NECESSITARIANISM.

Achilles and the tortoise argument see ZENO'S PARADOXES.

act/action (from Latin, *actum,* a thing done, from *agere,* drive, do) **1.** that operation, function, or activity which has been done or is being done. Examples: counting, jumping, thinking, willing, bribing. **2.** the exertion of energy resulting in a deed, performance, behavior, or event. Examples: slapping someone, hiding, painting, making a face. **3.** the effect produced in something. Example: blinding a person. **4.** a physical, bodily change or motion preceded by a personal act of WILL. **5.** A physical act or action is an operation or activity that results in some other physical change. Example: "The action of the moon upon the oceans causes tidal waves."
      See VOLUNTARY ACTION.

act, pure see PURE ACT.

activism (from Latin, *actum,* a thing done) **1.** the belief that action, as opposed to intellectual theorizing, is the way to truth and constructive social change. **2.** in metaphysics, the theory that activity (process, change, action) is the essential and necessary feature of reality.

acts, speech see SPEECH ACTS.

actuality 1. the domain of factual events. **2.** existence, reality. **3.** any state of existence that can be brought about by another state of existence. **4.** the having become something of a definite sort. Opposite to POTENCY. **5.** the achievement of the full potentiality of a thing. See ACTUALIZATION. Compare with ENERGIA.

actualization 1. the *process* of manifesting in reality the potential that is inherent in a thing. **2.** the *state* of completed realization in time of all the latent potential that is inherent in the nature of a thing. **3.** that which has achieved an (embodied) form. *Actualization* in this sense is in contrast with POTENTIAL/POTENTIALITY, that which has the *possibility* of achieving its (embodied) form. Example: a completed oak tree in contrast with the *entelecheia* of the acorn. **4.** in metaphysics and theology, the Absolute or God is thought to be completed, perfect, pure actualizations—pure actuality—since both manifest themselves completely, perfectly, and eternally in pure form, thus containing no potential that has to be realized.
      See entries under ENTELECHY.

ad hominem argument see FALLACY, TYPES OF INFORMAL (3).

adiaphora (Greek, *a,* not + *diaphora,* different, meaning "something that does not make a difference to something else") **1.** indifference. **2.** moral indifference. Used in Greek philosophy, especially Stoicism (see STOICS, THE) to refer to those morally indifferent things that in themselves are not and do not cause good or bad, right or wrong, virtue or vice—but are things in which these qualities may be found or by which they may be attained—such as knowledge, health, life, pleasure, money, art, social position, career.

aesthetic detachment, sometimes *psychic* or *psychical distance*. The state of being empathetically or contemplatively absorbed in an aesthetic situation, but not being involved in or responsive to the situation's own reality or to the reality it is depicting. Aesthetic detachment from a drama, for example, includes (a) detachment from concern about what is happening in the minds of the actors as they are acting; (b) detachment from what is happening behind the scenes to keep the drama going; (c) detachment from the desire to participate in the activity of the drama as it is unfolding; and (d) detachment from the belief that what is happening on the stage is continuous with the reality occurring outside the theater. Compare with AESTHETIC DISINTERESTEDNESS.

aesthetic disinterestedness that perception of an object or event in and for itself without any practical or cognitive purpose. To be distinguished from AESTHETIC DETACHMENT.

aestheticism 1. the belief that the aesthetic experience is the highest form of human experience. All other experiences are only means toward aesthetic experience. Nothing should interfere in this pursuit. **2.** the view that morality is the servant of art. (This is opposite to *artistic moralism*, which holds that art is the servant of a moral code.) The aesthetic experience, not moral behavior, is the SUMMUM BONUM of life.

aesthetics, sometimes *esthetics*. (from Greek, *aisthetikōs,* one who is perceptive of things through his sensations, feelings, and intuitions [the word *aisthēsis* means primary, rudimentary sensation]) **1.** the study of beauty, and of related concepts such as the sublime, the tragic, the ugly, the humorous, the drab, the pretty. **2.** the analysis of the values, tastes, attitudes, and standards involved in our experience of and judgments about things made by humans or found in nature that we consider beautiful.

Some typical questions in aesthetics: What do the word *beauty* and other words that refer to aesthetic responses mean? What is it about us and what is it about an object that make us call something *beautiful*? Is there a kind of experience that can be said to be uniquely *aesthetic*? What is the relationship between the aesthetic response to art and the aesthetic response to nature? What are the common and differing characteristics that exist among values such as beauty, good, truth, perfection, the pleasurable, the useful? How do aesthetic perception and feeling differ from other types of perceptions and feelings? Are there conscious or unconscious criteria influencing us in evaluating an object or event as *beautiful*? What roles do such things as psychic distance, emotional detachment, impartiality, and disinterestedness play in the aesthetic experience? Why is there a prevalent tendency in humans to respond aesthetically and to express themselves aesthetically in art and other forms of behavior?

aesthetic values see entries under OBJECTIVISM, RELATIVISM, SUBJECTIVISM.

aetiology, often spelled *etiology*. (from Greek, *aitia*, cause, the reason why a thing is what it is, + *lógos*, an account of, a description of, inquiry into, the study of) **1.** the study of the types of causes of phenomena. **2.** the inquiry into the cause(s) of a thing. **3.** the actual assigning or finding of a cause for something. See AITIA.

aeviternity (from Latin, *aevum*, eternity, uninterrupted and never ending time) **1.** the name for eternity as an infinite, past and future totality. Used in the context of transcending time and change. **2.** eternity imagined as that timeless or endless structure in which processes occur or in which they are predetermined. Compare with ETERNAL; ETERNAL, A PARTE ANTE; ETERNAL, A PARTE POST; SEMPITERNAL.

affective the general name for the emotional or feeling quality of experience as found in pleasure, pain, and a variety of emotions, such as love, hate, fear, anger. See FACULTY.

a fortiori (Latin, with greater force, all the more) **1.** refers to having to accept something on the basis of even stronger and better evidence. **2.** refers to the necessity of having to accept a further truth or argument as clearly more obvious on the basis of a truth one has already accepted. Example: "If you cannot get ready to go with me by this afternoon, then *a fortiori* you surely cannot be ready before breakfast, which is when I am leaving."

agapē (Greek, love; moral, spiritual love; brotherly love; compassion; charity. The plural *agapai* means love feast.) **1.** in general, *agapē* was used to designate the highest form of human love in contrast with EROS, sexual love, and with PHILIA, friendship. **2.** in PLATONISM, *agapē* is the love of the eternal, perfect ideas such as the good, beauty, truth. **3.** in Christianity, *agapē* is the love of man for God and of God for man. (*Agapē* was also used to refer to the love feast of early Christians that revolved around Holy Communion.)

agathon (Greek, good) **1.** in PLATONISM, the name given to the highest good—the supreme idea. **2.** the ARETE—the functioning excellence of a thing—is its *agathon*, its good, and its good is related to what it can fulfill or actualize out of its unique potential. See GOOD (PLATO AND PYTHAGOREANS).

agathos (Greek, good, noble, gentle, brave) often found together with the Greek word KALOS, which means *good* in the sense of beautiful. The Greek saying *kalos kai agathos* is translated as "He is good (in the sense of a beautiful appearance), and he is good (in the sense of his moral, spiritual actions)."

agent (from Latin, *agere*, to act; *agens*, that which is acting) **1.** one who, or that which, exerts power upon something and produces an effect. (A cause is often personified as an agent intending to bring about, to produce, its effect, or to make something happen.) **2.** in ethics, a self (person, EGO) (a) who is capable of deliberate action or (b) who is in the process of an action.

agnosticism (from Greek, *a,* not, no, + *gnōstikos,* one who knows or has knowledge of) **1.** the belief (a) that we cannot have knowledge of God and (b) that it is impossible to prove that God exists or does not exist. **2.** sometimes used to refer to the suspension of judgment (see EPOCHE) about some types of knowledge, such as about the soul, immortality, spirits, heaven, hell, extraterrestrial life.

agreement, method of see METHODS, MILL'S INDUCTIVE.

aitia (Greek, cause, the reason why a thing is what it is or acts as it does, the conditions responsible for the occurrence of something) **1.** cause in the sense of a mechanical or scientific description of the interacting events that produce the effect being studied. See CAUSE. **2.** "Cause" in the sense of presenting all the possible ways we can talk about (describe) how things come to be the way they are—how things develop in a process from a beginning point to their completed state. These *aitiai* (causes) are then seen to be the reasons for becoming—for the temporal development of all change from a state of potentiality to actuality. See CAUSES, ARISTOTLE'S FOUR. **3.** "Cause" in the sense of giving reasons for something being (becoming) the way it is rather than its being (becoming) something else. See AETIOLOGY; REASON, PRINCIPLE OF SUFFICIENT.

akrasia (Greek, bad mixture, ill-tempered, lacking in self-control, incontinent, immoderate) that condition of character in which one knows what should (must) be done but is unable to do it. Lack or weakness of willpower (self-determination, self-discipline, self-direction). See INCONTINENCE.

The Greeks, Plato and Aristotle, for example, used *akrasia* to refer to the state of a person's will that makes him or her unable to resist temptation or to do what the person knows is right and good. Contrasted with ENKRASIA.

alethic (from Greek, *aletheia,* truth, real as opposed to unreal, real as opposed to appearance) used as an adjective meaning "relating to truth." See MODE.

alienation (from Latin, *alienus,* alien; related to *alius,* another) that state of awareness in which things become foreign or strange to consciousness. Feelings range from indifference and unconcern to aversion and disgust toward objects, whereas before there may have been love, attraction, friendship, and excitement about these very objects. Alienation is characterized by qualities such as lack of the desire to identify and participate with the object of consciousness; lack of commitment to the goals within social groupings; and detached viewpoint with no inclination for involvement.

The source of alienation may be found in living in a depersonalized social environment; an inability to personalize, or humanize, one's social and physical surroundings; a sense of helplessness and powerlessness about influencing bureaucratic, social, and physical events; the inability to make sense of one's existence; the feeling that one is alone in the world, without guidance, goals, or values that can produce direction and certainty in life; that one's existence has been thrust upon one without intent or choice; that the universe is ultimately indifferent to one's values, aims, wishes, and desires. See ENNUI, ESTRANGEMENT, SELF-ALIENATION. Contrast with DEALIENATION.

als ob (German, as if; referring to something hypothetical, postulated, pragmatically acceptable but not necessarily true or real) associated with Hans Vaihinger's philosophy especially as expressed in his book *The Philosophy of "As If,"* in which knowledge is based not on objective truth but on assuming as true certain unverifiable fictional constructions that are useful as conceptual tools for the formation of intellectual systems. This philosophy is sometimes called *fictionism.*

alteration qualitative change. See CHANGE (ARISTOTLE).

altruism (from Latin, *alter,* another, other) **1.** the promotion of the good of others. (To be distinguished from (a) the promotion of the good *for* others as in benevolent tyranny, and (b) the promotion of the good *with* others as in the cult activities of a fraternity.) **2.** a selfless and benevolent love for humankind and dedication toward achieving the well-being of people and society.

Altruism may be motivated by (a) a disinterested sense of duty to humans and society, or (b) the disciplined attempt to overcome one's self-centeredness and selfish desires in love of others, which involves such qualities as compassion, sympathy, and selflessness. Altruism may involve (a) self-abnegation or self-denial, in which one's own good is thought less of, or not considered at all, or (b) a self-interest in which one's own good is taken into account and is a requisite for promoting or achieving the good of others. (The former is related to the concept of martyrdom and the latter to the concept of enlightened self-interest.) Contrast with EGOISM.

ambiguity, process-product the ambiguity committed when a statement can refer either to a process or to its product and it is unclear from the context which of the two is intended. Example: "Adam went to see the construction." The word *construction* can refer to a process or to a product. If it refers to a process, Adam went to see the builders in the act of constructing. If it refers to the end product of the act of constructing, Adam went to see that which was constructed.

ambiguity, semantical refers to a word(s) in a sentence in which the word(s) can have more than one meaning, sense, or reference, and there is doubt as to which is intended. Example: "Adam rented two apartments." One possible meaning is that Adam rented two apartments for his own use. Another possible meaning is that Adam rented out two apartments to others (or kept one for himself and rented out the other). See EQUIVOCATION.

ambiguity, syntactical see AMPHIBOLY.

ambiguity, type-token the ambiguity committed when an expression can refer either to a type or to a token and it is unclear from the context which is meant. Example: I write the sentence "Jane is a student" on the blackboard ten times. I then ask, "How many sentences have I written?" If the question intends to refer to *type*, then the answer is that I have written only one (type of) sentence. If the question intends to refer to *token*, then the answer is that I have written ten sentences. See TYPE/TOKEN DISTINCTION.

ambiguity of accent see FALLACY, TYPES OF INFORMAL (**9**).

amoral literally not moral. (The prefix *a* represents the Greek negation.) **1.** *amoral* may be contrasted with *nonmoral* (that area in which moral categories cannot be applied), and with IMMORAL (evil, sinful, wrong). Choosing a necktie is a nonmoral act: that is, one which does not involve moral values. Killing a person in violation of moral and social standards is *immoral*. Killing a person without any concern or commitment to moral or social concepts of good or bad is *amoral*. An amoral person in this sense is one who is indifferent to and does not care to abide by the standard moral codes of society. **2.** *amoral* has also been defined with reference to action or behavior that is morally value-free: that is, neither moral nor immoral, neither right nor wrong. (This definition makes *amoral* synonymous with *nonmoral* or *nonethical*.) Science has been called amoral in this sense of the term. Contrast with MORAL.

amphiboly (syntactical ambiguity) (from Greek, *amphibolos*, not regular speech; a sentence whose meaning is doubtful or confusing) An amphiboly results when, due to the grammatical structure (syntactics) of a sentence, it is unclear which of several possible meanings the sentence has. Example: "He rode a horse with a muzzle on his mouth." The *semantics* (meaning) of each of these words may be clear, but the *grammatical* relationship among the words produces a confusion of possible meanings. Grammatical constructions that produce amphibolous expressions include misplaced modifiers, loosely applied adverbs, elliptical constructions, and omitted punctuation.

analogical reasoning sometimes called *arguing from analogy* or *analogical inference*, that is, arguing by comparing the similarities between things: if two things are alike in many respects, it is probable that they will be alike in other respects. The specific argument form is: Since X and Y are observed to be alike in respects a, b, c..., they therefore are probably alike in further respects m, n, o..., which characteristics have been observed in one of the two things being compared but not yet in the other. Such specific arguments from analogy are never conclusive and do not serve as proof.

analogy (from Greek, *analogia*, *analogos*, proportionality, proportion; from *ana*, up, upwards, upon, throughout, continuous + *logos*, ratio, reasoned) originally a mathematical term. In such a context *analogy* signified a common or reciprocal relationship between two things or a similarity of two proportions. The Greek term came later to mean the (usually linguistic) comparison of similarities in concepts or things. **1.** the pointing out of similarities or resemblances between things. **2.** a form of (usually inductive) inference in which, from the assertion of similarities between two things, it is then reasoned that the things will probably also be similar in yet other respects.

The value (correctness, fruitfulness) of an analogy is often judged by criteria such as (a) the number of resemblances (similarities) that exist between the things compared; (b) the number of further resemblances suggested which on testing are verified as correct; and (c) the number of suggestions about resemblances implied in the analogy for further follow-up.

Analogies are pictorial, metaphorical, or model methods of thinking that may be highly suggestive of what to look for. But whether that which is suggested is the case can be determined only by empirical means, such as observation and experimentation.

analogy, refutation by logical see COUNTEREXAMPLE, METHOD OF.

analysis (from Greek, *analysis,* from *analyein,* resolve, unloose; from *ana,* up + *lyein,* loosen, untie) **1.** the mental (or actual) separation of something (a whole, an entity, a problem) into its component parts in order (a) to study the parts separately, or (b) to study their interrelationships, or (c) to study how they relate to the whole. **2.** the process of attempting to uncover the implicit meanings and presuppositions of a system of beliefs or of a statement.

analysis, linguistic also *linguistic philosophy*, the view that by analyzing ordinary language, we can better understand the nature of philosophical problems. Philosophical problems can be seen to be: (a) verbal problems without any basis in reality but based only on verbal confusions (see VERBAL DISPUTE) or (b) problems that dissolve of themselves once the linguistic confusions are seen. The aim of linguistic analysis is to make philosophical questions disappear. For example, the traditional problem of induction (see INDUCTION, PROBLEM OF) is a pseudo-problem. Once one is clear about the linguistic uses and meanings of words such as *evidence, reason, past, future, prediction,* and *recurrence,* there is no reason to see induction as a real problem. Some of the views found in linguistic analysis:

1. Language is not pictorially related to the external world, nor is it related isomorphically (in a one-to-one correspondence). Language does not resemble the things to which it is applied. **2.** Language is not a system of meanings obtained in the act of naming independently existing entities or facts. **3.** Language is a very diversified tool (for usage). **4.** The meanings of words and sentences are derived from their use within a context. They do not refer to or name anything independent of their usage. **5.** Words, sentences, and meanings perform a variety of functions such as naming, classifying, cataloguing, commanding, prescribing, describing, referring, expressing, evoking. (See LANGUAGE, FUNCTIONS OF.) **6.** The meanings of words and sentences must be considered in the context of the rules, habits, and conventions that control the uses of words and sentences. Meaning has little to do with the actual relationship between words and the objects that they represent.

Some of the antimetaphysical claims of linguistic analysis: (a) Language (propositions, statements) cannot present us with a picture of reality as a whole. (b) Language cannot represent (correspond to) reality (the facts that are being talked about). (c) Language is an attempt to say what can only be *seen* (had as experience; shown). By the very nature of all languages, it is impossible to go beyond (behind) their symbols. We would have to use their symbols, or other symbols, to talk about what is beyond those symbols, and we thus would still be involved in symbols. The attempt to go beyond language with the use of language is in effect to construct a metaphysical structure that reveals only its own content and system. (d) Philosophy clarifies concepts but does not give us scientific or metaphysical knowledge about the world.

Some linguistic analysts or linguistic philosophers are Ludwig Wittgenstein, John Wisdom, and Gilbert Ryle. In most cases it is difficult to draw a sharp line between linguistic analysis and ANALYTIC PHILOSOPHY. Compare with ORDINARY LANGUAGE PHILOSOPHY; POSITIVISM, LOGICAL. See LANGUAGE, PHILOSOPHY OF.

analytic, transcendental see TRANSCENDENTAL ANALYTIC (KANT).

analytic judgment see JUDGMENT, ANALYTIC (KANT).

analytic philosophy a twentieth-century philosophic movement particularly strong in England and the United States that concentrates on language and the attempt to analyze statements (or concepts, or linguistic expressions, or logical forms) in order to find those with the best and most concise logical form that fits the facts or meanings to be presented. Central to analytic philosophy is the forming of definitions—linguistic or nonlinguistic, real or contextual. (Contextual definitions primarily refer here to those that define the specific use of symbols whereby one set of symbols may be substituted for another.) The following are four of the many views that can be found in analytic philosophy:

1. Bertrand Russell: The aim of analytic philosophy is to translate grammatically misleading statements into logically correct forms. **2.** G.E. Moore: Analytic philosophy does not discover facts about the world but rather defines and clarifies concepts. The *analysandum* is the concept to be analyzed and the *analysans* is the logically equivalent concept that is substituted for it. They thus become synonymous, and this synonymity gives greater clarity. **3.** Ludwig Wittgenstein: The purpose of analytic philosophy is to translate all complex and descriptive statements (propositions, linguistic expressions) into elementary propositions. These are then put into ultimate, unanalyzable units that represent the simple irreducible units of the real world. A basic tenet is that philosophy cannot transgress the limits of language. Philosophy cannot describe or explain how language is related to the world. This relationship can only be shown. The proper task of philosophy is to make clear what can and what cannot be legitimately said. **4.** Rudolph Carnap: Analytic philosophy is the systematic uncovering of the logical syntax (the grammatical structure and its rules) of concepts and language, especially of the language of science, which is purely formal. The main concern here is not with the meanings (semantics) of words and not with the meaning relationship between our language and the real world but rather with the structural interrelationships of languages themselves. In some cases it is difficult to distinguish sharply between analytic philosophy and linguistic philosophy. See ANALYSIS, LINGUISTIC. Compare with ATOMISM, LOGICAL; EMPIRICISM, LOGICAL; ORDINARY LANGUAGE PHILOSOPHY.

analytic statement see STATEMENT, ANALYTIC.

anamnēsis (Greek, remembrance, recollection, mental recovery, recalling to mind) **1.** the bringing back to mind of a previous experience. **2.** the activity of recollecting knowledge attained in a previous existence. (In Plato and Platonism, *anamnēsis* is the knowledge gained from a remembrance of the perfect forms that the soul innately has as *a priori* knowledge or has experienced in an existence prior to its embodiment. Often referred to as Plato's Doctrine of Reminiscence (Recollection or Remembrance); see RECOLLECTION.

anangkē (Greek, necessity, that inner force which impels certain things to be done or prevents them from being done) *Anangkē* was used in three main senses in Greek philosophy: **1.** physical necessity understood as the constantly present, irrational, nonpurposeful, undirected, and uncontrolled element in the universe. **2.** the intrinsic resistance or recalcitrance of matter to be completely shaped by a rational force toward a good. (In Plato's *Timaeus* these qualities are the principal characteristics of matter that cannot be eliminated from the universe. Not even the DEMIURGE, who rationally manipulates all matter, can overcome those inherent and limiting qualities.) **3.** the logical necessity by which the conclusion of a valid categorical syllogism (necessarily) follows from its premises.

anarchism (from Greek, prefix *a*, not, the want of, the absence of, the lack of, + *archos*, a ruler, director, chief, person in charge, commander. The Greek words *anarchos, anarchia* meant having no government—being without a government). The *positive connotation:* Anarchism is the social ideology that refuses to accept an authoritarian ruling government. It holds that individuals should organize themselves in any way they wish in order to fulfill their needs and ideals. In this sense anarchism is not to be identified with NIHILISM but can be seen to have similarities to political libertarianism and antinomianism (see ANTINOMIAN). The *negative connotation:* Anarchism is the belief that denies any respect for law or order and actively engages in the promotion of chaos through the destruction of society. It advocates the use of individual terrorism as a means toward advancing the cause of social and political disorganization.

Anaxagoras of Clazomenae (c.500–c.428 BC) Greek philosopher born in Clazomenae, Ionia; died in Lampsacus, Mysia. He is regarded as the first philosopher to settle and teach at Athens (c.464–c.434), thus initiating the scientific and philosophic traditions of Athens. He taught such prominent figures as Pericles, Thucydides, and Euripides, and affected the thought of Socrates.

The teachings of Anaxagoras, like those of Socrates later, brought a charge of impiety—the belief in the traditional gods of Athens was being challenged and replaced by what the Athenians regarded as strange theories. Pericles defended him before the Athenian court, and Anaxagoras was acquitted. After the trial, Anaxagoras emigrated to Lampsacus, where he died shortly after his arrival.

Fragments of his *On Nature*, written in the Ionic dialect, survive. As with the other Ionian philosophers (for example, Thales, Anaximander, and Anaximenes), his interests were primarily naturalistic and cosmological. He developed a theory of the universe based on a dualism. In its natural state, the universe is a mass of matter in chaos. This unordered material mass is composed of combinations of small, invisible seeds, or particles or potentialities, that vary in size, shape, color, taste, and fluidity. The *nous*, or universal mind, pervades the entire universe, controlling the mass of unordered material, moving it by the function of mind, directing it, and ordering it into objects and patterns.

The seeds upon which the *nous* works are infinite in number, and each seed can be divided infinitely into its constituent qualities. All things past, present, and future are contained in this unordered mass, and in each seed. By means of motion (rotation), the *nous* brings about the order of the universe by separation and combination. Anaxagoras's naturalism led him to conclusions about eclipses, the sun being a mass of molten metal, the heavenly bodies having been rocks cast off from the earth, and men and animals originating from moist earth.

Anaximander (c.610–c.546 BC) Greek philosopher, natural scientist, mathematician, born in Miletus, Ionia; student of Thales. Regarded as the second of the Ionian, or Milesian, naturalists, placed after Thales and before Anaximenes, and as Thales' successor to the Milesian, School. When Anaximander was about 25, Thales predicted the solar eclipse of 585 BC.

Anaximander contended that the fundamental, ultimate stuff of the universe out of which all things arise was not Thales' water (or fluid), not Anaximenes' air, but the *apeiron*, that which has no limit, no boundary, no end point—the infinite—and which is everlasting (eternal), therefore imperishable and without origin, without beginning or end, and out of which all things arise and return in time, according to the rhythms of construction and destruction.

Among his scientific and mathematical achievements were the geometric arguments for the obliquity of the eclipse, the invention of the sundial and gnomon, the first map of the Greek world, the first map of the stars and constellations placing the earth at the center as a disk, and determination of the path of the sun. Anaximander also presented the first theory of evolution, which did not have an impact on human thought until Darwin's time: Examination of fossils taken from cliffs showed that (a) those taken from the lower parts of the cliffs were simpler in structure than those taken from the higher parts, and (b) the fossils were similar in structure and over time became more and more complex. Living forms in earlier times were not like what they were later; over time, he concluded, living forms are not eternal or unchanging, but evolve from simpler forms, a thought rejected by Greek and medieval thought, but revived in the 19th century.

In a fragment surviving from Anaximander's writings, he says that human beings as they were in his time could not have survived in the past to construct communities. In their infancy they would have been helpless in their struggle to survive and would have become extinct. Therefore, humans must have originated from previous living things "of another kind, because other animals—unlike us—are quickly able to look for their own food, whereas, as they are now, require prolonged care."

Anaximenes (fl. c.545 BC) Greek philosopher born in Miletus, Ionia. He was the third of the Ionian, or Milesian, naturalists, placed after Thales and Anaximander, and a friend and student of both men. He held that the fundamental stuff of the universe is a cosmic air (a) that held all things together—as the soul is air that holds us together, and (b) in which and from which all things arise as they are and are changed from what they are, in accordance with forces such as expansion (rarefaction) and contraction (condensation). This cosmic air is infinite in extent; eternally in motion, causing all the physical changes in the universe; pervades all things and all things that are present in the universe; is invisible, except as qualities such as motion, hot, cold, and damp; is that from which all things that have existed, do exist, and will exist have their beginnings.

angoisse sometimes *anomie* (French, anguish, anxiety, distress, agony), used to refer to: **1.** a feeling of free-floating dread or despair, **2.** a state of disorientation, **3.** a sense of isolation, **4.** also used in the sense of ANGST.

angst (German, *angst*, dread, despair, anxiety, anguish) the dread of nothingness, annihilation, meaninglessness, unconcern. See EXISTENTIALISM.

animism (from Greek, *anemos,* that which blows or that which breathes, wind; whence came Latin *animus*, breath, soul, life principle) **1.** the belief that all things are alive. **2.** the belief in the reality of soul immanent in and pervading all things—humans, animals, rocks, rivers, trees, the earth, the moon, the stars—as their guiding force. **3.** the belief that there is an invisible, intangible, nonmaterial soul that is the underlying ground for life distinct from the material body it inhabits and acts upon to cause the body to behave. **4.** in ancient cosmology, the belief that the universe—our world as well as all the heavenly bodies—possesses eternal souls that are the source of all motion and change. There was thought to be a hierarchy of souls attached to the various levels of existence. **5.** in metaphysics, the view that existence (being, the universe) as a whole is alive, or that there is a pulsating life-force or will that is intimately connected with and propelling its processes and direction. The universe itself is either a living, organic whole, or is infused with an inner living principle. Compare with HYLO-MORPHISM, HYLOZOISM, PANPSYCHISM, PANTHEISM, PERSONALISM, VITALISM. **6.** epistemologically, the belief in the tendency of human nature to project its own inner life qualities upon external inanimate (and animate) reality. In early thought, for example, trees, rivers, the moon were believed to have a will, feelings, thoughts, and intentions. Compare with ANTHROPO-MORPHISM. All forms of animism are not anthropomorphic, since in animism the objects may possess life qualities without possessing human form. Such animism occurs in many areas of language; for example, in common talk: "The door pushed me out of the room." Compare with EMPATHY, PERSONIFICATION, SYMPATHY. It is found in the language of metaphor and of poetry: "He is a wily old fox." See ANALOGY, METAPHOR. It is found in scientific language: "The pressure in the container burst open the lid." Contrasted with MECHANISM.

animism, teleological the theory that (a) parts are adapted (coordinated, adjusted) to other parts within a whole in order to achieve the purpose of the whole, and (b) the whole itself sets the purpose and causes the adaptation. See entries under TELEOLOGICAL and TELEOLOGY.

anoetic (from Greek, *a,* not, + *noētikos,* from *noein,* perceive, or from *nous,* mind) **1.** referring to the states of SENTIENCE, such as pure emotions or sensations that have not yet come to full cognitive awareness. In this sense the anoetic is a precognitive state. Contrast with NOETIC. Compare with PRECONSCIOUS. **2.** referring to the states of sentience that do not come into full cognitive awareness except with the application of deliberate means such as hypnosis. In this sense the anoetic is an acognitive (or noncognitive) state. The terms *anoetic, subnoetic,* and SUBLIMINAL are sometimes used interchangeably.

anomie see ANGOISSE.

anschauung (German, intuition) see INTUITION (KANT).

Anselm, Saint (1033–1109) Catholic medieval theologian born in Italy, became Archbishop of Canterbury, in England. Anselm is known for his statement *Credo ut intelligam,* variously translated as "I believe in order to understand"; "I do not seek to understand in order to believe"; also "One who does not believe will not experience (the faith)" and "One who has not experienced (faith) will not understand." Thus, for Anselm, faith precedes reason, and reason must substantiate that faith. Reason becomes the hand-maiden of faith.

Anselm's major works are *Monologium, Proslogion, Cur Deus Homo*, and *De Veritate*. Gaunilo's objections to Anselm's ontological argument for God's existence is contained in *Liber pro Insipiente*, and Anselm's reply is contained in *Liber Apologeticus*.

ante res (Latin, before [prior to] reality, or before [prior to] things) used by medieval philosophers (a) in the context of REALISM whereby universals were regarded as existing prior to the existence of material objects in which they could be found, and (b) in the context of natural law (see entries under LAW, NATURAL) whereby God's laws are prior to and the cause of natural phenomena. Compare with IN RES; POST RES

anthropocentric (from Greek, *anthrōpos,* man, mankind, + *kentron,* center) **1.** referring to any view which maintains that man is the center and ultimate goal of the universe. **2.** referring to the view that man's values are central to the functioning of the universe, and the universe sustains and progressively supports those values. **3.** occasionally, the term is used to refer in a negative way to the belief that reality can be correctly explained only on the basis of the forms of subjective human experience.

anthropomorphism (from Greek, *anthrōpos,* man, mankind, + *morphē,* form, shape, figure) **1.** the representation of God, the gods, or natural forces as having human form and attributes. **2.** the belief that God, or the gods, have characteristics similar to man's, such as consciousness, inten-tion, will, emotions, sensations. An extreme form of anthropomorphism maintains that God or the gods exist in the shape of man but are more per-fect and powerful. **3.** often refers to the belief that animals possess human abilities and qualities such as thought, communication, feelings, and moti-vation.

antientropic factor see ENTROPIC, ANTI-.

antilogism (from Greek, *antilogia,* contradictory, from *anti,* against, + *leg-ein,* speak, reason) **1.** any inconsistent triad of statements whereby if any two are true the third can be seen to be inconsistent, false, or contradictory (see EVIL, THEOLOGICAL PROBLEM OF). **2.** an argument whose conclusion is stated as a contradiction to its valid conclusion. Example: Socrates is a human. All humans are mortal. Therefore, Socrates is not mortal.

antinomian (from Greek, *anti,* against, + *nomos,* law) **1.** one who desires to be free from the regulations and laws of a society. One who wants to live either outside society in a state of nature (like the CYNICS) or within society but adhering to as few social norms as possible. (Antinomians, as opposed to activists or anarchists, do not directly engage in overthrowing the laws and political structure of a society.) See ANARCHISM. **2.** in theology, (a) one who believes that faith alone, not moral law, is necessary for salvation. (b) in a stronger theological sense, one who despises and holds himself or herself above all laws and social restrictions because of some special faith, grace, or knowledge that makes for salvation.

antinomies, the four (Kant) also *the four theses of rationalistic metaphysics,* each contradicted by an antithesis. Kant believed that solid arguments could be given for both the thesis and its antithesis (see ANTINOMY) for the following: (a) The universe has a beginning in time and is finite in space. The universe has no beginning in time and is not finite in space. (b) All things are made up of simple constituents. Nothing is made up of simple constituents. (c) All things have a cause. Not all things have a cause. (d) A necessary being exists that explains the universe. No necessary being exists. See DIALECTIC, TRANSCENDENTAL (KANT).

antinomy (from Greek, *anti,* against, + *nomos,* law) a contradiction between two principles each of which appears to be true but which cannot both be true. Often regarded as an extreme kind of PARADOX.

Antisthenes (c.455–c.360 BC) Athenian philosopher, founder of the Cynic School of Athens, a pupil of the Sophist Gorgias, and an admirer and imitator of some aspects of Socrates' life and thought.

Antisthenes taught that the ideal aim of life is to acquire virtue, which can be taught. The essence of virtue is self-control (self-discipline). Pleasure is never to be sought for its own sake. The works of Antisthenes are not extant, but the ancients attributed to him interpretations of Homer, philosophic dialogues, orations, and maxims.

antithesis (from Greek, *antithesis,* from *anti,* against, + *tithenai,* set) **1.** the opposition and contrast of words or concepts. **2.** that statement or ideology presented in opposition to a declared position (thesis). **3.** in dialectical materialism, the antithesis is the second member of a process of change and advance which counters the first member (thesis). Out of this opposition emerges a third member, called the SYNTHESIS, which incorporates the positive qualities or truths of both the thesis and antithesis and which transcends them both to become itself a thesis to be met by an antithesis, and so on. See DIALECTIC (HEGEL); LOGIC, DIALECTICAL; MATERIALISM, DIALECTICAL.

apatheia (Greek, from *a,* not, + *pathos,* suffering, pain) used especially by the Stoics to mean indifference to pleasure and pain; the state of tranquility or peace of mind and body resulting from emotional detachment from the everyday world. See STOICS, THE.

apeiron (Greek, limitless, boundless, without limit, INFINITE, endless, the indeterminate) **1.** the concept of the *apeiron* as infinite spatial extension of substance is found in many Greek philosophers (Anaximander, Anaximenes, Xenophanes, Melissus, the Atomists, et al.), but philosophers such as Plato, Aristotle, and the STOICS believed the universe to be finite. **2.** the concept of the *apeiron* as infinite divisibility or as an INFINITESIMAL continuum with reference to the analysis of motion, time, and magnitudes in space was accepted by Zeno. Aristotle accepted the *apeiron* with respect to counting numbers. **3.** Anaximander was the first to use the word *apeiron* to refer to the universe as spatially unbounded and from which opposite substances, attributes such as hot/cold, dry/wet, came into being, and in which they opposed each other. The *apeiron* was eternal, imperishable, primal, indeterminate, and the inexhaustible material source for the existence of all things. There was a trend in Greek philosophy toward hypostatizing this word (see HYPOSTATIZATION, REIFICATION/REISM). **4.** the Pythagoreans (a) put the *apeiron* and the *peron* (or PERAS) in their list of irreducible opposites that form the basic underlying structure and principles of all becoming and of all reality. The *apeiron* is classified in a dualism with such opposites as: the even number; the unintelligible; the many; the moving; the ugly; the bad. The *peron* is classified with the odd number; the intelligible; unity; nonmotion; beauty; the good. The Pythagoreans also used the word *apeiron* to refer to (b) the formless (that which must be put into an order); or (c) the inchoate flux of opposites or contraries (such as hot, cold; even, odd; wet, dry) that are put into an ordered and intelligible arrangement by the principle of *peras* (limit); or (d) the principle of disorder or disharmony causing things to lose their order.

aperçu (French, intuitive insight, immediate recognition or awareness, as opposed to insight stemming from cognitive processes).

apodeictic sometimes spelled *apodictic* (from Greek, *apodeiktikos,* derived from *apo,* from, + *deiknynai,* show; thus meaning showing that which one must prove). **1.** clearly provable or demonstrable. (Or clearly impossible, or undemonstrable.) **2.** necessarily true. **3.** absolutely certain. Aristotle contrasted apodeictic, which meant *certain beyond dispute*, with eristic dialectic, which meant *subject to dispute*. See DIALECTIC.

Apollonian spirit the impulse toward order, proportion, rationality, harmony, pattern, measure, and intellectual explanation. Its opposite is the DIONYSIAN SPIRIT. Both concepts are found in Friedrich Nietzsche's *The Birth of Tragedy* (1872). Compare with CLASSICISM.

apologetics (from Greek, *apologetikos,* speaking in defense of) **1.** methods that attempt to defend and vindicate a doctrinal position against its critics. **2.** in theology, the endeavor to rationally justify the divine origin of a faith.

a posteriori (Latin, that which follows after, from *a, ab,* from, out of, + *posteriori,* latter) after or coming from sense experience. Opposite to A PRIORI. Used in the context of concepts such as CONTINGENT, PROBABLE, EMPIRICAL, INDUCTION, scientific, verifiable, SYNTHETIC, factual, EXPERIENCE, OBSERVATION. See KNOWLEDGE, A POSTERIORI.

appearance (from Latin, *a, ad,* to, toward, + *parere,* come forth, become visible) **1.** that which is seen, or the sense content immediately present to consciousness. **2.** the sense content that is believed to have some vague or illusory semblance to that from which it originates. **3.** the way a thing seems to be (as opposed to the way it is in itself, or to an objective way of viewing it). **4.** the sense content that has no resemblance to that from which it originates or to which it is said to refer.

appearance/reality contrasting terms that refer to the distinction between what things are like (APPEARANCE) to the perceiver (knower, observer) and what they are like in themselves (REALITY). The distinction accepts the notion that there are things (or there is a reality) existing independently of our knowledge of their appearances (or its appearance) but emphasizes (a) (the strong view) that we can never know these things as they are in themselves (or as that reality is in itself), or (b) (the weak view) that only a few things can be truly known about things as they are in themselves (or about that reality as it is in itself). See NOUMENON, PHENOMENON.

Arguments used in support of the RELATIVITY OF SENSE PERCEPTION are also used to support the distinction between appearance and reality. See RELATIVISM, PROTAGOREAN.

apperception (from Latin, *ad,* to, toward, + *percipere,* perceive, mentally apprehend) **1.** the perception of one's own consciousness, in contrast to PERCEPTION, which is the mental state that refers to external things. Used in the context of concepts such as reflective consciousness, self-awareness, introspection, self-perception (perception of one's mental functioning), and self-reflection. (See SELF-CONSCIOUSNESS.) Used with reference to such acts as selecting, concentrating, attending, deciding, choosing, assimilating, intending, avoiding, and willing. **2.** the deliberate assimilating and reorganizing of ideas by an act of intellectual will. In this sense apperception requires qualities of willing and attending (the recognizing, interpreting, identifying, explaining, subsuming, rejecting of ideas). **3.** the mental activity that (a) brings faint items of knowledge (indistinct impressions, vague notions or feelings) out of the subconscious to the level of conscious attention and (b) puts them into intellectual patterns, thereby making sense of them.

apperception, empirical (Kant) the ego's awareness of actual, concrete, changing states of consciousness. This function was performed by the empirical ego in contrast to the pure ego, which produced a transcendental apperception. Contrast with APPERCEPTION, TRANSCENDENTAL. See EGO, EMPIRICAL (KANT).

apperception, transcendental sometimes referred to as the *transcendental* (or *pure*) *ego of apperception;* the *transcendental unity of apperception.* **1.** the inner, fundamental, and unchanging sense of a unity of our consciousness. That aspect of a person's consciousness that endures as a unity throughout immediate and momentary changes. **2.** for Kant, transcendental apperception is the structured unity (pure ego, self) of consciousness that precedes (is transcendent to) the content of our perceptions and makes possible their experienced order and meaning. This structured transcendent unity consists of (a) the intuitions of space and time, which are modes *by which* we perceive and are not objects *of* our perception, and (b) the categories of understanding such as quantity, quality, relation, and modality. See CATEGORIES OF THE UNDERSTANDING (KANT). Transcendental apperception was thus thought to be the necessary condition for having an experience and for synthesizing experience into a unity. Contrast with APPERCEPTION, EMPIRICAL. See EGO, TRANSCENDENTAL (KANT); IDEALISM, TRANSCENDENTAL (KANT).

appetitive (from Latin, *appetere,* strive after, long for) pertaining to the basic wants or desires, such as those for food and water, exercise, and sex. See FACULTY.

apprehension. (from Latin, *apprehendere,* seize, grasp) **1.** the process of conceiving, perceiving, or understanding an idea or concept. **2.** the act of becoming consciously aware of the bare presence of an object or idea. Contrasted with the act of naming, judging, and intellectually grasping an object. See COMPREHENSION.

a priori (Latin, that which precedes; from *a, ab,* from, out of, + *prior,* former, before) prior to and independent of sense experience. Opposite of A POSTERIORI. Used in the context of concepts such as necessary, certain, definitional, deductive, universally true, innate, and intuitive. See KNOWLEDGE, A PRIORI.

a priori **judgment** see JUDGMENT, A PRIORI (KANT); KNOWLEDGE, A PRIORI.

Aquinas, Thomas (1224–1274) Italian philosopher and theologian, known as *Doctor Angelicus* and regarded as the prince of all scholastic philosophers and theologians. Pope Leo XIII's *Encyclical* of August 4, 1879, states that the works of St. Thomas are to be taken as the foundation of Catholic theology. Aquinas's synthesis of philosophic thought, especially Aristotle's, into Christian thought is without parallel. (It can be said that he Christianized Aristotle's philosophy.)

In 1323, Aquinas was canonized by Pope John XXII. In 1567, Pope Pius V ranked Aquinas with the already recognized great Latin Church Fathers: Ambrose, Augustine, Jerome, and Gregory. Aquinas's two major works were his *Summa contra Gentiles* (3 volumes, 1259) and his *Summa Theologica* (12 volumes, 1265). They provide us with Aquinas's most important theological doctrines in the form of a simplified compendium. His writings began with his *Commentary on the Sentences of Peter Lombard* (1254) and continued until his death with commentaries on the Scriptures, Boethius, pseudo-Dionysius, Aristotle, etc.

archē (Greek, the beginning, the starting point, the origin of a thing, first) **1.** the basic, underlying substance or principle out of which all things come to be. Its first use as a philosophic concept in this sense is found in Anaximander, who conceived the *archē* as (a) eternal, with no beginning and no end, and (b) the source of all things that are, have been, and will be. **2.** that first and originating point from which a thing comes to be what it is.

ARCHETYPES

archetypes (from Greek, *archē,* first, + *typos,* pattern, stamp, mold) **1.** the original models from which things are formed, or of which things are copies. For example, Plato's ideal forms (beauty, truth, good, justice) are regarded as archetypes. See FORMS, PLATO'S THEORY OF IDEAL. In some interpretations of Plato, the good is the one and only archetype, from which all other forms receive their being. **2.** in the psychology of Carl Jung, the patterns of thought and the imagery that emerge from the collective unconscious of humankind. In literature they are referred to as *primordial images* or *archetypal symbols* and are found, for example, in recurring myths.

aretē (Greek, the goodness of a thing, that at which a thing excels) in Greek literature, when applied to persons it signified qualities such as valor, prowess, courage, and strength. In a moral sense it meant virtuousness, meritoriousness, and goodness of service. It is often translated as *virtue.* See entries under VIRTUE.

The philosophic meaning of *aretē* has to do with the *functioning excellence* of a thing. When something performs the function it is designed to perform and it does this excellently, then it has *aretē;* it is *virtuous* in that respect. Example: The *aretē* of a pruning tool is to cut branches. It was intended for this purpose. It does this better than anything else. Insofar as it performs its function well, it has *aretē.*

To determine human *aretē,* the Greeks asked: "What is unique to the human? What functions does a human perform that no other thing performs as well?" It is not locomotion, not growth, not sensating, not procreating; these and many other functions are shared in common with other beings such as animals. The *aretē* of humans will be found in that which they can do uniquely: reason. The use of the rational faculty is that which distinguishes a human from all other beings. A human's *aretē* consists of the development and use of reason to the utmost level of functioning excellence. (And for Aristotle, in this consists also an individual's ultimate happiness.) See AGATHON; entries under ESSENCE; EUDAIMONIA.

argument (from Latin, *arguere,* make clear) **1.** the reasons (proof, evidence) offered in support or denial of something. **2.** in logic, a series of statements called *premises* logically related to a further statement called the *conclusion.* Arguments are divided into two general categories: deductive and inductive. See DEDUCTION and INDUCTION.

argument, invalid see INVALID.

argument, open-question see OPEN-QUESTION ARGUMENT (G.E. MOORE).

argument, sound see SOUND (LOGIC).

Aristippus (c.435–c.386 BC) Greek philosopher born in Cyrenaica (now Libya). He was a pupil of Socrates and founder of the hedonistic Cyrenaic School of philosophy. He based his ethics on the pursuit of immediate pleasure tempered by rational control, or prudence, and the avoidance of pain. His writings are not extant.

aristocracy (from Greek, *aristos*, best, + *kratein*, be strong, govern or rule over) **1.** a government ruled by the best (aristocrats), who are chosen by such criteria as intellect, virtue, rank, status, power, achievement, fortune, and noble birth—or combinations of these. **2.** rule by a small class regarded as privileged and superior to the rest of the community and thereby has a natural right to lead.

Aristotle (384–322 BC) Greek philosopher born in Stagira, in Chelcidice, in the northwestern region of the Aegean. His father, Nichomachus, was a member of the medical guild called *the sons of Aesculapius*.

At age 17, Aristotle was sent to Plato's Academy in Athens, where he studied and taught under Plato from 367 to Plato's death in 347. During the next 12 years, Aristotle taught and conducted research in biology, zoology, botany, and physiology in various places. It was during this period that he taught the boy who later would become known as Alexander the Great. For another 12 years, Aristotle directed a school he founded in Athens. It was called the Lyceum and was also known as the Peripatetic School.

Aristotle's work comprises dialogues, constitutions, histories, literary criticism, poetry, essays, philosophies, treatises, scientific compilations, memoranda, notes, and lectures. A sampling of his philosophic and scientific works follows:

1. Analytics. (Aristotle used this term, but it is also known as *logic* or *organon*.) Works such as *Posterior Analytics; Sophistici Elenchi; the Topics; De Interpretatione; the Categories.*

2. Physics. (The Greek term is *physis*, the study of nonliving, or inorganic, natural phenomena.) Works such as *The Physics; De Caelo* (On the Nature of the Heavens); *De Generatione et Corruptione* (On Coming into Being and the Passing Away from Being); *Meteorologica.*

3. Psychology. Works such as *De Anima* (On the Nature of the Soul); *Parra Naturalia* (essays on such topics as sensation, perception, memory, sleep, and dreams).

4. Biology. Treatises such as *De Partibus Animalium* (On the Parts of Animals); *De Incessu Animalium* (On the Progression [Continuity] of Animals); *De Motu Animalium* (On the Movement [Motion] of Animals); *De Generatione Animalium* (On the Reproduction [Generation] of Animals).

5. Metaphysical. The Metaphysics—on ontology in the sense of the study of being-in-itself, being-as-being, and not being in some specific sense, such as being a rock, star, human, etc. Also referred to as *first philosophy*.

6. Ethics. Works such as the *Eudemian Ethics* (named for Eudemos, Aristotle's student); *Nichomachean Ethics* (named for Aristotle's son Nichomachos).

7. Politics. Aristotle's *Politics* has three clear divisions: (a) theory or philosophy of the state, found in the first three books; (b) pragmatic recommendations for governing a state; and (c) outline of an ideal state, reminiscent of Plato's final work, *The Laws*.

8. Literary Criticism. Includes *The Rhetoric* and *The Poetics*.

art (from Latin, *ars, artis,* skill) **1.** creations (works, productions) of humans that have aesthetic qualities or values. **2.** skills acquired in experience that make these creations possible: the ability to contrive and to systematically and intentionally use physical means to achieve desired results according to aesthetic principles, whether intuitively or cognitively understood. See FINE ARTS; TECHNĒ.

art, philosophy of the concern with the conceptual problems arising from our understanding of art. Questions such as these are asked in the philosophy of art: How is art defined? What makes a work of art beautiful, appealing, or ugly? How do we respond to a work of art? Does art symbolize? What kind of meaning or knowledge does art communicate? Is artistic expression a unique form of expression? Does art reveal a truth about anything? Why do humans create works of art? See AESTHETICS.

asceticism (from Greek, *askētikos,* one who exercises) in general, the view that man should deny his desires. **1.** the strong version: man ought to deny all desires without exception. **2.** the weak version: man ought to deny only the base desires of the body (lust, lasciviousness, sensuousness) and of the world (desire for material possessions, fame, achievement). The desires of the flesh must be repressed. Only in this way can one free the soul to attain virtue and salvation.

Both senses of asceticism have been associated with celibacy, austerity, simplicity, obedience, poverty, fasting, discipline, penance, mutilation of the body, the solitary and contemplative life, and self-denial.

a se (Latin, from itself, by itself) refers to an eternal self-sustaining, self-sufficient, and self-subsisting substance or ultimate existence that exists of itself by its own power and is not derived from any other source whatever. Its essence is to exist, and its existence is its essence. In medieval philosophy, applied only to God. See ASEITY; IN SE; PER SE.

aseity (from Latin, *aseitas,* being by, for, and of itself) the state of being of a thing (a) that is utterly, completely, absolutely independent of other things, (b) upon which all other things depend for their total existence, and (c) that manifests its nature (essence) in a perfectly pure way without manifesting nonessential (see PER ACCIDENS) characteristics. Traditionally, the word *aseity* has been applied to God. See PERSEITY.

assent (from Latin, *assentire,* feel, think) to intellectually accept the truth of a statement.

assent (Hume) 1. acceptance of an immediate feature of our consciousness about which we can do little (except accept it). Things that have the quality of assent: our desires, wants, wishes, drives, likes and dislikes, and impressions. **2.** an emotional attachment to or preference for something that is, at the moment had, beyond rational judgment as to its truth or falsity, goodness or badness.

association, laws of 1. the patterns or forms by which ideas are connected, such as similarity (resemblance), contrast, contiguity in space and time, causality, and propinquity. **2.** the forces or principles causing this patterning. See CONTIGUITY, LAW OF; CONTRAST, LAW OF.

associationism sometimes referred to as *associationistic psychology,* the theory (a) that all mental states are made up of unique, simple, discrete, irreducible elements (such as impressions, sense data, sensations) and (b) that these elements combine and recombine by laws of association (see ASSOCIATION, LAWS OF) to form our complex mental states. (Associationism is identified with John Locke, David Hume, and John Stuart Mill.) Compare with ATOMISTIC PSYCHOLOGY.

assumption associationism (from Latin, *assumere,* take, adopt, accept) **1.** a statement (idea, belief) that is accepted as true (a) without clear proof or (b) without presenting an argument to support it. **2.** a statement that is accepted in order to develop the ideas it can lead to. Example: "On the basis of acting *as if* x is true, what conclusion can then be drawn?" See POSTULATE.

ataraxia (Greek, imperturbability, lack of disturbance, equilibrium; from *a,* not, + *tarazein,* stir up, trouble, confound, agitate) *Ataraxia* is translated as *tranquility* or *imperturbability of mind and body* and was used especially by the Epicureans much as the Stoics used the word *apatheia,* to signify the goal of human life and the highest form of happiness. See HEDONISM (EPICURUS).

athanatism (from Greek, *athanatos,* immortal, from *a,* not, + *thanatos,* death) **1.** the belief in the survival of the soul (consciousness, mind, self, ego, personality) in some form or other, and in some place or other after death. **2.** the belief in immortality. Opposite of THANATISM.

atheism (from Greek, *atheos,* without God, from *a,* not, + *theos,* God) **1.** the belief that gods do not, or God does not, exist. **2.** the disbelief in any kind of supernatural existence that is supposed to affect the universe. **3.** the lack of belief in a particular God. (The Greeks called the Christians atheists for not believing in their gods, and the Christians called the Greeks atheists for not believing in their God.)

atomic fact the simplest, most rudimentary, elementary, and irreducible kind of fact consisting of a quality in some particular thing or a relation between particular things. There is a one-to-one (see ISOMORPHISM) relationship between an atomic proposition (atomic language) and an atomic fact. For example, subjects (proper names) correspond to terms (particulars); adjectives correspond to qualities; verbs correspond to relations. See ATOMISM, LOGICAL.

atomism, Greek the philosophy developed by the early Greek philosophers Leucippus, Democritus, and Epicurus, and the Roman, Lucretius, which maintained that reality is composed of atoms. The Greek word *ātomos* from which our word *atom* is taken means indivisible, having no parts, uncuttable, and is made up of the privative letter *a*, not, + *topos*, able to be cut. The atoms as minute material particles are the ultimate constituents of all things and have properties such as size, shape, position, arrangement, and movement. Atoms are eternally present, simple, separate, irreducible to anything further, impenetrable, unchangeable (their essential nature remains eternally the same), and invisible to the naked eye. There are infinitely many atoms in existence. Atoms in themselves do not possess qualities such as color, taste, heat, or smell. These qualities are produced by the activity of the atoms upon sense organs. The atoms are eternally in motion in empty space, colliding with each other and forming objects. Their sizes and geometric shapes interlock into configurations producing the variety of existing things. The existence of any individual thing can be explained in terms of the arrangements of the positions and figures of the atoms of which it is composed.

In general, atomism is the materialistic view that the universe consists of ultimately simple, independent, and irreducible entities that are only contingently interrelated (as opposed to necessarily interrelated) to form objects. See entries under MATERIALISM. See VOID (ATOMISTS)

atomism, logical the name given to the philosophic outlook primarily identified with Bertrand Russell and Ludwig Wittgenstein, characterized by such theories as: (a) Language and thought can be analyzed in terms of indivisible and discrete components called atomic propositions that correspond to ATOMIC FACTS. (b) Logic organizes atomic propositions into systems of knowledge. (c) A fundamental identity of structure exists between a symbol and the fact it represents. (d) The complexity of the symbol corresponds to the complexity of the facts symbolized by it. (e) There is a close similarity (possibly an ISOMORPHISM) between the structure of a formal (ideal) language and the real structure of the world. (f) Relations are externally real.

The major discussions of logical atomism center around concepts such as fact, atomic and molecular propositions, simples, properties, relations, thing, object versus sense data, the construction of logical and linguistic meanings. See ANALYTIC PHILOSOPHY.

atomistic psychology the attempt to explain mental phenomena and all experiences by reference to the combining and recombining of minute, indivisible, irreducible, successive occurrences of unchangeable items variously called *psychological atoms*, *logical atoms*, *impressions*, *sensations*, *sense data*, and *atomic facts*. Whatever the items are called, they are viewed as distinct and unique mental entities, separable and existing independently, needing nothing else to explain or support their presence. Compare with ASSOCIATIONISM.

attribute (from Latin, *attribuere,* from *ad,* upon, + *tribuere,* assign, bestow, bestow upon) **1.** a characteristic or PROPERTY of a thing. Attributes are linguistically expressed as adjectives or as an adjectival clause or phrase. (Substances, or things said to have attributes, are expressed as nouns.) Examples: sweetness is an attribute of honey; goodness is an attribute of God; thinking is an attribute of a human. **2.** in logic, *attribute* is used synonymously with PREDICATE—that which is asserted or denied about the subject of a categorical proposition. Example: "The chair is brown." *Brown* is an attribute of *chair*—the predicate of the sentence with *chair* as its subject. **3.** in metaphysics, attributes may be classified as essential, necessary, accidental, or contingent. See ACCIDENTAL ATTRIBUTE; QUALITY.

Augustine, Saint [Aurelius Augustinus] (354–430) Born in Tagaste, North Africa, and converted to Christianity in 386, baptized in 387. Augustine studied literature and rhetoric and was influenced by such writers as Cicero, St. Paul, St. Anthony, and Plotinus. In early life, he traveled and taught in Rome and Milan. From middle life on, he lived in Hippo, in North Africa.

Augustine can be seen as living at the end point of the Roman Empire and its religion, and the beginning point of the intellectual Christianization of the Empire. Emperor Constantine converted to Christianity c.314, and after a few years of conflict and dissension all future Emperors remained Christian. Augustine's major works are *Confession*; *De Doctrina Christiana*; *De Trinitate*; and *De Civitas Dei*.

Austin, John Langshaw (1911–1960) British analytic, linguistic philosopher, known as the philosopher of ordinary language; born in Lancaster and educated at Oxford, where he taught for many years.

Austin's well-developed philosophic scholarship was based on knowledge of such figures as Leibniz, Frege, Aristotle, and Plato. He is mainly known for his work in the analytic methods of studying philosophy and his emphasis on analysis and clarification of ordinary language, which reveals suppositions about, and insights into, the world around us. His major works include *Foundations of Arithmetic* (1950), a translation of Frege's *Gründlagen der Arithmetik*; *Philosophical Papers* (1961); *Sense and Sensibilia* (1962); and *How to Do Things With Words!* (1962).

autarkeia sometimes *autarkia*, Greek for self-sufficiency, individualism, or autonomy, which was thought to be the principal characteristic of happiness and the virtuous man in Greek ethical systems. In Aristotle, *autarkeia* is essential to EUDAIMONIA, self-realization, and the contemplative life. In Stoicism, *autarkeia* refers to the state of nondependence on another for the satisfaction of physical and emotional needs. See STOICS, THE.

authoritarianism the view that advocates unwavering obedience to some authority as the true source of knowledge (or political belief) that is beyond questioning, as opposed to the individual pursuit of knowledge or the free spirit of inquiry.

authority (from Latin, *auctor*, originator, leader, head) an individual or group considered to have valid knowledge and/or legitimate power. **1.** in its positive sense, authority is accepted for the benefits derived that could not be derived, or as easily derived, from any other source, especially under the social and personal limitations under which people must necessarily exist. **2.** in its negative sense, authority is regarded as oppressive and an illegitimate exercise of knowledge and power.

autocracy (from Greek, *autos*, same, self, + *kratos*, strength) a form of rule in which one individual has absolute, supreme control of a people.

automatism (from Greek, *autōmatos*, self-moving) the view that all living things are machines (automata) explainable by the mechanistic descriptions given by sciences such as physics, chemistry, and physiology.

autonomy (from Greek, *autos*, self, + *nemein*, hold away, assign) **1.** the power of self-regulation. **2.** the act of self-governing, self-determining, self-directing. **3.** independence from the will of others. **4.** the right to follow one's own volitions. An autonomous self is one that functions in an integrated way (as opposed to responding randomly and inconsistently to stimuli as they arrive), choosing and directing activities relevant to its own needs. Moral autonomy is the freedom to reach one's own moral values concerning right and wrong.

Averroës, Ibn Rushd (1126–1198) Muslim philosopher and theologian, born in Córdoba, Spain, of Spanish Arab ancestry. He was proficient both in Islamic studies and Greek sciences and philosophies. One of his works was a textbook of medicine.

Averroës published Arabic summaries of Aristotle's works and Plato's *Republic*. His works were widely read and discussed among Christian theologians, including Aquinas, and stirred up much controversy. His writings defending the right of Muslims to study and incorporate Greek philosophy into the Islamic tradition brought him commendation yet, in 1195, he was tried in Córdoba and exiled.

Avicenna [Ibn Sina] (980–1037) Islamic philosopher, physician, scientist, expositor, translator of Greek philosophy and mathematics; born near Bukhara. In addition to his accomplishments in many subjects, he mastered Greek philosophy, mathematics, and astronomy.

His book the *Shifa* (Healing of the Soul) was an encyclopedic systematization of all available ancient Greek knowledge. It is in four parts: *Logic*, including rhetoric and poetry; *Physics*, including psychology, botany, zoology, cosmology, cosmogony, meteorology, astronomy, space, time, causation, motions, and the concept of a vacuum; *Mathematics*, including Euclid's geometry and the principles of arithmetic and music; and *Metaphysics*, including commentaries on Aristotle's *Metaphysics*.

Avicenna's other major work was the *Canon*, a comprehensive collection of medical and pharmacological information. It follows Galen's tradition of the four elements (fire, air, water, earth) as the composition of all things; and the four humours (blood, phlegm, choler, melancholy). It was through Avicenna and Averroës that medieval Europe came to know the works of Aristotle. Avicenna's works influenced the philosophy, theology, medicine, and science of medieval culture. His attempt to harmonize Greek philosophy with the beliefs of Islam was the kind of synthesis that Aquinas and others attempted to accomplish for Christianity.

awareness the conscious act of attention to what is being experienced. Awareness may refer (a) to the attention given to the content of a sensation or experienced object, or (b) to the attention given to the act of attending itself. The former is synonymous with CONSCIOUSNESS, and the latter with one of the meanings of SELF-CONSCIOUSNESS (SELF-AWARENESS).

axiology (from Greek, *axios,* worthy, + *logos,* the study of) the analysis of values to determine their meaning, characteristics, origins, types, criteria, and epistemological status.

axiom (from Greek, *axioma,* that which is thought to be worthy) **1.** the most basic and necessary self-evident (or assumed) truth upon which a logical or mathematical system is built and which cannot be denied without destroying the consistency of the system. **2.** a fundamental statement that cannot be deduced from other statements and is the primitive beginning point from which other statements can be inferred. Axioms are not regarded as provable in the same sense as those statements deduced from them are provable. Their proof is related to the extent to which they can be used to construct a coherent and inclusive system. See ASSUMPTION.

Ayer, Alfred Jules (1910–1989) British philosopher born in London, educated at Oxford. He studied logical positivism at the University of Vienna and taught at University College, London, and at Oxford. His main works include *Language, Truth and Logic* (1936); *The Foundations of Empirical Knowledge* (1940); *Thinking and Meaning* (1947); *Philosophic Essays* (1954); *The Problem of Knowledge* (1956); *The Concept of a Person* (1963); and *The Central Questions of Philosophy* (1972).

B

Bacon, Francis (1561–1626) English philosopher born in London and educated at Cambridge, and known as the practical creator of scientific induction. He had a distinguished career in law, which ended when he was forced to admit that he was guilty of bribery and corrupt dealings in Chancery suits.

Among his many works are *Essays* (1597); *The Advancement of Learning* (1605); *Novum Organum* (1620); *De Augmentis Scientarium* (1623); and *The New Atlantis* (1624).

Bacon, Roger (c.1214–1292) English philosopher, natural philosopher, alchemist, encyclopedist, and philologist; born in the county of Somerset and educated at Oxford and the University of Paris. He was an advocate of Aristotelianism, then being introduced from recent findings and translations, mostly from Arabic into Latin. Bacon's works were condemned, and he was imprisoned from 1277 to 1292.

Besides Bacon's many scholarly commentaries on Aristotle, his Greek and Hebrew grammars, and his alchemical treatises, Bacon's major works are *Communia Mathematica* (1268); *Communia Naturalium* (1268); *Opus Maius* (1268); *Opus Tertium* (1268); *Compendium Studii Theologiae* (1292); and *Compendium Studii Philosophiae* (1292).

Baconian method a method proposed by Francis Bacon of obtaining knowledge of natural phenomena by induction that stressed (a) the importance of drawing inferences from examination of particular, concrete facts to make generalizations about these facts, and (b) the necessity of testing hypotheses by means of observations and experiments. The goal of Bacon's scientific, inductive methodology was to control, manipulate, and use natural phenomena for the benefit of humanity. The purpose of knowledge for Bacon may be summed up in the phrase "Knowledge is power." See IDOLS (BACON); TABLES OF INVESTIGATION, THE THREE (BACON).

bad faith (Sartre) 1. self-deception, especially the act of not admitting that one has freedom of choice (authentic choices) or not allowing oneself to see possible choices, and thereby avoiding responsibilities and the anxieties of making decisions. See *EN SOI* (SARTRE), *POUR SOI* (SARTRE) **2.** lack of self-acceptance, especially the act of not admitting—or deceiving oneself about—what is true about oneself. **3.** lack of self-assurance or self-esteem that prevents one from acting upon existence and provides the conditions for acting as a thing in existence.

beauty (from Latin, *bellus*, pretty) **1.** that which is pleasing. **2.** that quality or group of qualities which pleases a sense organ such as the eye or the ear, and/or pleases the intellect by proportion, unity, variety, symmetry, simplicity, grace, fitness, suggestiveness, intricacy, perfection, or excellence. **3.**

the quality or property of a thing that produces aesthetic pleasure or satisfaction. Comprises one of the triad of ideals—truth, goodness, beauty—with which classical philosophy has been especially concerned. Beauty has been viewed (a) as a formal property or quality inherent in the object itself that exists independently whether or not it is perceived (OBJECTIVISM [VALUE THEORY]), (b) as a name for the subjective emotional response the viewer has to the object viewed (SUBJECTIVISM [VALUE THEORY]), and (c) as a simple, indefinable, unanalyzable quality (such as *good* or *yellow*) whose presence is intuited or directly apprehended and cannot be empirically verified by scientific tests.

In the view of Plato and the Neo-Platonists such as Plotinus, (1) the soul strives toward possession and understanding of beauty. Beauty was regarded (as were truth, love, goodness, justice, and so on) as one of the active forces in the universe, an aspect of the ideal and spiritual powers propelling all reality. (2) The degree to which the property of beauty is present in an object determines the degree to which that object is beautiful. (3) To the degree to which an object imitates (partakes of) the ideal, perfect, unchanging form of beauty, to that degree it is beautiful.

Beauty arouses joy, cheerfulness, happiness, affinity, and attraction, and is contrasted with the SUBLIME, which arouses feelings of amazement and awe, and with the ugly (see UGLY, PARADOX OF THE), which arouses disgust and antipathy. In some philosophies the three are mutually exclusive, in others they can exist together and/or all can be pleasurable.

becoming 1. the act of changing from one form of existence to another. Mere change of position or of motion is not considered *becoming*. **2.** that kind of change actualizing the potentiality of something toward being something other than it once was, in a process of realizing its goal, purpose, or end. **3.** in Plato and the Platonists, *becoming* refers to ordinary sensuous experience and the mundane world in which things come and go, in contrast to the true BEING of the unchanging, eternal Ideas or Forms. Contrast with IDEAS (PLATO).

begging the question see fallacy, types of informal (**13**); PETITIO PRINCIPII.

behaviorism a type of reductive materialism that attempts to explain all consciousness in terms of overt behavior responses and/or covert dispositional states, and excludes any reference to mental states. Opposed to the subjectivism of introspection (and introspective psychology) as a source of knowledge about something called consciousness. Radical or metaphysical behaviorists believe that there are no inner private mental states distinct from behavior of some sort. (Some *radical behaviorists* enlarge the meaning of *behavior* to include neurological processes.) Mental-concept words such as *choosing*, *deciding*, *intending*, and *willing* do not stand for mental events or states. They are explainable in terms of either (a) the occurrence of publicly observable behavior, or (b) dispositional behavior (tendencies) for publicly observable events to occur. For example, thinking is explained in terms of subvocal speech, laryngeal movements, muscular contractions, skin and eye responses, etc. Emotions are explained in terms of visceral reactions. Language and speech are complex stimulus-response systems, and provide no ground for inferring unobservable mental states. *Methodological behaviorists* believe that mental states do (or might possibly) exist, but they cannot be of any scientific interest—they cannot be objectively examined, predicted, verified, confirmed, or quantified. *Epiphenomenalistic behaviorists* believe that nonbehavioral mental states do exist but have no causal influence on human behavior. See MIND, TYPES OF THEORIES OF (8); and entries under PSYCHOLOGY.

being contrasted with NONBEING, VOID, and with BECOMING. **1.** existing. **2.** whatever exists as the subject of distinctions or the object of a language. **3.** all that is, the totality of existence. *Being* in this all-inclusive sense is not a GENUS. We can generalize about any and all particular beings (bodies, objects, actions) but not about the everything-that-is. **4.** that which is regarded as the most fundamental reality. Being was thought by the early Greek philosopher Parmenides to be that which is eternal, one, all-inclusive, and unchanging. Parmenides' famous passage from which this was inferred: "That which is, is; and that which is not, is not and can never be." The things we perceive are many, transient, varied, changing, and therefore cannot be called true being. This Parmenidian use of the word implies the distinction between a true realm (reality) and one of illusion (appearance). *Being* came to refer to that existence behind or above phenomena as their cause, or as that in which they inhere. In this sense *being* is used synonymously with ultimate reality, substance, prime matter, God, the infinite reality, the absolute, the One, etc. When used in this way, the reference is not to any particular being (existing thing) but to pure being, being-in-itself, being-*qua*-being (being-as-being). The essence of such a being is to exist necessarily; its essence is existence and its existence is its essence (expressed by the Latin phrase *esse ipsum subsistens*). **5.** in Plato and the Platonists, being (the world of being) refers to the heavenly realm of the perfect, unchanging, and eternal Ideas (*forms*), in contrast to BECOMING (the illusory world of becoming or of sensations) in which things are in constant flux and change. Contrast with NONBEING (PLATO).

being, hierarchy of the view that there are gradations of reality, or a scale of beings. Example: nonliving things, plants, living things, rational beings, angels, God. Some frequent assumptions: (a) There is a division between the visible (tangible, material) world and the invisible (intangible, immaterial) world. (b) The latter is more spiritual and hence superior. (c) The more self-sufficiency and reason a thing possesses, the higher it is on the scale. (d) The most self-sufficient, rational, and superior being is the infinite immaterial substance called God. (e) All things emanate in hierarchical succession from this God of which all things are a part. (f) The further away from this source of being a thing is, the more it is composed of matter and the more evil it contains. See EMANATION.

being-as-such sometimes *being-qua-being, being-as-being, pure being, being-in-itself.* **1.** what existence would be like in itself, apart from human consciousness. **2.** that which possesses universal characteristics that belong to everything in existence and not only to a finite number of individual objects. See EXISTENCE. **3.** that which is the ground for the existence and the explanation of all things.

belief 1. a state of mind in which confidence, trust, faith is placed in a person, idea, or thing. **2.** a conviction or feeling that something is real or true. **3.** intellectual assent to an idea. **4.** that which is asserted or contained in an idea.

Belief may stem from an immediate, nonreasoned acceptance of an idea (a feeling, a hunch, a want) or from a deliberately thought-out argument. Compare with CERTAINTY, PSYCHOLOGICAL OR INTUITIVE; DOGMA; FAITH; OPINION.

Bentham, Jeremy (1748–1832) English philosopher, born in London. He began to study Latin at age 3, and even before he matriculated at age 13 at Oxford excelled at writing Latin and Greek verse. He studied law but never practiced. His interest lay in philosophically systematizing and codifying the law, reforming legal procedures, simplifying the law, and making the law more humane and less bureaucratic.

Bentham wrote *The Fragment on Government* (1776); *Rationale of Punishments and Rewards* (1825, originally published in French in 1811 as *Théorie des peines et des récompenses*); *Defense of Usury* (1787); *The Manual of Political Economy* (published in part in 1789); *Introduction to Principles of Morals and Legislation* (1789); *A Catechism of Parliamentary Reform* (written 1809, published 1817); *Book of Fallacies* (1824); *Rationale of Judicial Evidence* (1827); and *Constitutional Code* (1830).

He was the leader of the political radicals of his day, and his philosophy attracted prominent intellectuals, such as James Mill, John Stuart Mill, and the Austens. His work and writing created a strong radical movement in England that led to liberal reforms that persist today.

Bentham is known for his utilitarian tendencies and regarded his principle of utility as a basic rule for all legislators: ". . . that property in any object whereby it tends to produce pleasure, good, or happiness to the party whose interest is considered." John Stuart Mill adopted the principle in his *Utilitarianism.* Of the many philosophic concepts Bentham contributed, the best known, however, is his HEDONISTIC CALCULUS, and his major philosophic impetus was to foster social, penal, and legal reform. In his view of economics and politics, he was close to the laissez-faire doctrines of Adam Smith. Bentham staunchly defended individualism: Each person is the best and final judge of his or her own interests. The individual should never be hindered by an authority, state, or institution from securing his or her own interests. People are subject to two principal motives: avoidance of pain, and procurement of pleasure. The purpose of law in all its forms must be to secure and promote "the greatest happiness of the greatest number." Punishment, the infliction of pain or discomfort, is itself evil, though necessary to prevent greater evil.

Bergson, Henri (1859–1941) French philosopher born in Paris. Winner of the Nobel Prize for Literature in 1927. His principal works are *Time and Free Will: An Essay on the Immediate Data of Consciousness* (published in Paris in 1889, in New York City in 1910); *Matter and Memory* (Paris, 1896; New York, 1911); *Laughter. An Essay on the Meaning of the Comic* (Paris, 1903; New York, 1910); *Introduction to Metaphysics* (Paris, 1903; New York, 1913); *Creative Evolution* (Paris, 1907; New York, 1911); *Mind-Energy* (Paris, 1919; New York, 1920); *The Two Sources of Morality and Religion* (Paris, 1932; London, 1935); and *The Creative Mind* (Paris, 1934; New York, 1946).

Bergson's philosophy is evolutionary, but not materialistic. Life is intuited as an inner flow. Material and bodily changes are the mechanisms of that spiritual activity. Human activity in itself contains a freedom distinct from these mechanisms. For example, two radically different kinds of time exist: (a) the time of measurement (scientific time; objective time; conceptual time; mechanical time) and (b) the time of our immediate, intuitive, flowing experience. Measured time is mathematical, symbolic, part of a physical explanation, using standard units or moments measured by spatial marks on chronometers, clocks, etc. *Measured time* is seen as extended, homogeneous, and entering a future in a forward direction. Our inner, *intuitive time* is an irreversible, active flow that blends so much into itself that the activity or process of time is indivisible, yet heterogeneous (made up of a succession of different qualities and events), concrete rather than abstract, real rather than symbolic, immediate rather than objectively detached, actively ongoing, flowing, immediately and intuitively experienced and felt, and always a part of our consciousness. Measured time is illusory, but is regarded by scientists as *real time*.

Bergson, for his part, advocates the use of an intuited élan vital to get in touch with the true forces operating in all things. Knowledge of the élan vital serves as the true explanatory foundation for change, and for evolution in nature. See ELAN VITAL.

Berkeley, George (1685–1753) born in Ireland, became a Fellow of Trinity College, Dublin; in 1724, became Dean of Derry; in 1734, became Bishop of Cloyne. Berkeley established a school in Bermuda and then, for three years, lived in Newport, Rhode Island, where he attempted to raise funds for his school in Bermuda. When he failed, he left for England.

Berkeley has been labeled an IMMATERIALIST, an IDEALIST. He is considered one of the three leading British Empiricists (Locke, Berkeley, Hume) in contrast with the Continental Rationalists (Descartes, Spinoza, Leibniz). As a Christian theologian, Berkeley attempted to show (a) that all existence is a function of the mind (and will) of God; (b) that without God's thought there would be no existence, since existence is a product of God's thinking; (c) that natural events are signs and symbols, letters and words of God's thought and language, which we have to decipher and with which we have to bring our thoughts into harmony; and (d) that the source and foundation of all existence is not matter, but the living, active mind of God, who in perceiving (thinking) creates existence.

Some of Berkeley's most prominent scientific philosophic works are *Essays Towards a New Theory of Vision* (1709); *A Treatise Concerning the Principles of Human Knowledge* (1710); *Discourse on Passive Obedience* (1711); *Three Dialogues Between Hyles and Philonous* (1713); *De Motu* (1721); *Alciphron, or the Minute Philosopher* (1732); and *Siris* (1744).

best, principle of the a common Platonic notion that (a) all things have an inner tendency to strive for their good, for the best that is possible for them; (b) no person who knows his or her good (or the good) would choose an evil; and/or (c) everything in the universe is rationally arranged for the best. Related to Socrates' belief that 1. humans always choose what they regard to be the best or good (and do not ever choose what they regard to be bad or evil) and 2. evil is due to ignorance of what is good. See SOCRATIC PARADOXES.

best of all possible worlds, the (Leibniz) the world as it exists could not possibly be better than it is, since God's perfect wisdom, goodness, and omnipotence necessitate God to create the best of all the worlds possible to create. See COMPOSSIBLES (LEIBNIZ); REASON, PRINCIPLE OF SUFFICIENT (LEIBNIZ).

best of all possible worlds, the (Stoics) since the universe is rationally necessitated (fated) by the logos, it is good and hence the best possible. See STOICS, THE.

bioethics the study of the ethical problems that arise from the interrelation- ship between medical/biological research and technological advances on the one hand, and the rights and the future of humans on the other. Examples of specific problems: euthanasia, abortion, eugenics, genetic manipulation, cloning, genetic screening, genetic therapy, fetal research, exogenesis (developing an embryo outside the mother's womb), and brain control.

black-and-white thinking 1. thinking that is expressed in rigid extremes (polarities, contrasts) without qualifications and without sensitivity to the subtleties of the issues. **2.** thinking that infers that because something is true it is extreme, or something contrary to it must be false (or vice versa). Compare with FALLACY, TYPES OF INFORMAL (1).

body sometimes *material body*. **1.** used synonymously with MATERIAL OBJECT, or MATTER. Example: A body in motion will remain in motion. **2.** often designating the material composition of the human (or animal) in contrast with the mind, spirit, or soul. See entries under MIND.

Boethius, Anicius Manlius Severinus (c.480–524) Roman philosopher, writer, statesman, Christian theologian; born in Rome and regarded as the last of the Roman thinkers and the initiator of the Christian intellectual heritage. Boethius wrote voluminously in defense of Christianity, always in the context of preserving classical Greek Knowledge. Imprisoned on a false charge of treason, heresy, sacrilege, and inappropriate studies—of mathematics and astrology—Boethius was imprisoned for almost a year, during which time he wrote his major work, *De Consolatione Philosophiae*. Boethius was executed and became popularly regarded as a saint.

Bonaventure, Saint (1221–1274) Franciscan theologian, philosopher, mystic; born in Tuscany, Italy, he studied in Paris. He was canonized in 1482 by Pope Sixtus IV.

He opposed the Aristotelianism of his friend Thomas Aquinas and propounded instead the neo-Platonism of St. Augustine. His most important works are *Breviloquium*; *Itinerarium Mentis in Deum*; *De Reductione Artium ad Theologiam*; *Biblia Pauperum;* and a commentary on Peter Lombard.

Boole, George (1815–1864) English mathematician and logician, born in Lincoln; taught mathematics at Queen's College in Cork, Ireland, until his death. He made many contributions to logic and philosophy.

Foremost are his applications of algebra and its methods and notations to logic and to the theory of probability; his development of a calculus for logical operators or connectives and a logic of classes; his theory of the independence of some forms of logic from traditional deductive procedures; his stress on a metalogic, or higher level of logic, which became the foundation of all logico-mathematical thought based on his theories of Laws of Thought; and his development of a logic of variables without reference to quantifiers. The well-known Boolean Algebra stands for the variety of non-axiomatic mathematical and logical systems that have grown out of Boole's procedures.

Of Boole's many writings, the following have had a major impact: *The Mathematical Analysis of Logic* (1847); *An Investigation of the Laws of Thought* (1859); and *On the Calculus of Finite Differences* (1860).

bracketing (Husserl) the suspension (*bracketing off*) of the presuppositions and abstractions implicit in the sciences, such as *matter-of-fact*, *physical cause/effect relationship*, and *material object*. By purifying one's perspective in this way, one is able to see things as they actually appear to consciousness. The aim of philosophy is to describe, classify, and intuitively grasp the variety of kinds of experience and consciousnesses in their purest subjective state and in their concrete operations. See PHENOMENOLOGY (HUSSERL).

Brentano, Franz (1838–1917) German philosopher, logician, and psychologist; born in Marienberg and taught philosophy at Würzburg and Vienna. He became a Roman Catholic priest in 1864 and left the Church a decade later. Brentano wrote extensively on all subjects in philosophy as well as treatises and commentaries on such historical figures as Aristotle. Much of his writing was published posthumously, and more compilations and translations are in progress. Available in English is his *The Origin of Our Knowledge of Right and Wrong* (1902). Portions of his 2-volume *Psychologie* appear in *Realism and the Background of Phenomenology* (1960, edited by Roderick M. Chisholm).

Bruno, Giordano (1548–1600) Italian philosopher, theologian, poet, naturalist; born near Naples; studied philosophy under the Augustinian order in Naples and was ordained by the Dominicans. Suspected of heresy, Bruno fled to Rome in 1576 and shortly afterward left the Dominican order. In 1592, Bruno was charged by the Inquisition, and in 1600 burned at the stake.

Bruno believed, with Copernicus, that the sun is the center of our planetary system; that the universe is infinite in extent and this truth illustrates God's infinite power; that God and nature are different words for the same thing, so God represents the unity and coherence of the universe, and the universe represents that unity's changing diversity and variety; that God is revealed in the structure, change, and processes of nature, of the universe; that the human is a microcosm of the universe; that the human mind is an expression of the being, power, and reality of God; and that the authority of the Church could not, and should not, supersede human individuality or its intellectual expression and development.

Bruno's principal work is *De Immenso et Innumerabilibus* (1591).

bundle theory of the mind or self see MIND, BUNDLE THEORY OF THE (HUME).

C

calculus (from Latin, *pl. calculi,* piles or rows of stones or pebbles—which stood for numbers and were manipulated to produce arithmetical results) **1.** any formal system for solving logical problems. Inferences are drawn with the use of symbols, rules of inference, and methods of logical procedure. Used as a synonym for *logic* (as in *sentential,* or *propositional, calculus* and *predicate,* or *functional, calculus*). **2.** the principles regulating (a) the quantification of something (as in HEDONISTIC CALCULUS [BENTHAM]) or (b) the procedures and definitions to be followed in determining the application of concepts (as in the *calculus of classes* and the *calculus of probability*).

canon (from Greek, *kanōn,* a rule such as used by carpenters to set a straight line or to measure by; a rod [shuttle] such as used in weaving) a basic and important rule (principle, standard, criterion) to which logical and scientific methods must adhere. Example: John Stuart Mill's Five Canons of Induction. See METHODS, MILL'S INDUCTIVE.

capacity the potential for a thing to do something, to act or react. In humans, capacities may be innate or acquired through conditioning. In ethics, what a person is able (has the capacity) to do in relation to what the person ought to do. For example, the moral command not to steal has meaning only for one who is not a kleptomaniac and thus has the ability (capacity) not to steal. See DISPOSITION.

cardinal virtues see VIRTUES, CARDINAL.

carnal (from Latin, *carnalis*; from *caro, carnis,* flesh) **1.** animalistic. **2.** that which has to do with the body as the source of cravings, appetites, desires, sensuality, sexuality, lust, indulgence. **3.** material, worldly, hence temporal, transitory, and valueless. Contrast with SPIRITUAL.

Carnap, Rudolf (1891–1970) American philosopher born in Germany; philosopher of empiricism and positivism, logic, mathematics, science, and the conceptual structure of language; educated at the universities of Freiburg and Jena. His early philosophic foundations and inspiration were the logical and mathematical works of Bertrand Russell and Frege.

Some of Carnap's important works are *Philosophy and Logical Syntax* (1935); *Philosophy of Science* (1936); *Logical Syntax of Language* (1937); *Foundations of Logic and Mathematics* (1939); *Formalization of Logic* (1943); *Meaning and Necessity: A Study in Semantics and Modal Logic* (1947); *Logical Foundations of Probability* (1950); and *The Continuum of Inductive Methods* (1952).

Carneades (c.213–129 BC) Greek Skeptic philosopher and rhetorician. Born in Cyrenaica (now Libya). Founder of Plato's Third, or New, Academy.

Cartesianism those philosophies that existed for about a century after Descartes' death in which philosophers used his major philosophic assumptions and methodology to develop their own systems. (They did not necessarily adhere to every detail of Descartes' philosophy but did retain his rationalistic and mathematical/geometric method.) Descartes' main aim was to reconstruct the whole of human knowledge by means of a rational, deductive (basically geometric) system. See COGITO ERGO SUM. The Cartesians also attempted to construct one all-inclusive science, which would explain all natural phenomena (biological, chemical, physical, psychological) in terms of common quantitative and mathematical laws. See VORTEX THEORY (DESCARTES).

casualism the belief that all things happen by chance. Compare with ACCIDENTALISM; TYCHISM.

casuistry 1. in the positive sense, (a) the art (science, ideology, doctrine) that deals with questions of right or wrong conduct, or (b) the actual application of moral principles to particular conduct. **2.** in the negative sense, sophistical, equivocal, false, or misleading reasoning or teaching about one's moral conduct, duties, and principles. See ETHICS;CASUISTIC.

categorical 1. not hypothetical. **2.** unconditional. **3.** without qualification or exception. **4.** definite. **5.** obligatory, not conditional-on-a-wish. **6.** referring to the *names* of the categories of classification and/or the categories themselves that are being classified. See entries under CATEGORIES; CATEGORY.

categorical imperative, the (Kant) the necessary and absolute moral law believed to be the ultimate rational foundation for all moral conduct: "So act that you can will the maxim (principle) of your action to be a universal law binding upon the will of every rational person." The categorical imperative is not conditional (hypothetical) based on a wish or consequences, as in "If you wish to have healthy gums, take vitamin C." It is absolutely binding. Compare with HYPOTHETICAL IMPERATIVE (KANT). See DUTY; ETHICS (KANT).

categories (Aristotle) 1. all things that can be conceived and named are subsumed under one or more of the following ten classes or genera: *substance (ousia)*, for example, man, animal, plant; *quantity (poson)*, for example, 175 pounds; *quality (poion)*, for example, good, hot, brown; *relation (prosti)*, for example, dependent upon farming; *place (pou)*, for example, in the country; *time (pote)*, for example, 1978; *position, condition,* or *state (keisthai)*, for example, standing, being drunk; *possession (echein)*, for example, having hair; *action, activity (poiein)*, for example, plowing; *passion, passivity,* or *being affected (paschein)*, for example, becoming thirsty. The categories and their number vary slightly in Aristotle's writings. Substance (see SUBSTANCE [ARISTOTLE]) is the most important of them, and Aristotle has much to say about how the other categories are related to it. Nothing is intelligible unless put into the framework of these categories. Our understanding of things is formed by the categories, and things themselves are formed by the forces acting in nature that operate according to these categories. **2.** in Aristotle's *Metaphysics,* there is a presentation of what might be called *metacategories*, or the concepts that pervade and are common to all the categories as such. These are: *being* (existence), *oneness* (unity), *sameness* (identity), and *otherness* (variety). See TRANSCENDEN-TALIA.

categories (Plato) of the categories scattered throughout Plato's works, five basic ones are listed in his *Sophist:* being, rest, motion, identity, and differ-ence. Plato laid the foundation for philosophizing in terms of categories.

categories of logic, the (Kant) the categories of logic, also called The Logical Table of Judgments, are grouped in the following way:

I. QUANTITY	II. QUALITY
1. Universal	1. Affirmative
2. Particular	2. Negative
3. Singular	3. Infinite

III. RELATION	IV. MODALITY
1. Categorical	1. Problematical
2. Hypothetical	2. Assertorical
3. Disjunctive	3. Apodeictical

The study of these twelve categories was the subject matter of what Kant called *Transcendental Logic*, from which he deduced the cate-gories of the understanding. See CATEGORIES OF THE UNDERSTANDING, THE (KANT); DIALECTIC, TRANSCENDENTAL (KANT).

categories of the understanding, the (Kant) pure *a priori* concepts or principles that provide the necessary structure for the understanding to perceive and conceive what is given to it in experience. The Table of Categories, also called The Transcendental Table of the Pure Concepts of the Understanding, is grouped in the following way:

I. QUANTITY	II. QUALITY
1. Unity (the Measure)	1. Reality
2. Plurality (the Quantity)	2. Negation
3. Totality (the Whole)	3. Limitation

III.
RELATION
1. Substance/Subsistence
   (Inherence)
2. Causality/Dependence

3. Community/Interaction
   (Reciprocity)

IV.
MODALITY
1. Possibility/Impossibility

2. Existence/Nonexistence
   (Being/Nonbeing)
3. Necessity/Contingency

Some of the basic tenets in Kant's philosophy of the twelve categories: (a) They are necessary conditions for any experience—without them there can be no experience, no knowledge. All experience and knowledge presuppose them. (b) They are a complete list of the forms of our understanding. (They are the only ways by which things can be experienced and made meaningful.) (c) They do not describe or classify reality as it is in itself. (We can never know the noumenal realm/world and thus (1) can never know its intrinsic structure and (2) can never apply these categories to it. These categories refer only to the phenomenal realm/world.) (d) They are *applied* to (projected upon, imposed upon) the raw material provided in experience but are not and cannot be obtained from experience. They transcend experience. See APPERCEPTION, TRANSCENDENTAL (2); DEDUCTION, TRANSCENDENTAL; SUBSTANCE (KANT).

category 1. a class, division, genus, family, or type with which distinctions are made among things for conceptual analysis and classification. **2.** a class of things that has a predicate or to which some term can be applied. **3.** any basic idea, concept, notion, or principle fundamental to a system of philosophy. **4.** one of the ultimate conceptual forms by which knowledge is made possible and which is a unique class in the following senses: (a) It may be found in conjunction with other categories (classes, forms) but cannot be described by them or reduced to them since it has nothing in common with any other category (except metalinguistically). (b) It cannot be regarded as a member of any other higher class (except as a member of the all-inclusive class of ultimate being or substance). (c) It gives form to the content of our knowledge but does not itself provide that content. (d) It serves as the foundation for all meaningful communication in subject-predicate languages.

category mistake the improper semantical grouping of unrelatable classes of meaning that results in some form of ABSURD (meaningless, ridiculous, nonsensical, sound-without-sense) statement; no literal or meaningful translation of the resulting statement is possible that can avoid the absurdity. Example: "The redness of time hits until it sleeps." This sentence is syntactically (grammatically) but not semantically legitimate due to category mistakes.

catharsis see KATHARSIS.

causal chain sometimes *causal sequence, causal series*, the view that the cause-effect relationship is a time sequence in which the effect produced becomes the cause of an effect, which in turn becomes a cause of an effect, and so on; also a reverse sequence in which a cause is an effect of a previous cause which in turn was an effect of a previous cause, and so on.

causal principle also *principle of universal causation or principle of causation*, the theory that every event has a cause. (Causes may not be known for specific events, but nevertheless if it is an event, it has a cause.)

causal regress, infinite the view that the causal series of events leading into the past has no absolute beginning point; a cause can always be found for an event and these events extend backward infinitely. There is no so-called first cause. The principal concepts involved in this view: (a) Any two causes, regardless of how far apart they are, are only a finite distance apart. (b) No two causal events are an infinite distance apart, but the series itself is infinite. (c) For any distance that can be designated between two causes, there will be an even greater distance that can be designated in the infinite series of causes. (d) No matter how far away that cause is which is pointed out in the regress, there will be an infinite number of other causes before it.

causal uniformity, the principle of 1. the theory that similar causes produce similar effects and similar effects have similar causes. Commonly phrased: "same cause, same effect; same effect, same cause." Contrasted with CAUSES, PRINCIPLE OF THE PLURALITY OF. **2.** the theory that cause-and-effect relations can be stated in the form of general laws that assume that to some extent what happens in the future will be similar to what happened in the past. See UNIFORMITY OF NATURE, PRINCIPLE OF THE. Contrast with CAUSES, PRINCIPLE OF THE PLURALITY OF.

causa sui (Latin, cause of itself, self-caused) **1.** the term has been applied to God to refer to God's ability to cause God, to bring God into existence. The question "Where did God come from?" has been answered by saying that God is *causa sui,* that is, God's own cause. Aquinas argues against self-causation in the following way: God cannot cause Himself. If He existed to cause Himself, He did not need to cause Himself (since He already exists). And if He did not exist He could not be anything to be able to cause Himself. *Causa sui* is a contradiction in terms. **2.** *causa sui* has erroneously been used to refer to concepts such as self-activating, self-existence, necessary being, absolute nondependence, that which proceeds independently on its own and out of its own essence. It has also been confused with eternal, timeless, and uncaused.

cause 1. anything capable of changing something else. **2.** that which produces something (makes something happen; brings about the occurrence of something) without which that thing would not have resulted. That which is produced (or changed) is called the *effect* and the effect is explained by its cause. **3.** the conditions each of which is necessary for the occurrence of an event, and all of which are sufficient for its occurrence, and which precede the event in time. (A cause of an event may be thought of as the name for a multitude of relevant conditions none of which, exclusive of the others, can be called *the* cause.) **4.** when X occurs and Y invariably follows, then X is said to be the cause of Y (and Y the effect of X). **5.** the sufficient conditions(s) for the occurrence of an event. See REASONS.

cause, efficient see CAUSES, ARISTOTLE'S FOUR.

cause, final see CAUSES, ARISTOTLE'S FOUR.

cause, formal see CAUSES, ARISTOTLE'S FOUR.

cause, immanent the internal conditions in a thing that produce change, as opposed to external conditions affecting it. Example: the act of willing to move one's hand and thereby *causing* it to move. Contrasted with CAUSE, TRANSCENDENT.

cause, material see CAUSES, ARISTOTLE'S FOUR.

cause, transcendent the external conditions that produce change upon or in a thing, as opposed to internal conditions affecting it. Example: water causing a seed to open. In this sense, *transcendent cause* is used interchangeably with *efficient cause*. Contrasted with CAUSE, IMMANENT.

cause and effect relationship a relationship in which three fundamental concepts are inherent: (a) temporal precedence. The cause always occurs prior in time to its effect. Cause and effect cannot occur simultaneously. A cause cannot follow its effect. (b) *cause* is meaningful only when related to the word *effect* (and vice versa); that is, *to be a cause* or *to have a cause* can only be understood in the context of a related or relatable effect (and vice versa). (c) cause and effect are related in an invariable sequence (succession, regularity, conjunction) in which whenever one occurs and the other always follows, then the former is labeled a *cause* and the latter its *effect*.

cause and effect relationship (Hume) before Hume the following notions were generally assumed about the concept of causality: (a) *regularity of succession:* To say that C is the cause of E is to say that whenever C happens then E happens, or that any instance of C is always followed by an instance of E. (Hume's term for this invariable sequence of cause and effect was *constant conjunction*.) (b) *temporal precedence:* The cause precedes the effect. And (c) *necessary connection* (which is the notion Hume rejected): there is a power, or force in C which *must make E occur*. A bond or tie was thought to exist that cemented a cause to its effect. The regularity of succession of C and E is due to a physical and logical necessity compelling the cause to produce the effect. Some of Hume's criticisms of necessary connection: (1) Necessity cannot be observed to exist between a cause and its effect. No power, no force can be shown *making, producing, influencing* the effect. All that is observed is the constant conjunction (regular succession) of C followed by E. We can observe the fact of one thing being followed by another, but not any necessary connection purportedly existing between these facts. (2) No sensation (impression) exists from which our idea of such a power in the cause necessitating the effect can be derived. There is no sensation of any bond or tie necessarily connecting the cause with its effect. Events are conjoined but not connected. (3) One cannot infer an effect simply from observing or analyzing the event that is considered a cause. One cannot infer a cause simply from observing or analyzing another event that is considered an effect. Only our experience of what constant conjunction does take place gives us this notion of which causes are related to which effects. Necessary connection is a product of habits of the mind and has no external reality. People become familiar with constantly conjoined events and formulate a belief based on past experience. (4) Statements about causal connections cannot be logically necessary statements or truths. The idea of a cause can be clearly distinguished from the idea of its effect without contradiction. If they were necessarily connected, this could not be done—the thought of one would automatically entail (necessitate) the other. It is possible to imagine a cause not being followed by the expected effect. It is as well possible to imagine some effect that in our experience did not follow a particular cause. (There is no logical contradiction in saying that when I let go of this pencil it will float in midair rather than fall to the floor; no amount of experience will ever be amassed to prove that its floating in midair cannot happen.) No real, objective, inductive grounds can be given for inferences from causes to effects. (Kant attempted a resolution of what he saw as problems in Hume's account of causality by making causality one of his CATEGORIES OF THE UNDERSTANDING.) See KNOWLEDGE (HUME); SKEPTICISM (HUME).

causes, Aristotle's four 1. *material cause:* the substrate, substance *out of which* a thing comes to be and which persists; that *in which* a change takes place. **2.** *formal cause:* that shape (pattern, configuration) *into which* something is changed. The essence (the essential characteristic) being manifested in the process of becoming. **3.** *efficient cause:* that *by which* some change is brought about; that which initiates activity. (The efficient cause is often referred to as the *propelling cause.*) **4.** *final cause:* that *for the sake of which* an activity takes place; that end (purpose, goal, state of completion) *for which* the change is produced, or for which the change aims (strives, seeks). Its *telos* or *raison d'être.* (The final cause is often referred to as the *telic cause.*) These four causes answer the question of *why* and *how* a thing becomes what it becomes rather than becoming something else. Taken together they may be called *teleological causation.* For Aristotle, we understand a thing if we know four things about it: (a) what it is *made of* (material cause), (b) its *form* (formal cause which is taking shape or being expressed), (c) what (or who) *produced* (made) it (efficient cause), and (d) its *final state* (end, goal, purpose, state of completion) toward which the activity is progressing, toward which the change is striving.

These four causes operate both in art (TECHNĒ: all those things created by humans) and in nature (PHYSIS: all things not created by humans). An artist makes the head of Zeus out of marble. The material cause is marble. The formal cause is the form of Zeus taking shape in the marble; this is in the artist's mind as an idea which the artist is impressing upon the marble. The efficient cause is the force of the hammer and chisel applied over a period of time by the artist. The final cause is the end product, the completed art work, for the accomplishment of which the whole process is taking place.

In artistic creation, Aristotle's four causes have a transcendent teleological character. The artist is separate from (transcends) his or her medium. The artist gives a thought objective reality in a physical medium. In natural creation, Aristotle's four causes have an immanent teleological character. The form being developed is inseparably linked with its matter. The reason for an object's developing the way it does is an integral part of the thing itself. Examples are an acorn developing into an oak tree, or a fetus developing into a child. The material cause is the material stuff of which the acorn or fetus is made. The efficient cause in the case of the acorn is the rain, sun, soil, temperature, wind; in the case of the fetus, the complex biochemical changes in the mother's womb affecting the fetus. The formal cause for the acorn is the seed's own character to become an oak tree rather than a maple tree or a piglet; and for the fetus the formal cause is the pattern by which the fetus is developing toward maturing into a child. The final cause is the point of actualization of the process where what was striven for is reached.

Aristotle's four causes assumed (1) a continuity and interdependence among all phenomena and (2) a hierarchical gradation in nature from inert matter receiving qualitative and quantitative change; to plants, which have the functions of nourishment and reproduction; to animals, which in addition possess sensation, mobility, and many types of mental functions; to the human being, who in addition possesses the supreme function of reason. Aristotle's word for cause (AITIA) meant *the reason for something happening*. It denoted all the ways to describe in a language (the Greek language) how things come to be the way they are; how they develop from a beginning process to a completed state, potentiality to actuality. But for Aristotle, these four causes were not merely linguistic tools for talking about phenomena; they were actual operating principles in the universe to produce what is in existence. See CHANGE (ARISTOTLE); EXPLANATION, TELEOLOGICAL.

causes, principle of the plurality of the view that the same effect can be produced by different causes. Examples: Death may be caused by drowning, a heart attack, a hit on the head. A sneeze may be caused by pollen, by an itch, by a cold. Contrasted with CAUSAL UNIFORMITY, THE PRINCIPLE OF.

This formulation sometimes includes the view that the same cause can at different times produce different effects.

certain (from Latin, *cernere,* perceive, decide, determine, resolve) **1.** INDU-BITABLE. **2.** thoroughly established as unquestionably true. There are no degrees of certainty as there are for notions such as clarity, CONFIRMATION, and reliability. A thing may be certain but not necessarily self-evident or tautologically true. That which is certain is known, but that which is known need not be certain. Contrast with DOUBT.

certainty, psychological or intuitive the feeling of assurance (certitude) that something is true and undeniable. Related to mental states or atti-tudes such as acceptance, belief, trust, certitude, dependability, reliability, unquestionability, indisputable, fixed, and settled. Example: The certainty that is associated with our belief that the sun will rise tomorrow morning, or that we exist. Opposite to SKEPTICISM; DOUBT. Compare with BELIEF.

chance (from Latin, *cadere,* fall—as in the falling of the dice) in general, to come to pass, to happen without design, intention, or purposiveness and without expectation or prediction. The word *chance* has been understood in a variety of contexts: **1.** ignorance of the causes producing an event; a chance event is an event whose cause is unknown. **2.** not directed by intel-ligent foresight. **3.** the coming together of unexpected, unpredictable, unintentional, and independent series (coincidences) of causes. Such events are not physically necessitated nor are they determinable by the mind. (Chance precludes necessity [and design]; what occurs by chance cannot occur by necessity [or by design].) **4.** lawless: no law can explain it. (Although chance can be understood by laws of PROBABILITY.) **5.** uncaused events. (This is an erroneous use.) See TYCHĒ. Compare with ACCIDENTAL-ISM, RANDOM, TYCHISM.

change (from Latin, *cambiare,* exchange or barter) involving—in lessening degrees of essentiality—the concepts of (a) succession (time); (b) an iden-tity that is involved in a change, or something that can be identified which remains relatively the same within a changing state; (c) some degree of variation or alteration of this identity (becoming different in some respects from what it once was); and (d) often a direction or growth.

change (Aristotle) Aristotle used the word KINĒSIS to include any kind of change or movement (motion). Aristotle discusses change in a rich variety of ways: **1.** change (motion) is eternal (a tenet that all Greek philosophers except the Eleatics, who denied change, accepted as necessary and indu-bitable). The essence of time is such that it excludes the possibility of a time—a state—without change. There could never have been a time at which there was no time; hence, there could never have been a time with-out change (motion). **2.** all physical change requires these essential ele-ments: (a) *matter* (a substrate, substance): that which continues throughout the change, or that which is changing; (b) *privation:* the absence or lack of a particular form; (c) the *form* that appears during (or throughout) the change. All physical change consists of matter developing (or acquiring) a form it did not previously possess. (An alternative way of putting it: All physical change consists of a form developing in matter, where form was not previously present in the same way.) **3.** change may be divided into types such as: (a) *qualitative change:* (sometimes referred to as *alteration*). Changes of the characteristics (qualities, properties, attributes) of an object. Examples: a green leaf turning brown; iron rusting; a liquid changing color. (Sometimes referred to as *accidental change.*) In qualitative change, the substance (the identity, or the substantial nature) of the thing does not change. (b) *spatial-temporal change* (sometimes referred to as *change of place,* or *locomotion*): change of the positions of objects. (c) *quantitative change:* change of number of a thing. This includes (1) change of size and shape (alteration of a thing's boundaries), (2) increase or decrease of size, shape, or number (augmentation or diminution), and (3) increase or decrease of motion or movement. Example: the multiplication or growth of living cells. Quantitative change usually involves both spatial and qualitative change. (d) *substantial change:* development of a thing's form or identity, the activity of a potential (a nature, or form, or essence, or potency) becoming actualized, becoming an existent. There are two general kinds of substantial change: (1) *generation:* the coming-to-be of something; a thing's becoming what it is intended to be; and (2) *degeneration:* the passing-away from its developed, actualized state; the process of losing or destroying that which the thing was intended to be. See GENESIS (ARISTOTLE); CAUSES, ARISTOTLE'S FOUR; MATTER/FORM (ARISTOTLE); and entries under SUBSTANCE that refer to Aristotle.

change (Cratylus) the Greek philosopher Cratylus (a younger contemporary of Socrates) took Heraclitus's view of change to the extreme. Heraclitus observed that everything is in constant change, and no one can step into the same river twice. Cratylus extended this to say that no one can even step into the same river once, because not only is the river changing to prevent us from stepping into the same river a second time but we are changing also during the time it takes us to attempt to step into the river that first time. See SKEPTICISM (CRATYLUS).

change (Heraclitus) the Greek philosopher Heraclitus of Ephesus was one of the first philosophers to use the concept of change as the foundation of his philosophy: Unending FLUX is the most fundamental characteristic of the universe. He is famous for saying: "All things change (flow, separate, dissolve)." "Nothing remains the same." "You cannot step into the same river twice." Compare with LOGOS (HERACLITUS).

chaos (Greek, *chaos,* gap, chasm; from *chainein,* gape) **1.** the disorganized, confused, formless, and undifferentiated state of primal matter before the presence of order in the universe. **2.** that condition of the universe in which chance is the principal ruler. **3.** an uncontrolled state of affairs. **4.** in Greek philosophy, the universe as it was before rational principles (laws) manifested themselves throughout the universe and brought about the world order as it is now. This is sometimes regarded as a principle itself, which prevents order or demolishes order. Compare with COSMOS. See DEMIURGE.

character (from Greek, *charaktēr,* from *charassein,* make sharp, engrave; often the sign or token imprinted on something to indicate such things as ownership, origin, name, or brand) **1.** the name for the sum total of a person's traits, which includes such things as behavior, habits, likes, dislikes, capacities, dispositions, potential, values, and thought patterns. **2.** the relatively fixed structure or feature of a personality that causes such traits. **3.** the relatively fixed framework of a personality in accordance with which such traits manifest themselves.

characteristic, defining the quality a thing must have in order to be defined (classified, named) as that thing. Example: The defining characteristic of *bachelor* is to be unmarried. See CLASS.

characteristic, distinguishing sometimes *differentiating characteristic.* The distinctive quality that marks off (differentiates, distinguishes) a thing from other things.

choice the decision reached between (or among) alternative possibilities. Some characteristics of choices: (a) They cannot be classified as true or false, but are classified as good or bad, right or wrong, preferable or not preferable. (b) The choices one continues to make are said to habituate one's character toward them. (c) Choices reveal the essential traits of a personality. (d) Choices require awareness of alternatives, deliberation, and intentional activity. (e) Choices may be related to, but can be distinguished from, motives, intentions, wishes, desires, consequences, and principles of conduct.

choosing the traditional meaning: a voluntary act preceded by deliberation; conscious selection; the mental act that causes an action to take place, which action is (usually) the one preferred from among alternative courses of action. Choosing rationally or voluntarily, as opposed to choosing irrationally or involuntarily in a forced manner, involves characteristics such as: (a) an *inclination* (or necessity) to act (usually in the face of a problem). (b) *deliberation* about the problem. (c) a *decision* to act. (d) the perception of *alternatives*—of more than one possibility of action. (e) the evaluation of the *consequences*—the weighing of the relative merits of the results that may follow each alternative. (f) a *choice* as to how to act or proceed. (g) the *action* engaged in. (Usually the one preferred among the alternatives.) (h) *volition*—the deliberate concerted effort in and commitment to making the choice and the action a reality. (i) sometimes: *appraisal* of what has occurred. See VOLUNTARY ACTION; WILL.

Chryssipus (c.280—c.207 BC) Greek Stoic philosopher born in Soli, Cilicia; worked in Athens, where he was a disciple of Cleanthes, the second head of the Stoic School, after Zeno. His more than 700 writings on logic, language, ethics, physics, and psychology exist today only in fragments. We know of his philosophy from these fragments, from quotations and the cataloguing of his works, and from ancient commentators and philosophers.

circularity also *circular reasoning* or *arguing in a circle* **1.** applied to ideas (arguments, reasoning, definitions) that repeat themselves. **2.** applied to arguments that assume the conclusion that is to be proven. See DEFINI-TIONS, TYPES OF (1); FALLACY, TYPES OF INFORMAL (13).

clairvoyance (from French, *clair,* clear, + *voyant,* seeing) **1.** the ability to obtain information about objects or people by means other than our five senses. This includes reading thoughts (see TELEPATHY). **2.** the ability to perceive or discern objects not perceptible by our ordinary sensory means of perceiving. Clairvoyance is considered a direct and immediate transfer of information by *nonsensory* and noninferential means. See PARAPSYCHOL-OGY.

class any group (collection) of things possessing common characteristics (properties, qualities, attributes). The common characteristics of the class define the class; they are called the *class-defining characteristics*. These may be multiple and complex characteristics, or a singular and simple characteristic. *Students* names a class. It is the name given to a group of characteristics that we believe a student has: engaged in study, registered at school, going to classes, being tested, etc. The Latin GENUS is often used as a synonym. See SET.

class, complementary that collection of all things which do not belong to a given class. Example: the complement of the class *students* is the class of all those things that are *not* students: trees, clouds, planets, houses, cars, roads, satellites, etc. It is customary to form a complementary class by prefixing its name with *non*. The complement of the class *students* would be the class *nonstudents*. *Nonstudents* may be called a complementary term, or the complement of *students*.

class, singular sometimes *unit class* or *unique class*, a class with only one member.

classicism an expression of a temperament, or the product of that temperament, that is based on a desire for order, harmony, proportion, moderation, and perfection derived from the application of reason and intelligence directing emotion and feeling. Contrasted with ROMANTICISM.

Cleanthes (c.331–232 BC) Greek Stoic philosopher, born in Assos, in Troas. He studied for 19 years under Zeno of Citrium, founder of the Stoic School, and after Zeno's death succeeded him as leader of the the Stoic School.

clear and distinct ideas see IDEAS, CLEAR AND DISTINCT (DESCARTES).

cogito ergo sum (Latin, I think, therefore I am, or I am thinking, therefore I exist) Descartes' phrase for an immediate, necessary, and indubitable intuition, in which he recognizes himself clearly and distinctly as a RES COGITANS (a thinking thing or self). He cannot doubt that he thinks (doubts), for in the very act of doubting he proves the act of thinking (doubting) to be true. *Cogito ergo sum* serves as the self-evident truth or axiom from which Descartes developed his rationalistic system of explanation. See SKEPTICISM (DESCARTES).

cognition (from Latin, *cognitio,* from *cognoscere,* become acquainted with, know) **1.** intellectual knowledge. **2.** the act of knowing.

Cohen, Morris Raphael (1880–1947) American philosopher who stressed naturalism and logical empiricism; born in Minsk, Russia; educated at the City College of New York and at Harvard, where he studied under Josiah Royce and William James. Cohen taught at the City College of New York for decades and lectured widely at American universities.

His most important works include *Reason and Nature: An Essay on the Meaning of Scientific Method* (1931); *An Introduction to Logic and Scientific Method* (1934, with Ernest Nagel); *A Preface to Logic* (1945); *The Meaning of Human History* (1947); *Studies in Philosophy and Science* (1949); and *Reason and Law: Studies in Juristic Philosophy* (1950).

coherence (from Latin, *cohaerere,* adhere together, stick together, be united) **1.** connection by some common idea (principle, relationship, order, concept). **2.** following logically without any inconsistency or gaps. Logical congruity. Opposite to INCOHERENCE. Contrasted with INCOMPATIBLE. Compare with COMPATIBLE; CONSISTENT. See TRUTH, COHERENCE THEORY OF.

collectively considering the members of a CLASS (group, SET) as one unit. What can be said about a class collectively may not be true of all, or any, of the members of the class. Opposite to DISTRIBUTIVELY.

comedy (Aristotle) a play in which the actions of the main characters are worse than the actions of ordinary people in daily life. Compare with TRAGEDY (ARISTOTLE).

commitment (Sartre) the free choice of principles of conduct and a way of life, in spite of the lack of any good reasons for accepting them. Their only defense is allegiance to them, and action on their behalf. See EXISTENTIALISM.

common consent argument for God's existence also known as the *consensus gentium* argument, the attempt to prove the existence of God by appeal to the universally held belief in all cultures in all ages that there is a God (of some kind or other). This is the argument holding that God exists on the grounds that there is universal consent (belief, assent, assurance) that God exists. See FALLACY, TYPES OF INFORMAL (16); GOD, ARGUMENTS FOR THE EXISTENCE OF.

common sense 1. that which seems sensible (rational, correct) to people of good perception and abilities. **2.** that power or faculty used to come to conclusions which others in their right minds would also come to. **3.** everyday, ordinary, common understanding. **4.** the natural beliefs shared by normal individuals, plain individuals, or the general judgment of individuals. **5.** those ideas necessarily employed in practical activity. **6.** a general trust in the senses and common knowledge that puts them beyond argumentation.

Truths of common sense are directly perceived, and no proof is needed for their support.

common-sense beliefs, fundamental the common-sense outlook on the world that is characterized by assumptions about reality such as: (a) An external world exists distinct from consciousness and would remain in existence even if there were no consciousness. (b) Minds similar to our own exist externally in bodies similar to our own. (c) We all have a personal identity or unity about us that endures through time. (d) Individuals can act in a self-determining way. (e) Order exists independently of consciousness. (f) Cause and effect exist as relationships in nature. (g) Things exist in time and space.

common-sense realism see REALISM, COMMON SENSE.

compatibilist (ethics) one who believes that determinism, which denies the existence of free will, is compatible with the *facts* or beliefs grounded in human experience such as (free) choices, moral decisions, self-initiation, moral *oughts* and *shoulds*, responsibility, accountability, blame, praise, punishment, and other concepts that imply the existence of freedom of the will in humans. Contrasted with *incompatibilist*. See entries under FREE WILL.

compatible (from Latin, *compati*, have compassion; from *com*, with, + *pati*, bear, suffer) **1.** capable of coexisting in harmony. **2.** statements (meanings, ideas) that are capable of being related logically and/or conceptually (a) without being inconsistent and/or (b) without leading to an inconsistency. Opposite to INCOMPATIBLE. Compare with COHERENCE.

complement (from Latin, *complementum*, that which fills up or completes; from *com*, with + *plere*, fill) see CLASS, COMPLEMENTARY.

composition, fallacy of see FALLACY, TYPES OF INFORMAL (15).

compossibles (Leibniz) things that (a) are not contradictory, (b) belong to a possible world, and (c) can therefore at some time exist together. Physical laws (and ultimately God) determine the actualized existence in time of all such possible worlds. In Leibniz's theory of compossibles there is an infinity of possible combinations that will never exist and has never existed; that is, an infinite number of possibilities or noncontradictions that will never be realized and yet are known by God's omniscience. See REASON, PRINCIPLE OF SUFFICIENT (LEIBNIZ); BEST OF ALL POSSIBLE WORLDS, THE (LEIBNIZ).

comprehension (from Latin, *comprehendere*, grasp) the act of UNDERSTANDING (imagining, conceiving, apprehending) the meaning or intent of something. Some of the ways in which this is achieved: (a) subsuming particular items under general and abstract explanations or classes; (b) applying general and abstract principles to particular cases; (c) inferring possibilities and anticipating future events based on past occurrences; (d) deducing implications or conclusions from a series of statements; (e) relating or ordering seemingly disparate experiences; and (f) comparing the unfamiliar (the relatively unknown) with the familiar (the known). Compare with APPREHENSION, PREHENSION.

compresence (from Latin, *com,* with, together, + *presentare,* be present before one) the presence of two or more things together in consciousness, a coexistence that is fundamental to the act of knowing.

compulsion (from Latin, *compellere,* drive together, compel) the act of being forced (coerced, necessitated, driven, influenced, irresistibly forced, constrained, etc.) to do or to respond to something. An extreme form of compulsion is not being able to do other than what one is doing—a situation without choice. A less extreme form of compulsion is being *able* to do otherwise but not possessing the freedom or opportunity to do so. Compulsions are divided into *internal* compulsions: those originating within one's own psyche (examples: obsessions, desires to do or say something); and *external* compulsions: those originating from outside forces (examples: political coercion, being knocked down). See entries under FREEDOM, FREE WILL. Compare with VOLUNTARY-INVOLUNTARY ACTIONS.

Comte, Auguste (1798–1857) French philosopher born in Montpellier; philosophic eclectic and synthesizer, founder of the Positivistic School.

His major work is his *Cours de philosophie positive* (written between 1830 and 1842). It traces the development of the sciences from astronomy, physics, chemistry, and biology to sociology—tracing three major stages of intellectual and cultural development. In the *theological* stage, thought is predominantly religious and God-oriented, and the will, spiritual entities, and forces are causes of phenomena. In the *metaphysical* stage, natural processes are caused by abstract, disembodied concepts and laws. In the *positivistic* phase, events are explained in terms of observed relationships and sequences.

Comte's later works include *A General View of Positivism* (French 1848, English 1865) and *The Catechism of Positive Religion* (French, 1852, English 1858).

conation (from Latin, *conari,* attempt, strive, struggle) the Latin *conatus* is often used for the term *conation,* the volitional (willing) aspect of consciousness. The tendencies, urges, or powers impelling effort toward action, and specifically toward self-preservation. Sometimes used with reference to deliberate VOLUNTARY ACTION directed toward something desired. See WILL.

conceive (from Latin, *concipere,* conceive, take, seize) **1.** to grasp with the mind. **2.** to form a conception of, to imagine. **3.** to comprehend, to understand. **4.** to suppose. **5.** to plan out.

Sometimes contrasted with *imagine,* which is included in the class of *conceive. Imagine* suggests a pictorial understanding, whereas *conceive* also includes nonpictorial understanding of abstractions (for example, of infinity). See IMAGE, MENTAL; IMAGINATION.

concept (from Latin, *concipere,* conceive) **1.** a mental impression, a thought, a notion, an idea of any degree of concreteness or abstraction, used in abstract thinking. **2.** that which enables the mind to distinguish one thing from another. **3.** what is meant (or imaged) by the term used to designate it. **4.** sometimes used to refer to the universals abstracted from particulars.

concepts, polar see POLARITIES.

conceptualism 1. the theory that universals (general abstract concepts or ideas) exist in particular things as their essence, and never exist separately from them, but the mind abstracts (conceptualizes) them out of particular things and creates symbols or names for them which are retained and related to each other in understanding as abstractions. (In this sense, conceptualism is a compromise between REALISM and NOMINALISM.) **2.** the theory that universals are concepts (abstract entities) that exist only as products of the mind, but are more than mere names; that is, they are mind-dependent but common to minds regardless of the names or language used. See UNIVERSALS (CONCEPTUALISM).

conceptualization involves a combination of the following: (a) knowing the meanings of what is to be understood (conceived) indicated by such things as using a symbol, or referring to the things correctly without ambiguity, ambivalence, imprecision, or vagueness; (b) having an image of the thing to be understood; (c) recognizing (identifying) the thing to be understood when confronted by it; (d) being able to bring the thing to be understood to consciousness as an abstraction and/or as an image; and (e) being able to communicate some of its essential characteristics to others. Compare with COMPREHENSION.

conclusion (from Latin, *concludere,* conclude; from *con,* with, + *claudere,* shut) **1.** a statement that has been inferred from other statements. **2.** that statement which is the logical consequence (implication) of the premises of an ARGUMENT. Often conclusions are indicated by symbols or by words such as: *therefore, thus, it follows that, for, consequently, implies, this proves that, this indicates that, hence.*

concomitant (from Latin, *con,* with, + *comitari,* accompany) **1.** accompanying or attending each other. **2.** associated or conjoined with each other, usually indicating a temporal, spatial, or causal interrelationship of things. Used in phrases such as *concomitant circumstances, concomitant variations,* and *concomitant effects.* See METHODS, MILL'S INDUCTIVE.

concrete (from Latin, *concrescere,* grow together) that which is real, vivid, known by direct experience, belonging to actual existence, and specific. The individual, the practical, the particular, as opposed to the general, the abstract, the IDEAL, the VAGUE.

concreteness, fallacy of misplaced the phrase coined by Alfred North Whitehead to refer to what he considered the fallacy of taking an abstract characteristic and dealing with it as if it were what reality was like in its concrete form. See PROCESS PHILOSOPHY; REIFICATION/REISM.

concretion (from Latin, *concrescere,* grow together; from *con,* with, + *crescere,* grow—in the sense of unite into one being) the bringing together or the developing together of a variety of elements or processes and thereby creating unities.

concretion, principle of (Whitehead) Alfred North Whitehead's phrase for *God:* that drive given to things, or which things possess, impelling them toward actualization of their form; the creative urge by which new unities grow together, emerge, and advance, producing greater interrelatedness. See PROCESS PHILOSOPHY.

concretism see REIFICATION/REISM.

condition, necessary 1. a condition X is necessary for condition Y if whenever X does not occur, then Y does not occur. Example: Oxygen is a necessary condition for the occurrence of fire; if oxygen is not present then there can be no fire. **2.** the condition in the absence of which a specific event cannot take place. **3.** that condition in the absence of which a thing could not have events happening to it. Example: That I exist may be considered a necessary condition for the occurrence of events happening to me such as feeling pain caused by a pin. Compare with CONDITION, SUFFICIENT; NECESSARY EXISTENCE.

condition, necessary and sufficient the condition whereby E will occur if and only if C occurs, and C will occur if and only if E occurs.

condition, sufficient 1. that condition in the presence of which an event occurs. Example: Rain is a sufficient condition (but not a necessary condition) for a street being wet. **2.** that condition in the presence of which a thing exists (or subsists). Example: The presence of a combustible material, heat, and oxygen in proper combinations is the sufficient condition for the existence of fire. Compare with CONDITION, NECESSARY.

conditional (from Latin, *conditio,* agreement, condition) **1.** dependent on a state of affairs (condition) without which it will not take place. Found in phrases such as *a conditional wish* and *a conditional promise*. **2.** implying or expressing a supposition. **3.** a compound sentence of the form "If . . . then."

conditional, counterfactual sometimes *contrafactual,* or *contrary-to-fact conditional;* conditional statements that have the form: "If event p had occurred, then event q would have occurred." Example: "If the train had come by two minutes earlier, I would have been killed." The antecedents of counterfactuals (a) are meant to be false (and cannot help but be false), (b) refer to a state of affairs that would have been true if certain conditions had obtained, and (c) in some way or other are intended as true statements even though they are not in *fact* true. Most counterfactuals are expressed in the subjunctive mood and are used for expressing disposition-type statements (tendencies, abilities, potencies, capacities). Counterfactuals are often used in a historical context. Example: "If Alexander the Great had not died so young, he would have conquered China."

conduct (from Latin, *conducere,* bring together) **1.** in general, synonymous with behavior. **2.** one's manner of action. **3.** in philosophical psychology, any type of human activity or response in which the personality is involved. **4.** in ethics, any voluntary behavior or intentional disposition to act for which a person may be held responsible relative to standards of right and wrong.

configuration (from Latin, *configurare,* form together, out of, or from) the structural pattern that interacting or interrelated parts take. In most general cases, interchangeable with GESTALT, FORM, and WHOLE.

confirmation (from Latin, *confirmare,* from *con,* with, + *firmare,* make firm) partial or tentative evidence or VERIFICATION. Not all empirical statements can be verified (observationally or through experimental testing). Examples: "All crows are black." "All gases expand as their temperatures rise." Observation and experimental evidence for such statements are based on a limited or finite number of instances from which inductive generalizations such as the above are made. But the statements are universal and refer also to the many unobserved cases in the past and in the future. Other examples: "If X is a chemical compound, then when put under some specific pressure and temperature it will become a solid." "Salt is soluble in water." For statements such as these, for hypotheses, for unobservable entities in science, there can only be confirmation (partial evidence) but not verification. Probability theory is used as a quantitative procedure for confirmation of laws, hypotheses, or concepts. See HYPOTHESIS.

confirmation, principle of sometimes *confirmation principle, principle of confirmability,* or *confirmability principle;* a weaker variation of the principle of verification (see VERIFIABILITY, PRINCIPLE OF). Some logical positivists, recognizing that statements (hypotheses, theories, etc.) can never be completely verified or completely refuted by observation, proposed the principle of confirmation in place of the principle of verification. A few of the main points involved in the principle of confirmability: (a) Statements are more or less confirmed (or disconfirmed) by observation evidence. (b) Statements are confirmed if the consequences deduced from them are true and if not as many true consequences can be deduced from competing statements. (c) Statements may not be directly testable but are confirmable if other observational statements tend to confirm them (or imply their confirmability). (d) Statements are confirmable if they can be defined precisely enough so that their degree of probability can be calculated.

conflagration (Stoics) (from Greek, *ekpyrōsis,* from *ek,* out of, + *pyr,* fire; the Greek term meaning "being burned up or consumed entirely") in the Stoic view, the universe eternally goes through cycles of being dissolved into fire. A new cycle in essential respects similar to all the previous cycles emerges to be eternally repeated. See RECURRENCE, ETERNAL.

connotation (from Latin, *con,* with, + *notare,* mark) **1.** the associations (feelings, attitudes, emotions, images, thoughts) suggested by a word either to the user of the word or to the listener. Examples: "He isn't man enough to do it." The word *man* is not used for its literal meaning but for the expressive or emotional meanings that have come to be associated with it (such as courageous, responsible, mature). The word *snake* in its literal sense means a reptile without legs, but it carries associations of being slippery, devious, slimy, upsetting. **2.** sometimes used to mean *denotation*, which more properly is the literal, actual meaning of a word. The SIGNIFICATION or designation of a word, which states the main characteristics that determine the things (referents) to which the word can be correctly applied. See CONNOTATION (INTENSION); DEFINITION, TYPES OF (2).

connotation (intension) the collection of characteristics (properties, qualities) common to all (and only to those) things referred to by a word, also those characteristics *intended* by the use of the word. The connotation of the word *dog* would consist of the specific characteristics applicable to, or common to, all dogs. This is the denotative, informative, or descriptive meaning of CONNOTATION. See DENOTATION and INTENSION.

conscience (from Latin, *conscire,* know, be conscious, from *con,* with, together, + *scire,* know) the sense, feeling, or awareness (a) of what one ought to do and what one ought not to do, and/or (b) of what is morally correct, right, good, permissible, etc., and morally incorrect, wrong, bad, prohibited, etc. This MORAL SENSE is (1) *intuitive* and/or *immediate;* that is, no argumentation or process of reasoning is involved, and (2) *urgent*; that is, there is a feeling of obligation to do its bidding. **1.** traditionally, conscience has been associated with: (a) an inner *restraining force*—an inner voice such as SOCRATES' DAIMŌN, which prohibits some actions (and occasionally suggests some); the "Thou shalt not" aspect of human behavior. (b) an *individualism* in which the dictates of personal conscience supersede social sanctions (the inner moral law takes precedence over the secular order); (c) a *directing force* for moral behavior stemming from the core of a person's humanity, especially in situations where ethical codes may not provide an answer, expressed in such phrases as "Let your conscience be your guide." **2.** the FACULTY interpretation: The mind has different faculties that are the sources of man's different abilities. For example, the rational faculty is the cause of rational action. The willing faculty (the ability to do, to decide, to choose) is the origin of volition. The conscience faculty is used to distinguish between right and wrong, good and bad. It is the source of ethical behavior, deciding what is morally the best thing to do and impelling obedience. See ETHICS. **3.** the behavioristic interpretation: Conscience is the sum total of an individual's conditioned responses to internal and external stimuli. These responses have been reinforced basically by social and peer approval and are broken only with internal conflict and difficulty. The internalization of norms of behavior. See DAIMŌN.

consciousness (from Latin, *conscire,* know, be aware of) often used synonymously with MIND, consciousness has been regarded as the center or focal point of AWARENESS, FEELING, PERCEPTION, and KNOWLEDGE. **1.** a relation between an object being known and a knowing subject. **2.** a relation existing among (a) an activity of knowing, (b) the content being known, and (c) the awareness of them both. See SELF-CONSCIOUSNESS. **3.** the constituents and operation of awareness (of the mind) at any given moment. **4.** the actual mental states as they occur (pain, jealousy, an image, a concept). **5.** the ability to (symbolically) identify mental states. See INTROSPECTION. **6.** consciousness has ascribed to it characteristics such as: (a) It is a primitive—something that cannot as such be analyzed or traced further and that cannot be built up out of other more rudimentary concepts or states. (b) Consciousness is a *brute fact*—something that just happens and cannot be reduced to anything else similar to it as its source (although on another level of analysis it can correctly be said to be caused by cerebral functions). (c) Each consciousness is characterized by its uniqueness, individuality, unity, continuity in time, privacy (no one can know another's consciousness as it is in itself), intentionality, and self-relection. (d) Consciousness has irreducibile *modes* (levels, aspects, abilities, dimensions) such as: content (images, sensations, perceptions, feelings, emotions, cognitions, etc.), quality, mood, intensity, comprehensiveness, direction, volition, selectivity, attention, intention, memory, etc. See entries under EGO and SELF.

consequentialism (ethics) the view that the correctness (rightness, goodness) of moral conduct is judged in terms of its results (consequences). See ETHICS, TELEOLOGICAL.

consistent (from Latin, *consistere*, stand still or firm, be stable; from *con*, with, + *sistere*, cause to stand) Concepts are consistent (a) if their meanings do not contain contradictory terms (for example, squared circle) that mutually exclude each other, or (b) if they do not contain inherent contradictions (for example, "A thing X can be wholly in two different spaces at the same time"), or (c) if they are not outright contradictions (for example, "Adam is a male and he is not a male"). Compare with COHERENCE. Contrast with CONTRADICTION.

construct, theoretical sometimes *theoretical construction, theoretical fiction, hypothetical construct, hypothetical construction,* and *hypothetical fiction.* **1.** an inferred, nonobserved entity. **2.** an entity or process whose existence is postulated (assumed, hypothesized, supposed) and used within a system of explanation to explain observable phenomena. Examples: meson, quanta, the subconscious.

contemplation (from Latin, *contemplari*, contemplate, meditate, gaze at attentively) **1.** in metaphysics, the life of thinking for the sake of thinking that results in happiness achieved through the actualization of the individuals's highest faculty, reason (see EUDAIMONIA). **2.** in epistemology, synonymous with knowledge or the act of acquiring knowledge; the activity of thinking or of pondering. **3.** in religion, synonymous with *meditation,* the act of attempting to behold some spiritual object or gain spiritual insight. **4.** in mysticism, *mystical contemplation* or *the contemplation of the mystic* is used with reference to the method of experiencing complete or partial absorption into the *one* (God; nature; the unity of all things). See entries under MYSTICISM.

context (from Latin, *contexere,* weave together; from *con*, with, + *texere*, weave) the sum total of meanings (associations, ideas, assumptions, pre-conceptions, etc.) that (a) are intimately related to a thing, (b) provide the origins for that thing, and (c) influence our attitudes, perspectives, judgments, and knowledge of that thing.

contextualism (metaphysics) the view that rejects the distinction between APPEARANCE on the one hand and a REALITY supposedly behind the appearance on the other. Such distinctions are regarded as relative to, and making sense in terms of, the purposes of a specific line of inquiry (or language). There is no absolutely correct or real context.

contiguity, law of in philosophical psychologies (such as atomistic and associationistic psychologies), the association of ideas or combination of ideas (a) that have coexisted or (b) that have succeeded one another so that one brings the other to consciousness. See ASSOCIATION, LAWS OF.

continence (from Latin, *continere,* hold together, repress) **1.** self-restraint, self-command, self-mastery, self-governance; especially with reference to strong passions. (Sometimes continence refers specifically to the exercise of sexual self-restraint, total or partial.) **2.** in ethics, that moral state of the individual in which irrational bodily desires are controlled by reason. Contrast with INCONTINENCE.

contingent (epistemology) (from Latin, *contingere,* touch on all sides, happen; from *con*, with, + *tangere*, touch) refers to knowledge that is obtained by empirical means (as opposed to logical means) and must thus be regarded as only probably true. Compare with A POSTERIORI. Contrast with A PRIORI.

contingent (logic) refers to any statement that is not necessarily true (that is, its denial does not produce a self-contradiction), and is logically possible. Contrast with TAUTOLOGY.

contingent (metaphysics) in general, something that is liable to happen, but not certain to happen; it could happen or not depending on the circumstances. The contingent includes all those things that are not necessary and that are not impossible. **1.** an event that is not necessitated to happen. **2.** refers to the causal or temporal dependence of an event on the existence of other events (themselves not necessitated) without which the event will not occur. Contrast with entries under NECESSARY.

continuity, law of (Leibniz) the theory that all change in nature occurs in degrees; there are no discontinuous changes; and no so-called jumps anywhere in any process in the universe.

continuum 1. that which has an uninterrupted sameness about itself within a process of change or growth; a continuity of common characteristics recognizable within an activity. **2.** that which (a) exhibits no change about itself but remains the same in some particular way relative to certain other features about itself that are changing, and/or (b) remains the same with itself relative to other things around it which change. **3.** the imperceptible and/or gradual change of a thing's characteristics in time. Example: the continuum of development of a seed to a plant. **4.** the area (often regarded as uninterrupted or as gapless, except in abstraction) between different things or qualities. The greater the difference, the greater is the tendency to polarize the continuum with words such as *the end points, the extremes, the poles, the opposites* of the continuum. Examples: the continuum between hot and cold; the continuum between illusion and reality.

contradiction (from Latin, *contradicere,* speak against; from *contra,* against, + *dicere,* speak) **1.** any statement that is necessarily (by logical definition) always false. **2.** any statement whose final truth column contains all falses. **3.** the negation of a statement. See LAWS OF THOUGHT, THE THREE. Contrast with CONSISTENT.

contradiction, self- a statement or concept that contradicts itself; that both affirms and denies its basic meaning. Examples: "The ball dropped upward." "Adam is one bachelor I know of who is married." "Self-caused." "Causeless event." "Uncaused effect."

contraries (metaphysics) see OPPOSITES (METAPHYSICS).

contrast, law of (from Latin, *contrastare,* stand in opposition to; from *contra,* against, + *stare,* stand) in philosophical psychology, qualities such as hot and cold, light and dark, which are distinctive (different) in comparison with each other, tend to be associated together in consciousness; that is, they tend to bring one another to mind. Sometimes classified as one of the laws of association. See ASSOCIATION, LAWS OF.

convention (from Latin, *conveniens,* suitable, fit, proper, acceptable) **1.** any commonly agreed-upon statement whose truth is based not on the way things are in nature but on that agreement itself. Examples: (a) Laws and moral rules are regarded as social contracts under which people agree to live in order to secure safety, protection, order, an education, fulfillment of their needs, and so on. (b) That an object is called *red* is a convention, since another name could have been chosen. **2.** in Greek philosophy, convention (NOMOS, law, common agreement, standard acceptance) was contrasted with nature or the natural (PHYSIS).

conventionalism 1. in the philosophy of science, the view that physical laws (theories, hypotheses) are convenient shorthand expressions (conventions) for organizing and explaining experience. Other expressions can be found—and will be found—that perform similar tasks. Thus, physical laws are postulates; they are not absolute. They are relative to our framework of knowledge and to our technology. They cannot reveal reality as it is in itself but reveal only what and how consciousness puts things in relationships.

They are commonly accepted in scientific circles because they bring about greater simplicity of explanation, control, comprehensiveness of understanding, prediction, and ways to deduce further concepts than competing laws can bring. Physical laws are subject to revision and ultimately will be abandoned if they cannot perform these functions. Compare with INSTRUMENTALISM. **2.** in logic, the truths and principles of logic are arbitrary conventions agreed upon in order to build up a formal system. No one set of axioms (or rules of inference, or postulates, or conceptual method) is primary and fundamental to all logical systems. The truth of axioms in a logical system is a matter of conceptual agreement as to where to begin and how to proceed. **3.** sometimes *linguistic conventionalism, pragmatism in language,* or *linguistic pragmatism.* The view that languages or calculi can be set up syntactically in a number of ways. The decision to accept one language rather than another is a decision made on the basis of combinations of such things as convenience, simplicity of procedures, practicality, comprehensiveness, usefulness, and applicability. See LANGUAGE, FORMAL.

corporeal (from Latin, *corporeus*; from *corpus,* body) sometimes *corporal.* **1.** material, consisting of MATTER. **2.** PHYSICAL, having physical dimensions. **3.** extended, that which occupies space. **4.** bodily, having a BODY as opposed to being a SPIRIT or SOUL. **5.** tangible, opposite to INCORPOREAL. See FORM, CORPOREAL.

correspondence see TRUTH, CORRESPONDENCE THEORY OF.

corrigible (from Latin, *corrigere,* to correct) **1.** subject to error. **2.** capable of correction. Opposite to INCORRIGIBLE.

cosmogony (from Greek, *kósmos,* world, universe, + *gignesthai,* be born) sometimes used synonymously with COSMOLOGY **1.** a theory of the origination of the universe. This may be expressed in the form of myths, speculation, or science. **2.** the systematic inquiry into the origin of the universe.

cosmological argument for God's existence 1. any of the arguments that proceed from what are regarded as observed facts about the universe, such as motion, cause, contingency, order, to the conclusion that God exists as the origin of and ground for these facts, such as PRIME MOVER, FIRST CAUSE, NECESSARY BEING, and orderer. Proceeds from an analysis of the existence of things to the existence of God and to one or more of God's characteristics. This is in contrast with the ontological argument (see entries under ONTOLOGICAL ARGUMENT FOR GOD'S EXISTENCE), which proceeds from the acceptance of the definition of God (God's essence) to God's existence. **2.** a cosmological argument may refer to any argument for God's existence based on the derivative and dependent nature of the universe upon something other than itself; based on the contingency of the universe and its utter dependence on a necessary being (God) who begins, supports, and maintains it (as the sound of a harp is dependent on a harpist).

All cosmological arguments stress (a) the behind-the-scene activity of this necessary being and (b) how different from the universe in essential characteristics that necessary being (God) is. God is nondependent, whereas the universe is dependent on God. God is self-moving, whereas the universe has motion imparted to it. God is eternal, whereas the universe has a beginning in time. God is self-actualized, whereas the universe is in a state of potential being partly actualized in time. God is immutable (unchanging), whereas the universe is in continual change. See GOD, ARGUMENTS FOR THE EXISTENCE OF.

cosmology (from Greek, *kósmos,* world, universe, + *logos,* the study of, the underlying reasons for, an account of) **1.** the study of the universe as a rational and orderly system. **2.** sometimes used synonymously with METAPHYSICS: The study of the most general and pervasive concepts that can be applied to the universe (such as space, time, matter, change, motion, extension, force, causality, eternity). **3.** often used to refer to that branch of science, specifically a section of astronomy, which attempts to hypothesize about the origin, structure, characteristics, and development of the physical universe on the basis of observations and scientific methodology. See COSMOGONY.

cosmos (from Greek, *kósmos,* order, the form or structure of a thing. One meaning of *kósmos* was the ordered adornment, the harmonious ornamentation, such as necklaces and earrings, that women wore to beautify themselves. An early use of the word was applied to the starry heavens designating that they were created to adorn and beautify the earth) **1.** the order (or harmony) of the universe. Contrasted with CHAOS. **2.** the ordered universe. **3.** the universe itself as a single, integrated whole or system. Used as a synonym for UNIVERSE.

counterexample, method of 1. the method of refuting something by pointing out an instance that denies it or is in some way contrary to it. Example: A black swan is a counterexample to the assertion "All swans are white." **2.** in logic (also called *refutation by logical analogy*), the method of arguing by which the validity of an argument-form is refuted by showing an instance in which the same argument-form can be given true premises yet have a false conclusion.

courage (from Latin, *cor,* heart) the state of mind or action that enables one to face a danger without being overcome by the attendant fear. In Greek philosophy, courage was one of the cardinal virtues. See VIRTUES, CARDINAL. A courageous person is not one who has no fear, and not one who is overcome by fear, but one who is able to control fear and act according to a sense of duty or rational judgment. It was regarded by Aristotle as the mean between (the excess of) foolhardiness and (the defect of) cowardice. See MEAN, THE (ARISTOTLE).

Cratylus (dates unknown) Greek Athenian philosopher, an elder contemporary of Plato (c.428–c.348 BC). (Plato's dialogue *Cratylus* is named for him.) A disciple of Heraclitus, Cratylus amended Heraclitus's "One cannot step into the same river twice," making it "One cannot step into the same river even once." That is, nothing can be said about anything, since all things are in change and never remain the same to have anything said about them.

creatio ex nihilo (Latin, creation out of nothing) see CREATIONISM. Contrast with EX NIHILO NIHIL FIT.

creation (from Latin, *creare*, create, cause to exist, bring into being) **1.** the bringing something new into existence out of something previously existing. This is the sense of creation in Plato's *Timaeus;* the rational guiding principle of the universe (see DEMIURGE) shapes eternally existing matter into new forms by following the eternally perfect ideal forms. See FORMS, PLATO'S THEORY OF IDEAL. **2.** the activity of constructing, making, building, shaping, or the product of such activity.

creationism 1. the view that the universe and its life forms were produced (and are being produced) by a supernatural agent. **2.** all things begin and continue to exist only through the decision, plan, and activity of a supernatural being (God). **3.** matter (the universe) was created instantaneously by God out of nothing. **4.** the human soul is separately created and presented by God at birth (or at conception).

credo quia absurdum est (Latin, I believe because it is absurd) sometimes expressed: *Credo quia impossibile est* (I believe because it is impossible). Often referred to as *Tertullian's dictum.*

credo ut intelligam (Latin, I believe in order that I may understand) the dictum that serves as the basis of Anselm's ONTOLOGICAL ARGUMENT, and expressed in the first part of Chapter 2 of his *Prologion* (also spelled *Proslogium*): "I do not seek to understand in order that I may believe, but I believe in order that I may understand. For this I also believe; that if I did not believe, I could not understand." See FAITH, FIDES PROECEDIT INTELLECTUM.

criterion (from Greek, *kritērion,* a means for judging; from *kritēs,* judge, one who decides) **1.** a standard (rule, test, method) for judging or measuring something. For example, in ethics, one of the principal concerns is to find the criterion (or criteria) by which we can call acts moral or immoral, good or bad, right or wrong. **2.** that which enables one to know (discriminate, classify, decide) such things as: whether a statement is analytic or synthetic, true or false, etc.; whether a thing exists or not (and what type of existence it has); whether a linguistic usage is correct; whether a concept is applicable; whether certain characteristics define a thing, etc.

cybernetics (from Greek, *kybernētēs,* steersman, pilot, controller, governor) **1.** the study of feedback mechanisms, communication systems, and controls found in machines and in living organisms. **2.** the study of how mechanical systems can be regarded as adaptive. **3.** the study of the self-regulatory features of artificial automata (and living organisms) that display *purposiveness* and other functions that have been traditionally assigned to the activity of a mind.

CYRENAICS

cynic words such as *cynic, cynicism,* and *cynical* have pejorative connotations of moroseness, pessimism, doubt, belittlement, contempt for other's opinions, lack of faith in ideals and humanity, and a belief that humans are selfish, hypocritical, insincere, and self-indulgent.

Cynics, the a school of Greek philosophers whose founders included Antisthenes of Athens (a friend of Socrates) and Diogenes of Sinope (who, according to legend, carried a lighted lantern around in the daytime to seek an honest man). The traditions of the sect lasted from the fourth century BC well into the Roman sixth century AD. The Greek word for dog (transliterated as *kyōn* or *cyōn*) may have been derogatorily applied to them; hence their name *cynics, the dog philosophers,* since they appeared to live freely like dogs, roaming, scrounging, and begging, unfettered by cultural restraints. The sect may have been named after the gymnasium Cynosarges, which was its first gathering place and which was probably founded by Antisthenes. The Cynics taught that virtue is the highest good. Its essence is self-control and independence. Happiness comes from acting virtuously, which to them also meant using one's native intelligence to survive. They distinguished between natural values (conformity with the rhythms of nature) and artificial values (those imposed by individuals on individuals). Ignorance of one's simple nature and its simple needs (but instead following the corrupt ways of society) leads to unhappiness. Embracing unnatural values (external and material things) such as fame, wealth, success, achievements, pleasures, reputation, and academic degrees leads to unhappiness. Desires lead to unhappiness. Individuals should live in a state of nature with a minimum of desires and needs. The individual who wants nothing, lacks nothing, and has a minimum of needs is like the gods who have no needs to be satisfied. Lack of moderation, lack of the power to abstain, and overindulgence lead to unhappiness. Self-sufficiency can be achieved only through self-discipline, which involves training the body and disciplining the mind. Only then can the individual have the rational presence to act virtuously, fulfilling his or her highest capacities. In general the Cynics were ascetics, antinomians (against the established norms, customs, traditions, laws of society), anti-intellectuals, nonacademic, nonsystematic, and highly individualistic. They ridiculed luxury and sensual pleasures and idealized poverty. They despised the speculative theories of the academics, which they thought had no practical benefit for the individual but enslaved him or her with false obligations (such as duty to family; care of property; loyalty to the rulers, the wealthy, and the military; and patriotism).

Cyrenaics a Greek hedonistic philosophy founded by Aristippus of Cyrene, hence the name Cyrenaics. The Cyrenaics believed that the highest good in life is obtaining pleasure for oneself—intense pleasure of the moment, regardless of any consequent pain. Live for present pleasures; there may not be any future. Pleasure is the only good desirable for its own sake.

CYRENAICS

Pleasure is the only criterion for deciding right and wrong. Intense, immediate physical pleasure is the best. Manipulate anything and anyone by shrewdness, intelligence, and wit in order to secure these intense pleasures. All things—wealth, power, fame, luxury—are not good in themselves or desirable in themselves but are for the attainment of pleasure. See HEDONISM (ARISTIPPUS) and compare with other entries under HEDONISM.

D

daimōn (Greek, sometimes transliterated as *daemon* or *demon*, also found as *daimonion* or *daemonion*) Some of the variety of meanings: **1.** *daimōn* was used interchangeably with *theo,* a god, or *thea,* a goddess. In a general way it meant deity or divine power. **2.** a divinity whose characteristics are somewhere between the traditional gods and the most idealized of humans, which serves as an intermediary (similar to a guardian angel) between humans and the gods. (In Plato's *Symposium* the *daimōn* communicates to the gods the prayers of humans and reveals to humans the commands of the gods. Socrates refers to a *daimonion ti,* a divinelike something or other, that wants him to refrain from, or engage in certain actions.) See CONSCIENCE, SOCRATES' DAIMŌN. **3.** *daimōn* also referred to one's genius, one's fortune or lot, and to one's tendency of spirit. **4.** used as a synonym for PSYCHE to mean soul (self, spirit) attached to an individual at birth that determines the individual's fate or fortune. See *EUDAIMONIA.*

Darwin, Charles Robert (1809–1882) English naturalist born in Shrewsbury and educated at Edinburgh and Cambridge; developed a biological theory of natural selection that influenced all subsequent forms of human thought. His voyage of scientific observation from 1831 to 1836 convinced him that species, contrary to popular belief, were not immutable. His first major work attracted widespread attention: *The Origin of Species by Means of Natural Selection* (1859). It was followed by three other works that influenced the course of philosophic thought: *The Variation of Animals and Plants under Domestication* (1868); *The Descent of Man and Selection in Relation to Sex* (1871); and *The Expression of the Emotions in Man and Animals* (1873).

Darwinism, social the theory that society is a state of struggle for existence in which the fittest (strongest) wins. The strongest is characterized by EGOISM, ruthlessness, competition, ambition, manipulation, scheming, intelligence, energy, wealth, and power: "Might makes right." *Social selection* operates in society much the same way as NATURAL SELECTION operates in nature, whereby the unfit (weakest) is eliminated. The unfit are characterized as being noncompetitive, altruistic, idle, lazy, powerless, and poor. The good of society as a whole is served in this social struggle for existence. The self-made millionaire has traditionally been regarded as the exemplar of the fittest.

Dasein (German) used in a number of senses: **1.** fact or factuality. **2.** being, existence, usually of any kind. (Used interchangeably with the German *Existenz*). **3.** that kind of existence applicable to things (as opposed to individuals, who initiate activity). The third meaning is identical with the French *être-en-soi* and is used by Heidegger. See *EN SOI* (SARTRE).

data, empirical see EXPERIENTIAL.

data, experiential see EXPERIENTIAL.

datum (from Latin, *datum*, given) plural *data*, sometimes *presentment* or *presentational immediacy* **1.** in logic, that which is given, presented, or admitted as a fact from which inferences can be made. **2.** in epistemology, the specific content that appears in CONSCIOUSNESS, that which is given in consciousness as fundamental to knowledge.

dealienation the process of denying the tendency toward SELF-ALIENATION (self-estrangement) in which the *self* emotionally and intellectually feels itself removed from and uninvolved in its surroundings and actions. The process of feeling that one's self is self-directed and self-relating in a meaningful and consenting way. Compare with ALIENATION, ESTRANGEMENT.

deduction (from Latin, *deducere*, lead from; from *de,* from, away, down, + *ducere*, lead, draw) **1.** reasoning from a general truth to a particular instance of that truth. Example: All dogs are mortal. Charlie is a dog. Therefore Charlie is mortal. **2.** the process of making explicit the logical implications of statements or premises. **3.** the process of inference from statements (premises) in which a necessarily true conclusion is arrived at by rules of logic. Contrasted with INDUCTION.

deduction, transcendental (Kant) the name given by Kant to the attempt to show that there is one set of categories basic and ultimate to all human understanding and experiencing. See CATEGORIES OF THE UNDERSTANDING (KANT).

definiendum (Latin, that which is to be defined) the word (expression, phrase, symbol) being defined.

definiens (Latin, that which does the defining) the words used to define something; the part of a definition that gives the meaning of the definiendum.

defining, rules for Many rules have been presented since Plato and Aristotle for constructing good definitions. There are many kinds of definitions used for different purposes and with different intentions. Most of the rules have exceptions. Rules for defining can be looked at as general guidelines to control extreme subjectivity and relativity in expressing meanings and to limit capriciousness and confusion in communication. Some of the rules: **1.** a definition must indicate the essential characteristics (the essential properties, attributes, qualities, or features, the true nature, the essence) of the thing being defined and not its accidental characteristics, that is, those which merely happen to apply, but need not apply, to the thing being defined. **2.** wherever applicable, a definition should give the genus and differentia of the thing being defined. **3.** the definiendum should not appear in the definiens. **4.** on initial contact with a word to be defined, the *definiens* in some sense must be clearer and more familiar than the *definiendum.* (In dictionary definitions that which is contained in the definition of a word is more readily understood by the use of relatively explicit and familiar terminology.) **5.** the *definiendum* must be logically equivalent to (synonymous with) the *definiens*. **6.** a definition should be precise and not too broad and not too narrow. (A definition is too broad if the *definiens* applies to things to which the *definiendum* does not. A definition is too narrow if the *definiendum* applies to things to which the *definiens* does not.) **7.** a definition must be concise, with no superfluity, irrelevancies, or redundancy. **8.** a definition must not be ambiguous. **9.** a definition must not be obscure, but must be expressed in terminology that can easily be understood. **10.** a definition must not be vague. **11.** a definition must not be expressed in metaphors or figurative language. **12.** a definition must not be defined in negatives. **13.** a definition must not be stated in opposite or correlative terms.

definition (from Latin, *definire,* limit, end, be concerned with the boundaries of something) **1.** the meaning of a word (either its ordinary, commonly accepted meaning, or the meaning stipulated [intended] by the user). **2.** the description of the essential characteristics (properties, attributes, qualities, features) of a thing or idea. The principal function of definitions is to present meanings for terms that are not clearly understood in a context of other terms (and their meanings) that *are* clearly understood. Definitions increase vocabulary and impart information. They attempt to prevent ambiguity, obscurity, unintelligibility, imprecision, vagueness, and complexity (by, for example, making it possible to substitute single words for long and sometimes cumbersome meanings). Definitions are, in a general sense, stipulative. They are resolutions—declared intentions as to (a) how to use words in a certain manner, and (b) how they are used.

definition, family resemblance view of see FAMILY RESEMBLANCE (WITTGENSTEIN).

definition, Socratic theory of see SOCRATIC THEORY OF DEFINITION.

definition, types of The twenty types of definitions given here are not exhaustive of the types of definitions that can be presented, nor have their nomenclature and classifications been standardized. Many fuse into one another. **1.** *circular definition* (often given in the Latin phrase *circulus in definiendo,* circularity in defining), presenting the meaning of a word either (a) by using the same word with the same meaning in the DEFINIENS, or (b) using a grammatical variation of the same word (the DEFINIENDUM) in the *definiens*. Examples: "A preacher is one who preaches." "A Medicare official is one who officiates in the Medicare program." Usually regarded as a fallacious method of definition, although most types of definition contain this circular quality. See CIRCULARITY. **2.** *CONNOTATIVE definition,* one in which the *definiens* presents or explains the concept (idea) symbolized by the *definiendum.* A connotative definition gives meaning to a word by describing the common characteristics possessed by all the things denoted by the word. Emphasis is put on implicitly or explicitly stating the GENUS and DIFFERENTIA of a thing. The *definiens* attempts to present the unique characteristics of the *definiendum*. Example: A bird is "a vertebrate with feathers." **3.** *contextual definition* (sometimes called *definition in use*), a definition that defines a word by establishing a context for it, or by indicating the context that gives it meaning. Example: "X is defined as soft when it yields easily to my touch." **4.** *denotative definition,* giving a list of examples to which the word in question can be correctly applied. Example: A bird means such things as "a sparrow, eagle, cardinal, kiwi, penguin." **5.** *essence definition* (also *essential definition* or *real definition*), giving the ESSENCE of a thing. From among the characteristics possessed by a thing, one is unique and hierarchically superior in that it states (a) the most important characteristic of the thing, and/or (b) the characteristic on which the others depend for their existence. Example: A human is "an animal that reasons." Other characteristics that depend on reason for their existence: (1) an animal that laughs, (2) an animal that creates and uses tools, (3) an animal that creates and uses symbols and language, (4) an animal that cooks its food, and (5) an animal with an opposable thumb. Definition by essence looks for a single, objectively existing essence. **6.** *functional definition,* defining in terms of the functions the thing performs. Example: Defining a referee in connection with what that person does in the game he or she is refereeing (such as blow the whistle to stop play, apply penalties, enforce rules, etc.). Words such as philosopher, president, charity, liver, student, manager, predator, and gene can be functionally defined. Functional definitions are extrinsic; they do not stress the defining characteristics peculiar to the thing itself but the functions of the thing and its relations to other things. **7.** GENUS ET DIFFERENTIA definition, defining by giving the characteristics (*differentia*) of a class that distinguish it from other subclasses that also fall within a more general class (genus). Example: A human is an "animal (genus) that is rational (*differentia*)." **8.** *historical definition,* defining in reference to the history of the thing being defined. Example: Defining a graduate in terms of his or her participation for a time in a series of events. A person would not be called a graduate unless he or she participated in a history of events that lead up to graduation. Other words that can be historically defined: sufferer, retiree, physician, veteran, and athlete. Historical definitions are extrinsic. They do not stress the characteristics peculiar to the thing itself but present its external relations to other things and the sequential events involving it. **9.** *lexical definition* (sometimes called *customary* or *reportive definition*), reporting the meaning that a word has in common (ordinary, established) usage. Example: Nibble means "bite lightly or gently; eat in small bits." **10.** *loaded definition,* giving the meaning of a word in a prejudicial or biased way, often associated with propaganda. Example: Dr. Johnson's definition of fishing as a fish on one end of a line and a fool on the other. **11.** *nominal definition* (sometimes called *verbal definition*), any definition that explains the meaning of a *word* or *symbol,* as opposed to a *real definition,* which gives the definition of a *thing.* Example: "A *triangle* is (names) a plane figure with three connected straight sides that form three angles that total 180°." **12.** *operational definition,* indicating the actions (operations, activities, procedures) that the word symbolically implies and which when performed serve as its meaning. Example: "The word *length* means taking a measuring stick such as a foot ruler, laying it on the object to be measured so that one end of the stick coincides with one end of the object. The object is marked where the other end of the stick ends, and the stick is then moved along the object in a straight line until the first (previous) end point coincides with the previous position of the second end. The process is repeated as often as possible. Note the total number of times the operation has been performed. This total number constitutes the length of the object." See OPERATIONALISM. **13.** *ostensive definition* (sometimes called *demonstrative definition*), defining by pointing to (demonstrating, showing, illustrating, feeling) actual examples of the thing being defined. Example: "The word *bird* means this" (*point to a bird*). **14.** *persuasive definition* (sometimes called *rhetorical definition*) giving the meanings of words in an emotive (expressive) way in order to influence the attitudes (feelings, emotions, goals) of others. Example: "The true meaning of *teacher* is one who relates to his or her students on a personal level and enthusiastically guides them to sources of information." (Often associated with advertising.) **15.** *precising definition* (sometimes called *restricting definition*), a specific form of *stipulative definition* whereby specific and explicit meanings are attached, and can only be attached, to a word. Example: "For the purpose of our discussion, the word *argument* is to mean a conclusion drawn from more than one sentence according to the formal rules of inference presented in this book." **16.** *real definition* (sometimes used interchangeably with *essence definition* and on occasion with *connotative definition*), a definition that presents the essential characteristic (nature, structure, form, essence, property, attribute, etc.) of a thing as opposed to a *nominal definition,* which gives the meaning of a word or symbol. **17.** *recursive definition* (sometimes called *inductive definition*), a definition in which a variation of the word defined occurs in the *definiens,* thereby avoiding the appearance of a circular definition. Example: "A *mother* is a female parent." **18.** *stipulative definition* (sometimes called *legislative definition*), (a) the *definiens* is intentionally limited in meaning and/or is assigned a specific meaning for consistency and clarity of communication and as a matter of preference, thus indicating how the user of the word intends to have that word understood. Example: "We propose to restrict the meaning of the word *college* to four-year institutions of higher learning." (b) a new word chosen somewhat arbitrarily that is assigned a meaning for the sake of such things as brevity, expressing a new concept, secrecy, added precision, avoidance of emotive connotations, or standardization. Example: When Norbert Wiener coined the word *cybernetics* he gave it the stipulative definition "the science of communication and control systems." **19.** *synonymous definition* (sometimes called *dictionary definition*), a definition in which the *definiendum* and *definiens* are interchangeable; the giving of a list of cognate words, or identical meanings. The paradigm for synonymous definitions is the translation of words from one language to another language. Examples: "To hate means to loathe." "The word *kyōn* means dog." **20.** *syntactical definition*, one that defines the notational conventions prescribing the ways in which certain signs (symbols, expressions) will represent, or be substituted for, particular items.

deism (originally from the Greek, *theos,* god; transliterated into Latin as *deus*) in general, the belief in the existence of God. The term *deism* was first used in Christianity by the Calvinists during the latter part of the sixteenth century; in England, it appeared during the early seventeenth century. For the most part, deism holds to the following beliefs: **1.** God as the FIRST CAUSE created the universe. **2.** God created the unchangeable laws by which the universe is governed. **3.** God is in no way immanent in God's creation, but totally different from it, transcending it as, for example, a watchmaker transcends the watch he or she has made and set in motion. **4.** reason is in harmony with revelation (or revelation must conform to reason). **5.** the Bible must be analyzed according to reason, and its doctrines should not be made into mysteries. **6.** God has a preordained plan for the universe; all things are predetermined. **7.** the highest duty and sole aim of human life is to fulfill the purpose of the natural laws God has created. **8.** in some versions: God occasionally suspends physical laws in order to revitalize the natural system. **9.** in some versions: God can intervene in the lives of humans, and provide grace and/or moral guidance. See GOD CONCEPTS.

demiurge (from Greek, *demiourgos*, one who does work for people, skilled workman, craftsman, maker, creator) a term used by Plato, principally in his dialogue on cosmology *The Timaeus*, to refer to the principle (force, power) of creation in the universe. The demiurge, also given as demiourgos, follows the eternal, unchanging, perfect ideal forms, shaping chaotic and recalcitrant matter into the best possible rational patterns. See ANANGKĒ and CREATION.

Democritus (c.460–c.370 BC) Greek atomist and materialist philosopher born in Abdera, Thrace. He was dubbed "the laughing philosopher" by his contemporaries because of his cheerful disposition and habit of laughing at human foibles. Over 72 works are attributed to him, ranging from astronomy, physics, botany, and biology to cosmology, ethics, and philosophy.

demonstration (from Latin, *de,* from, down, away, + *monstrare*, show), sometimes called *derivation* or *justification.* In logic, the formal proof used in an argument (usually a deductive argument) that shows the inferences used to reach the conclusion.

De Morgan, Augustus (1806–1871) English mathematician, logician, philosopher, and historian of science and logic; born in India and educated at Cambridge. He taught mathematics at the University of London. His philosophic and technical analysis of logic and the theory of probability influenced the interpretation, understanding, and direction of modern symbolic and categorical logic. De Morgan's many writings include *Essay on Probabilities* (1838); *Arithmetical Books* (1847); *Formal Logic* (1847); *Syllabus of a Proposed System of Logic* (1860); and *Budget of Paradoxes* (1872).

denial see NEGATION.

denotation (from Latin, *denotare,* from *de,* from, down, away, + *notare,* mark) **1.** the application of the meaning of a word (term, symbol, etc.). **2.** the naming of instances that a word has; citing the referents for a word; giving examples of the thing to be defined or explained. Example: The characteristics of being a bird may not be entirely clear or agreed upon, but listing examples sometimes helps convey the meaning: sparrow, pigeon, eagle, vulture, kiwi, duck. The complete denotation of a word would be the entire list of all the things to which the word has applied or will apply. **3.** EXTENSION, the collection of all those things to which the word applies; the things (instances, items, objects, individuals) that can be subsumed under a word or conception and thereby be partly definable. See DEFINITION, TYPES OF (4).

deontology (from Greek, *deon,* moral duty, that which is morally binding, the morally right, obligation, imperative, necessity, + *logos,* the study of the underlying reasons of a thing, the science of, an account of) the study of the concept of DUTY (obligation, responsibility, commitment) and its related concepts. See ETHICS, DEONTOLOGICAL. *Deontic* is occasionally used for *deontological. Deontic* in general refers to anything having to do with the concept of necessity (see LOGIC, DEONTIC), or with duty.

Descartes, René (1596–1650) French philosopher, mathematician, scientist; born at La Haye, Touraine. His early education included study of Latin and Greek, logic, mathematics, physics, metaphysics, and ethics; later, he studied law.

By 1618, when Descartes was 22 and living in Holland, he prepared two manuscripts, *Essay on Algebra* and *Compendium of Music*. He left Holland in 1619 and traveled in Poland, Hungary, Bohemia, and Bavaria. He met mathematicians while staying in Ulm on the Danube, a village known for its mathematicians. It struck him that the method of analytic geometry could be applied to all fields of study, including philosophy. Descartes had three dreams he was to perceive as revelations: In one he found himself lame and was forced by a storm to find shelter in a church. In a second dream, he heard thunder and saw sparks of fire around him. In the third dream, he opened a volume of poetry to a line by Ausonius, *"Quid vitae sectabor iter?"*(What life shall I follow?). After extensive further travel, he returned to Holland in 1628, a country that was to be his sanctuary for the rest of his life.

His works include *Discourse on Method*, an introduction to *Dioptric, Meteors*, and *Geometry* (all published in 1636 and 1637); *Meditations on First Philosophy* and *Objections* (to his philosophy by Arnauld, Gessendi, Hobbes and others) and his *Replies* to them all (all three works published in 1640 and 1641); *Principles of Philosophy* (1644); *Treatise on the Passions of the Soul* (1649); and *Rules for the Direction of the Mind* (published in 1701).

descriptivism (ethics) see ETHICS, DESCRIPTIVISM IN.

design, argument from sometimes simply the *design argument*. Kant refers to it as the *physico-theological argument*. Refers to any of the wide assortment of arguments for God's existence that rely on the apparently purposeful design in the universe, to prove the existence of a God that is a cosmic mind (designer). See GOD, ARGUMENTS FOR THE EXISTENCE OF; TELEOLOGICAL ARGUMENT FOR THE EXISTENCE OF GOD.

destiny (from Latin, *destinare*, decree beforehand, make fast, determine, settle) one's predetermined lot, usually divinely foreordained; FATE. Sometimes personified as a power that cannot be resisted.

determinism 1. the view that every event has a CAUSE. **2.** given a set of conditions X, it will always be followed by nothing other than a set of conditions Y. (And given that set of conditions X, the set of conditions Y could not have been preceded by anything other than that set of conditions X.) **3.** the view that (a) all things in the universe are governed by, or operate in accordance with, causal laws; (b) everything in the universe is absolutely dependent on and necessitated by causes; (c) given sufficient knowledge of the workings of any particular thing, we would be able to see not only its future but the future of all things completely mirrored in it (see MONADS [LEIBNIZ]); or, as for example in Laplace (d) given sufficient knowledge of the mass, position, and direction of every particle in the universe at any given time, and an infinite mathematical ability, one can predict every future event. Compare with entries under FREE WILL; INDETERMINISM.

deus ex machina (Latin, god from out of a machine; in ancient theater, a device for bringing a god to the stage to resolve plot intricacies) used derogatorily to mean that God or some other supernatural cause is artificially brought in to provide an explanation or resolution of a problem.

Dewey, John (1859–1952) American philosopher, psychologist, educator, ethicist; born in Burlington, Vermont. He had a distinguished career as a teacher, including professorships at the University of Chicago and Columbia University, in New York.

Dewey's published numerous works, a few of which are given here: *Leibnitz's Essays Concerning the Human Understanding* (1888); *Outlines of a Critical Theory of Ethics* (1891); *The Significance of the Problem of Knowledge* (1897); *Logical Conditions of a Scientific Treatment of*

Morality (1903); *The School and the Child* (1907); *The Influence of Darwin on Philosophy* (1910); *The School and Society* (1915); *Creative Intelligence* (1917); *Human Nature and Conduct* (1922); and *The Quest for Certainty* (1929).

dialectic (from Greek, *dialektikē*, the art of conversation, discussion; or *dialektikós*, one skilled in logical argument or debate—originally referred to debating tournaments in which the primary aim was to refute an opponent's arguments or lead the opponent to contradictions, dilemmas, or paradoxes. In general, a dialectician was one who left nothing unquestioned) **1.** the art (*technē*) of asking and answering the proper questions in a discussion at the proper time and in the proper way so as to bring knowledge out into the open. **2.** the art of gaining better knowledge on a topic by exchanging reasoned views and arguments. **3.** the art of obtaining true knowledge on a topic by use of a formal reasoning process. (*Dialectics* is the term sometimes used to designate the branch of logic that presents the rules and modes of reasoning correctly; also to designate the systematic, logical analysis of concepts to show what they entail.) **4.** the method of arriving at a definition for a concept by means of examining the common characteristics found in a number of particular examples of that concept. **5.** the method of classification whereby there is a repeated division of a concept into its respective subclasses.

dialectic (eristic) see ERISTIC.

dialectic (Hegel) 1. the process whereby a thought or an existing thing necessarily leads to or changes into its opposite (or contradictory), thereby arriving at a new synthesis (unity). **2.** the process of change in thought and the universe in which a higher level of knowledge (truth) and of existence (unity) is reached by means of the necessary opposition of contradictories. **3.** the process of necessary change involving a triad (three elements) consisting of (a) an existing thing or thought (*thesis*), (b) its opposite or contradictory (ANTITHESIS), and (c) the unity (SYNTHESIS) resulting from their interaction and which then becomes the basis (*thesis*) of another dialectical movement. Sometimes referred to as *triadic dialectic*. Hegel's dialectic is developmental and evolutionary in character, and its end point is complete perfection. See LOGIC, DIALECTICAL; MATERIALISM, DIALECTICAL (MARX-ENGELS).

dialectic (Heraclitus) the process of change in the universe whereby all things pass over into what they are not, and were not (OPPOSITES).

dialectic (Plato) 1. used specifically in Plato's *Republic* to refer to the unique and complex education required of the philosopher-ruler from childhood on as he ascends to the vision of the supreme good by which all his decisions and behavior are thereafter guided. **2.** Plato also used *dialectic* to refer to the rational, philosophical method in general.

dialectic (Socrates) 1. Socrates' method of asking questions to bring out a point for elaboration and with others following the answers to their logical conclusions (which ultimately conform to the good, the true, and the beautiful). **2.** Socrates' question-and-answer method of getting his listeners to accept the truth of particular instances that have something in common, and from that acceptance to also assent to the true universal element, the generalization, or the ESSENCE evident in those particular instances. (The UNIVERSAL or essence that is found provides the basis for the definition of the concept or thing, and also gives insight into the ideal forms it exemplifies.) **3.** the method of inquiry into and the finding of the real (essence) definitions of things. **4.** the method of separating (*dialegontas*) things according to their class, nature, or kind. **5.** the give-and-take in discussion whereby an opponent is made to admit a series of points only to find that acceptance of them leads to an inconsistency with what the opponent believes. See SOCRATIC METHOD; SOCRATIC QUEST, THE; SOCRATIC THEORY OF DEFINITION.

dialectic (Zeno) The REDUCTIO AD ABSURDUM method of argumentation attributed to Zeno the Eleatic whereby a belief is refuted by showing how its acceptance leads either (a) to a logical contradiction or (b) to a logical conclusion that in no way is acceptable to reason (or common sense). See ZENO'S PARADOXES.

dialectic, transcendental (Kant) in Kant's *Critique of Pure Reason* one of the divisions of his Transcendental Logic (see CATEGORIES OF LOGIC [KANT]). The purpose of such a dialectic was to find those judgments that presume to go beyond the limits of finite human experience. Such judgments in Kant's view are not only presumptuous but also illusory. The four antinomies (see ANTINOMIES, THE FOUR [KANT]) and the notion of God as the FIRST CAUSE are cited by Kant as examples of such judgments.

dialectical materialism see MATERIALISM, DIALECTICAL (MARX-ENGELS).

dialectics, historical (Marxism) The following are some basic views: **1.** humankind and history are in tension yet in an inseparable harmony. **2.** insofar as humans are in conflict with the historical dialectical forces operating in the universe, then these forces will be alienated, unexpressed, unrealized. **3.** humankind is a product of the negating ideologies of its particular epoch. By means of revolution humans can eliminate the gap between themselves and these perfecting but alienated historical forces at work in the universe. **4.** people are humanized by transcending their immediacy, by overcoming the impersonality of social (class) forces, and by identifying themselves with those historical dialectical forces that are rational and person-oriented. **5.** the final state of development is social and ethical perfection. See LOGIC, DIALECTICAL.

dianoia (Greek, referring in general to the act of thinking or to the faculty of thought) **1.** in Plato, *dianoia* is a type of discursive knowledge between DOXA (mere opinion or faith) and NOĒSIS (true intuitive knowledge. See NOUS.) **2.** in Aristotle, *dianoia* is used in general to mean intellectual activity that critically (a) appraises the differences among concepts, (b) is able to see them in combinations and relationships, and (c) can extrapolate from (a) and (b). *Dianoia* is subdivided into (1) THEORIA and EPISTĒMĒ (in their sense of knowledge sought for its own sake), (2) TECHNĒ (knowledge used to make something), and (3) PHRŌNESIS (knowledge wisely applied to conduct). **3.** in Aristotle's works on logic he uses *dianoia* specifically to mean *syllogistic reasoning*. See VIRTUES, DIANOETIC (ARISTOTLE).

dichotomy (from Greek, *dichotomia*, from *dicha*, two, + *temnein*, cut) **1.** the division of things into two basic parts that are regarded as fundamentally and/or irreducibly different. Examples: A human is composed of a soul and a body. Two realities exist: the supernatural and the natural. Sometimes, *dichotomy* is used pejoratively referring to divisions that are artificial or arbitrary. **2.** refers to any mutually exclusive relationship of two things (classes, statements, entities, events). Frequently, such relationships are also regarded as exhaustive. **3.** in logic, dichotomy (dichotomizing) refers to the method or process of classifying or dividing into a genus and species according to differentiae. See DIFFERENTIA. Compare with DIS-PARATE; DISTINGUISH.

dichotomy, is/ought see IS/OUGHT DICHOTOMY.

dichotomy, mind/body see MIND/BODY DICHOTOMY.

difference, method of see METHODS, MILL'S INDUCTIVE.

difference in identity, principle of 1. regardless of how similar (identical) things are, any thing in the universe can be said to be different from any other thing in at least one respect; for example, that they occupy different spaces (are numerically distinct), exist at different times, are distinct or different objects of thought or being. **2.** no two things can be identical in all respects (otherwise they would not be *two* things). Compare with IDENTITY IN DIFFERENCE, PRINCIPLE OF.

differentia (Latin, difference) **1.** the distinguishing characteristic or specific difference of a thing from other things. **2.** he characteristic of a thing that (a) is used to make class divisions, or (b) distinguishes one subclass from another subclass within a class. Example: having all three sides equal is the *differentia* between equilateral triangles and all other types. See GENUS ET DIFFERENTIA DISTINCTION.

dikaiosynē **(Plato)** (Greek, justice) *Dikaiosynē* is the word most often used by Plato for what has been translated as *justice* but which in general means *an inner sense of righteousness; knowing when to do the fair and right thing.* (There are connotations in this Greek word and its cognates of such concepts as rightness, lawful, judgment, justified, judicial, punishment, penalty.) Plato uses the word distinctively and in several senses: **1.** that intuitive response (principally a characteristic of the philosopher-king, who has attained knowledge of the ideal forms) to a situation that automatically expresses a sense of what is good, correct, proper, the best, the most rational for that situation. **2.** doing, within the context of a highly integrated community such as in Plato's *Republic,* (a) that for which one is best suited by heredity and training, and (b) that which will help achieve a functioning harmony of all parts of the community in order to produce the general good. **3.** having the three faculties of the soul (reason, will, desires) integrated, not in conflict or tension, governed by rational principles, and thereby able to respond in a rational, tranquil, and morally correct way to all circumstances and problems. See VIRTUES, CARDINAL.

dilemma, moral a situation in which mutually exclusive moral actions or choices are equally binding.

ding an sich, das (German expression used by Kant and Kantians, meaning *the thing in itself*) **1.** refers to anything beyond and hence unknowable to consciousness and to any possible experience. **2.** the transcendent, independent reality that is beyond any possibility of being known by humans. See DIALECTIC, TRANSCENDENTAL (KANT).

Dionysian spirit the irrational impulse in humans that accepts and craves ecstatic, spontaneous experiences in life and is associated with the will to life and power. Its opposite is the APOLLONIAN SPIRIT. Both concepts were developed in Friedrich Nietzsche's *The Birth of Tragedy* (1872). Compare with ROMANTICISM.

discourse, universe of see UNIVERSE OF DISCOURSE.

discursive see REASONING, DISCURSIVE.

disparate (from Latin, *disparatus*; from *dis,* away, between, + *parare,* prepare; or from *par,* equal) **1.** dissimilarity in basic kind and/or quality. For example, the sensations of color and cold are disparate. **2.** two ideas are disparate if neither calls up something of the other. **3.** two things are disparate if they cannot be put into a genus/species relationship. Compare with DICHOTOMY.

disposition (from Latin, *disponere*, dispose; from *dis*, away, + *ponere*, place) the tendency (propensity, bent, inclination) to behave in a certain way. Dispositions differ from emotions (feelings) in that they do not report on the mood a person is in at a given time, but report a general set of tendencies. Example: "She is afraid of crowded places" indicates a tendency to be in the emotional state of fear in crowded places. *Emotional dispositions* (such as emotional commitments to a person or idea; prejudices; preferences) are contrasted with *cognitive dispositions* (such as the tendency to believe; anticipations; expectations). See STATE, DISPOSITION. Contrasted with STATE, OCCURRENT.

dispute see VERBAL DISPUTE.

distinction see DISTINGUISH. Also *GENUS ET DIFFERENTIA* DISTINCTION; SENTENCE/STATEMENT DISTINCTION; TYPE/TOKEN DISTINCTION; USE/MENTION DISTINCTION.

distinguish 1. point out the differences between (or among) things. **2.** recognize that one thing (quality, feature, predicate, object, etc.) is not another.

When either 1. or 2. is done, a *distinction* is made. A *real distinction* is one that distinguishes according to differences that exist in the qualities of the things being distinguished (such as mind and brain or animal and radios). An *abstract distinction* is one that distinguishes qualities or differences according to abstract principles, which in reality are not separable or distinguishable (except in abstraction) from the thing of which they are a part. For example, we may say that only an abstract distinction can be made between the qualities of mind and the qualities of brain, though the *objects* thus distinguished are not separable in reality. Abstract distinctions are sometimes referred to as *mental* (or *conceptual*, or *arbitrary*) distinctions. Compare with DICHOTOMY.

distributively considering each member of a class (group, set) singly. What can be said about a class distributively may not be true of the class taken as a whole. Opposite to COLLECTIVELY. See TERM, DISTRIBUTED.

division, fallacy of see FALLACY, TYPES OF INFORMAL (18).

dogma (from Greek, *dogma*, that which seems to one, an opinion, a belief, a public ordinance) **1.** a doctrine (BELIEF, ideology, tenet, opinion) that has been formally and authoritatively proclaimed either by a leader or by an institution such as a church. **2.** that which one who accepts the authority must think about a specific thing.

dogmatism 1. unmerited positiveness in asserting the truth of a doctrine. **2.** the rejection of any examination of an idea and the assertion that the idea is true by authority and is beyond questioning.

dogmatists (Kant) a term used somewhat pejoratively by Immanuel Kant to apply to philosophers, principally metaphysicians, who believed that: (a) the universe can be known by means of inferences derived from a few self-evident principles without recourse to observation, control, experimentation, or testing; (b) humans have the ability to transcend experience and, independently of sense experience, arrive at truth about the real nature of things.

double-aspect theory of mind see entries under MIND, DOUBLE-ASPECT THEORY OF.

double effect doctrine (ethics) the doctrine that an act done with good intentions and according to moral principles can have good results but also unintended repercussions and/or side effects that (a) are not themselves worthwhile or morally acceptable, or (b) are morally acceptable only because they are inextricably associated with that act.

doubt (from Latin, *dubitare,* waver in one's opinion) **1.** hesitate or be undecided about the truth of something. **2.** question the veracity of an idea or consider it questionable. **3.** be inclined not to believe the truth of an assertion. Contrast with CERTAIN.

One is in doubt about the truth of an assertion whenever one does not commit himself or herself to its truth (or to the truth of its negation).

doubt, Descartes' method of the first of four rules presented by Descartes in Part II of his *Discourse on Method*, offering the most succinct formulation of his method of doubt: Nothing is to be admitted as true unless (a) it is free from all prejudicial judgments, and (b) it is so clearly and distinctly presented to the mind that in no circumstance can it ever be doubted. See METHOD (DESCARTES).

Descartes' method of doubt was to doubt anything and everything until he arrived at something that could not in any way be doubted by any rational being. (The idea so arrived at would be indubitably CERTAIN and universally true.) From this absolutely certain and true idea, one could then derive in logical fashion other certainties and truths. A system so constructed would be an organized group of interdependent ideas, each consistent with all others and each implying the others; thus, the system would be comprehensive and flawless. See SKEPTICISM (DESCARTES).

doxa (Greek, opinion, seeming, judgment) used in general to refer to an inferior type of knowledge, for example, in comparison to EPISTĒMĒ. See DIANOIA; ESSENTIALISM (PLATO).

dualism any philosophic view that insists on the existence of two independent, separable, irreducible, unique realms. Examples: supernatural/natural, God/universe, spirit/matter, soul/body, visible world/invisible world, world of the senses/world of the intellect, thinking substance/material substance, actual reality/possible reality, noumenal world/phenomenal world, force of good/force of evil. The universe can be explained only by means of both realms. Contrasted with MONISM; PLURALISM. See GOD CONCEPTS (4).

dualism, Descartes' soul/body Descartes held that the human being is a union of two separable and distinct substances: body and soul. The body is part of the physical universe and mechanical in operation, as are all things in the physical universe. The body on its own can—and does—operate with its own *life*, and many of its activities are not caused by the *soul*. The soul is connected to all parts of the body, but it performs most of its functions at the pineal gland in the brain. By acting on the pineal gland, the soul produces such mental events as thinking, perceiving, willing, emoting, and sensing. Compare with MIND/BODY INTERACTIONISM and other MIND/BODY entries.

dualism, mind/body 1. the belief that minds are distinct from bodies. Human beings are not merely a collection of material particles. **2.** the belief that mind and body are two irreducibly distinct and separable substances whose essential attributes are different in every respect. See MIND, TYPES OF THEORIES OF. Compare with MIND/BODY DICHOTOMY and other MIND/BODY entries.

dualism, theological see GOD CONCEPTS (4).

Duns Scotus, John (c.1265–1308) Scottish scholastic philosopher and theologian; born in Duns, Scotland, and known as the *Doctor Subtilis*. He became a Franciscan and studied at Oxford. Like others of his time, he wrote and lectured at Oxford, Cambridge, and Paris on Peter Lombard's *Sentences*, in defense of Scholasticism against the innovations of

Aristotelian philosophy then being introduced, especially by Aquinas. His main works (undated) are considered to include *Commentaries on the Sentences of Peter Lombard*, also known as *Ordinatio*; *Quaestiones Subtilissimae in Metaphysicam* (a treatise on Aristotle's *Metaphysics*); and *Tractatus de Primo Principio*.

duration (Bergson) For Henri Bergson every true duration (*durée réelle*) is (a) incomplete, (b) changing (dynamic), (c) unique (novel), and (d) continuous. Duration is a continuum of successive but heterogeneous movements. It is TIME conceived (perceived) as indivisible. Each moment contains an element of uniqueness or novelty; no moment completely reflects the past or the future. Nature is in a dynamic process of change; nothing is immutable. All change is continuous and congruous with all change externally related to it. Duration precludes any discontinuity with other existing changes or movements.

duty 1. that which one is required and expected to do (or not to do) in reference to such things as one's humaneness, status, occupation, responsibilities. **2.** that which one ought to do, and/or one feels obliged to do. **3.** that which one feels morally compelled to do, usually opposite to what one is inclined (wishes, desires) to do. Related to concepts such as CONSCIENCE, moral principles, VIRTUE, the GOOD, the RIGHT, OBLIGATION. See CATEGORICAL IMPERATIVE, THE (KANT).

duty (Kant) see ETHICS (KANT).

duty, *prima facie* see PRIMA FACIE DUTIES (ROSS).

dyad/dyadic (from Greek, *dyas,* two) *Dyad* means two units regarded as one; *dyadic* means binary, composed of two parts, or dual without necessarily implying a monism or identity or the two. Examples of dyadic thought: reality is both one and many; unchanging and changing; moving yet unmoving; unified yet varied; same yet different; good and evil; spontaneous and necessitated.

dynamis (Aristole) (Greek, power, force, strength) **1.** that power (energy, force) which causes change, and/or **2.** that state of potential a thing has to produce change or to become other than what it is. Compare with ENERGEIA; POTENTIAL/POTENTIALITY.

dynamis (Plato) (Greek, power) used by Plato to mean: **1.** the power of transferring or imparting activity or change to something else. **2.** the ability to receive power (force, motion, activity). **3.** the capacity to be influenced by forces (change, movement, etc.).

dynamism (from Greek, *dynamis,* power, strength, the ability to do a thing) **1.** the theory that everything in the universe is composed of FORCE (tendency, will, power) or forces. **2.** the universe is a totality of forces. Dynamism uses the concept of force as the fundamental unit of explanation in contrast, for example, with atoms, matter, mass, motion, ideas, souls.

dysteleological (from Greek, *dys,* hard, ill, bad, difficult, + *telos,* end, goal, purpose, + *logos,* the study of) referring to processes of maladjustment in the universe such as inherent limits to organic adaptation, accident, disease, and death. Such processes thwart achievement of purpose and/or indicate forces other than only adaptive (good) forces at work in the universe. Contrast with TELEOLOGY.

dystopia (from Greek, *dys,* bad, + *topos,* a place) a place or state not of ideal perfection, but of ideal imperfection in regard to individuality, humanness, dignity, and uniqueness. Novels such as *Brave New World* and *1984* have been called *dystopian.* Opposite to UTOPIA.

E

Eckhart, Johannes (c.1260–1328) German Dominican theologian, regarded as the founder of mysticism in Germany; born in Hochheim, near Gotha. He was prior of the Dominican Order in Erfurt and vicar of Thuringia. In 1300, he went to the University of Paris to study. In 1320, he lectured in Paris and taught in Strasbourg, and in 1323, became regent of the Dominican House of Studies in Cologne, where he was accused of heresy. His writings were subsequently condemned by Pope John XXII. His extant works are sermons and tractates.

eclecticism (from Greek, *eklektikos*, one who selects; from *eklegein*, pick out, choose from) **1.** the choosing of ideas (concepts, beliefs, doctrines) from a variety of systems of thought in the process of constructing one's own system. **2.** selection from diverse schools of thought that which is considered of value so as to create from the diversity an acceptable unified system.

economy, principle of see OCKHAM'S RAZOR.

ecstasy (from Greek, *ekstasis*, being out of place, displacement, entrancement, astonishment, trance; from *ek*, out, + *estanai*, set, stand—therefore, stand outside oneself) **1.** a state of joy, rapture, exaltation. **2.** a state of being overpowered by an emotion. **3.** a state of being beyond the realm of reason and even self-control. **4.** a mystical, prophetic, or poetic trance.

The feeling involved is so intense and overwhelming that it is interpreted as an experience of *standing outside of one's ordinary consciousness*, and as a climactic focus or absorption of all the faculties into an undifferentiated unity in which there is no discrimination among things such as body, spirit, mind, intellect, will, desires, or needs. See MYSTICAL EXPERIENCE.

eduction (from Latin, *educere*, lead forth; from *e*, out, + *ducere*, lead) **1.** the eliciting (extracting, drawing out) of a point or an idea by ANALYSIS or INFERENCE. **2.** direct inference of a PARTICULAR from particulars. **3.** arguing from particulars. **4.** in metaphysics, the drawing out (or the ACTUALIZATION) of a substantial form potentially in matter.

effect see entries under CAUSE.

efficient cause see CAUSES, ARISTOTLE'S FOUR.

effluences (effluxes), theory of (from Latin, *efflux*, from *effluere*, flow out of; from *ex*, out of, + *fluere*, flow—therefore, that which flows out of something) sometimes called *theory of effluvia* or *theory of simulacra*, a pre-Socratic theory primarily found in Empedocles and Democritus. Physical objects shed (spurt out, give off) *aporroai*, films (images, effluences), which fit into sense-organ pores, meeting with like effluences in the body. This process causes the sensations and perceptions that form the basis of our knowledge of the external world. This theory lasted in MATERIALISM throughout the medieval period. Compare with EIDŌLA.

egalitarianism the view that all humans are equal and should be treated equally in liberties, rights, respect, acceptance, opportunities, etc. See EQUALITARIANISM for a fuller discussion.

ego (from Greek, *egō,* I, I at least, for my part, for myself) used as a synonym for SELF and some meanings of AGENT; PERSONAL IDENTITY; PERSON; SUBJECT; CONSCIOUSNESS.

ego, empirical (Kant) the active individual self (subject, ego) in its processes and contents as perceived by immediate INTROSPECTION, and which qualitatively distinguishes one person from another (or which provides his or her particular character). Contrasted with EGO, TRANSCENDENTAL (KANT).

ego, pure that nonempirical (invisible, intangible, nonmaterial, unchanging, unverifiable) entity (soul, spirit) (a) that is the underlying cause of all human mental functions and (usually) (b) whose existence cannot be known directly by introspective analysis but must be *inferred* from the content of our introspection. (For Kant, a pure ego must be presupposed without empirical evidence in order to explain the unity of our consciousness.) See EGO, TRANSCENDENTAL (KANT).

ego, transcendental (Kant) that unfathomable subject (self) presupposed by (implied by, indicated by) the unity of our consciousness. In other philosophies usually referred to as *pure ego* (see EGO, PURE). Contrasted with EGO, EMPIRICAL (KANT).

ego of introspection, the 1. the intuitively felt (or perceived) unity of consciousness. **2.** the system of internal mental states (an individual self or identity) that endures throughout change and moments of time. **3.** the personal awareness of a series of interconnected, internal mental acts, or states, or contents. **4.** the cognition of a conceptual distinction (a) between one's own consciousness and a realm of nonconsciousness, and (b) between one's own consciousness as immediately given (and directly known), and all other things that can never be known in this unique way. See INTROSPECTION.

egocentric illusion (from Greek, *egō,* I, + *kentron,* center, pivotal point) **1.** the apparent fact that each self cannot help perceiving itself as the focal point and center of the universe, though in reality no self is such. **2.** the view that everything in the universe is organized to satisfy our ego, needs and goals, and wishes and desires.

egocentric predicament 1. the apparent situation that each person can have knowledge only of his or her own experiences. One cannot get beyond one's experiences to know anything about the world as it exists apart from oneself. One cannot know anything about another's experiences as they exist to that other person. **2.** all knowledge is a product of our own individual consciousness, and no knowledge is possible of anything outside our consciousness. See entries under SOLIPSISM. **3.** the term was invented by Ralph Barton Perry to name the fact that we are all limited to and by our own unique and peculiar perceptual world. We cannot go beyond this world to know what the external world is like in itself, since that knowledge would inevitably have to be structured in terms of our perceptions. See *DING AN SICH, DAS.*

egoism 1. in general, excessive self-love and preoccupation with oneself, and excessive reference to one's own knowledge, experiences, manners, customs, or beliefs. **2.** specifically, gratification of self, the belief that the aim of life is to procure satisfactions (pleasures) for oneself, as humans are by nature selfish, self-seeking, self-interested, self-loving creatures. (In strong forms of egoism, humans act to fulfill only their own desires and interests even at the expense of others.) Opposite to ALTRUISM. See DARWINISM, SOCIAL.

egoism, altruistic sometimes given as *egoistic altruism,* the view that self-interest is compatible with benevolent actions and motives. It is possible to satisfy our own interests in the act of seeking the best interests of others. The achievement of the happiness of others creates happiness in us. The loss of happiness in others diminishes the happiness in us. Thus, benevolence (see ALTRUISM) is not to be regarded as a secondary motive in humans.

egoism, ethical the view that (a) each person *should* aim to promote his or her own well-being and interests; (b) the *SUMMUM BONUM* of life should be to procure the most satisfactions (pleasures, goals, desires, needs) possible for oneself; and (c) one's own success and happiness should be of primary and ultimate worth, and all other values should stem from this.

Some forms of ethical egoism are referred to as *enlightened* (or *rational*) *self-interest,* of which altruistic egoism (see EGOISM, ALTRUISTIC) is the exemplary form.

egoism, psychological 1. the thesis that all individuals do *in fact* seek their own interests at all times, that there is no purely unselfish act. See SELFISHNESS. **2.** the theory that all human actions are consciously or unconsciously motivated by a desire for one's own well-being and satisfactions; it only appears that one acts for the benefit of others.

egotism connotes (a) offensive self-conceit, self-adulation, self-praise, and (b) offensive living for the selfish satisfaction of one's own interests, desires, needs, and appetites. Not necessarily to be equated with EGOISM.

eidetic (from Greek, *eidos,* that which is seen, form, shape, figure, appearance, type, species, idea) referring to an idea or image that resembles the characteristic property or constitutive ESSENCE of a thing. (Husserl uses *eidos* to mean essence.)

eidōla also IDŌLA (Greek, images, likenesses, ideas, phantoms, idols) used in Greek philosophy primarily by the Atomists to refer to the groups of particles that flow as effluences (images, films, copies) from physical objects and stimulate the sense organs to produce sensations and perceptions, which are the sources of our knowledge of the external world. Compare with EFFLUENCES (EFFLUXES), THEORY OF.

In Democritus, *eidōla* were emissions of material particles from an object that were like the form of the object. They imprinted themselves on the sense organs and produced sense experiences of external objects. In Epicurus, *eidōla* were the physical images of external objects that perpetually peeled off from the surface of things and flew about at random, imprinting themselves on us to form perceptions of things.

eidōla (art) The term may refer to the human-created pictorial images of actual things or to the representations of images. *Eidōla* imitate or are only a semblance (PHANTASMA) of their originals. This imitation of the original exists within two extremes: **1.** a likeness (*eikon* or ICON) that has many of the characteristics of the original such as in a model or sculpture of a thing, or **2.** a likeness that has only the appearance of being like the original, such as something painted in linear perspective on a two-dimensional canvas.

eidos see IDEAS (PLATO).

einfühlung German, most frequently translated as EMPATHY.

élan vital (French, vital impetus, vital principle, vital impulse) a term used in nonmechanistic and creative evolutionary theories (such as Bergson's) to answer such questions as why living organisms have evolved into greater and greater complexity in the course of evolutionary time. The *élan vital* is (a) the driving force propelling life on to higher and higher levels of structure and organization and (b) the creative force giving direction to evolution. It is likened to a flow or current of consciousness, with which all the universe is imbued and which determines the direction of evolution. Bergson speaks of the *élan vital* as a supraconsciousness, a nonempirical, intangible, invisible, nonverifiable acting force. The term VITALISM is taken from this French term.

Eleatics, the the school of philosophy founded by Parmenides in Elea (a city in what is now southern Italy). Melissus of Samos and Zeno of Elea are two famous disciples. Eleaticism is characterized by an extreme MONISM: reality is one, motionless, unchanging, undifferentiable, and eternal. Melissus defended the eternality of the *one* by showing that its denial implies the untenable position of the creation of something from nothing, or the destruction of something into nothing. See MATTER, PRINCIPLE OF THE CONSERVATION OF. Zeno defended extreme monism by showing the contradictory nature of the language of change (motion, movement, activity, process); since the linguistic description of change is contradictory, there is no change. See DIALECTIC (ZENO) and ZENO'S PARADOXES.

elements (from Latin, *elementa,* the first principles of things, the rudimentary nature of something) **1.** the simple substances out of which (or by which) something comes to be. See ELEMENTS, THE FOUR. **2.** the simple constituents of a complex; in this sense used synonymously with *component.* Elements are regarded as primary and irreducible.

elements, the four water, air, fire, and earth, which some Greek philosophers believed to be the ultimate irreducible primary simple constituents (or masses) of the universe. All things were composed of the combination and various proportions of these four elements. The amounts of the elements and the changes the elements underwent determined the kind of object a thing was and how it behaved. Each of these material elements had two inherent forces, or qualities: cold and wet (water), hot and wet (air), hot and dry (fire), cold and dry (earth). "Like causes like"; "Like attracts like"; "Unlikes repel" etc. are principles used in the philosophers' physical explanations. Any of the four elements could blend into or become another element, provided that the other three contained a common quality. Theories of the four elements remained from Greek times as the primary mode of scientific, physical, and material explanation well into the 17th century. Compare with HUMOURS, THE FOUR.

emanation (from Latin, *emanare,* flow out of; from *e,* out, + *manare,* flow) a creation theory that all reality proceeds (by necessity) from a central principle of perfect being that is one and eternally present. The emanation conception of creation often uses the analogy of the sun and the light that radiates from it. The sun is the source of the light; the *one* is the source of all existence. Light emanates from the sun and is dependent on it but not identical with it. Take away the sun, you then take away light. The universe is an outpouring of the *one* and is dependent on it for its existence and order but is not identical with it. Take away the *one,* you then take away the universe. The farther you are from the sun the less bright the light. The farther away from the *one* a thing is, the less spirituality and perfection it possesses. Matter is the farthest away from the *one*; intelligence is the closest to the *one,* followed by pure psyche (soul, spirit). The theory of emanation is primarily associated with the neo-Platonic philosophy of Plotinus. See BEING, HIERARCHY OF; HEN; ONE, THE.

embodied mind see MIND, EMBODIED.

emergent, an sometimes called *gestalt property* of organized structures, the new qualitative synthesis produced by structures organized in certain patterns that cannot be predicted from examination of the constituent parts of the whole. Examples: Water (liquidity, fluidity) is the quality that emerges from the combination of two parts of hydrogen and one part of oxygen under certain conditions. Both hydrogen and oxygen are gases that burn. The emergent quality (water) could not have been predicted from knowledge of the properties of hydrogen and oxygen. The mind (consciousness, awareness) is regarded as a new quality that emerges when certain neural processes become organized in a specific way; change the organization of these physical structures, and another quality (mind) will emerge. See EVOLUTION, EMERGENT.

emergent mentalism see MENTALISM, EMERGENT.

emotion (from Latin, *emovere,* remove, shake, stir up; from *e,* out, and *movere,* move) **1.** a mode of feeling. **2.** a particular, irreducible, unanalyzable feeling; a quality of consciousness, immediately present, known only by having it, and not accessible as a felt quality to the consciousness of anyone else. In general, any of the feeling, affective passion states referred to by emotion terms (love, hate, fear, anger, etc.). **3.** emotions (a) are occurrent states (see STATE, OCCURRENT) of consciousness such as immediate feelings or moods that may be of short or long duration, and (b) may also be dispositional states (see STATE, DISPOSITION) that tend one toward other emotions, attitudes, or activities. An example of (a): the joy of solving a puzzle. An example of (b): sympathy inclining one toward helping someone in need. **4.** All emotions involve covert and overt bodily changes, whether recognizable or not, such as changes in digestion, heartbeat, blood pressure, hemoglobin count, adrenalin secretion, amounts and kinds of hormones, blushing, panting, trembling, paling, fainting, crying, and nausea. **5.** Classifications of emotions may be made according to their being desirable or not desirable, harmful or not harmful, useful or not useful, etc. **6.** Emotions may be thought of in terms of whether or not they are related to an increase in the efficiency of and in the energy available for behavior such as thinking, perceiving, concentrating, selecting, and acting. Examples: Fear may be associated with the prevention of learning, inhibited perception, and decreased concentration. On some occasions fear may be associated with certain kinds of learning, intensification of perception, and improved concentration about specific things in the environment. Grief may be associated with decreased efficiency in relating to people or desire to get things done; or it may be associated with the opposite effect in some personalities. See PATHOS. Compare with FEELING; SENSATION.

emotivism see ETHICS, EMOTIVE THEORY OF.

empathy (from Greek, *empathēs,* being in a state of emotion, being much affected by or at something; empathy was constructed out of the Greek *en,* in, into, and *pathos,* suffering, emotion, feeling, passion) sometimes referred to by the German EINFÜHLUNG **1.** the projection of one's own inner feelings on an object or activity. Examples: "Those pillars are straining under the tension of the roof's weight." The feelings had while (empathetically) watching a boxing match and undergoing, physically and mentally, what is thought to be taking place in the combatants. **2.** the abstract understanding of the inner feelings of another consciousness but without oneself experiencing them at that moment. Example: knowing a friend's grief but not being involved emotionally in the grieving. See ANIMISM; SYMPATHY.

Empedocles (c.493–c.433 BC) Greek natural philosopher, poet, statesman; born in Sicily. As a statesman he was an ardent supporter of constitutional democracy. His philosophy, expressed in poetic form, was influenced by Pythagoras and Parmenides. Empedocles is known for his physical theory of the four original roots, or elements, of all things: fire, earth, water, and air, which are moved by the forces of love (attraction) and hate (repulsion). Fragments of his hexameter poem *On Nature* are extant, as well as some verses of *Purification*.

empirical (from Greek, *empeiros,* experienced, practiced in a thing, directly acquainted with some knowledge) sometimes *empiric,* referring to knowledge founded on experience, observation, facts, sensation, practice, concrete situations, and real events. *A posteriori* knowledge (see KNOWLEDGE, A POSTERIORI) as opposed to A PRIORI KNOWLEDGE (see KNOWLEDGE, A PRIORI). Contrast with EXPERIENTIAL.

empiricism (from Greek, *empeiria,* experience, concrete acquaintance or familiarity with something) **1.** the view that all ideas are abstractions formed by compounding (combining, recombining) what is experienced (observed, immediately given in sensation). **2.** Experience is the sole source of knowledge. **3.** All that we know is ultimately dependent on sense data. All knowledge is directly derived or indirectly inferred from sense data (except some definitional truths of logic and mathematics). **4.** Reason cannot on its own provide us with knowledge of reality without reference to sense experience and the use of our sense organs. Information provided by our senses serves as the basic building block of all knowledge. Contrasted with RATIONALISM.

empiricism, logical holds to views such as: (a) Modern logical analyses are applicable to the solution of philosophical and scientific problems. (The traditional problems of philosophy are divided into two classifications: 1. problems of fact, which science deals with, and 2. problems of methodology and conceptual analysis, which philosophy deals with. All other problems are either irrelevant or meaningless.) (b) There are limits to empiricism. The principles of formal systems of logic and of inductive inference cannot be proved by reference to experience. (c) All true propositions (except logical truths) are reducible to sense datum propositions (basic propositions) which are about immediately given sense data. See MEANING, EMPIRICIST THEORY OF; POSITIVISM, LOGICAL. Compare with ANALYTIC PHILOSOPHY.

empiricism, radical 1. the theory that relations as well as particulars exist in the external world. **2.** the theory that immediate experience is the only origin of and sanction for all knowledge. (Radical empiricism is called SENSATIONALISM when *immediate experience* is interpreted as *immediate sensations*.)

empiricists, the British those traditionally included: Locke, Berkeley, Hume; sometimes also included: Francis Bacon and Thomas Hobbes. Contrasted with RATIONALISTS, CONTINENTAL (EUROPEAN).

end 1. the object (goal, PURPOSE, aim) whose attainment is intended by an agent. **2.** that ultimate state of ACTUALIZATION of a FORM, ESSENCE, or process beyond which there is no further need for development. **3.** the rela-

tive state of fulfillment that must be reached in order for a process to
progress to another stage or to a final stage.

end, man as an (Kant) the ethical rule that all humans must be treated as
ends in themselves, and not as means to ends. All persons are morally self-
governing agents living under natural moral law. All are able to realize the
good will that is the only thing good in itself without qualification. See
ETHICS (KANT).

endeiktikon (Greek, that which marks or points out, or indicates) referring
to indicative words, signs, or symbols whose referents are not observed or
experienced in a direct way. For example, words such as *soul, spirit, substance, mind, matter,* and *essence* are considered as *endeiktic* (indicative
signs) when believed to refer to entities inaccessible to empirical testing or
experience.

ends, heteronomy of (Kant) the condition of the will in which the will is
guided (governed, directed, motivated) by ends that are sought for the
benefit of oneself or another (such as reputation, pleasure) rather than for
the development and betterment of one's own moral will, and/or obeys
moral laws that are not its own. Opposite to WILL, AUTONOMY OF THE
(KANT).

ends, kingdom of (Kant) the unity of all rational people under a universal
moral law.

ends/means controversy, the a dispute regarding dichotomous statements
such as: "The end justifies the means"/"The end never justifies the means";
"Evil means lead to good ends"/"Evil means never lead to good ends"; and
"Actions must be judged only by their consequences"/"Actions cannot be
judged on the basis of their consequences."

energeia (Greek, energy; from *en,* in, + *ergon,* work, and from *energos,*
active) a term used as in Aristotle to refer to force, the active exercise of,
activity, the power of acting, the process of becoming actualized, the development of a thing's potentiality into its actualization. The *energeia* of
things varies in duration. Contrasted with POTENTIALITY and POSSIBILITY.
Compare with ACTUALITY; DYNAMIS (ARISTOTLE); ENTELECHY (ARISTOTLE).

energy 1. the POWER, FORCE, strength exerted by a thing. **2.** the power to
produce a change. **3.** the inherent capacity to act (move) and to cause
action (motion).

The concept of energy entails concepts such as (a) space, (b) time, (c) a
flow or transformation, (d) a quantity, (e) (often) a direction, and (usually)
(f) a physical medium that has the first five characteristics. Often regarded
as the basic physical reality on which all phenomena depend for their existence; all phenomena are manifestations of the various processes, transfor-
mations, or levels of energy. In this sense, MATTER is not conceived of as a
SUBSTANCE, or as the ultimate unchanging building block of the universe.
Rather, matter becomes *identical* or interchangeable with the concepts of
(1) energy, (2) process, or (3) matter regarded as a *form* of energy.

In most cases *energy* is a more general term than MOTION, force, or power.

energy, principle of the conservation of see MATTER, PRINCIPLE OF THE CONSERVATION OF.

enkrasia Greek word used by philosophers such as Plato and Aristotle to refer to that state or strength of a human's will that is able to resist temptation and/or is able to do what it knows is right and good. Contrasted with AKRASIA.

ennui (French, from the Latin *in odio,* in hatred) boredom, tedium, weariness usually arising from overindulgence, satiety, or the lack of capacity to be stimulated. See EXISTENTIALISM.

ens (Latin, being) **1.** used interchangeably with the Latin RES. **2.** sometimes used to refer to being-as-being, without any qualifications (properties, determining features). In theology, the ultimate *ens* refers to God, in whom ESSENCE and EXISTENCE are identical. In metaphysics, the ultimate *ens* refers to the ABSOLUTE. See *A SE.*

en soi (Sartre) (French, in itself, in oneself) a phrase used by Sartre to refer to existence in which one acts (is acted upon) as a mere existing thing, suppressing (or out of ignorance not realizing) the fact that authentic, free choices are open for one's every action. The quality of *être en soi* (be in itself) belongs to things and to humans insofar as they act like inactive objects. Sartre contrasts *en soi* with *POUR SOI. En soi* is related to self-deception and inauthentic existence and in particular to an individual who lives avoiding responsibility, to self and others, in order also to avoid the anxiety, distress, and malaise that accompany the act, or fulfillment, of responsibility. Individuals live *en soi* when they are involved in BAD FAITH (SARTRE). See EXISTENTIALISM.

entelechy (Aristotle) (from Greek, *entelecheia,* being complete) **1.** in Aristotle's philosophy, synonymous with complete actuality where there is no further potentiality to be realized, where the thing's essence has been fulfilled. **2.** also in Aristotle's philosophy, entelechies are regarded as the regulators of orderly activity, causing things to do that which is natural to them and to seek their specific natural ends or completion. Compare with *ENERGEIA.*

entelechy (Leibniz) the dominant monad within a complex. The ultimate entelechy is the dominant monad, or God. See MONADS (LEIBNIZ).

entity (from Latin, *entitas,* from ENS, thing) **1.** a being. **2.** an existent. **3.** that which has a real, substantial existence.

entity, neutral sometimes called *neutral stuff,* a qualityless existent or being, usually one that has characteristics of neither mind nor matter. See MONISM, NEUTRAL.

entropic, anti- sometimes *antientropic* or *anabolic factor,* the forces at work in the universe that tend to prevent an increase in the ENTROPY of a system or render a system less entropic.

entropy (from Greek, *entropē*, a turning in; from *en*, in, + *tropē*, a turn, a transformation) **1.** the disorganization of a physical system. **2.** the tendency of a closed nonequilibrium physical system toward a state of equilibrium or lack of potential. **3.** the transformation of energy in a closed system away from one level (kind, quality) where energy is available to do physical (mechanical) work. The *less* energy the system has ready to be used as work, the higher its entropy. Example: a bucket of ice melting to water. Energy must be brought into the system to make that water into steam or ice again. The water has reached an entropy level; a level of thermal equilibrium.

Epictetus (c.50–130) Greek Stoic philosopher, a Phrygian slave born in Hierapolis. His master in Rome freed him and saw to his education in Stoic philosophy. He lived and taught Stoicism in Rome until c.94, when he removed to Epirus—all philosophers were exiled by the Roman emperor, Domitian.

The philosophy of Epictetus stressed *apatheia*, an indifference toward, or transcendence of, pleasure, pain, suffering, feelings, and emotions—leading to acceptance of life, and serenity in it. The aim of life was to desire nothing but freedom, self-control, and contentment. Epictetus is not known to have written anything, but his student Flavius Arrianus compiled the sayings of Epictetus in eight volumes of *Discourses*.

Epicureanism SEE ATOMISM, GREEK; HEDONISM (EPICURUS).

Epicurus (341–270 BC) Greek philosopher, an atomistic materialist and qualitative hedonist, born on the island of Samos. After studying in Athens in his youth, Epicurus taught at Mytilene (also called Lesbos) and Lampsacus. About 306, he established an outdoor school in Athens and there taught for the rest of his life. His philosophy (especially his views on pleasure) was greatly influenced by Plato and by the Cyrenaic beliefs of Aristippus. Epicurus was mainly interested in ethics, although he wrote on the atomic structure of the universe—a development of the materialism of Leucippus and Democritus. His principal ethical tenet was *ataraxia* as the highest good for humans to aim at—imperturbability, or tranquility, of mind, body, and spirit.

epiphenomenalism (from Greek, *epiphaneia*, appearance; from *epi*, on, upon, over and above, + *phainein*, appear, show, become evident) a theory of the relationship of body and mind. (a) Consciousness is an epiphenomenon (an aftereffect, a by-product) caused by certain cerebral processes; (b) consciousness does not affect the body but exists as a powerless neutral state; and (c) conscious states do not affect other conscious states. The usual analogies given in epiphenomenalism: Just as the body causes its shadow and the shadow has no causal efficacy on the body or on other shadows, so the brain causes consciousness, but consciousness cannot affect the brain. Just as a locomotive produces steam or smoke, which do not causally affect the locomotive, so the body produces consciousness that has no causal connection with its source in brain processes. See MIND, TYPES OF THEORIES OF (5).

epistēmē (Greek, true knowledge, scientific knowledge, systematic knowledge) opposite to *DOXA*. Contrasted with *POIETIKOS; TECHNĒ; THEORIA*. See *DIANOIA;* ESSENTIALISM (PLATO).

epistemic pertaining to knowledge.

epistemology (from Greek, *epistēmē,* knowledge, + *logos,* the study of, theory of) theory of knowledge, the study of (a) the origins, (b) the presuppositions, (c) the nature, (d) the extent, and (e) the veracity (truth, reliability, validity) of knowledge. The branch of philosophy that asks questions such as: Where does knowledge come from—how is it formulated, expressed, and communicated? What is knowledge? Is sense experience necessary for all types of knowledge? What part does reason play in knowledge? Is there knowledge derived only from reason? What are the differences among concepts such as: belief, knowledge, opinion, fact, reality, error, imagining, conceptualizing, idea, truth, possibility, certainty?

epochē (Greek, a cessation) used, for example, by the Greek skeptics to mean: **1.** a provisional suspension of judgment about the truth or falsity, or the belief or disbelief in ideas until a better determination can be made, or **2.** a deliberate denial of knowledge in order to arrive at certainty from a clean slate. Compare with AGNOSTICISM; SKEPTIC; and entries under SKEPTICISM.

equalitarianism 1. the belief that all humans are socially and politically equal (the belief sometimes also favors economic equality). Each individual is to be counted as one. A common trait is seen to exist in all people requiring that they be treated equally. This trait may be reason, or a soul, or a moral sense, or suffering, or being created by God. **2.** the view that everyone ought to be treated with the same consideration and concern. Each individual should receive equal treatment under law and equal opportunity for such things as an education, development of capacities, and fulfillment of human needs. This is to be taken as a regulative procedure of social and ethical conduct that in the end produces a more abundant good for humankind than do other attitudes. **3.** the nondiscriminatory treatment of all persons regardless of race, religion, sex, sexual preference, status, wealth, intelligence, physical abilities, etc. See EGALITARIANISM.

equivocation (from Latin, *aequivocus,* calling something by the same name and same meaning; from *aequus,* equal, + *vocare,* call) **1.** refers to the inconsistency of giving different meanings (or senses) to the same word. See entries under AMBIGUITY. **2.** an equivocation is committed when a word is used with one particular meaning in one part of a presentation and then deliberately or unintentionally used with another meaning in another part of the presentation. Example: "A crime should be punished. It is a crime the way he wastes his money on alcohol. Therefore he should be punished." The two uses of *crime* are different. In the first, the word means *legal infraction or violation*; in the second it means *morally inexcusable and reprehensible act*. The fallacy of equivocation occurs when conclusions are reached by using words that have changed their meanings within the argument. See FALLACY, TYPES OF INFORMAL (19).

Words (or actions) are *equivocal* when given two or more possible meanings without certainty as to which meaning is intended. Opposite to UNIVOCAL. To *equivocate* is to use the same language in different senses, and in the derogatory meaning of *equivocate*, to use language in a willful way to mislead or deceive by the use of double, or varied, meanings. *Equivocator* means one who says one thing and really means another, whereas a *hypocrite* is one who says one thing and does another, and a *prevaricator* (see PREVARICATION) is one who evades the truth by quibbling with words and/or shuffling their meanings to suit the user's purpose.

Erigena, John Scotus (c.815–c.877) Irish philosopher, theologian, and Greek scholar; born in Scotia (now Ireland); considered to be the first synthesizer of medieval theological and philosophic streams of thought, and the originator of the Scholastic tradition. Erigena wrote many translations of Christian writers and commentaries on them, but his two principal works are *De Praedestinatione* (851) and *De Divisione Naturae* (c.865).

eristic (from Greek, *eris*, strife, conflict) sometimes called *eristic dialectic* **1.** argumentative. **2.** characterized by spurious reasoning. **3.** referring to the exchange of ideas in which the aim is not truth but the intentional use of any kind of argument and manipulation of language to win a dispute or persuade someone of the truth of a point in question.

The phrase *eristic dialectic* is sometimes used pejoratively, specifically to refer to the Sophists' claim to debate in such a way as to make the worse appear the better, and the better appear the worse. Opposite to APODEICTIC. See DIALECTIC and SOPHISTIC.

erōs (Greek, love) **1.** in Greek mythology the god of love. (Hesiod depicted *Erōs* as the first of the gods to emerge from Chaos, drawing all things together into an order. Later writers spoke of him as the son of Aphrodite.) **2.** the creative and binding force in the universe. **3.** the love of beauty; the source of inspiration for the search in life for beauty and the good. **4.** possessive love. **5.** sensual and/or sexual (erotic) attraction; physical love. **6.** desire. **7.** the passionate attachment to (or enthusiasm toward) another, or which is created in another. Compare with AGAPĒ, PHILIA.

erotetic (from Greek, *erōtēsis*, a question, a questioning) referring to the asking of questions, or to the procedure of questioning. Some forms of DIALECTIC are erotetic.

In Aristotle's logic, an *erōtēma* was a question used as a premise in a syllogism that had to be responded to before the argument could proceed.

eschatology (from Greek, *éschatos*, the last, the furthest, the outermost, the last time, + *logos*, the study of) the beliefs associated with last or final events such as death, a judgment day, the end of the earth, the final moment of history, and people's relationship to them.

esoteric (from Greek, *esōterikos,* inner, interior) referring to private or secret doctrines (ideologies, beliefs) understood and shared only by the initiated. Opposite to EXOTERIC.

ESP an abbreviation for *extrasensory perception, extrasensory phenomena,* or *extrasensory powers.* See PARAPSYCHOLOGY.

esse (Latin, exist, be) **1.** the *act* of being (as opposed to a *state* of being). **2.** used to refer to the active expression of an essence. Compare with *ENS.*

esse est percipi (Latin, to be is to be perceived) Berkeley's phrase that was the cornerstone of his philosophy. The view that for something to exist it must either be perceived or be engaged in the act of perceiving. Berkeley called things that are perceived *sensible things* or *sensible qualities;* sometimes he called them *ideas* or *sensations.* Examples: pains, pleasures, itches, colors, sounds, tastes, smells, tangible shapes. These sensible qualities exist as passive products or objects of a mind (or a spirit). They cannot exist when they are not being experienced. Minds are active beings that will and perceive. (Perceiving is an activity.) Only active minds together with their sensible qualities exist. Only because the world is continuously perceived by God does it continue to exist when humans are not perceiving it. See IMMATERIALISM (BERKELEY).

essence (from Latin, *essentia,* from *esse,* be) **1.** that which makes a thing what it is (and without which it would not be what it is). **2.** that which makes a thing what it is rather than its being or becoming something else. **3.** that which a thing possesses and which makes that thing identifiable as the particular thing it is (and without which it would not be identified as that thing). **4.** the necessary and essential defining characteristic of a thing. **5.** the fundamental, prime, ultimate power of a thing. **6.** the abstract idea (or law) of a thing by which we can recognize further particular instances of it.

Essence is often contrasted in abstraction with EXISTENCE. But for philosophers who take the concept of essence seriously, a thing could not exist without having an essence. Essence and existence are said to be identical in such things as God, the universe (eternal matter), the absolute. Sometimes, essence is used synonymously with FORM and IDEA. See *OUSIA.*

The plural, *essences,* is sometimes used to refer to the spirits, souls, immaterial agencies in things.

essence (Aristotle) 1. that something which the thing is to be in its final completed state. **2.** the essential nature (internal principle) of a thing that makes it what it is at any given state in its teleological development and makes it become what it will finally be. See FORM (ARISTOTLE). **3.** that which is the underlying identity or nature of a thing throughout the process of change from potentiality to actuality. In this sense Aristotle is using essence (*ousia*) and substance synonymously (see entries under SUBSTANCE that refer to Aristotle). **4.** that which is necessary and unchanging about a concept or thing. Compare with DYNAMIS (ARISTOTLE).

essentialism 1. the belief that things have essences. **2.** the theory that a definition describes or reveals the essence of a thing and/or of the perfect ideal form of which it is an imperfect copy. To the extent to which it does this, it is indubitable, true, exact, precise, incontrovertible. To the extent that it does not do this, it is untrue, false, inadequate, inexact, imprecise, disputable.

essentialism (Plato) there are two general levels of knowledge: (a) that of the eternally perfect, immutable, invisible, abstract forms (ARCHETYPES, essences) and (b) that of visible, tangible (sensed) objects. The aim of philosophy is to gain an understanding of the real world of forms. This is achieved by means of pure rationality (contemplation, mathematical-type reasoning): the abstract intellectual grasp of the ideal forms of which particular objects are imperfect imitations. Plato called this knowledge EPIS-TĒMĒ.. Common knowledge has to do with the understanding of the sensed world by means of sense perception, experience, observation of particulars. Plato called this knowledge DOXA: opinion.

esthetics see AESTHETICS.

estrangement (from Latin, *extraneus*, strange; from *extraneare,* treat or regard something as a stranger [sometimes an unwanted and unknown stranger]) **1.** the act of keeping something at a distance, or withdrawing and withholding one's emotions and confidence in things, usually because the world appears unfriendly. See ALIENATION. **2.** the state of feeling produced by the act described above. See SELF-ALIENATION. Contrast with DEALIENATION.

eternal (from Latin, *aeternus*, from *aevum*, age) **1.** everlasting, of infinite duration, endless continuation in time without beginning or end, SEM-PITERNAL, perpetual. **2.** having no succession, but existing all at once, an unchanging timelessly present *one*. See AEVITERNITY.

eternal, *a parte ante* the infinite extent of time before (*ante*) any present moment.

eternal, *a parte post* the infinite extent of time after (*post*) any present moment.

eternal recurrence see RECURRENCE, ETERNAL.

eternal return see RECURRENCE, ETERNAL.

ethical imperativism see IMPERATIVISM.

ethical intuitionism see ETHICS, INTUITIVE.

ethical naturalism see NATURALISM, ETHICAL.

ethical nihilism see NIHILISM (ETHICS).

ethical relativism see RELATIVISM (VALUE THEORY).

ethics (from Greek, *ēthikos*, from ĒTHOS, usage, character, custom, disposition, manners) **1.** the analysis of concepts such as *ought, should, duty, moral rules, right, wrong, obligation, responsibility*, etc. **2.** the inquiry into the nature of morality or moral acts. **3.** the search for the morally good life.

ethics (Kant) doing something out of a desire to do it and doing something out of a feeling of moral OBLIGATION (DUTY) to do it are different states. Moral merit cannot be given to actions done out of instinct or inclination. Moral merit can be given only to those actions done out of a sense of duty as prescribed by reason. The only unqualified good is the *good will*. To have a good will is to act always from a sense of duty. Duty is awareness of the moral law and complete submission to the moral law. Moral law is in opposition to inclination, and it is expressed in the form of a categorical imperative (No matter what, you must . . . .). Moral law is unconditional. Desire is variable. The methods for obtaining the satisfaction of desires are variable. But the moral law applies at all times, in all places and to all people, and with respect to every moral instance. Duty, good will, moral law are *a priori* concepts. No one can ever know them merely by describing behavior. See CATEGORICAL IMPERATIVE, THE (KANT); ETHICS, FORMALISTIC (KANT); END, MAN AS AN (KANT); ENDS, HETERONOMY OF (KANT); ENDS, KINGDOM OF (KANT); POSTULATES OF PRACTICAL REASON, THE (KANT); WILL, AUTONOMY OF THE (KANT); and WILL, FREE ELECTIVE (KANT).

ethics, axiological the theory that the values inherent or involved in a moral act determine the act's worth and correctness. See AXIOLOGY.

ethics, casuistic (from Latin, *casus,* case; from *cadere,* fall, happen) sometimes referred to as CASUISTRY **1.** the application (or stretching) of ethical rules to judge (favorably or adversely) a particular ethical situation. **2.** using conniving or false arguments to morally defend an action insupportable by moral rules. **3.** using dubious moral rules to defend an action. Compare with RATIONALIZE.

ethics, deontological sometimes, but rarely, simply *deontics* (see DEONTOLOGY). The theory (a) that the rightness or wrongness of a moral action is determined, at least partly, with reference to formal rules of conduct, rather than consequences or results of an action, and (b) that some actions in conformance with these rules are obligatory (compulsory, categorically imperative, necessary) regardless of their results. Sometimes called a *formalist* theory (see ETHICS, FORMALISTIC), since it is based on following the fixed, formal status of moral law. Related to *ethical intuitionism* (see ETHICS, INTUITIVE; INTUITIONISM [ETHICS]) when it is thought that the formal rules of conduct are obtained by intuition. Contrasted with approaches such as the pragmatic, the utilitarian, and the teleological, which stress the results of an act as determining the moral act's worth and correctness. Opposite to ETHICS, TELEOLOGICAL.

ethics, descriptive sometimes called *descriptive morality*, seeks to know (a) what ethical rules (or moral actions) are common among people, (b) whether they are universal, and (c) what effects their application has.

ethics, descriptivism in sometimes called *ethical descriptivism*, the view that ethical statements (values) are obtained much as factual (descriptive) statements are obtained and are meaningful and usable much in the same way. For the most part related with ethical objectivism and descriptive ethics (see ETHICS, DESCRIPTIVE). Contrasted with *emotivism* (see ETHICS, EMOTIVE THEORY OF) and PRESCRIPTIVISM in ethics.

ethics, emotive theory of also called *emotivism*, a noncognitive theory: ethical knowledge is different from other kinds of knowledge such as factual, scientific, conceptual, cognitive, logical. Words such as *right, wrong, bad, good, should*, and *ought to* (a) do not refer to qualities in things, (b) cannot be said to be true or false (since they do not describe any states of affairs), (c) cannot be formally deduced or demonstrated by means of a logical system, and (d) cannot be empirically verified by such things as experimentation, observation, or testing procedures. Ethical words function similarly to interjections (terrific!), imperatives (do it!), prescriptions (thou shalt . . .), optatives (would that . . .!), or performative utterances (I apologize). Ethical statements are expressions of such things as blame, praise, prohibition, or derogation used (1) to influence conduct and/or (2) to express emotions, feelings, attitudes, or (3) to evoke similar emotions. They request, exhort, command, persuade, advise, cajole. Ethical disagreement (disagreement about convictions or values) is actually disagreement about attitudes. For some emotive theorists, ethical statements may indirectly be cognitive, in that they may provide information about one's attitudes, beliefs, ideas, commitments, and convictions.

ethics, evolutionary see DARWINISM, SOCIAL.

ethics, formalistic sometimes called *ethical formalism* or *deontological ethics*. Universal ethical rules are obligatory regardless of their consequences to us or to others. See ETHICS, DEONTOLOGICAL.

ethics, formalistic (Kant) sometimes referred to as *ethical formalism*. Correct moral choices (action, behavior) can be made according to many motives and standards such as prudence (If I wish this, then I must do such and such), sympathy, goodness, benevolence, love, compassion. But the highest motive and standard must be a sense of duty—the unqualified submission to the universal, exceptionless moral law. See CATEGORICAL IMPERATIVE, THE (KANT); ETHICS (KANT).

ethics, intuitive sometimes called *ethical intuitionism* **1.** moral values are intuitively apprehended, or given. **2.** (usually) these intuitively apprehended moral values are (a) objectively real, universally obligatory, common to all human beings, and (b) the ability to discern them by INTUITION is latent in everyone. **3.** (a) certain kinds of human actions are directly, intuitively, and self-evidently known to be intrinsically wrong or right, bad or good, and/or (b) certain ultimate, universal moral principles or rules are directly, intuitively, and self-evidently known as binding on human nature.

Intuitively known moral universals and values are often claimed to be (a) unobservable, (b) nonnatural (underived from an examination of natural phenomena), (c) innate, (d) simple, (e) self-evidently true, (f) immediately and directly present to (or perceived by) conscience, and (g) requiring no justification.

ethics, is/ought dichotomy in sometimes called *fact/value dichotomy*. From a description of facts it is impossible to assert moral strictures or arrive at ethical convictions. Example: you cannot deduce the moral dictum "Humans ought to speak the truth" from the fact that humans do speak the truth (or do not speak the truth). See IS/OUGHT DICHOTOMY; and entries under NATURALISTIC FALLACY.

ethics, monistic sometimes called *ethical monism*, the theory that only one intrinsically worthwhile ethical good such as pleasure exists. All things are done for the sake of that good.

ethics, moral faculty theory in 1. the theory that one can perceive the difference between good and bad, right and wrong, with the aid of an ethical FACULTY or sense, in the same way that one can perceive the difference between yellow and blue, a sound and a smell, with the aid of perceptual faculties. One can know that this paper is white by perceiving it. So one can know that something is ethical or not by perceiving the situation. **2.** the view that there is a faculty which directs us toward moral values such as benevolence, the common GOOD, DUTY, sacrifice, love of mankind. Compare with MORAL SENSE. See CONSCIENCE.

ethics, naturalistic 1. the theory that ethics is empirical. Ethical statements have their source in what is occurring in nature and in human nature. Ethics can be derived from an examination of nonethical conditions such as the social interaction of people, their needs and drives. **2.** ethical terms can be defined in nonethical (natural, descriptive, factual) terms. **3.** ethical statements can be reduced to factual statements about natural processes or events. See NATURALISM, ETHICAL.

ethics, noncognitive the position that statements containing implicit or explicit references to moral values do not contain descriptive knowledge, are not informative in that sense, and hence are neither true nor false.

ethics, normative moral philosophy that provides humanity with general guidelines or knowledge about such things as (a) what is good and right (bad and wrong), (b) what people ought to do (and ought not to do) in specific situations, (c) what should be pursued in life, (d) how life should be lived, and (e) what we should do to others and what they should do to us.

ethics, objectivism in see OBJECTIVISM (VALUE THEORY).

ethics, perfectionism in see PERFECTIONISM (ETHICS).

ethics, pluralistic sometimes called *ethical pluralism*, the theory that (a) a number of intrinsically worthwhile ethical values or goods (such as charity, love, sharing, benevolence, kindness) exist, and (b) the *SUMMUM BONUM* of an individual is to participate in as many of them as he or she can.

ethics, subjectivism in 1. the theory that ethical judgments such as *good* mean that I approve of certain actions and that I personally feel or think the same way. **2.** moral values are expressions of human emotions, attitudes, reactions, feelings, thoughts, wishes, and desires, and have no objective reference in the world. **3.** there is no way of rationally or objectively solving moral conflict, or arriving at moral judgments or values. Compare with SUBJECTIVISM (VALUE THEORY).

ethics, teleological 1. the theory that the consequences (see CONSEQUEN-TIALISM [ETHICS]) of a moral act (as opposed to its intention, motive, moral principle, etc.) determine the act's worth and correctness. One may have the best of intentions, or follow the highest moral principles, but if the result of a moral act is harmful or bad it must be judged as a morally or ethically wrong act. PRAGMATISM, UTILITARIANISM, and other related theories presuppose teleological ethics. Opposite to ETHICS, DEONTOLOGICAL. **2.** an ethics in which the moral worth of an act is judged in terms of the extent to which that act accomplishes its purpose or end (or the purpose or end of the ethical system adhered to). **3.** an ethics in which the rightness or wrongness of an act is judged with reference to some end result that is regarded as desirable and good. Whatever achieves this end result is morally good, and whatever thwarts its achievement is morally bad.

ethnocentrism (from Greek, *ethnos,* nation, + *kentron,* center, central) the belief of a people or group that their own ways (values, religion, race, nation, culture, language) are superior to all others.

ēthos (Greek, character, one's habitual way of living, one's moral motivation or purpose) **1.** the character, tone, disposition, values, and sentiments of a person, community, or people. **2.** in Plato, one's *ēthos* is the character produced by habitual responses. **3.** in Aristotle, one's *ēthos* is the character produced by moral as opposed to intellectual habits. (Aristotle describes different *ēthoi* (plural) found at different stages in human development. Aristotle also used *ēthos* to refer to a drama's presentation of character as opposed to action, incidents, suffering, thought, diction, etc. Compare with PATHOS. **4.** in Stoicism, *ēthos* refers to that which motivates behavior or conduct. (This is reminiscent of Heraclitus's saying that the *ēthos* of an individual is his daimōn.)

etiology see AETIOLOGY.

être en soi see EN SOI(SARTRE).

être pour soi see POUR SOI (SARTRE).

eudaimonia (Greek, a vital spiritual well-being, happiness; from *eu,* well, good, + DAIMŌN, spirit, god, inner force, genius) Aristotle's word for the happiness attained when an individual's potentiality for a full rational life is realized to the utmost and the individual fully expresses all his or her varied capacities. This striving for self-realization is the essence of being human. See GOOD (ARISTOTLE).

euphemism (from Greek, *euphēmismos,* from *euphēmizein,* use words that have a good omen or appearance; from *eu,* well, + *phēmē,* voice, speech, or from *phanai,* speak, make appear) sometimes referred to as a *eulogism,* an inoffensive or better-sounding word or expression substituted for one that is unpleasant, harsh-sounding, or insensitive.

event (from Latin, *eventus,* from *evenire,* happen, come out, occur; from *e,* out, + *venire,* come) **1.** that which occurs (happens). **2.** a change in the properties (qualities, characteristics, attributes, relations) of a thing. **3.** a change (movement, activity, process) between or among things. (Contrasted with object, thing, state of.)

evidence (from Latin, *e,* out, + *videre,* see) **1.** proof or fact. **2.** that which tends or is used to prove or support something. **3.** that which is accepted as conclusive (clear, obvious, acceptable, confirmed) support of a statement (proposition, hypothesis, law).

evil 1. that which is injurious, painful, hurtful, or calamitous. **2.** morally bad or unacceptable, sinful, wicked, vicious, or corrupt. **3.** that which impedes the achievement of goals, ideals, happiness, or general well-being. **4.** misfortune.

evil, moral evil that is the result of deliberate human action. Contrasted with EVIL, NATURAL.

evil, natural evil that is the result of usual or unusual natural occurrences. Examples: diseases, famines, drought, volcanic eruption causing death. Contrasted with EVIL, MORAL.

evil, theological problem of an ANTILOGISM that stems from assuming three things, only two of which are compatible (sometimes called *the incompatible triad*): (a) the omnipotence of God, (b) the omnibenevolence of God, and (c) the existence of evil.

Epicurus presented the problem this way:

Is God willing to prevent evil, but *not able* to prevent evil? Then he is not omnipotent.

Is God able to prevent evil, but *not willing* to prevent evil? Then he is not omnibenevolent.

Is God *both* willing and able to prevent evil?

Then why does evil exist?

Hume presented the same problem thus:

If evil in the world is the intention of the Deity, then He is not benevolent.

If evil in the world is contrary to His intention, then He is not omnipotent.

But evil is either in accordance with His intention or contrary to it.

Therefore, either the Deity is not benevolent, or He is not omnipotent.

evolution (from Latin, *evolutio,* an unrolling, unfolding, developing) **1.** the development of a thing into a more complex organization and/or different organization. **2.** the development of a thing's potential toward a further result, purpose, or end.

Evolutionism is the general name given to developmental views of life or the universe. See NATURAL SELECTION (DARWIN).

evolution, emergent as a speculative COSMOGONY, emergent evolution deals with more than the evolution of living forms on earth. It presents the general outlines of the evolutionary process of the universe (the totality of spatio-temporal existence). Its principal aim is to delineate the succession of levels in the universe that show such characteristics as unity, variety, and progressive increase in complexity. The basic categories or concepts used in its analysis are: (a) discontinuity (emergence), (b) levels (qualities), (c) novelty, and (d) creative advance. **1.** *discontinuity*: differs from the gradualism (the continuity of changes among life forms) of Darwinism. Evolutionary events are *discontinuous* with previous events. Novelty, that which comes into existence for the first time, does so abruptly. **2.** *level*: that part of the universe having related qualities (properties, aspects, characteristics) which have emerged from previously existing levels. Each succeeding level contains the constituents of the preceding level. **3.** *novelty*: the evolutionary process produces existents that have never in any way been in existence before. The novel features produced can neither be reduced in explanation to their constituent parts nor predicted from them. They are cumulative features of a creative advance (*NISUS*). Examples: life, mind, fluidity, translucence, conscience, sensation. Each novel quality may be thought of holistically as more than the sum of its parts (see GESTALT; HOLISM). In a sense, this is allied with the notion that there is more in the effect than that which is contained in the cause. **4.** *creative advance:* there are small cumulative advances in the rearrangements and reorganizations of the constituents at each level, but there is also a broad, general creative direction toward an all-encompassing, interrelated, perfect whole. (For most emergent evolutionists that perfect whole will never be completely realized but is the infinite goal toward which the universe strives.)

Emergent evolution is associated with such names as C. Lloyd Morgan, Jan Christiaan Smuts, Samuel Alexander, Henri Bergson. See EMERGENT, AN; VITALISM.

excluded middle, law of see LAWS OF THOUGHT, THE THREE.

existence (from Latin, *existere,* appear, exist, emerge, have actual being; from *ex,* out of, + *sistere,* cause to stand) **1.** that which exists. **2.** that which has actuality (being). **3.** anything that is experienced.

Asserting *that* a thing is, in contrast with ESSENCE, which asserts *what* a thing is (what a thing truly is according to its inherent nature). See OBJECTIVE EXISTENCE (REALITY).

existential in EXISTENTIALISM, refers to: **1.** the vivid experience of the reality and varied dimensions of the present. **2.** the awareness that one *is* and that one is an acting, choosing being creating and expressing one's self-identity in the process of acting and choosing responsibly. **3.** the experience of being intensely involved in living, its fulfillments and predicaments.

existential import refers to statements that assert or assume the real existence of the objects that they denote.

existentialism also called *existential philosophy, existentialist philosophy,* a relatively modern view in philosophy (although with historical roots as far back as Greek and medieval philosophy) associated in its inception with Sören Kierkegaard and Friedrich Nietzsche. Its primary and best-known exponent in contemporary philosophy is the French philosopher Jean-Paul Sartre. Other existentialists: Camus, Jaspers, Heidegger, Marcel. There are many varieties of existentialism ranging from atheism to theism, from phenomenalism and phenomenology to forms of Aristotelianism. Some of the following themes are common to existentialists: **1.** EXISTENCE precedes ESSENCE. Forms do not determine existence to be what it is. Existence fortuitously becomes and is whatever it becomes and is, and that existence then makes up its *essence*. **2.** an individual has no essential nature, no self-identity other than that involved in the act of choosing. **3.** truth is subjectivity. **4.** abstractions can neither grasp nor communicate the reality of individual existence. **5.** philosophy must concern itself with the human predicament and inner states such as alienation, anxiety, inauthenticity, dread, sense of nothingness, and anticipation of death. **6.** the universe has no rational direction or scheme. It is meaningless and absurd. **7.** the universe does not provide moral rules. Moral principles are constructed by humans in the context of being responsible for their actions and for the actions of others. **8.** individual actions are unpredictable. **9.** individuals have complete freedom of the will. **10.** individuals cannot help but make choices. **11.** an individual can become completely other than what he or she is. See ALIENATION; *ANGOISSE*; BAD FAITH (SARTRE); COMMITMENT (SARTRE); *ENNUI; EN SOI* (SARTRE); ONTOLOGY (EXISTENTIAL PSYCHOLOGY); *POUR SOI* (SARTRE).

existentialism, humanistic some of the beliefs: **1.** the universe (a) is not in itself intelligible (humans make it intelligible); (b) does not conform to any rational, logical order or process; and (c) is not created, supported, or designed by an omnipotent, benevolent God. **2.** all things are contingent; nothing is necessarily decreed to occur as it occurs. **3.** all meaning, order, explanation, classification is given to reality by consciousness and is not part of any reality other than the reality of consciousness. **4.** reality cannot be reduced to a neat system since it is inherently unintelligible, non-categorizable and amorphous. **5.** there is no objective moral realm; moral values do not exist outside of consciousness. Compare with HUMANISM, PHILOSOPHICAL.

ex nihilo nihil fit (Latin, nothing comes out of nothing, or out of nothing, nothing can come, or nothing can be made out of nothing) sometimes simply *nihil ex nihilo* or *creatio ex nihilo nihil fit*. Contrasted with *CREATIO EX NIHILO*.

exoteric (from Greek, *exōterikos*, being outside something; from *exōteros*, outer, utter, exterior) **1.** open to everyone; pertaining to that which is not secretive and understood only by a selected few, but is easily comprehended by the public. **2.** referring to the public, or popular, presentation of ideas (doctrines, beliefs) easily understood by laymen (noninitiates, nonexperts). **3.** specifically, *exoteric* refers to some of Aristotle's (mostly early) writings (*exōterikoi logoi*), which were written for general, popular reading outside his school and contained ideas easily grasped by the populace (in contrast to the *esōterikoi logoi* or technical writings intended for student use within his school). Contrast with ESOTERIC.

experience (from Latin, *experientia*, trial, experience) **1.** living through events, feelings, emotions, sufferings, happenings, states of CONSCIOUSNESS. **2.** knowledge derived from personal activity, practice, practical skills. **3.** the capacity or talent to perform something derived from the above. **4.** states of consciousness such as being in pain, imagining a unicorn, doubting a belief, thinking about the sum of 2 plus 2, enjoying a musical composition. (There is philosophic controversy as to whether or not there is a difference between such immediate experiences and the AWARENESS that one is having them.) Compare with EXPERIENTIAL; PERCEPTION; SENSATION.

experience, mystical see MYSTICAL EXPERIENCE.

experience, pure see PURE EXPERIENCE.

experience, religious see RELIGIOUS EXPERIENCE.

experiential referring to any kind of experience, in contrast to EMPIRICAL, which is confined to sensation/perception/observation types of experiences that are shared by people. For example, *experiential data* include the knowledge (understanding, intuitions, insights, information) obtainable by such means as INTROSPECTION, self-analysis, private conscious states, etc., whereas *empirical data* are limited to the knowledge obtained through the senses and/or checked by the senses.

experientialism the theory that immediate, concrete experience is the only source of knowledge and the only method of testing the value and truth of knowledge (theories, hypotheses, etc.).

explanation (from Latin, *explanare,* flatten, make level or plane, explain) in general, making something intelligible, rational, or familiar. An explanation of phenomena differs from a proof of phenomena in that if one requests an explanation, this assumes the existence of the phenomena to be explained, whereas if one requests a PROOF, this assumes that the phenomena may not have occurred and some evidence of their occurrence must be presented.

explanation, functional explanation of phenomena in terms of describing the interrelated activities (functions, actions) that elements of a thing undergo during its existence. A functional explanation of "Why does the heart beat?" would be in terms of the further activities that depend upon the heart's activities, such as circulation of blood, and/or the physical, chemical, and possibly artificial processes (functions) of those parts of the heart and body on which the beating of the heart depends. Opposed to explanations in terms of purposes, intentional striving for goals, or drives to fulfill an end. Contrasted with EXPLANATION, TELEOLOGICAL.

explanation, holistic see HOLISTIC EXPLANATION.

explanation, mechanistic the description of how parts interact mechanically with other parts within a complex. Opposite to EXPLANATION, TELEOLOGICAL. See MECHANISM.

explanation, organismic see ORGANISMIC EXPLANATION.

explanation, scientific making something intelligible by describing *what* the structures and processes of a thing are, and/or showing *how* a thing does what it does. Contrasted with EXPLANATION, TELEOLOGICAL.

The foundation of scientific explanation: (a) forming generalizations (theories) from facts (empirical observations) by use of inductive-deductive methods; (b) connecting these facts with a consistent and systematic body of generalizations and related facts already accumulated and accepted (confirmed, verified); (c) drawing out the logical and empirical implications and consequences the facts may have for the body of generalizations itself, (d) constructing a JUSTIFICATION (CONFIRMATION; VERIFICATION) for the facts and for the generalizations; and (e) showing that facts can be calculated (deduced), quantified, or predicted from the body of generalizations. See METHOD, SCIENTIFIC.

explanation, teleological **1.** explanation in terms of some purpose (end, goal) for which something is done. **2.** explanation in terms of goal-directed or purpose-directed activity. Usually the goal or purpose is preset or planned. **3.** explaining the present and past with reference to something in the future (a goal, purpose, end, result) that is being striven for or for the sake of which the process takes place. Opposite to mechanistic explanation (see EXPLANATION, MECHANISTIC), which explains the present and any future event in terms of prior conditions. **4.** explanation in terms of the structures and activities of the parts of a whole being adapted (coordinated, adjusted, fitted, suited) to each other toward the fulfillment of the purposes or needs of that whole. See ANIMISM; CAUSES, ARISTOTLE'S FOUR; ORGANISMIC EXPLANATION; and entries under TELEOLOGICAL.

explication (from Latin, from *explicare,* unfold, display; from *ex,* out of, from, + *plicare,* fold) **1.** explanation. **2.** the process of making obvious (explicit) and (sometimes) precise that which is implied or implicit in a statement. **3.** in categorical logic, showing how the meaning of the predicate is contained in the meaning of the subject. See STATEMENT, ANALYTIC. Opposite to SYNTHETIC. **4.** the giving of a full and detailed account of something.

expressive see MEANING, EXPRESSIVE.

extension **1.** DENOTATION. The sum total of things to which a word applies. The extension of the noun *human* is all those things that possess the (intensional) characteristics of humans, such as being a rational mammal that is a biped. The extension of a word is determined by its CONNOTATION (INTENSION). **2.** the range of things to which a concept refers or over which it has meaning.

In general, *extension* refers to the objective world, as opposed to *inten-*

sion, which refers to how we *mean* to see or look at the world. Also, for the most part extension has to do with classes and intension with qualities (properties, attributes, characteristics, etc.). See LAW OF INVERSE VARIATION (INTENSION/EXTENSION); MEANING, EXTENSIONAL. Compare with INTENSION.

extension (metaphysics) (from Latin, *extendere*, stretch out) also *extended*, occupying physical space and existing in time: that which is tangible, can be divided, has shape or figure, and is capable of being changed and/or moved. See entries under SUBSTANCE.

extension, empty refers to words that have meaning but do not denote anything. Example: The word *centaur* does not denote; it has no extension; thus, it is said to have an empty extension.

extensionality, thesis of 1. the theory that every (empirical) statement is either an elementary proposition of fact (a logically simple statement) *or* a truth-function of such statements. **2.** the theory that every intensional statement can be translated into an extensional statement; all intensionality can be reduced to extensionality; there is no intensional logic since all extensional statements contain no intensionality. See EXTENSION; INTENTION.

external relations see RELATIONS, EXTERNAL.

externalization sometimes called *extrojection* or *external reference*, the tendency or the act of the mind to regard sensations as externally real objects.

extrapolation the process of assigning probability values for events, or of predicting events that extend beyond the patterns established by the known empirical data, but which are suggested or which can be inferred from such data.

extraspection the ability to have, or the feeling that one has, direct and immediate communication with or understanding of external minds. Compare with INTROSPECTION; RETROSPECTION; TELEPATHY.

extrasensory phenomena or perception see ESP and PARAPSYCHOLOGY.

extrinsic (from Latin, *exter*, outside, + *secus*, beside, otherwise) **1.** external. **2.** unessential. Opposite to INTRINSIC.

extrinsic good (value) see GOOD, EXTRINSIC.

extrinsic-intrinsic good (value) see GOOD, INTRINSIC-EXTRINSIC.

F

fact (from Latin, *facere*, do, make) **1.** an actually occurring event, quality, relation, state of affairs; that which is actual, real; that which is. **2.** a situation or state of affairs that has taken place. **3.** a true description of what is happening or of what has happened. A *fact* in the senses above makes such a description true or false. These views assume that facts exist independently of our thoughts about them. **4.** the meaning contained in true statements. **5.** a judgment (interpretation) of what we regard reality to be like. The view in 4 and 5 assumes that facts do *not* exist independently of our thoughts about them. **6.** that which corresponds to a true statement. See TRUTH, CORRESPONDENCE THEORY OF.

fact, atomic see ATOMIC FACT.

fact, brute an ultimate fact for which no further explanation (reason, account) need or can be given. Example: "The universe is eternal."

fact/value dichotomy see IS/OUGHT DICHOTOMY.

faculties of the soul (Plato) The soul is divided into three faculties: (a) the APPETITIVE, (b) the spirited, and (c) the rational. When the faculties are in harmony about ideals and knowledge of the good, an individual has peace of soul. When they are divided, an individual is in a state of disorder and conflict. See SOUL (PLATO).

faculty (from Latin, *facultas*, from *facilis*, easy, + *facere*, make) a power (ability, endowment) of the mind (soul or body) that produces certain operations or functions. A general list of faculties: (a) *vegetative*, or *nutritive:* causes activities such as metabolism, respiration, nutrition, growth, and reproduction; (b) *locomotive:* causes movement, directional change; (c) APPETITIVE: causes our basic wants, drives, desires, and bodily needs; (d) AFFECTIVE, or *sensory:* causes sensation, perception, feelings, emotions, pleasures, pains, and is the basis of most forms of memory and imagination; (e) *volitional:* causes our will to live and our drive (energy) to attain our desires, wants, needs, and interests (see VOLITION; WILL); and (f) RATIONAL, *cognitive,* or *intellectual:* causes knowledge and activities such as abstract thinking, conceptualizing, judging, interpreting, using language, knowing the good, and directing the will toward it. See CONSCIENCE.

faculty psychology the theory that: **1.** consciousness and mental states such as those of willing (VOLITION), thinking, imagining, and feeling are caused and explainable by the faculties of the mind that correspond with those states of consciousness, such as the faculty of volition, the faculty of reason, the faculty of imagination or fancy, the spirited faculty, and the appetitive faculty. **2.** the mind (or soul) operates according to the faculties in 1. Taken together they form the entity or substance called the mind, soul, spirit, which in some mode of interaction with the body is the source of our consciousness or mental states. Contrasted with FUNCTIONAL PSY-CHOLOGY.

faith (from Latin, *fides,* faith, trust, loyalty) **1.** acceptance of a system of beliefs believed to be true. **2.** belief in the creeds of a religion. **3.** steadfast belief and trust in God (usually one who has revealed Himself and can be known). **4.** belief in something despite the evidence against it. **5.** belief in something even though there is an absence of evidence for it. **6.** belief in something because of past evidence for it; confidence based on reliability. **7.** trust in the truth of something that cannot be rationally or empirically supported but which is presupposed by some form of empirical knowledge. See BELIEF; CREDO UT INTELLIGAM; FIDEISM.

faith (ethics) used mostly in the sense of *keeping faith* (as opposed to *keeping the faith*), which implies such things as keeping promises, being loyal, trustworthy, fair, reliable, etc.

faith (Kant) the acceptance of regulative principles or ideals that cannot be demonstrated theoretically or empirically but nevertheless are needed and used efficiently in scientific, practical, and moral affairs.

faith, bad see BAD FAITH (SARTRE).

fallacy (from Latin, *fallacia,* deceit, trick) **1.** a logical error; reasoning that does not follow the rules of inference or that violates them. **2.** an argument that is misleading in the sense that it is incorrect but may, or is used to, convince people of its correctness. **3.** a defective (false, incorrect, erroneous, mistaken) argument in which the conclusion is not justified by the statements supporting it. Fallacies can be divided into two broad groupings: *formal fallacies* and *informal fallacies.* See the following entries under FALLACY. Compare with INVALID; PREVARICATION; SOPHISM.

fallacy, classification of informal Informal fallacies (see FALLACY, INFORMAL) may be classified in a variety of ways. Three general categories: (a) *material fallacies* have to do with the facts (the matter, the content) of the argument in question. Two subcategories of material fallacies are: (1) *fallacies of evidence,* which refer to arguments that do not provide the required factual support (ground, evidence) for their conclusions, and (2) *fallacies of irrelevance* (or *relevance*), which refer to arguments that have supporting statements that are irrelevant to the conclusion being asserted and therefore cannot establish the truth of that conclusion. (b) *linguistic fallacies,* which have to do with defects in arguments such as ambiguity (in which careless shifts of meanings or linguistic imprecisions lead to erroneous conclusions), vagueness, incorrect use of words, lack of clarity, linguistic inconsistencies, and circularities. (c) *fallacies of irrelevant emotional appeal,* which have to do with affecting behavior (responses, attitudes). That is, arguments are presented in such a way as to appeal to one's prejudices, biases, loyalty, dedication, fear, guilt, and so on. They persuade, cajole, threaten, or confuse in order to win assent to an argument.

fallacy, formal 1. an invalid argument; an error in deductive logic (reasoning) in which the conclusion does not follow with necessity from the premises. See INVALID. **2.** an invalid inference; a misconstrued or wrong inference that may seem to follow a correct rule of inference but does not, such as denying the antecedent of a conditional statement in order to deny its consequent. 3. an error of logical form (see FORM, LOGICAL), a violation of a rule of inference or the principles of logic.

Formal fallacies are committed only by deductive arguments.

fallacy, informal 1. any error in reasoning to conclusions that does not follow the formal structures and rules of logical validity. **2.** an argument whose conclusion (a) is not adequately supported and/or (b) does not necessarily have to be the conclusion that can be drawn.

Informal fallacies are committed by inductive reasoning or arguments.

fallacy, types of informal sometimes called *semiformal* or *quasi-formal fallacies*. The following list of 40 informal fallacies is by no means exhaustive. No attempt has been made to subsume them under general categories such as in FALLACY, CLASSIFICATION OF INFORMAL. **1.** *black-and-white fallacy*, arguing (a) with the use of sharp (black-and-white) distinctions despite any factual or theoretical support for them, or (b) by classifying any middle point between extremes (black-and-white) as one of the extremes. Examples: "If he is not an atheist then he is a decent person." "He is either a conservative or a liberal." "He must not be peace-loving, since he participated in picketing the American embassy." **2.** *fallacy of argumentum baculinum* (the Latin translates as *argument according to the stick* or *argument by means of the rod*), arguing to support the acceptance of an argument by means of a threat, or use of force. When reasoning is replaced by force, the result is termination of logical argumentation, and other kinds of behavior are elicited, such as fear, anger, and reciprocal use of force. **3.** *fallacy of argumentum ad hominem* (the Latin translates as *argument against the man*) arguing against a person, or rejecting a person's views by attacking or abusing his or her personality, character, motives, intentions, qualifications, etc., as opposed to providing evidence why the views are incorrect. Example: "What John said should not be believed because he was a Nazi sympathizer." **4.** *fallacy of argumentum ad ignorantiam* (the Latin translates literally as *argument to ignorance*, but is better translated as *argument from ignorance*) (a) arguing that something is true because no one has proved it to be false, or (b) arguing that something is false because no one has proved it to be true. Examples: (a) spirits exist since no one has as yet proved that there are none; (b) spirits do not exist since no one has as yet proved their existence. Also called the *appeal to ignorance:* the lack of evidence (proof) for something is used to support its truth. **5.** *fallacy of argumentum ad misericordiam* (the Latin translates as *argument to pity*) arguing by appeal to pity in order to have some point accepted. Example: "I've got to have at least a B in this course, Professor Wodehouse. If I don't, I won't have a chance of getting into medical school." Also called the *appeal to pity.* **6.** *fallacy of argumentum ad personam* (the Latin translates as *argument to personal interest*) arguing by appealing to the personal likes (preferences, prejudices, predispositions, etc.) of others in order to have an argument accepted. **7.** *fallacy of argumentum ad populum* (the Latin translates as *argument to the people*) also called *appeal to the gallery, appeal to the majority, appeal to what is popular, appeal to popular prejudice, appeal to the multitude,* and *appeal to mob instinct*; arguing in order to arouse an emotional, popular acceptance of an idea without presenting a logical justification of the idea. An appeal is made to such things as biases, prejudices, feelings, enthusiasms, and attitudes of the multitude in order to evoke assent rather than to rationally support the idea. **8.** *fallacy of argumentum ad verecundiam* (the Latin translates as *argument to authority* or *to veneration*) (a) appealing to authority (including customs, tradition, institutions, etc.) in order to gain acceptance of a point at issue and/or (b) appealing to the feelings of reverence or respect we have for those in authority, or who are famous. Example: "I believe that the statement 'You cannot legislate morality' is true, because President Dwight Eisenhower said it." **9.** *fallacy of accent*, sometimes classified as an *ambiguity of accent*, arguing to conclusions from undue emphasis (accent, tone) on certain words or statements. Classified as a *fallacy of ambiguity* whenever this emphasis creates an ambiguity or AMPHIBOLY in the words or statements used in the argument. Example: "The queen cannot but be praised." **10.** *fallacy of accident*, also called by its Latin name *a dicto simpliciter ad dictum secundum quid* (freely translates as *from a general truth to a particular case regardless of the qualifications of the latter*) (a) applying a general rule or principle to a particular instance whose circumstances *by accident* do not allow proper application of that generalization. Example: "It is a general truth that no one should lie. Therefore, no one should lie when a murderer at the point of a knife asks you for information you know would lead to a further murder." (b) the error in argumentation of applying a general statement to a situation to which it cannot be applied and was not necessarily intended to be applied. **11.** *fallacy of ambiguity* an argument that has at least one ambiguous word or statement from which a misleading or wrong conclusion is drawn. **12.** *fallacy of amphiboly* arguing to conclusions from statements that are amphibolous—ambiguous because of their syntax (grammatical construction). Sometimes classified as a *fallacy of ambiguity*. **13.** *fallacy of begging the question* (a) arriving at a conclusion from statements that themselves are questionable and have to be proved but are assumed true. Example: "The universe has a beginning. Every thing that has a beginning has a beginner. Therefore, the universe has a beginner called God." This assumes (*begs the question*) that the universe does indeed have a beginning and also that all things that have a beginning have a beginner. (b) assuming the conclusion or part of the conclusion in the premises of an argument, sometimes called *circular reasoning, vicious cir-*

cularity, or *vicious circle fallacy*. Example: "Everything has a cause. The universe is a thing. Therefore, the universe is a thing that has a cause." See PETITIO PRINCIPII. (c) arguing in a circle—one statement is supported by reference to another statement, which statement itself is supported by reference to the first statement. Example: "Aristocracy is the best form of government because the best form of government is that which has strong aristocratic leadership." **14.** *fallacy of complex question* or *loaded question* (a) asking questions for which either a *yes* or a *no* answer will incriminate the respondent. The desired answer is already tacitly assumed in the question, and no qualification of the simple answer is allowed. Example: "Have you discontinued the use of opiates?" (b) asking questions that are based on unstated attitudes or questionable (or unjustified) assumptions. These questions are often asked rhetorically of the respondent in such a way as to elicit an agreement with those attitudes or assumptions from others. Example: "How long are you going to put up with this brutality?" **15.** *fallacy of composition* arguing (a) that what is true of each part of a whole is also (necessarily) true of the whole itself, or (b) that what is true of some parts of a whole is also (necessarily) true of the whole itself. Example: "Each member (or some members) of the team is (or are) married; therefore, the team also has (must have) a wife." Inferring that a collection has certain characteristics merely on the basis that its parts have them proceeds erroneously from regarding the collection DISTRIBUTIVELY to regarding it COLLECTIVELY. **16.** *fallacy of consensus gentium* (the Latin translates literally as *unanimity of the nations*, freely as *widespread agreement*) arguing that an idea is true on the basis (a) that the majority of people believe it and/or (b) that it has been universally held by all men at all times. Example: "God exists because all cultures have had some concept of a God." **17.** *fallacy of converse accident* sometimes called *converse fallacy of accident* (also called by its Latin name *a dicto secundum quid ad dictum simpliciter*, freely translated as *from a particular truth as if it were generally valid*) the error of generalizing from atypical or exceptional instances. Example: "A drink of warm brandy each night helps older people relax and sleep better. People in general ought to drink warm brandy to relieve their tension and sleep better." See *fallacy of accident*, number 10 above. **18.** *fallacy of division* arguing that what is true of a whole is (a) also (necessarily) true of its parts and/or (b) also true of some of its parts. Example: "The community of Pacific Palisades is extremely wealthy. Therefore, every person living there is (must be) extremely wealthy (or therefore Adam, who lives there, is [must be] extremely wealthy)." Inferring that the parts of a collection have certain characteristics merely on the basis that their collection has them erroneously proceeds from regarding the collection collectively to regarding it distributively. **19.** *fallacy of equivocation* an argument in which a word is used with one meaning (or sense) in one part of the argument and with another meaning in another part. A common example:

"The *end* of a thing is its perfection; death is the *end* of life; hence, death is the perfection of life." **20.** *fallacy of non causa pro causa* (the Latin may be translated as *there is no cause of the sort that has been given as the cause*) (a) believing that something is the cause of an effect when in reality it is not. Example: "My incantations caused rain to fall." (b) arguing so that a statement appears unacceptable because it *implies* another statement that is false (but in reality is not). **21.** *fallacy of post hoc ergo propter hoc* (the Latin may be translated as *after this therefore the consequence [effect] of this*, or *after this therefore because of this*) sometimes called *fallacy of false cause*, concluding that one thing is the cause of another thing because it precedes it in time. This is a confusion between the concept of succession and that of causation. Example: "A black cat ran across my path. Ten minutes later I was hit by a truck. Therefore, the cat's running across my path was the cause of my being hit by a truck." **22.** *fallacy of hasty generalization* sometimes called *fallacy of hasty induction* an error of reasoning whereby a general statement is asserted (inferred) based on (a) limited information, or (b) inadequate evidence, or (c) an unrepresentative sampling. **23.** *fallacy of ignoratio elenchi* (the Latin translates literally as *ignorance of the refutation*), also called *irrelevant conclusion,* an argument that is irrelevant; that argues for something other than that which is to be proved and thereby in no way refutes (or supports) the points at issue. Example: A lawyer in defending his alcoholic client who has murdered three people in a drunken spree argues that alcoholism is a terrible disease, and attempts should be made to eliminate it. IGNORATIO ELENCHI is sometimes used as a general designation for all fallacies that are based on irrelevancy (such as *ad baculinum, ad hominem, ad misericordiam, ad populum, ad verecundiam,* and *consensus gentium*). **24.** *fallacy of inconsistency* arguing from inconsistent statements, or to conclusions that are inconsistent with the premises. See *fallacy of tu quoque,* number 36 below. **25.** *fallacy of irrelevant purpose* arguing against something on the basis that it has not fulfilled its purpose (although in fact that was not its intended purpose). **26.** *fallacy of is-to-ought* arguing from premises that have only descriptive statements (*is*) to a conclusion that contains an *ought* or a *should.* See IS/OUGHT DICHOTOMY. **27.** *fallacy of limited* (or *false) alternatives* the error of insisting without full inquiry or evidence that the alternatives to a course of action have been exhausted and/or are mutually exclusive. **28.** *fallacy of many questions* sometimes called *fallacy of the false question* asking a question for which a single and simple answer is demanded, yet the question (a) requires a series of answers and/or (b) requires answers to a host of other questions, each of which should be answered separately. Example: "Have you left school?" **29.** *fallacy of misleading context* arguing by misrepresenting, distorting, omitting, or quoting something out of context. **30.** *fallacy of prejudice* arguing from a bias or emotional identification or involvement with an idea (argument, doctrine, institution, etc.). **31.** *fallacy of red herring* ignoring a criticism of an argument by shifting attention to another subject. Example: "You believe in abortion, yet you don't believe in the right-to-die-with-dignity bill before the legislature." **32.** *fallacy of slanting* deliberately omitting, deemphasizing, or overemphasizing certain points to the exclusion of others in order to hide evidence that is important and relevant to the conclusion of an argument and that should be taken into account in an argument. **33.** *fallacy of special pleading* (a) accepting an idea or criticism when applied to an opponent's argument but rejecting it when applied to one's own argument, or (b) rejecting an idea or criticism when applied to an opponent's argument but accepting it when applied to one's own. **34.** *fallacy of straw man* presenting an opponent's position in as weak or misrepresented a version as possible so that it can easily be refuted. Example: "Darwinism is in error. It claims that we are all descendants from an apelike creature, from which we evolved according to natural selection. No evidence of such a creature has been found. No adequate and consistent explanation of natural selection has been given. Therefore, evolution according to Darwinism has not taken place." **35.** *fallacy of the beard* arguing (a) that small or minor differences do not (or cannot) make a difference, or are not (or cannot be) significant, or (b) arguing so as to find a definite point at which something can be named. For example, insisting that a few hairs lost here and there do not indicate anything significant about my impending baldness; or trying to determine how many hairs a person must have before he can be called bald (or not bald). **36.** *fallacy of tu quoque* (the Latin translates as *you also*) (a) presenting evidence that a person's actions are not consistent with that for which he is arguing. Example: "John preaches that we should be kind and loving. He doesn't practice it. I've seen him beat up his kids." (b) showing that a person's views are inconsistent with what he or she previously believed and therefore (1) that person is not to be trusted, and/or (2) that person's new view is to be rejected. Example: "Judge Egener was against marijuana legislation four years ago when he was running for office. Now he is for it. How can you trust a man who has changed his mind on such an important issue? His present position is inconsistent with his earlier view and therefore should not be accepted." (c) sometimes related to the *fallacy of two wrongs make a right*. Example: The Democrats for years used illegal wiretapping; therefore, the Republicans should not be condemned for illegal wiretapping. **37.** *fallacy of unqualified source* using as support in an argument a source of authority that is not qualified to provide evidence. **38.** *gambler's fallacy* (a) arguing that since, for example, a penny *has* come up tails ten times in a row then it will come up heads the eleventh time or (b) arguing that since, for example, an airline *has not* had an accident for the past ten years, it is then soon due for an accident. The gambler's fallacy rejects the assumption in probability theory that each event is independent of its previous happening. The chances of an event happening are always the same no matter how many times that event has taken place in the past. Given those events happening over a long enough period of time, then their frequency would average out to 1/2. See entries under PROBABILITY. The *gambler's fallacy* is sometimes referred to as the *Monte Carlo fallacy* (a generalized form of the *gambler's fallacy*): the error of assuming that because something has happened less frequently than expected in the past, there is an increased chance that it will happen soon. **39.** *genetic fallacy* (a) arguing that the origin of something is identical with that from which it originates. Example: "Consciousness originates in neural processes. Therefore, consciousness is (nothing but) neural processes." Sometimes referred to as the *nothing-but fallacy*, or the REDUCTIVE FALLACY. (b) appraising or explaining something in terms of its origin, source, or beginnings. (c) arguing that something is to be rejected because its origins are known and/or are suspicious. **40.** *pragmatic fallacy* arguing that something is true because it has practical effects on people: it makes them happier, easier to deal with, more moral, loyal, stable. Example: "An immortal life exists because without such a concept men would have nothing to live for. There would be no meaning or purpose in life and everyone would be immoral."

For a few of the other remaining informal fallacies see PATHETIC FALLACY and entries under NATURALISTIC FALLACY.

false 1. to say that an idea (belief, proposition, opinion) is false is to say that the FACT to which it refers does not exist (has no being). **2.** not conforming to reality or truth. **3.** not having good supporting evidence. **4.** wrong. **5.** the member of a two-truth value set that denies the truth value assigned to a statement. Contrasted with entries under TRUTH.

In science, to *falsify* is to show that the evidence in support of an empirical statement is not verified or confirmed by scientific methodology.

family resemblance (Wittgenstein) the phrase used to refer to an approach in defining that opposes the traditional method of searching for the real ESSENCE or the defining characteristic of a thing. Meanings are associated by a number of elements—features that have family resemblances—(a) each of which is possessed by several things, and (b) several of which are possessed by each thing without there being any one element (or definite set of elements) possessed by all the things defined in the same way.

fatalism 1. the belief that all events are necessitated (determined) to happen the way they do in fact happen no matter what we do to try to avoid them or prevent them. Even our attempts to countermand FATE are inevitably thwarted. "What will be will be." **2.** the individual is the product of predeterministic forces operating in the universe. A person cannot in any way direct his or her behavior or destiny, or that of history. No one can help being what he or she is and acting as he or she does. **3.** certain events will inevitably come to pass in our existence at a particular time and at a prescribed place. See PREDETERMINISM.

fatalism (theology) 1. the belief that God, as all-knowing and all-powerful, foresees and necessitates according to God's foresight how every event in the universe will occur. **2.** all that the individual is and becomes is caused by God's rational power operating in conformity with God's will. Nothing that one can do will alter that fixed plan. Only that which God has decreed to happen happens and that which happens is that which God has decreed to happen. **3.** God necessitates certain events to happen to each individual according to God's foreknowledge of the individual's faith and merit as a believer. These events are fated to occur in this life or as salvation in an afterlife. See PREDESTINATION (THEOLOGY).

fate (from Latin, *fatum,* oracle, that which is ordained to happen by the gods) **1.** PREDESTINATION, the necessity in things compelling them to happen as they do. **2.** DESTINY, one's appointed lot. **3.** Divine Providence, regarded as the rational, purposeful, good, and necessary outcome of an intelligence. **4.** one's fortune as shaped by forces over which there is no control.

Sometimes fate is regarded as an arbitrary, capricious, impersonal, and menacing force, will, or agency. Sometimes fate is personified and pictured as an agent external to the universe determining (necessitating) its processes by an act of intelligence and/or will.

feeling 1. sentience, sensating, experiencing a sensation in itself apart from any direct reference to the object producing it or to the PERCEPTION (COGNITION, CONATION) of which it is a part. Feelings are regarded as pure subjective states that reveal aspects of the subject's CONSCIOUSNESS but not (necessarily) the qualities of its source. **2.** used to refer to any experience, or any quality of experience whatever. ("I feel hot." "It feels hot." "I feel neglected." "I feel a thought coming on." "It feels like rain.")

Feelings can be classified as (a) occurrent states (see STATE, OCCURRENT) of consciousness happening at a given moment ("I feel morose") or (b) disposition states (see STATE; DISPOSITION) that express tendencies towards something ("I feel that Adam will win this bout").

fictionism see ALS OB.

fideism (from Latin, *fides,* faith) **1.** the doctrine that religious truth is founded on FAITH and not on reason or empirical evidence. **2.** faith is superior to reason or science as a source of knowledge. **3.** all other sources of knowledge (a) must conform to and support knowledge obtained by faith, or (b) are based on a faith in presuppositions that cannot be justified by reason or evidence.

fides proecedit intellectum (Latin, faith precedes understanding, faith must be had before one can understand) an expression used since the time of Augustine to assert the primacy of FAITH, the subordination of the intellect to faith, the subservience of reason to revelation. See CREDO UT INTELLIGAM.

final cause see CAUSES, ARISTOTLE'S FOUR.

fine arts those arts whose primary function is to produce an aesthetic experience of beauty without regard to what economic or practical use they may be put. Some of the arts that may fall under this category are architecture, poetry, painting, music, and sculpture.

The general contrast to fine art may be called *useful* or *mechanical art*. This refers to products having definite practical human uses (such as chairs, automobiles, houses, umbrellas), which may be made to possess aesthetic qualities yet serve principally a nonaesthetic function. See TECHNE.

finite (from Latin, *finire,* stop, limit) **1.** having a limit or end point, for example in a series. **2.** being bounded or contained; having a magnitude. **3.** being limited in such qualities as power, abilities, imagination, or size. Opposite to INFINITE.

first cause 1. the uncaused being usually called God, that is, the initial cause of the existence of the universe. Before this first causal event there was either (a) no universe in existence and God created the universe out of nothing (see CREATIO EX NIHILO), or (b) the universe existed statically without out any causal series or interrelationships activating it. **2.** the uncaused being that is the continual causal ground for the particular cause-effect patterns that occur at any given time in the universe. This being may be as in 1, or it may be the support at each moment of events that stretch back infinitely. Compare with PRIME MOVER; UNCAUSED CAUSE; UNMOVED MOVER. See COSMOLOGICAL ARGUMENT FOR GOD'S EXISTENCE.

first mover see PRIME MOVER.

first philosophy (Aristotle) translation of Aristotle's *prōtē philosophia,* which had to do with **1.** the study of being as being; the study of the general and pervasive characteristics of all types of existence, the causes and first principles of being, and with **2.** the study of the kind of being that is IMMUTABLE and TRANSCENDENT. 1 is nearly synonymous with modern conceptions of METAPHYSICS and ONTOLOGY. 2 is nearly synonymous with modern conceptions of THEOLOGY. Compare with METAPHYSICS (ARISTOTLE).

first principles 1. statements (laws, reasons, rules) that are self-evident and/or fundamental to the explanation of a system and upon which the system depends for consistency and coherence. They are thought to need no explanation. **2.** the basic laws that cause things to be what they are. They are brute facts and have no cause. **3.** the rudimentary and ultimate truths that serve as the foundation of moral action.

five ways, the (Aquinas) sometimes called *quinque viae* (Latin: five ways) refers to the five proofs or arguments that Aquinas presents in his *Summa Theologiae* for the existence of God: **1.** UNMOVED MOVER. **2.** FIRST CAUSE. **3.** the ultimate source of necessity. **4.** the hierarchy of perfections in the world and their source in something completely perfect. **5.** the governance of the world or teleological direction. See GOD, ARGUMENTS FOR THE EXISTENCE OF.

flux (from Latin, *fluxus,* a flowing) **1.** change or that which changes. **2.**

motion (flow) or that which moves (flows). Generally associated with Heraclitus's philosophy. *Flux* is one of the translations of the Greek *hroē*, river, stream, flood, a flowing, a changing, as in the famous statement attributed to Heraclitus, *panta hrei:* "all things change (are in a state of flux)." See CHANGE (HERACLITUS).

force (from Latin, *fortis*, strong) **1.** that which is able to affect something else. **2.** any activity (action, power, ENERGY, strength) that changes the condition (characteristics, qualities, motion, spatial relationship) of a thing. **3.** any action that overcomes resistance or suppresses another action. **4.** the cause of CHANGE (MOTION, activity, action). Compare with entries under POWER. See DYNAMISM.

form (from Latin, *forma*, form, shape, figure, pattern, imprint, organization, plan, mold, stamp) **1.** an image of the shape or structure of a thing. **2.** the shape, structure, CONFIGURATION of a thing. **3.** the orderly arrangement of things. **4.** that aspect under which a thing is conceptualized or appears and by which it is classified. **5.** the ESSENCE of a thing.

form (Aristotle) 1. ESSENCE, OUSIA. **2.** that which is in matter and makes (forms) it into the object it is. See CAUSES, ARISTOTLE'S FOUR. For Aristotle, form could not exist independently of matter except in abstraction. See HYLĒ (ARISTOTLE).

form (Kant) the A PRIORI ingredient in all experience whereby what is presented to us as raw sensation by *sensuous intuition* is categorized and unified by the mind into perceptions and judgments. Nothing is meaningful unless structure (form) is imposed upon it by the mind.

form, accidental that which is secondary but dependent on the essential form of a thing and which leads the essential form into a nonnecessary mode of existence. Example: The essential form of man is reason. That he becomes a mathematician rather than a dramatist is *forma accidentalis* (accidental form), a mode secondary to the *forma essentia* (essential form) yet dependent on it. Contrasted with FORM, ESSENTIAL OR SUBSTANTIAL.

form, corporeal that which gives a thing its bodily (material) configuration and characteristics and which is the source of its tendency to continue in existence and to struggle to survive. See CORPOREAL.

form, essential or substantial 1. that which makes a thing exist as it is, that which causes an existing thing to be what it is. **2.** that which makes a thing become what it becomes, that which gives a process the pattern it has in its becoming or being something. **3.** matter and change in themselves are indifferent to the composition, configuration, or direction they take. It is substantial or essential form that gives them the particular activity, organization, and purpose they have. **4.** the aspect of a thing that enables us to (a) to recognize the class (species, order, family) to which it belongs and (b) to differentiate it from other things. Contrasted with FORM, ACCIDENTAL.

form, immaterial the form (spirit, soul) that can, and at times does, exist independently of matter and material objects but which is created by God to manifest itself in a material object (the body) in order to fulfill its essential nature (or form).

form, logical 1. the pattern (structure) of a statement or an argument, or a process of reasoning, as opposed to its content (subject matter). **2.** the pattern found in the relations of variables and in their truth values. **3.** the inferential relations among statements or arguments independent of their meanings.

form, material the form that needs matter for it to exist and be active as a form.

form, pure immaterial that form (pure spirit) which exists independently of matter and which at no time relates to matter, neither affecting matter nor needing to have its essence revealed through a material manifestation.

formal referring to that which has to do with the abstract pattern, structure, or principle of a thing as opposed to its parts, subject matter, or contents.

formal cause see CAUSES, ARISTOTLE'S FOUR.

formal language see LANGUAGE, FORMAL.

formal logic see LOGIC, FORMAL.

formalism any system that stresses FORM (principles, rules, laws) as the significant or ultimate ground of explanation or evaluation.

forms, Plato's theory of ideal also called *Plato's theory of ideas*. There are two worlds: (a) the transcendent (noumenal) world of absolute, perfect, unchanging ideal forms of which The Good (see AGATHON) is the primary one (usually interpreted as including BEAUTY and TRUTH) and the source of all the others, such as justice, temperance, courage; and (b) the phenomenal world (the world of appearances) composed of things in a state of flux attempting unsuccessfully to emulate (imitate, participate in, partake of) the ideal forms.

The love (attraction, affinity) that things have for the perfection inherent in these ideal forms inspires (causes, motivates) things in the phenomenal world to change, move, act, seek goals. The phenomenal world is the world of our sensuous, ordinary, everyday experiences, which are changing, illusory, unstable, erroneous, and finite. The world of eternal forms is the real, true, permanent world of which reason after proper discipline occasionally gives us a glimpse. Abstractions—such as of equality, circularity, redness, humanness—that one can conceive and recognize in a variety of things provide simple indications that forms exist. The forms exist independently of consciousness. See ARCHETYPES; IDEAS (PLATO); KNOWLEDGE (PLATO); MOTION (PLATO).

four causes, Aristotle's see CAUSES, ARISTOTLE'S FOUR.

four elements see ELEMENTS, THE FOUR.

freedom 1. self-determination, self-control, self-direction, self-regulation. **2.** the ability of an agent to act or not to act according to his or her dictates (willingness, commands) and/or preferences (desires, drives); being able to act in conformity with that which one wills; being the cause of one's own actions. **3.** being compelled or directed by desirable internal motives, ideals, wishes, and drives as opposed to external or internal compulsion, coercion, or constraint. **4.** the ability to choose and the opportunity to satisfy or procure that choice. Compare with LIBERTY.

freedom (Plato) 1. being governed (mastered, determined) by reason, enlightened by knowledge of the ideal good; obeying reason rather than being a servant to passions and to involuntary and ignorant actions. **2.** having the will guided by righteousness (DIKAIOSYNĒ). Lack of freedom is being guided by the bad, being subservient to evil. The evil tyrant is to be pitied because being ignorant of the good, the tyrant is a slave to evil. Plato and Platonism assumed as an ideal (a) the primacy of man's reason, and (b) the subordination of man's will to reason. God's will is perfectly free because it is directed by perfect goodness.

freedom for see LIBERTY.

freedom from 1. the absence of undesirable external or internal interference, containment, coercion, or restraint, imposed by other people, society, institutions, natural forces, or one's inner self in the realization of desired goals or interests. **2.** the absence of undesirable conditions in life, such as freedom from pain, freedom from hunger, freedom from poverty, freedom from anxiety, freedom from fear, freedom from responsibility.

freedom of see RIGHTS.

freedom to the opportunity to achieve the desired goals (ideas, objectives, purposes, ends) that one has selected for oneself without being obstructed.

free will, sense of 1. the feeling (a) of making uncaused, uncompelled choices, or (b) initiating uncaused actions. **2.** the feeling that given the same circumstances I could have done otherwise than that which I did in fact do. **3.** the feeling that I can will something, can exert energy in some desired direction, and have it successfully implemented. **4.** the feeling that alternative courses of action are open to me at any given moment and that the future is not fated.

free will, theory of 1. the belief that, given again the same conditions, humans can will to do otherwise than what they did do. **2.** the belief that acts of free will are caused by inner mental states (willing) of an agent but (a) *not* by material changes in the brain and (b) *not* by external stimuli. **3.** the belief that the will is free in the sense of not being caused or determined by anything else. That is, it is independent of antecedent physiological, neurological, psychological, and environmental conditions. Acts of free will are alleged to be *uncaused events*, such as uncaused assents, dissents, choices, decisions. See INDETERMINISM (ETHICS). Opposite to DETERMINISM; PREDESTINATION (THEOLOGY); PREDETERMINISM.

free will problem, the 1. if all human actions are caused, then how can concepts found in our everyday experience such as blame, responsibility, duty, obligation, commitment, dedication to ideals, self-control, self-direction, self-determination, and freedom be made meaningful? **2.** if every human act is caused, then how can this be made compatible with a human's sense of free will? See FREE WILL, SENSE OF. **3.** if each human decision is caused, then how can this be made consistent with humans' common and universal feeling that had they an opportunity to do it over again (a) they *could* have decided to do the opposite, or to do something else, or (b) looking at the past situation with present hindsight they *would* have decided differently, and hence *can* if the situation arises again?

free will problem, the (theology) 1. God is omniscient and therefore knows beforehand as an eternal truth each choice (action) that each human will decide on. If this is the case, then humans cannot *freely* choose (act) otherwise than the way in which God knows they will (and if they do act contrary to God's knowledge, then God cannot be omniscient). If God knows humans' sins before they commit them, and the sins must occur according to God's knowledge, then how can humans avoid those sins, and how can humans be said to have free will? **2.** if God has complete foreknowledge of everything that will happen, and is also omnipotent, then God must have organized all things to happen the way in which God has foreknowledge that they will happen. If this is the case, then how can it be maintained that humans have free will?

Frege, Friedrich Ludwig Gottlob (1848-1925) German mathematician, logician, and philosopher; born in Wismar (Weimar) and regarded as the founder of mathematical logic. He taught at the University of Jena and developed a logical notation for the quantifier-variable that replaced traditional concepts of the quantifier and its uses, and set the foundations for analysis of truth and provability of mathematical statements. His use of logical analysis and mathematical methods in resolving philosophic problems influenced the logical, mathematical, and philosophic outlooks of Whitehead, Russell, Wittgenstein, and Husserl, among others.

Frege's extensive writings are still largely untranslated. Two important translations are Peter Geach and Max Black (editors), *Translations from the Philosophical Writings of Gottlob Frege* (1952), and J.L. Austin's *The Foundations of Arithmetic: A Logico-mathematical Enquiry into the Concept of Numbers* (1953).

function (from Latin, *functio,* performance, execution) **1.** the usual (proper, normal, characteristic) activity of a thing within a system. **2.** the power or faculty of acting in a certain way unique to that class of things. **3.** the conceptual operation of relating ordered sets of things that have some correspondence or dependency between them.

functional explanation see EXPLANATION, FUNCTIONAL.

functional psychology the doctrine that conscious processes or states such as those of willing (volition), thinking, emoting, perceiving, and sensating are activities or operations of an organism in physical interrelationship with a physical environment and cannot be given hypostatized, substantive existence. These activities facilitate the organism's control, survival, adaptation, engagement or withdrawal, recognition, direction, etc. The entire organism can be analyzed as a feedback and stimulus response system. See CYBERNETICS.

Consciousness is not produced by faculties, a soul or a mind, but is the variety of functions found in the human considered as a biological, physical creature interacting with an environment. Functional psychology opposes the FACULTY view in psychology (see FACULTY PSYCHOLOGY) that, for example, the WILL is a faculty of the self (mind, personality, consciousness) which *causes* us to make decisions or exert energy toward a goal. Acts of choice and striving are not acts that obey a will. Compare with BEHAVIORISM.

functional unity any self-regulating, self-directing, self-organizing, or self-maintaining unit (system). Such integrated systems are regarded as organic wholes as in biology, or as unitary wholes as in CYBERNETICS, in which parts of the whole interrelate with each other (a) enabling the system to accomplish a specific activity (function, task), and/or (b) enabling the system to persist in its activity merely as an ordered system. That activity which a part within the whole plays in its interrelationships with other parts in support of (a) and/or (b) is called its *function* within the system.

fundamentum divisionis (Latin, fundamental division) the method or criterion by which a genus is subdivided.

future (from Latin, *futurus*, about to be) **1.** that which is to be. **2.** that which is to come after any present moment or instant of time. **3.** the time yet to come.

future, the that part of eternity which includes all events that are not occurring and have not occurred but that will occur.

G

gambler's fallacy see FALLACY, TYPES OF INFORMAL (38).

Geist (German, spirit, ghost, soul, mind, that which gives life to a thing) in German idealistic philosophy the term is used to refer to the ultimate reality and source of all things.

generalization 1. that general or universal concept arrived at by an examination of particular things. **2.** a statement referring to something that is regarded as (a) true about all members of a class ("all men are mortal") or (b) true about a number of the members of a class ("some artists are wealthy").

generalization, inductive also called *generalization from experience,* inductive reasoning that proceeds from the experience or observation of characteristics found in some things to a statement about all members of that class.

generation (from Latin, *generare,* generate) **1.** origination. **2.** production. **3.** formation. **4.** the process of beginning an activity. **5.** in Aristotelianism, the name for the process of change from some particular substance (or form) to another substance so different that another name must be given to it. Example: a caterpillar changing into a butterfly.

genesis (from Greek, *genesis*, origin, source, the productive cause of a thing, the beginning, the generation of something; used as a suffix, signifies development, evolution, a growth process) **1.** the mode of coming into being such as biological growth, or artistic creation. **2.** the origin of a thing's existence, such as its manner of birth, its descent, or its beginning.

genesis (Aristotle) Aristotle's view of genesis (becoming, change, beginning, growth) involves three fundamental concepts: (a) the existence of a permanently existing *substratum*, or underlying support, which he called *hypokeimenon* or *hylē*; (b) the changing of qualities into their opposites *(enantia),* or into what they were not before; and (c) the absence of *sterēsis* or the lack of the opposing (or differing) qualities. See CHANGE (ARISTOTLE); SUBSTANCE (ARISTOTLE); NATURE (ARISTOTLE).

genetic fallacy see FALLACY, TYPES OF INFORMAL (39).

genus (from Latin, birth, rare, kind, sort; the plural is *genera*) **1.** any CLASS of objects that can be divided into subclasses or subordinate SPECIES. **2.** that class of things being divided into species. Example: In the statement, "dogs are animals," *animals* is the genus. But in "animals are living things," *living things* is the genus, and *animals* becomes the species.

genus, summum (Latin, the highest class [category, set, substance]) **1.** refers to a supreme genus that is not a member (not a species) of any higher genus; the most inclusive class in any classification and which is not a subclass of any more inclusive class. Example: *Being* may be regarded as a *summum genus* that includes within it the general classes of: things, objects, bodies, organisms, animals, humans (which general classes can be further divided). **2.** *summum genus* may be used to refer to what is to be regarded within a context as the highest genus (or one of the highest genera). Example: *quality*, which includes color, blue, azure, teal, turquoise.

genus et differentia distinction a *genus* possesses features that can be predicated of, and are essential to, other kinds (types, classes) of things. The *differentia* is that which is possessed by, or can be predicated of, the members of only one class. Example: In "People are animals that laugh," *animal* is the *genus* and can apply to several other classes such as whales, cats, horses. *Laughing* is the *differentia*. It is a property limited to the class of *people*. See DEFINITION, TYPES OF (7).

genus/species (Aristotle) one of the principal tasks of science is to divide objects into the classifications of genus and species that are the real kinds or categories in which by their nature they belong and strive to stay. Example: All objects that are colored belong to the genus *color*, because they all have in common the property of being colored. Particular red objects belong to a species of that genus. Particular yellow objects belong to another, different species of that same genus. Red and yellow objects belong to different species because they have different properties; one has the property of being red, and the other has the property of being yellow. See SPECIES.

Gestalt (German, form, configuration, organized WHOLE, pattern) **1.** a unified whole, such as an organism (a) that has parts which act in an integrated fashion, (b) that is greater than the sum of its parts, (c) that has a substantive existence over and above the interaction of its individual parts, and (d) that is able to affect the behavior of its parts. **2.** in a nonmetaphysical sense, *gestalt* merely refers to the CONFIGURATION or sense of totality that a perception has. Example: When a melody is heard (perceived), a dynamic unity or wholeness appears to perception, yet its tones are in themselves diverse and succeed each other in a particular time sequence. Change the time sequence, and its *gestalt* is altered. See EMERGENT, AN.

Gestalt philosophy three of its basic philosophical tenets: (a) Our environment is seen as organized wholes (tables, chairs, houses) that can be broken down further into their constituent parts or sensa rather than being built up out of basic, irreducible, discrete impressions. (b) Consciousness has the same essential form (GESTALT, structure) as does its correlated psycho-neural-physical source. (c) Reality is any world to which the physical organism responds in the process of organizing perceived structures or wholes.

given, the 1. anything that is immediately presented to consciousness. **2.** the direct, immediate, irreducible sense data (presentments, appearances, impressions) or feelings, which serve as (a) the ultimate foundation of and reference point for what is known and (b) the material from which inferences and judgments are made. Compare with PROTOCOLS; SENSA.

gnōsis (Greek, a knowing, knowledge, an inquiry to ascertain knowledge about what happened).

gnōthi se auton (Greek, know thyself, knowledge of oneself) an injunction found inscribed on the Greek temple at Delphi (and others) which served as the basis of Socrates' philosophy of self-analysis and self-realization in order to arrive at better knowledge and conduct.

God a term variously conceived but used to apply to that which is considered to be a (or *the*) fundamental source of one's existence and/or values.

God, arguments for the existence of see COMMON CONSENT ARGUMENT FOR GOD'S EXISTENCE; COSMOLOGICAL ARGUMENT FOR GOD'S EXISTENCE; DESIGN, ARGUMENT FROM; FIVE WAYS, THE (AQUINAS); TELEOLOGICAL ARGUMENT FOR THE EXISTENCE OF GOD. Also see entries under ONTOLOGICAL ARGUMENT FOR GOD'S EXISTENCE.

God concepts these fall into a general classification that refers to the *number* of gods and the *degree* to which it is believed God is *identical with,* or is an IMMANENT or TRANSCENDENT force operating in the universe. The following is a list of some of the God concepts adhering to this classification: **1.** *polytheism* (from Greek, *polys,* many, + *theos,* god). The belief in the existence of many gods. **2.** *kathenotheism* (Greek, from *kath'en,* one by one, + *theos,* god) a form of *polytheism,* or, depending on the perspective, a form of *monotheism,* or *monism.* Of the many gods named and believed in, each in turn (thus, one by one) at a designated time of the year is worshiped and given the allegiance and respect customary to a supreme deity, in the realization that each god symbolizes only one of the innumerable facets of a more complex and fundamental reality or God that is the source of all things. **3.** *henotheism* (from Greek, *heis* or *enos,* one, + *theos,* god) a form of polytheism. Of the many gods that exist, one is their supreme ruler, to whom the others must give their loyalty and obedience. **4.** *dualism* the belief that two gods exist, one a force for good, the other a force for evil, both vying for control of the universe. See DUALISM. **5.** *monotheism* (from Greek, *monos,* one, single, alone, one-and-only, + *theos* god) the belief that there is one-and-only-one God. **6.** *pantheism* (from Greek, *pan,* all, + *theos,* god) the belief that God is identical with the universe. All is God and God is all. The universe taken as a whole is God. God and nature (universe, the totality of all that there is) are synonymous, two words for the same thing. **7.** *panentheism* (from Greek, *pan,* all, + *en,* in, + *theos,* god) all things are imbued with God's being in the sense that all things are *in* God. God is more than all that there is. God is a consciousness and the highest unity possible. **8.** *panpsychism* (from Greek, *pan,* all, + PSYCHĒ soul, spirit, mind) the belief that God is completely immanent *in* all things in the universe as a psychic force (mind, consciousness, spirit, soul). See PANPSYCHISM (METAPHYSICS). **9.** *theism* (from Greek, *theos,* god) in most interpretations: God is partly immanent in the universe and partly transcendent. See THEISM. **10.** *deism* (from Latin, *deus*, god) in most interpretations: God is totally transcendent, *wholly other* to the universe, and none of God's being is immanent in the universe. See DEISM.

golden mean, the see MEAN, THE (ARISTOTLE).

golden rule, the 1. do unto others as you would want others to do unto you. **2.** do not do to others what you would not want done to you.

good 1. any object of interest, value, or desire. **2.** that which is the object of, or valued by, the rational will. **3.** that desired by the will. **4.** the product of contemplative activity or the feelings surrounding such activity. The word *good* conveys laudatory qualities such as approval, commendation, excellence, admiration, and appropriateness; and has meanings such as virtuous, beneficent, beneficial, favorable, genuine, and praiseworthy. Compare with entries under PLEASURE; UTILITARIANISM.

good (Aristotle) that which in fact a thing aims to achieve in accord with its inherent nature. Example: The good for the individual is that which one is, by one's essential nature, committed to seeking. This is the full actualization of his or her essence (reason), the development of his or her rational faculties to the utmost, that which Aristotle calls EUDAIMONIA, which is translated as *happiness* but means the vital well-being that comes from exercising one's potentialities for a rational life. The good is not always identified with what one wishes, since wishes are not based on one's essential rational nature. Only when one wishes to express one's essential nature and seeks to do this are the two coherent with each other.

good (G.E. Moore) good, like yellow, a simple, indefinable property. The terms differ in that yellow is known by the use of our senses, whereas good is intuited. See OPEN-QUESTION ARGUMENT (G.E. MOORE).

good (Plato and Pythagoreans) the good of anything is (a) its existence in an intelligent (rational) order (proportion), and in the case of the individual (b) the individual's being activated by the highest intellectual (rational) ideas. See AGATHON.

good, contributory that which is desired or valued because of (a) the part it plays within an activity or whole that is itself desired or valued (considered a good), and/or (b) the part it plays in a process that is developing toward something which is desired.

good, extrinsic that which is desired or valued not for its own sake but for the sake of something else, for the beneficial consequences it brings. Example: enduring the discomfort of having a decayed tooth removed in order to be relieved of pain. See EXTRINSIC.

good, inherent 1. the quality in an object or experience that provides the basis for our seeing it as desirable or to be valued.

2. an ideal, objectively existing quality common to all good things and good experiences. Example: aesthetic form.

good, instrumental that which is desired or valued as a means of obtaining another good. Example: money. See INSTRUMENTALISM.

good, intrinsic 1. that which is desired or valued in and for itself. **2.** an end sought for its own desirability. Example: pleasure. See INTRINSIC.

good, intrinsic-extrinsic that which is desired or valued both for its own sake (in and for itself) as well as for the sake of something else, for the beneficial consequences it brings. Example: listening to a Bach fugue for the sheer enjoyment of it but also in order to pass a music test on the next day.

good, the (Plato) see AGATHON.

good, the highest see SUMMUM BONUM.

good will, the (Kant) see ETHICS (KANT).

greatest happiness principle see UTILITARIANISM.

Greek atomism see ATOMISM, GREEK.

H

habit (from Latin, *habitus,* state, appearance, dress; from *habere,* have) behavior, associations, or inclinations (a) acquired by repetition, (b) activated and expressed with little or no thought, and (c) performed without much resistance. Compare with HEXIS (ARISTOTLE), INSTINCT.

happiness 1. a pleasurable feeling-tone, which may vary in intensity, associated with one's life, or with certain activities in one's life; the sense of being pleased, joyous, content, satisfied, fortunate, blessed, favored, graced. **2.** the achievement of the highest value or goal in life (that which all individuals strive for) but interpreted variously as the procurement of pleasure, the realization of one's potential, exercising one's duty, being virtuous, following natural law, living a life of moderation, complete freedom to rationally determine one's own destiny, etc.

happiness (Aristotle) see *EUDAIMONIA.*

happiness (Kant) an ideal that cannot be realized (at least in this life). It consists of three fundamental aspects, which themselves cannot be fully realized in practice: (a) self-sufficiency, (b) integration (harmony) of the self, and (c) self-determination (freedom of the will).

happiness (Mill) identical (a) with pleasure and (b) with the absence of pain. Contrast with UNHAPPINESS (MILL).

happiness (Plato) see ARETĒ.

hedonic referring to (a) the pleasure-producing quality of a thing, or (b) the tendency of a thing to produce pleasure, or (c) the state of pleasure actually produced.

hedonics the aspect of ethics that deals with the relationship of DUTY to pleasure.

hedonism (Aristippus) the view that the aim of life should be the pursuit by any means whatever of as much physical pleasure for each moment as possible without taking heed of the consequences that might follow. See CYRENAICS.

hedonism (Epicurus) the view that the highest good in life is the absence of (a) pain and (b) vexing pleasures that bring pain or discomfort as their consequence. The aim of life should be ATARAXIA: tranquility (imperturbability) of body, mind, and spirit.

hedonism, egoistic (psychological) the theory that all human actions should be motivated by the desire to secure one's own pleasure, and by the desire to avoid pain to oneself, even if the pleasure or good of others has to be sacrificed.

hedonism, ethical (from Greek, *hēdonē,* pleasure, and *hēdys,* sweet, pleasant) the doctrine that (a) pleasure is the highest good (or the sole good) in life, (b) pleasure is an intrinsic good (or the only intrinsic good), (c) pleasure should be sought, and (d) the ethical worth (value, good) of human actions is determined by whether or not they produce pleasure. Ethical hedonism insists that each individual is obligated to himself or herself to live so as to obtain as much pleasure and as little pain as possible.

hedonism, psychological the theory that all human actions are in fact motivated by the desire to secure pleasure, and by the desire to avoid pain, and it is impossible to do otherwise.

hedonistic calculus (Bentham) sometimes called *hedonic calculus*, *utility calculus*, or *felicity calculus*. Jeremy Bentham devised a method of choosing an action, based on the amount of pleasure (as opposed to pain) that the action would provide. The amount of pleasure was determined by its intensity, duration, propinquity (nearness), certainty, fecundity (fruitfulness or fertility), and purity (not mixed with unappealing feelings such as pain or boredom and not followed by such feelings). See UTILITARIANISM.

hedonistic paradox 1. the person who constantly seeks pleasure for himself or herself will not find it, yet the person who helps others find pleasure will in the process find pleasure for himself or herself (or has a greater chance of finding it). **2.** pleasure is not something to be sought after directly; it is not to be thought of as an end in itself separate from an activity or an experience. It is attainable only as an attitude or feeling accompanying other things.

Hegel, Georg Wilhelm Friedrich (1770–1831) German philosopher and educator, with appointments at several European universities.

He studied the original sources of Christianity, with the aim of finding insights devoid of dogma, historical tradition, and prejudices. At Weimar, where he served as professor *extraordinarius*, he published *The Phenomenology of the Mind* (1807); at Heidelberg, in 1817, he prepared his *Encyclopedia of the Philosophical Sciences in Outline* and, in 1821, published *A Groundwork of the Philosophy of Rights*. Major themes of this work included: (a) The basic principles of morality, ethics, law, and social institutions are interconnected phases in a logical progression of a universal, rational mind (or will). (b) The *real* is the rational, and the rational is the only *real*. (c) All values originate in the organization and progression of events, a vital interconnection of all parts of society and nature. (d) Freedom, liberty, can never be separated from an orderly set of events.

Many of Hegel's published writings, such as his *Aesthetics*; *The Philosophy of Religion*; *The Philosophy of History*; and *The History of Philosophy*, were organized by editors who worked from notes taken by Hegel's students. Hegel completed the first part of his *Science of Logic* in 1831, the year in which he died suddenly of cholera.

Heidegger, Martin (1889–1976) German philosopher, existentialist; born in Messkirch, Baden; educated at the University of Freiburg, where he studied under Husserl, founder of phenomenology. He taught at Marburg and Freiburg. His main work is *Being and Time* (*Sein und Zeit*, 1927).

Heisenberg's principle of uncertainty see UNCERTAINTY, HEISENBERG'S PRINCIPLE OF.

Hempel, Carl Gustav (1905–   ) American philosopher of science and mathematics, born in Oranienburg, Germany; studied physics and mathematics at Göttingen, Heidelberg, and Berlin; came to the United States in 1937. He has taught at Yale and Princeton and is identified with the Logical Positivists. His most important books are *Fundamentals of Concept Formation in Empirical Science* (1952) and *Aspects of Scientific Explanation* (1965).

hen (Greek, one) the *single one*, that which includes all other things and is not included in anything, the source of all being, change, or emanation, the nondependent *first*, the ultimate reality. Also: a unit, a unity, an individuality (in contrast to multiplicity, manifold, aggregate, having parts, etc.). See EMANATION; ONE, THE.

henotheism see GOD CONCEPTS (3).

Heraclitus of Ephesus (c.540–475 BC) Greek philosopher, known as "the philosopher of change," "the dark philosopher," "the weeping philosopher," and "the obscure." After Heraclitus, Cratylus became the leading proponent of Heraclitus's philosophy of change.

here an indexical sign (such as *this, I, now, that*) (a) used to refer to spatio-temporal position and (b) having no descriptive content unless accompanied by further meanings. See SIGN, INDEXICAL.

heterogeneity (from Greek, *heterogenēs,* from *heteros,* other, + *genos,* race, descent, birth) **1.** having unlike qualities or parts throughout. **2.** the theory that things have unlike qualities or parts present in them no matter how similar they are. Opposite to HOMOGENEITY.

heterological referring to an expression whose meaning does not characterize (apply to) itself. Example: The word *Greek* is not a Greek word. Contrasted with HOMOLOGICAL.

heuristic (from Greek, *heuriskein,* discover) providing assistance in discovering (or in presenting) a truth or solving a problem, for example, a model or a useful hypothesis. Contrasted with PROOF.

heuristic principle a principle that is neither asserted nor evaluated as true but that is assumed for specific purposes at hand (such as to inquire into, explain something) because of its previous success or usefulness as an investigative tool.

heuristics the discipline that studies the methods by which truth (fact, ideas, etc.) are discovered and (sometimes) communicated.

hexis **(Aristotle)** (Greek, habit, state, characteristic) those predispositional structures in a thing that influence its activity and/or well-being and are not easy to change. They may be acquired (habits) or an inherent condition and are usually associated with emotions and feelings.

hierarchy of being see BEING, HIERARCHY OF.

historicism occasionally given as *historism* **1.** the theory that things are what they are because of their historical development; the descriptive account of a thing's history as sufficient explanation for it. **2.** the theory that inexorable laws determine all historical events, which are what history attempts to understand and use for prediction.

Hobbes, Thomas (1588–1679) English philosopher, born at Westport, now part of Malmsbury, and educated at Oxford. During his life, he was known in intellectual circles of Europe and knew such figures as Descartes, Gassendi, Galileo, and Bacon.

His first philosophic work was the *Little Treatise*, using geometry as the methodology of scientific explanation to account for the presence of sensation in terms of the motion of matter. In an autobiography he wrote in Latin verse, Hobbes states that one of his earliest philosophic questions was "What is sense?" Upon reflection it became apparent to him that if things were always at rest, or in uniform motion relative to one another, no discriminations could ever be made, and knowledge, perception, and education would be impossible. His general conclusion was that in motion (in the diversity of motion) can be found the cause of all things that have *being* and that *have become* as they are. (Hobbes later explained that the mind itself is a form of matter-in-motion and is the place where motions conjoined.)

Love of Euclidean geometry led Hobbes to employ geometrical explanations for the variety of motions—the very same scientific attempt that Galileo and others were making at the time. Previous philosophers believed that *rest*—to be in a place, at a time, and with a desire to remain there—was the natural tendency of all things. Hobbes held that rest was not the natural state, or tendency, of natural, material bodies. Motion, change, activity was for Hobbes the natural state and the natural predisposition of all natural, material bodies. In agreement with Galileo, Hobbes held that matter would continue in motion unless that motion was hindered by other motions to change direction and rate of motion.

Hobbes presented his philosophic position on these general principles in three treatises: *De Cive* (1642) discusses the correct methods of regulating social behavior and fostering correct social values and relationships. *De Corpore* (1655) explains all physical events and all material bodies in terms of motion and matter-in-motion. In *De Homine* (1658) he proposes that different and particular material motions, movements, are the causes of phenomena such as sensation, perception, emotions, feelings, thought, memory, and knowledge. Seen together, these three works were attempts at a systematic materialistic and mechanical integration of *matter* (body), *man*, and *citizen of society* and the state—attempts to find a common, fundamental, unified, mechanistic thread of analysis, explanation, and connection.

In 1640, Hobbes was circulating his *The Elements of Law, Natural and Politique*, comprising *Human Nature* and *De Corpore Politico*. In 1641, he published *The Leviathan; or the Matter, Form and Power of a Commonwealth, Ecclesiastical and Civil.*

Of all his works—too numerous to list here—*The Leviathan* is the volume known best today. In it he explained his political views: (1) The Church—all churches—should in all ways be subordinated to the will of the State. (2) The State has absolute, unconditional power, and only in this way could personal rights and individual and popular representation be maintained. (3) Under the social contract theory of the operation of a State with a constitution, the people rule. (4) The sovereignty of a State originated in the people via transference to the monarch of the people's rights for such things as protection, security, and self-preservation. (5) The State must be as strong as possible. (6) People must give absolute obedience to the monarch so that peace and order are maintained. (7) Freedom and liberty in the hands of people result in anarchy. (8) There must be a rational and enlightened concern for the commonwealth by the State, the sovereign, and individuals.

holism sometimes given as *wholism,* the theory that there is a real, fundamental, and irreducible difference between living and nonliving, between organic and inorganic, activity. The parts of living (organic) wholes function differently within the whole from the way they do outside it. Organic wholes must be studied as wholes, since knowing how parts act outside a whole does not enable us to know how those parts will act within a whole. See EVOLUTION, EMERGENT.

holistic explanation 1. an explanation of phenomena in terms of the functions (purposes, properties, activities) of a whole (form, totality, unity) that is the guiding principle of its parts. **2.** an explanation of the activity of the parts of a whole in terms of the functions of that whole. See ANIMISM, TELEOLOGICAL. Compare with entries under EXPLANATION.

homogeneity (from Greek, *homogenēs,* from *homos,* same, + *genos,* race, descent, birth) **1.** the state of having the same qualities or parts throughout. **2.** the theory that things have a similar quality or part that is present in them no matter how unlike they are. Opposite to HETEROGENEITY.

homoiomeries (Anaxagoras) the basic building blocks (*homoioi*) of the universe that can be divided, yet remain of the same kind. All things possess parts and are constructed from parts that are similar to their whole, to the whole from which they are taken. These homoiomeries may be divided infinitely and will continue to resemble each other. Example: Bone is made up of elements that look like bone. Those elements may be divided into parts that themselves look like bone.

homoiomeries (Aristotle) (from Greek, *homoiōma,* likeness, image, resemblance, counterfeit) those parts of a whole that resemble one another when separated from the whole. (In some interpretations the parts also resemble the whole.) Examples: wood, metal, hair, liver tissue. Aristotle did not believe this division can go on indefinitely. He thought there is a point of division at which the part no longer resembles other parts taken from the whole.

homological sometimes given as *autological,* referring to that whose meaning characterizes (applies to) itself. Example: The word *polysyllabic* is itself a polysyllabic word. Contrasted with HETEROLOGICAL.

homo mensura **theory** the theory that man (*homo*) is the measure (*mensura*) of all things. See RELATIVISM, PROTAGOREAN.

humanism, philosophical a philosophy that (a) regards the rational individual as the highest value; (b) considers the individual to be the ultimate source of value; and (c) is dedicated to fostering the individual's creative and moral development in a meaningful and rational way without reference to concepts of the supernatural. Compare with EXISTENTIALISM; NATURALISM.

human rights see RIGHTS, HUMAN.

Hume, David (1711–1776) Scottish philosopher born in Edinburgh and educated at Edinburgh University. During a stay in France, he wrote what is now regarded as his most important philosophic work, *The Treatise of Human Nature* (1739), a complete exposition of his philosophy. (Kant remarked that it was Hume who awoke him from his "dogmatic slumber.")

Another important work was Hume's *Philosophic Essays concerning the Human Understanding* (1748), in 1758 retitled *An Enquiry concerning the Human Understanding.* In 1751, Hume published his *An Enquiry concerning the Principles of Morals.* His *Dialogues concerning Natural Religion,* his last philosophic work, was published posthumously in 1779. (He also wrote a 5-volume *History of Great Britain* during the period 1746–1749.)

Hume has been classified as one of the three principal British Empiricists, along with Locke and Berkeley. Some of Hume's characteristic philosophic beliefs follow: (1) All that is contained in the human mind is derived from sense-impressions and ideas that are vague or faint images derived from these impressions. (2) No facts can be connected, proved, or explained by *a priori* reasoning. (3) Space and time are the way (simultaneously or successively) in which impressions occur to us. (4) Existence is not a separate idea, independent and accompanying any specific idea we have, but is identical with the idea of whatever we think of. "Any idea we please to form *is* the idea of a being; and the idea of a being is any idea we please to form.") This is the basis of Hume's and Kant's assertion that *existence* is not a predicate, property, or attribute—which serves as the basis for the major criticism of the ontological argument for God's existence. Since existence is not a predicate, then existence is not necessary for God to be completely perfect. (5) There is a distinction between matters of fact, discovered by empirical observation and by empirical-logical inference; and relations of ideas, discovered by intuition and logical demonstration. (6) There is no power or necessity binding a cause to its effect. Cause and effect are related in a temporal sequence, regularity of succession, contiguity, and constant conjunction. They are a matter of the association of our ideas, not of a productive power that brings about an effect from a cause, or causes a cause to necessitate a particular effect. (7) The mind is not an entity or substance, but a "bundle of impressions and ideas" related by connections such as resemblance, causality, and succession in a memory-type system. No *mind, self, spiritual substance, spiritual entity*, or *soul* exists independently, separately causing or connecting this bundle of impressions. There is no *mind* . . . in which this succession or bundle of impressions inheres.

humours, the four (from Latin, *humor*, moisture, vapor, fluid) from early Greek medicine, four body fluids that were evident to physicians: blood, yellow bile (choler), black bile (melancholy), and phlegm. The theory of the four humours (and the theory of the four elements) persisted well into the 17th century and served as a basis for medical explanations. These humours, or fluids, had to be kept in balance with one another in order to achieve physical, mental health, and a good temperament. How to create and maintain this balance was the concern of medicine. Compare with ELEMENTS, THE FOUR.

Husserl, Edmund Gustav Albrecht (1859–1938) German philosopher, born in Prossnitz, Austria; educated in sciences, mathematics, and philosophy at the universities of Leipsig, Berlin, and Vienna; taught at Göttingen and Freiburg. His major works were *Logical Investigations* (1900); *Philosophy as Rigorous Science* (1911); *Ideas* (1931); *Formal and Transcendental Logic* (1929); *Cartesian Meditations* (1931); *The Crisis of the European Sciences and Transcendental Phenomenology* (1936); and *Phenomenological Psychology* (published posthumously, 1962).

hybris sometimes given as *hubris* (Greek, overbearing pride, insolence, wanton violence, arrogance, going beyond one's abilities and making a fool of oneself, attempting to emulate the gods). *Hybris* was regarded as an evil that tended to result in a disaster or one's downfall.

hylē (Greek, matter, material, the primary substance of change) sometimes used synonymously with HYPOKEIMENON. Originally, *hyl[ame]* meant *wood* and especially the wooden structures holding a ship together or holding up a building; also, any material from which something could be made. In later, philosophic Greek, it came to mean the *substance* underlying reality, or the *matter* of which something is composed. *Hylism* is used to mean materialism.

hylē (Aristotle) the common material stuff found in a variety of things. In itself it had no distinct characteristics **1.** until form was *imparted* to it (in one interpretation of Aristotle), or **2.** until the form inherent in that matter began to become actualized (in another interpretation of Aristotle). This latter interpretation holds that no matter can exist without form being in some way associated with it, and no form can exist without its being imbued in matter. See FORM (ARISTOTLE); GENESIS (ARISTOTLE).

hylomorphism (from Greek, *hylē,* matter, + *morphē,* form, figure, shape) **1.** the theory that the universe is composed of matter and form in inseparable unity throughout. Wherever matter exists, form will also exist. Wherever form exists, matter will also exist. **2.** the view that form as directing energy gives matter its activity and pattern. Matter is that which is being structured into a process or pattern. **3.** the view that form is that which endures throughout change and does not itself change, thereby guaranteeing a continuity and identity to the individual thing. Matter is the changed and continually changing ingredient which without form could have no substantial or individual existence. Compare with ANIMISM.

hylozoism (from Greek, *hylē,* matter, + *zōē,* life) **1.** the theory that all matter possesses some degree of life qualities, and all life possesses a material basis. Matter and life are inseparable (except in abstraction). **2.** the theory that the universe is everywhere alive; all matter is innately life-active. Reality can be best understood as a self-sustaining, living organism. Compare with PANPSYCHISM (METAPHYSICS).

hypokeimenon (Greek, substratum, underlying ground, that which stands as the support for something) see GENESIS (ARISTOTLE); in logic, that which is presupposed by something else.

hypostasis (from Greek, standing under as support, substance, subsistence; from *hypo,* under, + *histanai,* cause to stand) that substance (ultimate ground, subsistent principle, essential nature, self-subsistent reality, subject) (a) in which attributes inhere and/or (b) which supports a subsisting personality. See *SUBSTANTIA* and entries under SUBSTANCE.

hypostatization sometimes called *abstractionism* and often used interchangeably with REIFICATION/REISM **1.** attributing actual existence to something that is only a name or an abstraction. **2.** regarding an abstraction or a relation as if it were an existing object. Example: Treating the concept *nation* as an entity over and above the relations, structures, activities, etc. that it designates.

hypothesis (from Greek, *hypothesis,* supposition, assumption, foundation, that which is laid down as a rule of action, principle) **1.** that which is assumed (or conjectured) without direct empirical evidence for the purpose of accounting for some fact or facts. **2.** a provisional or tentative proposal for the explanation of phenomena that has some degree of empirical substantiation or probability.

In science, a hypothesis describes what will (or would) occur under certain conditions. Observations are made and/or experiments are conducted to determine if the hypothesis is accurate or tenable (relative to other proposed hypotheses) in accounting for the facts, and/or to determine if what the hypothesis can be made to predict does come about. A predictive hypothesis is of great importance in science and is confirmed if its predictions come about. If its predictive and/or explanatory power is high, a hypothesis may be elevated to the status of a theory or law. If the prediction is not substantiated, this is good reason for not accepting the hypothesis, at least not without modification. An ideal hypothesis not only predicts but explains all the facts that have to be explained about a particular phenomenon. A hypothesis often serves also to suggest further investigations, observations, or experimentation. All hypotheses are subject to change as additional factual information is gathered and/or as new theories and laws are advanced. See CONFIRMATION; METHOD, SCIENTIFIC. Compare with THEORY, SCIENTIFIC.

hypothetical construct see CONSTRUCT, THEORETICAL.

hypothetical-deductive method sometimes called *hypothetico-deductive method.* See EXPLANATION, SCIENTIFIC.

hypothetical imperative (Kant) an imperative, and that system of morals based on such an imperative, which is conditional on a wish to possess a desired value or good. *If* you wish to have health, *then* you must (or ought) to do such and such. An imperative directing one to act on the basis of prudence and/or self-interest and not on the basis of DUTY or obligation to moral principles. Contrasted with CATEGORICAL IMPERATIVE, THE (KANT).

I

I an indexical sign (see SIGN, INDEXICAL) such as *now, this, here, that*, (a) used by someone to refer to himself or herself without reference to any particular aspect of himself or self, and (b) containing no descriptive content.

icon sometimes given as *ikon* (from Greek *eikōn*, image) **1.** an image, likeness, or representation of something. See EIDOLA (ART). **2.** a picture or a sign that is like in image to the thing it indicates or represents. See SIGN, ICONIC.

idea (from Greek *idéa*, form, pattern) **1.** anything that is a content (object, item) of consciousness; any act of awareness. **2.** a mental image or picture of something. **3.** the real likeness, representation, or essence of a thing embodied in an object and grasped by intelligence. **4.** any general notion, thought, mental impression, or concept. **5.** anything fantasized, fictionalized, or imagined. **6.** a belief, opinion, supposition, or doctrine held. **7.** something designed or intended to take place, such as a plan. **8.** an archetype, ideal, or pattern to be followed.

idea, abstract see ABSTRACTION.

ideal 1. a standard of perfection, excellence, beauty, goodness. **2.** a perfect type; embodying a perfect exemplar. **3.** archetypal idea (see ARCHETYPES); the perfect form grasped simply, consistently, and comprehensively. **4.** the perfect object or goal of our desire and willing.

ideal of reason, the (Kant) refers to reason's (unattainable) search for (a) knowledge of the totality of things, its conditions, structure, and possibilities, and (b) knowledge of its unconditioned and absolute ground. Kant calls this search the *transcendental illusion*. See ILLUSION, TRANSCENDENTAL (KANT).

idealism sometimes called *mentalism* or *immaterialism*. **1.** the theory that the universe is an embodiment of a mind. **2.** reality is dependent for its existence on a mind and its activities. **3.** all reality is mental (spiritual, psychical). Matter, the physical, does not exist. **4.** no knowledge is possible except of mental states and processes, and that is all that exists. Reality is explained in terms of such psychic phenomena as minds, selves, spirits, ideas, absolute thought, etc., rather than in terms of matter. **5.** only mind-type activities and their idea-type content exist. The external world is not physical.

idealism (Berkeley) see IMMATERIALISM (BERKELEY).

idealism (Plato) the view that true, absolute reality is the realm of the perfect, independently existing, unchanging, timeless forms (ideas), and the true object of all knowledge. See FORMS, PLATO'S THEORY OF IDEAL.

idealism, absolute the theory that the absolute (see ABSOLUTE, THE) regarded as a mind, ego, self, spirit, soul is the fundamental, undetermined reality in the universe: (a) upon which all things depend for their existence, but which depends on nothing else for its existence, (b) from which all things can be rationally deduced, (c) from which all finite things flow in a progressive development of its thought, and (d) in which all things exist as a thought. A monistic or pantheistic philosophy.

idealism, absolute (Hegel) Hegel denied the Kantian distinction between that which is given in our experience (such as sense impressions) and the categories used to structure and understand it. Things exist in our consciousness but in interrelationship to other things that also exist there. These relationships and connections of things are real, as real as qualities, as real as attributes. They can be understood as parts of a monistic system of an evolving substance in which the essential self-subsisting core is absolute spirit. The essence of this absolute spirit is (a) self-actualization into perfection and (b) its all-encompassing determining nature. See ABSOLUTE, THE.

idealism, critical (Kant) refers to Kant's theory of knowledge. The essence of critical idealism is Kant's sharp distinction between what is given to us in our experience (sense impressions), and the structures (forms of intuition and the categories) that the mind uses to arrange, interpret, and evaluate that which is given. See entries under CATEGORIES (KANT).

idealism, epistemological the theory that (a) nothing can be known except minds (selves) and their mental content. The extreme version of this is: nothing can be known except the operations of our mind and its content (see entries under SOLIPSISM); (b) knowledge of the mind is the fundamental and only source for constructing knowledge of anything else at all; and (c) all knowledge exists as a content in, and is caused by, a mind.

idealism, metaphysical the theory that (a) no object can exist without a mind (subject, self, ego) perceiving it (see ESSE EST PERCIPI), and (b) only minds and their content (ideas, images, perceptions, etc.) exist. Metaphysical idealism assumes an epistemological idealism. See IDEALISM, EPISTEMOLOGICAL.

idealism, pantheistic sometimes called *monistic idealism*, the theory that all finite minds (foci of psychic activity) are inseparable parts or aspects (modes, features, attributes) of the absolute thought (God, mind, spirit, soul), which can be separated only in abstraction.

idealism, personal synonymous with PERSONALISM.

idealism, pluralistic the theory that all finite minds or foci of psychic activity (a) are autonomous, unique, and irreducible, (b) interrelate, (c) are singular, private activities, and (d) may or may not relate to an absolute *one* or mind.

idealism, subjective the theory that (a) the knower and the thing known do not have independent existence; all knowledge is knowledge of our conscious states and processes and not of any external world; (b) that which is known is created by the human mind—matter is not real; (c) the absolute (God) creates the human mind to know that which the human mind creates for itself to know—all that is known exists for and in our minds; (d) that creative act of the absolute in (c) results from an act of thought by the absolute itself; (e) the only reality is mind and its processes and content; and (f) mental reality is all that can ever be known.

idealism, transcendental (Kant) knowledge of the external world is produced by our transcendental unity (logical ego) of apperception. Rational thought processes *per se* cannot give us synthetic knowledge of the external world. Sensation *per se* cannot give us knowledge. Our perceptions are organized by the pure *a priori* intuitions of space and time and by the categories of our understanding. These categories, and not how things are in themselves, are the conditions that make experience possible and intelligible. The transcendental unity (self, ego) is the source of these intuitions and categories and is that which applies them to raw *experience*. Nothing can be known of this transcendental unity. It is the *condition* for knowledge but not an *object* of knowledge. All we can know about it is *that* it *is* but we cannot say *what* it *is*. See APPERCEPTION, TRANSCENDENTAL.

ideas (Berkeley) the content of sense experience (perception) or the act of perceiving, and totally dependent on a soul (mind) and ultimately dependent on God's thought or perception. See IMMATERIALISM (BERKELEY).

ideas (Descartes) Descartes described three types of ideas: **1.** *innate ideas*, which proceed from the structure, activity, or potential (capacity, ability) of thought (the mind) itself. The three principal innate ideas are of (a) God, (b) the self (mind, ego, thinking substance), and (c) matter (body, external physical objects, material substance). **2.** *factitious ideas*, which are constructed by the mind in order to understand what things are (or might be) like (such as a scientist's physical or chemical model of a material object). **3.** *adventitious ideas*, which come as stimuli from the external world (such as of sound [a musical note], of sight [the moon], of heat [a fire]). Adventitious ideas do not come into the mind from the outside as qualities or entities but are formed by the mind from physical motions that affect the brain. See IDEAS, CLEAR AND DISTINCT (DESCARTES).

ideas (Hume) less intense and vivid images or copies of sense impressions retained in memory. See KNOWLEDGE (HUME).

ideas (Kant) those necessary, formal, and regulative concepts of reason to which no corresponding object can be given in sensation (such as that of the unity of the ego). See IDEALISM, TRANSCENDENTAL (KANT).

ideas (Locke) objects of understanding; anything that the mind attends to, is aware of, concentrates on, *has* as a representation, or is *given*. This includes that which the mind perceives (a) as its activity, such as willing, thinking, doubting, tending, feeling, and (b) as the immediate content of its perception or thought. See KNOWLEDGE

(LOCKE) and various entries under IDEAS (LOCKE) that follow.

ideas (Plato) 1. timeless, perfect, unchanging, immaterial, eternal ARCHETYPES (forms) of which existing things are imperfect copies. **2.** the eternal perfect forms used by the DEMIURGE as blueprints to be followed in its act of organizing matter into things. **3.** the essences (forms, universals) found in all things that resemble (imitate) the perfect forms and which when compared with our innate knowledge of the perfect forms make them recognizable (intelligible, namable) to us. **4.** universals (such as redness, circularity) that apply to more than one thing, as opposed to particulars (such as *this* red ball, *that* circular table). **5.** the ideal standard by which particular things are judged to be an approximation. **6.** any object of pure intelligence as opposed to objects of sensation. **7.** that enduring state of something as opposed to its becoming, or changing state.

Plato's word for idea was *eidos,* translated as *idea* or *form,* sometimes as *constitutive nature* or ESSENCE, and occasionally as *type* or *species* (see FORMS, PLATO'S THEORY OF IDEAL). Every major general word such as *good, beauty, justice, equality,* and *circularity* has a corresponding abstract idea (FORM or ARCHETYPE) that is an eternal, unchanging, incorporeal spiritual substance grasped only by the highest form of reasoning. All the many particular instances of these ideas (general classes) imitate, participate in, emulate their corresponding idea. This idea is the ideal standard by which its particular instance is identified and judged as to its shortcomings. Also it is the *cause* of their being what they are, since all things are urged on (activated) by a desire (longing, love) to be like their ideal. See ANAMNĒSIS, BEAUTY, MIMĒSIS; SOUL (PLATO).

ideas, clear and distinct (Descartes) the formulation that an idea is *clear* if it can be conceived as a whole and without inconsistency (for example, the conception of a circle); that an idea is *distinct* if it is never confused with another idea (for example, a circle is never confused with a square). Descartes believed that: **1.** those ideas and only those ideas that are perceived clearly and distinctly are to be accepted as true, and **2.** an idea may be clear without being distinct but cannot be distinct without also being clear. The three clear and distinct (self-evident) ideas about reality that provide the basis of his philosophy are (a) *extension* (matter occupying space), (b) *figure* (shape, size, spatial dimensions), and (c) *movement* (motion). See IDEAS (DESCARTES); METHOD (DESCARTES).

ideas, complex (Locke) ideas that are built up into combinations out of simple ideas—see IDEAS, SIMPLE (LOCKE). Complex ideas include abstract ideas, general ideas, universals, abstractions, some ideas of reflection and introspection, etc. Complex ideas are divided into (a) *modes,* (b) *relations,* and (c) *substance.* (The latter two are called *mixed modes;* they are arbitrary mental constructions and do not correspond to real entities.) A *simple mode* refers to the forms a particular simple idea can take (such as unity, spatiality), and a *complex mode* refers to the combination of simple ideas into a complex idea (such as that of number or amount). *Relations* consist of the contrasting (associating, etc.) of ideas (such as cause/effect, identity/diversity, oneness/multiplicity, place/time). *Substance* refers to the recognition that external objects continue to exist independently of consciousness and includes (1) the general idea of substance (matter, an underlying physical ground), (2) the particular idea of substances, and (3) the collective idea of substances.

ideas, innate 1. ideas (knowledge, concepts, beliefs) that are not derived in any way from our sense organs (experience) but preexist and originate in the mind itself. **2.** ideas that are potentially present in the mind at birth and that are brought to consciousness under certain conditions. **3.** ideas that are present to the mind as a tendency or predisposition to think a certain way.

Theories about innate ideas assume that innate ideas efficiently apply to, and provide an insight into, reality unobtainable from any other source.

ideas, simple (Locke) ideas that cannot be broken down any further into component parts. They are irreducible, primitive, indefinable, unmixed (such as red, pain, point, a sound, a smell, etc.). Usually associated with the immediate objects of our perception. Simple ideas appear to (are in) the mind as a unity; the mind of its own cannot in any way create, imagine, invent, or construct them, but needs them in order to have knowledge. The mind has the ability to store them in memory, remember (recall) them, and contrast and associate them in new combinations (see IDEAS, COMPLEX [LOCKE]) that are not found in our experience of them as simple ideas.

According to Locke, on most occasions we do not have experiences of simple ideas as discrete, autonomous, independent units. Simple ideas are found in integrated clusters that are broken up by the mind into their unique components. For example, the experience of a hot piece of metal combines such simple ideas as that of heat, hardness, smoothness. Some simple ideas, such as of heat, touch, sight, and smell, come only from one corresponding sense. Others, such as of shape, space, figure, and numbered amounts, come from the intermingling of senses.

ideas of practical reason (Kant) ideas that have no empirical foundation but are necessary for the function of morality, such as the ideas of God, freedom, and immortality. See ETHICS (KANT).

ideas of pure reason (Kant) sometimes called *ideas of theoretical reason*, ideas that have no corresponding objects but are necessary to the function of reason, such as the ideas of a soul, of the existence of an external world, and of God. See entries under CATEGORIES with reference to Kant.

ideas of reflection (Locke) 1. those ideas we have whenever we introspect on what we are doing when we engage in such activities as thinking, willing, doubting, hearing, touching, seeing. **2.** what the mind perceives in an awareness of, or reflection on, its functions. Compare with REFLECTION (LOCKE).

ideas of sensation (Locke) 1. the immediate quality (content) of perception, such as that the table is green, heavy, and large. **2.** that which is given in sensation.

identical 1. two things are identical if all the characteristics of one are also possessed by the other and vice versa. **2.** two things are identical whenever the totality of what can be said to be true about one is also the totality of what can be said to be true about the other. (All objects that are identical belong to the same class, and all identical classes belong to the same class. Identical objects belong to a class if-and-only-if the others do also.)

identify 1. recognize or establish *what* a thing is, or *that* it is what it is. **2.** recognize or claim that a thing is the same (in at least one respect) at a given moment in time as it was at a previous moment in time.

identity (from Latin *idem,* the same) **1.** exactly the same, as in *identical houses*; a relation of complete and absolute sameness or resemblance between two things; referred to as *strict* identity. See IDENTICAL. **2.** not a relation of complete sameness or resemblance between two things, but a meaning relation that remains the same in our application of it, between the name (sign, symbol) of a thing and the thing being named. **3.** neither 1. nor 2., but a relation of sameness that exists among those names themselves that refer to the same meanings or things. See "IS" OF FORMAL EQUIVALENCE.

identity, law of (logic) see LAWS OF THOUGHT, THE THREE.

identity (metaphysics) 1. permanence. **2.** relative permanence. **3.** that which endures throughout change. **4.** that which endures throughout change relatively longer than other things that can be seen to change. **5.** oneness, that which endures as a self-regulating unity throughout change. **6.** sameness, that which can be identified as being the same from among a diversity or plurality of things. **7.** that which is the same with itself.

identity, numerical one and the same thing; that which is the same with itself; self-sameness. Example: The Vice-President of the United States and the officer presiding over the U.S. Senate are identical. Things that share the same place (space) and time are numerically identical. If things are identified as being numerically identical, they have all their characteristics in common.

identity, personal see PERSONAL IDENTITY.

identity, principle of (logic) see LAWS OF THOUGHT, THE THREE.

identity, problem of 1. change exists. All things become other than what they were. In spite of this we experience something about things that we can identify as remaining the selfsame thing. What is that enduring selfsame thing? **2.** things within a class are all different, yet something about them can be classed as being similar. There is difference yet at the same time sameness. There is sameness yet at the same time difference. What is it that is the *same* among the differences? See UNITY IN VARIETY AND VARIETY IN UNITY, PRINCIPLE OF (METAPHYSICS).

identity, theory of mind/body see MIND/BODY, IDENTITY THEORY OF.

identity in difference, principle of 1. regardless of how different things are, any thing in the universe can be said to be identical with (similar to) any other thing in at least one respect (that they exist, occupy space, exist in time, are objects of thought, etc.). **2.** no two things can be different in all respects. Compare with DIFFERENCE IN IDENTITY, PRINCIPLE OF.

identity of indiscernibles, principle of (Leibniz) sometimes called *Leibniz's Law* **1.** no two things in the universe are exactly alike in all respects. When they are looked at closely enough, some differences will always be found. Thus, no two things are indiscernible from one another. **2.** no two things can be exactly alike in every respect except numerically. (No two things can differ only numerically.) Thus, no two things are identical, since each thing in the universe possesses something that no other thing in the universe possesses. **3.** all things that differ numerically (are spatially separated) have discernible differences. All things that have discernible differences are numerically distinct.

Leibniz's metaphysical inferences from his *principle of identity of indiscernibles*: (a) If things differ only spatially, this difference indicates the necessity of a further difference within their essential being (otherwise they would be identically the selfsame nature and therefore need not be different even spatially. (b) Difference is one of the most fundamental aspects of every existing thing (as are force, activity, and a unique rate of change). (c) All properties (characteristics, attributes) of a thing are necessary, essential, and unique to that thing. (d) There are no accidental attributes of a thing; a thing is what it is because of all the attributes it possesses and would be something else if it possessed attributes different from those. See REASON, PRINCIPLE OF SUFFICIENT (LEIBNIZ).

ideology (from Greek *idéa*, idea, + *logos*, the study of, the science of) **1.** literally and as used in classical metaphysics, the science of ideas, the study of their origins. **2.** in modern usage, *ideology* has a pejorative sense, as dogmatic, visionary theorizing or speculation that is false or unrealistic. **3.** in a nonpejorative sense, any system of ideas regarding philosophic, economic, political, social beliefs and ideals.

idola see EIDOLA.

idols (Bacon) described in Francis Bacon's *Novum Organum*: the four hindrances (preconceptions, prejudices, predispositions, biases) that Bacon believed prevent the proper use of the inductive method to obtain scientific knowledge.

1. *the Idols of the Tribe:* anthropomorphic projection and wishful ways of thinking that are inherent in the very nature of all human beings, all tribes, and all races, whereby their way of viewing things is regarded as the standard by which things really are. **2.** *the Idols of the Den (Cave):* private, unique personal prejudices. **3.** *the Idols of the Market:* failure to use language correctly and to define terms precisely. **4.** *the Idols of the Theater:* the blind acceptance of tradition and authority. See BACONIAN METHOD.

ignoratio elenchi (Latin, arguing or refuting by ignoring the issues at hand) refers to any fallacy of irrelevance whereby a conclusion is proved that does not have anything to do with the question at issue and thereby in no way refutes the argument it opposes. For further discussion see FALLACY, TYPES OF INFORMAL (23).

illocutionary expression/act (illocution) (from Latin, *il,* the assimilated form of *in,* in, + *loqui,* speak, utter) sometimes shortened to *illocutionary* **1.** something that is done *in* the very (or *by* the very) utterance of some statement or by an act. Something over and above the utterance of the statement, or the act, is implied. Examples: "Where have you been all this time?" "I think that is enough." A great diversity of things are classified under illocutionary expressions/acts, such as predictions, promises, requests, orders, commands, questions, pleas, persuasions, and expressions of feeling. **2.** the act that is performed in performing a LOCUTIONARY EXPRESSION/ACT (such as the act of stating what was just stated). See PERLOCUTIONARY EXPRESSION/ACT (PERLOCUTION).

illumination (from Latin *illuminare,* enlighten) intellectual or spiritual enlightenment, usually described as a sudden flash of insight or understanding.

illusion, egocentric see EGOCENTRIC ILLUSION.

illusion, transcendental (Kant) the illusion that is a consequence of the belief that such things as the *a priori* forms of intuition and the categories of understanding are descriptions of the true nature of reality in itself, not merely ways by which our consciousness structures that unknowable reality. See IDEAL OF REASON, THE (KANT); SKEPTICISM (KANT).

image, mental (from Latin *imago,* an image, a representation) **1.** any mental occurrence, such as a conception, an idea, or a picturing of something. **2.** abstract mental pictures (representations, copies) of external objects, much as a map is a picture of an area. **3.** an imitation or representation of a mental occurrence, as of an idea, a sensation, a product of the imagination or of fancy. Compare with CONCEIVE.

imagination 1. the power (faculty) of producing images and recombining them in new combinations apart from their actual occurrence in reality. **2.** the process of reviving perceptions as images, altering them, and merging them into new patterns or unities. **3.** the ability to idealize or objectify experiences. **4.** the activity of constructing ideas (concepts, images, models) that give insight into and help explain phenomena.

The pejorative use in such phrases as "It was only a product of my imagination" implies some mental construction that is totally unreal, the formation of imagery that does not accurately or in any way represent what has taken place. None of the above definitions necessarily implies such a use, though they may imply a creative fictionalizing or reconstruction of reality.

imitation see MIMĒSIS.

immanent (from Latin *immanere,* remain in) indwelling, inherent, operating from within, being actually present in something. Opposite to TRANSCENDENT.

immaterial (from Latin *immaterialis,* not matter, not the stuff of which things are made) not consisting of matter. Synonyms: incorporeal, spiritual, nonmaterial, nonphysical. Things that have been regarded as immaterial: God, spirits, angels, the soul, daimons, ghosts, the formal cause or principle in things, the *ÉLAN VITAL,* the mind, consciousness, the will, the intellect, emotions, feelings, sensations. A few of these (such as the last nine or so) have sometimes been considered as immaterial things but also dependent on material activity of some sort for their existence or activity.

immaterialism sometimes called MENTALISM, the doctrine that **1.** matter does not exist. Only ideas (immaterial or nonmaterial entities) and the psychic sources of these ideas exist. **2.** nothing exists or can ever be known to exist except in terms of ideas and the minds having them. (It is impossible to have an idea of something existing apart from its being thought of by a mind, since only in the very act of its being thought of is it an idea.) **3.** matter without any mind qualities existing independently of a mind perceiving and bringing it into existence is a *contradiction in terms.* (It is self-contradictory to hold that the universe consists of relations and qualities that are independent of a mind.) Immaterialism is a form of idealism. See entries under IDEALISM.

immaterialism (Berkeley) 1. the objects of our perception (mind) are ideas (sensibles, sensations). **2.** ideas are mental. See IDEAS (BERKELEY). **3.** the essence of ideas is to be perceived (see *ESSE EST PERCIPI*) and to be caused by a mind. (Ideas can never exist without a mind receiving them or producing them.) **4.** what we call physical things (such as tables, marbles, grass) are orderly collections of mind-dependent ideas. (They exist insofar as they are perceived by a mind and cannot exist unless they are perceived.) **5.** like causes like. Minds (spirits) exist to cause ideas (sensations, sensibles, perceptions). Matter, being totally unlike ideas, cannot cause ideas. It is meaningless to talk about matter apart from the presence of a mind perceiving it or causing a perception of it. The word *matter* is like the word *universal*—only a name (see NOMINALISM) standing for a collection of ideas (sensible qualities). **6.** we cannot have general ideas of things in abstraction or abstracted from their particular existing qualities. For example, I cannot have an idea of *redness* but always only of a particular red object such as a red handkerchief, a red ball, a red sunset, a red patch, a red surface (so with *matter*). **7.** there is no physical (material) reality that exists behind our ideas causing them. (Both primary and secondary qualities depend on a mind.) **8.** all knowledge except that of God and of one's own existence is derived from sense perception (experience) of particular things. **9.** although we as minds (spirits) are the immediate cause of ideas produced by our imagination, God is the ultimate cause of all our ideas and sensations. **10.** physical things (matter) are really ideas in God's mind, and we perceive these ideas as tables, marbles, grass. **11.** things (ideas) we perceive are signs or symbols in God's language as God attempts to communicate with us. The universe is God's expression in a language. The order, pattern, and regularity of all things indicate this. **12.** reality and its immediately felt unity cannot be reduced to a series of mindless, discontinuous, unrelated, nonmental aggregates. See MOTION (BERKELEY).

immediacy, presentational see PRESENTMENT/PRESENTATION.

immoral (from Latin *immoralis*; from *im*, not, + *mos, moris* manner, custom, conduct) not moral; acting contrary to morality and/or conscience; not conforming to the accepted rules of right conduct; unvirtuous. Contrast with AMORAL; MORAL.

immoralist one who refuses to accept the binding conditions or claims of a moral system.

immortality (from Latin *im*, not, + *mortalitas*, mortality) **1.** the unending continued existence of a life in some form. **2.** personal survival after death; the belief that the individual in some form and in some kind of existence survives the death (dissolution, destruction, total degeneration) of his or her body. This may be thought of in terms of the REINCARNATION, TRANSMIGRATION, or METAMPSYCHOSIS of a soul or the passing of a soul into an eternal realm, such as Heaven or Hell or Nirvana. Most forms of immortality hold to the prior existence of the soul in bodies or objects.

immutable (from Latin *immutabilis*, unchangeable) **1.** absolutely unchanging; constantly the same; invariable. **2.** not capable of changing. **3.** not capable of being changed.

imperative, categorical see CATEGORICAL IMPERATIVE (KANT).

imperative, hypothetical see HYPOTHETICAL IMPERATIVE (KANT).

imperativism sometimes called *ethical imperativism*, the view that morality is directive language: a set of commands or recommendations to act or not to act in certain specified ways.

implication, logical 1. sometimes called *definitional implication*, deducibility of one statement from another. Example: "Adam is married" logically implies that Adam has a wife or that Adam is a husband. **2.** sometimes synonymous with *logical entailment*, the relationship of two statements whereby if the first is true, then the other is also necessarily true. **3.** the necessary relationship between the premises and the conclusion of a valid argument. Used in this sense it is synonymous with *logical inference.*

impossible, logically referring **1.** to that which is a self-contradiction (such as a polygon with only two corners, or a thing being wholly present in two different spaces at the same time, or **2.** to logically false statement forms (such as p and not-p). All nonself-contradictions are logically possible. Contrast with POSSIBLE/POSSIBILITY.

impression (from Latin *im*, in, on, upon, + *primere*, press, stamp) **1.** the immediate and momentary conscious effect produced by stimulation of the senses. **2.** an indistinct, general notion, remembrances, opinion, or idea.

impression (Hume) the immediate, noninferential, noninterpretive sense datum presented to consciousness, or which appears in consciousness; sensation; sense image; that direct irreducible and primitive experience on which all knowledge is based. See KNOWLEDGE (HUME).

improbabilism the theory that it is not possible for the empirical sciences to assign positive probability values to hypotheses or theories in order to show their degree of confirmation. They can show only the improbability and the falsifiability of hypotheses or theories. Compare with PROBABILISM.

inauthenticity see BAD FAITH (SARTRE).

inclination (from Latin *in*, in, + *clinare*, bend, lean) **1.** a disposition, propensity, or tendency (a) to act in a particular way or (b) to be favorable toward something. **2.** used (for example, in Kant) to refer to the sum total of personal states and tendencies, such as feelings, moods, motives, intentions, attitudes, emotions, desires, wants, and drives.

incoherence (from Latin *in*, not, + *cohaerere*, adhere together) not connected logically and/or conceptually; incongruity in thinking; inconsistency. Opposite to COHERENCE. Compare with COMPATIBLE. See INCOMPATIBLE.

incompatibilist (ethics) one who believes that determinism (which denies the existence of free will) is *not* compatible with the *facts*, or beliefs grounded in human experience, such as (free) choices, moral decisions, self-initiation, moral *oughts* and *shoulds*, responsibility, accountability, blame, praise, punishments and other concepts that imply the existence of *freedom of the will* in humans. Contrasted with COMPATIBILIST. See entries under FREE WILL.

incompatible (from Latin *in*, not, + *compati*, have compassion) **1.** not compatible; not capable of coexisting in harmony; discordant. **2.** mutually inconsistent, referring to statements that cannot be consistently related logically and/or conceptually. Opposite to COMPATIBLE. Compare with INCOHERENCE.

incompatible or inconsistent triad a set of three statements of which only two can be held as true (the third is thus falsified by their truth). Example (1) God creates all things that exist. (2) Evil exists. (3) God does not create evil. See ANTILOGISM; EVIL, THEOLOGICAL PROBLEM OF.

inconsistency, fallacy of see FALLACY, TYPES OF INFORMAL (24).

inconsistent triad see ANTILOGISM; EVIL, THE THEOLOGICAL PROBLEM OF; INCOMPATIBLE OR INCONSISTENT TRIAD.

incontinence (from Latin *in*, not, + *continere*, hold together, repress) **1.** the inability to control one's lust (base physical desires) for the attainment of more rational and higher values. **2.** the desiring and choosing of an evil in the presence of a conflict between (a) knowledge of what is good (right, correct) and (b) those uncontrolled passions (desires, appetites, cravings, drives) for something that is recognized as evil (bad, incorrect, destructive). In the context of Aristotle's philosophy, an incontinent man feels the conflict between his tendency to immoral or depraved conduct and his tendency to follow rational moral principles, and allows the base part of himself to win out; the licentious man feels no such conflict. Compare with continence, licentious. See AKRASIA.

incorporeal (from Latin *in*, not, + *corporeus*, from *corpus*, body) not corporeal; immaterial; nonmaterial; bodiless; matterless; unextended; nonspatial; having no physical dimensions; intangible. Opposite to CORPOREAL.

incorrigible (from Latin *in*, not, + *corrigere*, to correct) **1.** not capable of correction. **2.** not subject to error. **3.** that against which nothing would count as evidence. **4.** absolutely certain. Example: The assertion (claim, affirmation) *that* we are having a feeling or a thought (mental claims) is incorrigible. Opposite to CORRIGIBLE.

independence, logical see STATEMENT, LOGICALLY INDEPENDENT.

indeterminacy, principle of see UNCERTAINTY, HEISENBERG'S PRINCIPLE OF.

indeterminism (ethics) (from Latin *in*, not, + *determinare*, from *de*, from, down, away, + *terminus*, limit) sometimes referred to as LIBERTARIANISM. **1.** the theory that the mind (consciousness, self, soul, personality) is an agent free to cause effects such as moral decisions. **2.** a rational being has freedom of the will to choose without being compelled (determined) to this choice by causes independent of that act. **3.** ethical choices are not influenced, and/or not caused by antecedent events. See entries under FREE and FREEDOM.

indeterminism (metaphysics) 1. the theory that some events do not have causes. **2.** the theory that some events (a) cannot be explained by being subsumed under general, universal laws or principles, and (b) cannot be predicted, not because of our lack of knowledge but because of an inherent characteristic in the universe such as chance, randomness, uncertainty, spontaneity, novelty, or an undetermined openness for possibilities to happen in the future.

indifference, principle of (probability theory) sometimes called *principle of insufficient reason* and *principle of nonsufficient reason*. If there are X possibilities for combinations (events) to occur, and no reason can be given why one should be more likely to occur than another, then the probability of each combination occurring is $1/X$. Example: If this principle is assumed, in craps, the probability of throwing double-six would be calculated at $1/36$ since there are 36 ways in which two dice can fall and only one is favorable for that double-six occurrence (based on the assumption that no reason can be given why any particular one of the 36 possibilities is any more likely than any other to occur). Also referred to as the principle of *nonsufficient reason*. See REASON, PRINCIPLE OF NONSUFFICIENT. Compare with REASON, PRINCIPLE OF SUFFICIENT.

indiscernible not recognized in any way as being different; recognized as being exactly alike. See IDENTITY OF INDISCERNIBLES, PRINCIPLE OF (LEIBNIZ).

individual (from Latin *individuus,* indivisible) **1.** an entity; existing as a distinct unity (unit) incapable of being divided actually or conceptually without losing its identity. **2.** a PARTICULAR. Opposite to general, UNIVERSAL. **3.** a single thing. **4.** PERSON; SELF; EGO.

individualism (political theory) 1. the theory that the principal concern of all political and social groupings is to preserve the rights, guarantee the independence, and enhance the development of the individual person. The state is a means used by individuals in the attainment of these goals and is never an end in itself. Society exists for the sake of its individual members. **2.** government must never interfere with the individual's pursuit of his or her wishes unless this can be shown to produce harm to other individuals. The best form of government is the least amount of government. **3.** all government must stem from the self-directing and self-regulating powers of individuals and must not be imposed by regulations and external coercion.

individuate 1. to discriminate (distinguish, identify, single out) from among others of a class or species. **2.** to give something individuality or a particular character.

individuation (metaphysics) 1. development of a particular (individual) thing from its corresponding universal or form. **2.** determination of the particular (individual) from its universal or general type. The *principle of individuation* refers to the cause (such as matter, or form, or God) of 1 or 2.

indubitable (from Latin *in,* not, + *dubitare,* waver in opinion, be undecided, hesitate in belief) **1.** referring to that which cannot be doubted because there are no reasons that can be found to doubt it. **2.** not doubtful in any way. **3.** unquestionably true; absolutely certain; incontrovertible; undeniable; irrefragable; sure beyond a doubt. *Indubitable* and INCORRIGIBLE are sometimes used synonymously. See CERTAIN.

An *indubitable statement* is one that cannot be doubted (rejected, disbelieved). Examples: "I exist," "I am now thinking."

induction (from Latin *in,* into, + *ducere,* lead) sometimes called *inductive reasoning, inductive generalization, empirical generalization,* or *enumerative induction* **1.** reasoning from a part to a whole, from particular instances of something to a general statement about them, from individuals to universals. **2.** reaching a conclusion about all (or many) members of a class from statements describing only some of them. Example: "All observed X's have had the characteristic Y; therefore, all X's are Y's." It is often believed that in this procedure the probability of the truth of the generalization is increased by each instance that verifies it. **3.** a form of nondeductive inference in which the conclusion expresses something that goes beyond what is said in the premises; the conclusion does not follow with logical necessity from the premises. Contrast with DEDUCTION.

induction, ampliative reasoning from a limited number of observed instances to a general causal relationship.

induction, eliminative the process of supporting or confirming a statement or hypothesis by falsifying those competing with it. An indirect method of CONFIRMATION.

induction, intuitive the view that we can experience necessary truths about the world, that something is essentially of a certain and necessary pattern and existence. Experience can show us what physically *must* happen. All necessity is not logical necessity. See UNIVERSALS (ARISTOTLE).

induction, intuitive (Aristotle) see UNIVERSALS (ARISTOTLE).

induction, perfect also called *formal induction* or *induction by complete enumeration*, stating a truth about all members of a class on the basis of having observed that truth in every member of that class. (In Aristotle, perfect induction is the process of arriving at a *genus* from examination of all its *species*.)

induction, principle of (metaphysics) the belief that things that have happened regularly in the past will continue to happen in the future. The future will resemble the past. Compare with UNIFORMITY OF NATURE, PRINCIPLE OF THE.

induction, problem of the problem of inferring a true statement about all members of a class on the basis of observing only some members of that class. Example: The truth of the statement "All crows are black" is based (a) on our seeing a great number of black crows, and (b) also on our not having seen any crows of another color. How is one logically justified in proceeding from *some* to *all*, since not all crows have been observed?

inductive methods, Mill's see METHODS, MILL'S INDUCTIVE.

ineffable 1. incapable of being expressed or communicated; unutterable; indescribable. **2.** that about which nothing at all can be said (such as God or reality in itself) due (a) to its inconceivability by the finite mind and/or (b) to its existing permanently outside the realm of human consciousness.

inert (from Latin *inertis*, unskilled, idle) **1.** unable to move itself (as in the phrase *inert matter*). **2.** unable, actively and on its own, to resist motion from being impressed on it. **3.** not having its own active powers. **4.** powerless; not being able to produce the expected or required effect. **5.** idle; not active (as in the phrase *inert personality*). **6.** the inherent or habitual indisposition of activity.

inertia, principle of (Newton) Newton's First Law of Motion. See MOTION, NEWTON'S THREE LAWS OF.

in esse (Latin, in being, in existence, actually existing).

in facto (Latin, in deed) in final, complete form. Example: A house is *in facto* when it has been completed and ready for habitation. Compare with IN INTELLECTU.

inference (from Latin *in*, in, + *ferre*, bring) **1.** the logical or conceptual process of deriving a statement from one or more statements. **2.** a CONCLUSION reached. **3.** DEDUCTION; deriving a conclusion from premises that are accepted as true. **4.** INDUCTION; deriving a conclusion from factual statements taken as evidence for the conclusion. See EDUCTION.

inference, invalid see INVALID.

inference, valid see VALID.

inference (deductive logic) 1. the procedure by which a statement is affirmed or denied on the basis of other statements that are accepted as true or false. This aspect of deductive logic is concerned (a) with the possible true/false relationships of statements for which a true or false claim is made: (b) in the context of the truth values of the logical connectives by which they are related. The interest is not in whether statements are in fact true or false, but whether, if they are claimed as true (or false), then how their true-false combinations can be related to other statements in true-false combinations. **2.** the procedure of establishing the validity of a conclusion from premises accepted as true by the use of principles of inference. Compare JUSTIFICATION; PROOF.

in fieri (Latin, in the process of becoming) in the act of beginning to be what it will be when completed. Example: A house is *in fieri* during the time it is being worked on by the builders.

infinite (from Latin *in* not, + *finire,* finish, limit, end, complete) **1.** unlimited; inexhaustible; endless. **2.** having no boundary; indefinitely large. Opposite to FINITE.

infinite, actual/potential (Aristotle) Aristotle denied (a) that there can be any physical object that can be divided indefinitely; (b) that there is any physical object infinite in number; and (c) that there is any physical object infinite in extent. He denied Zeno's notion that a line segment can actually be divided into an infinite number of indivisible units or unextended points. Aristotle believed that this could be done only theoretically or *potentially*. There is no actual infinite class; the members of a class may be increased without limit, but the class never reaches a completed totality (and in this sense there are classes that are *potentially infinite*). Many finite things are potentially infinite in that they will appear again and again without end (and have appeared without a beginning point).

infinite, the actual the infinite considered as a whole.

infinitesimal immeasurably and/or incalculably small; indefinitely small.

informal fallacies see entries under FALLACY.

ingression (from Latin *ingredi,* enter into) **1.** the coming together of potential occurrences, thereby creating existing complexes. **2.** the developing together, or growing together, of diverse things, thereby creating concrete wholes. *Ingression* is a term used by Alfred North Whitehead and by process philosophers. See PROCESS PHILOSOPHY.

in intellectu (Latin, existing in the intellect, or existing in the mind) referring to a thing's existing as an abstract idea or concept but without excluding the possibility that it also exists in reality. Compare with IN FACTO.

innate ideas see IDEAS, INNATE.

inner sense see SENSE, INTERNAL.

in res sometimes given as *in re* (Latin, existing in reality, existing in an actual material way or thing, existing in the external world even apart from any consciousness of it) used by medieval philosophers in the context of an Aristotelian realism (see REALISM, ARISTOTELIAN) whereby universals were regarded as existing *in things, in reality*, not in an ideal world of forms prior to reality (see REALISM, PLATONIC) and not only as names for similarities (see NOMINALISM, *ANTE RES, POST RES*).

in se (Latin, in itself) when applied to God (or substance, or ultimate being, or the universe), referring to an eternal, self-subsisting ultimate being in which all things are found. Compare with *A SE*.

instinct (from Latin *instinguere,* incite, instigate) **1.** an unlearned, natural impulse to act in a certain way. **2.** an involuntary, unreasoned, inherited tendency to act or to perform a specific action under the proper internal and external stimuli. **3.** predilection; a natural (innate, spontaneous) and/or ingrained aptitude or knack for doing something.

instrumentalism sometimes called *experimentalism,* the philosophic position that ideas (laws, theories, hypotheses, etc.) are tools (instruments, devices, means) by which certain conceptual manipulations and calculations can take place in resolving the puzzles in life and scientific inquiry. Ideas are used to control, predict, explain, organize, and create possibilities for human experience. Whether ideas are true or false is not a serious question; rather, one may seriously consider whether ideas are useful or powerful enough to explain and cause change and satisfy human needs and purposes. Thinking is to be judged according to its success in helping an organism adjust and thus survive socially and environmentally. *Instrumentalism* is associated with the philosophy of John Dewey and has affinities with CONVENTIONALISM; PRAGMATISM; and OPERATIONALISM. *Experimentalism* is the *term* Dewey preferred and used.

insufficient reason, principle of see INDIFFERENCE, PRINCIPLE OF (PROBABILITY THEORY).

intellect (from Latin *intelligere,* understand; from *inter,* between, + *legere,* collect, choose) **1.** the cognitive faculty; the faculty of knowing (as opposed in FACULTY PSYCHOLOGY to the faculty of willing and the faculty of feeling). **2.** the function of reason that makes ideas (concepts, abstractions) possible. **3.** the ability (or capability or power) (a) to know, to conceptually understand, and (b) to relate that which is known or understood. See FACULTY and entries under REASON.

intellect, active/passive see REASON, ACTIVE/PASSIVE (ARISTOTLE).

intellectual virtues see VIRTUES, DIANOETIC (ARISTOTLE).

intellectus see RATIO.

intellectus agens (Latin, the active intellect) the intellect as an agent affecting sensations (or phantasms) and perceptions and making them abstract so that they can be handled and known as universals.

intellectus possibilis (Latin, the possible intellect) the passive intellect (as opposed to the active intellect) whereby concepts (ideas, universals) are received (or developed or recognized) from the abstraction presented by the active intellect.

intelligence 1. the activity of an organism in adjusting to situations by the use of combinations of functions such as perception, memory, conceptualizing, abstracting, imagining, attending, concentrating, selecting, relating, planning, extrapolating, predicting, controlling, choosing, and directing. Contrasted with instinct, habit, rote, custom, and tradition. **2.** the process of coping with problems (issues, perplexities) by means of abstract thinking. Higher levels of intelligence contain elements such as (a) symbolization and communication of abstract thinking, (b) its critical analysis, and (c) its reconstruction to apply to further possibilities and/or to related situations, either practical or theoretical.

intension 1. the way in which something is intended to be understood. **2.** the way in which something is understood. (Compare with COMPREHENSION.) **3.** sometimes used synonymously with CONNOTATION. See LAW OF INVERSE VARIATION (INTENSION/EXTENSION); MEANING, INTENSIONAL. Compare with EXTENSION.

intent (from Latin *intendere*, intend, attend; from *in*, in, + *tendere*, stretch) **1.** the meaning (import, purpose, motive) of a thing. **2.** the directional activity (plan, design) toward purposely accomplishing something. **3.** being disposed to act in a certain way toward a specific object in order to achieve some desired result.

intention 1. meaning; import. **2.** PURPOSE; design. See INTENT. **3.** a predisposition to act to change something. **4.** a tendency to perform a specific act in order to attain some END.

intentionalism the view that the essential and defining characteristics of consciousness are (a) that it is able to have (understand) meanings (INTENSION) and (b) that it is able to direct itself conatively by intending.

intentionality 1. the ability of consciousness to (a) create a mental object that need not exist in the external world, (b) refer (apply) its content to reality, and (c) direct activity toward results. **2.** the ability of consciousness to refer to something that is not like itself or that is not like its own activity. **3.** the condition in which something directs, points to, or refers to something beyond itself.

In phenomenology, the *thesis of intentionality* (or *intentionality thesis*) refers to the belief that every act of consciousness possesses the above-listed qualities—all consciousness is consciousness of objects. The act of consciousness is called the *intentional act*, and the object is called the *intentional object*. Brentano and Husserl are the leading exponents of this view.

interactionism, mind/body see MIND/BODY INTERACTIONISM.

interjections, pure words such as "Ugh!" "Terrific!" "Out of sight!" "Hi!" and "Alas!" Usually these words do not call up specific objects or images in the listener. See LANGUAGE, FUNCTIONS OF (10).

internal (from Latin *internus,* inward) **1.** inherent; intrinsic. **2.** that which is within consciousness as opposed to that which is external to consciousness. **3.** the inner or essential nature of a thing such as its qualities or characteristics. **4.** (a) the activity (or relationships) of the parts within a whole and/or (b) that which is contained within a whole.

internal relations, doctrine of see RELATIONS, DOCTRINE OF INTERNAL.

intrinsic (from Latin *intrinsecus,* inward) **1.** inherent; in and of itself. **2.** essential. **3.** internal. Opposite to EXTRINSIC.

introjection (from Latin *intro,* inwardly, + *jacere,* throw) **1.** the process whereby external objects are internalized as representational images of reality. **2.** the theory that the mind is composed of a complex of ideas (images, concepts) that have been internalized, and that the mind knows the external world by projecting this internal complex upon the world.

introspection (from Latin *intro,* inward, within, into, + *specere,* look) **1.** looking into—giving mental attention to—one's mind, self, or consciousness. **2.** examining (observing) one's mental states and functions in an attempt to describe, study, or enjoy them. When introspection attends to previous happenings as opposed to immediately occurring mental states, it is called RETROSPECTION. Compare with REFLECTION (LOCKE). See EGO OF INTROSPECTION, THE.

intuition (from Latin *intueri,* look on) **1.** immediate noninferential apprehension or cognition of something. **2.** the power (ability) to have immediate, direct knowledge of something without the use of reason. **3.** innate, instinctive knowledge or insight without the use of our sense organs, ordinary experience, or reason.

Intuition has been regarded as a true and certain source of knowledge, and as the only source of knowledge of some realms of being such as of the ideal forms, of God, or of the essences of things.

intuition (Kant) in general, the process of sensing, or the act of having a sensation. See SENSIBILITY (KANT). Intuitions are of two kinds: **1.** *empirical (a posteriori)* intuition of things by means of our sense organs; **2.** *pure* or *formal (a priori)* intuition, which structures what is given by the empirical intuition into sensations that have the quality of being in space and time. *Anschauung* is the German word for intuition, used by Kant, and has the connotations of *insight; perception; that which is directly and immediately provided to and organized by the mind.* See KNOWLEDGE (KANT).

intuitionism (ethics) see ETHICS, INTUITIVE.

invalid (from Latin *invalidus,* not strong, inadequate) referring to a deductive argument that is not valid: The conclusion does not necessarily and with certainty follow from the premises. The premises do not establish undeniable logical support for the conclusion. It is possible for the premises to be true, yet the conclusion be false. Denial of the conclusion leads to no contradiction about what is claimed in the premises. Contrast with VALID.

INVERSE VARIATION, LAW OF (INTENSION/EXTENSION)

inverse variation, law of (intension/extension) see LAW OF INVERSE VARIATION (INTENSION/EXTENSION).

involuntary act see VOLUNTARY ACTION; VOLUNTARY-INVOLUNTARY ACTIONS.

ipso facto (Latin, in accordance with fact itself).

irrational (from Latin *ir,* the assimilated form of *in,* not, + *rationalis, ratio,* reason) **1.** not in accordance with, or contrary to, reason; absurd; foolish; nonsensical. **2.** not endowed with reason (rational powers, rational faculty). **3.** not exercising reason or rational judgment; not acting rationally. **4.** chaotic; inexpressible as a sensible order or arrangement. **5.** having no realistic or rational foundation (ground or explanation).

"is" useful in a number of ways: **1.** to relate things such as a subject and its predicate (as in "The rose is red"); **2.** to point things out (as in "This is a sparrow"); **3.** to classify or put into a list (as in "A whale is a mammal, and a snake is a reptile"); **4.** to provide identification for something (as in "He is a police officer"); **5.** to identify (as in "This is Mary Nagelmann"); **6.** to establish a meaning (or definition) relation (as in "A bachelor is an unmarried man"); **7.** to show an identity relation (as in "Lauri is Lauri" or "The Bard is Shakespeare"); **8.** to refer to what a thing is made up of (as in "This is butter, chocolate, and sugar"); **9.** to express a tenseless meaning or sense (as in "The sum of four plus four is eight"); **10.** to refer to something in a present sense (as in "He is breaking up the porch"); **11.** to refer to a past condition (as in "What Aristotle believed about substance is the backbone of his entire philosophy"); **12.** to refer to the future (as in "It is going to be a terrible sight").

"is" of formal equivalence the identity of meanings or truth-values related by the word *is,* as in "Lightning *is* an electric discharge between clouds or a cloud and an object on earth."

"is" of identity 1. numerical identity; a relationship of selfsameness or one-and-the-same thing, as in "This marble is this marble," "I am that which I am," "That (moon) is the moon," "The USSR was the Union of Soviet Sociaist Republics." **2.** isomorphic identity; a relationship of things being *exactly the same* in every respect (except spatio-temporally), such as in "Marble *x* is identical to marble *y.*" Or in a weaker form: "Jane is the identical image of her twin sister Beth."

"is" of predication sometimes referred to as the *copulative is,* identifying (applying, referring, relating) a quality (predicate, characteristic, attribute) to a subject, as in "The grass *is* green," "Water *is* a liquid," "School *is* a bore."

isomorphism (from Greek *isos,* equal, + *morphe,* form) **1.** likeness of form (pattern, order, structure); structural similarity. **2.** the one-to-one correspondence of similarity between the structure of one thing and that of another. That which establishes the identity relationship among things.

is/ought dichotomy also called *fact/value dichotomy.* Statements containing the verb *is* are related to descriptive or factual claims and are of a dif-

150

ferent order from those containing the verb *ought* or *should*, which are related to judgments, evaluations, or commands. It is impossible (logically, formally, conceptually) to derive an *ought* or *should* statement from an *is* (factual) statement, a NORMATIVE statement from a statement of facts; it is impossible to have a valid deductive argument in which the premises state descriptions and the conclusion states prescriptions or imperatives. See ETHICS, IS/OUGHT DICHOTOMY IN.

J

James, William (1842–1910) American philosopher and psychologist born in New York City, brother of novelist Henry James. Educated at Harvard and Harvard Medical College. He taught physiology, psychology, and philosophy at Harvard.

His 2-volume *The Principles of Psychology* (1878) was the first of his many important works. It was followed by *The Will to Believe and Other Essays in Popular Philosophy* (1897); *Human Immortality* (1898); *The Varieties of Religious Experience* (1902); *Pragmatism: A New Name for Some Old Ways of Thinking* (1907); *A Pluralistic Universe* (1909); *The Meaning of Truth: A Sequel to "Pragmatism"*(1909); *Some Problems of Philosophy: A Beginning of an Introduction to Philosophy* (1911); and *Essays in Radical Empiricism* (1912).

Jaspers, Karl Theodor (1883–1969) Swiss philosopher, psychiatrist, existentialist, phenomenologist; born in Oldenburg, Germany; educated at the universities of Heidelberg, Munich, Berlin, and Göttingen. Some of Jaspers' main concepts deal with the phenomenological description of the inner self; the boundaries and indefiniteness of consciousness, space, and time; the act of self-analysis and self-examination; the uniqueness, freedom, and ineffability of every human existence; the confronting of one's personal existence to others; the intentional and conative characteristic of all consciousness and thought; and the awareness of the religious aspects and the spirituality of existence in its intuitive and nonrational forms.

Jaspers was a prolific writer, but much of his work has not been translated into English. The important translations include *Man in the Modern Age* (1933); *The Question of German Guilt* (1947); *The Perennial Scope of Philosophy* (1949); *The Way to Wisdom* (1951); *Reason and Anti-Reason in Our Time* (1952); *Tragedy Is Not Enough* (1952); *The Origin and Goal of History* (1953); *Reason and Existence* (1955); *Myth and Christianity* (1958); *The Idea of the University* (1959); *Truth and Symbol* (1959); *Nietzsche and Christianity* (1961); *The Future of Mankind* (1961); *The Great Philosophers* (1962); *General Psychopathology* (1963); and *Nietzsche* (1965).

joint method of agreement and difference see METHOD, MILL'S INDUCTIVE.

judgment (from Latin *jus,* law) **1.** that deliberate function of consciousness involving such activities as identifying, comparing, discriminating, and evaluating whereby values and/or knowledge are asserted or interpreted. **2.** good sense; the power (ability, faculty) of judging wisely or correctly. **3.** decision; the result of an appraisal that results in an opinion or decree.

4. the assertion (or denial) of something. (In traditional categorical logic, the asserting or denying a predicate of some subject.) **5.** JUSTIFICATION; the process by which the truth or falsity of statements is determined. **6.** the process of forming or the state of a belief, opinion, assertion, conclusion. Used interchangeably with words such as knowledge, statement, proposition, concept, evaluation, decision.

judgment, analytic (Kant) knowledge in which what is thought (said, meant) in its predicate has already been thought in its subject. Examples: "Matter occupies space and exists in time." "A thing cannot be both true and false at the same time in the same respect." All analytic judgments are necessarily true or necessarily false. Contrast with JUDGMENT, SYNTHETIC (KANT).

judgment, *a priori* (Kant) knowledge that is necessary, universal, transcendental to experience, not derived from experience yet applicable to all experiences. Examples: "Every cause is followed by an effect." "There are no uncaused events."

judgment, logical (Kant) see CATEGORIES OF LOGIC, THE (KANT).

judgment, synthetic (Kant) knowledge in which what is thought in its predicate has not been thought in its subject. Examples: "Bananas are green and then turn yellow." "Lead is heavy." Contrast with JUDGMENT, ANALYTIC (KANT).

judgment, synthetic *a priori* (Kant) see KNOWLEDGE, SYNTHETIC *A PRIORI* (KANT).

jus naturalis (Latin, natural law) also given as *jus naturale* and *jus naturae*, law of nature. *Jus* is also found as *ius*.

justice (from Latin *justus*, just, or *justitia*, justice) **1.** fairness; equitableness. **2.** correct treatment; merited reward or punishment. **3.** rectitude; correctness and impartiality in the application of principles of rightness and of sound judgment. **4.** the embodiment of the virtues (ideals, values, principles) of a society. **5.** the establishment of a harmony between one's rights and the rights of others (society, the public, government, or individuals). See VIRTUES, CARDINAL.

justice (Plato) see DIKAIOSYNĒ (PLATO).

justice, commutative (Aristotle) acceptable and uncoerced exchange of goods (values, benefits) as contrasted with undesired and excessive manipulation, profiteering, exploitation.

justice, corrective/rehabilitative justice whose aim, for example, is not punishment for the sake of punishment or for revenge, but for the purpose of changing the character and the environment of the offender so that similar actions by that offender will not occur again.

justice, distributive proportionate or equal distribution; EGALITARIANISM. Allocating fairly to members of a community such things as money, property, privileges, opportunities, education, rights.

justice, distributive (Aristotle) that proper proportion determined objectively by reason, such as between a person's actions and their reward, and between a person's status (abilities, performance) and its compensation.

justice, retributive sometimes called *retaliative* or *retaliatory justice*, justice whose principal aim is revenge and/or vindictiveness as sometimes interpreted as being indicated by the statement "An eye for an eye and a tooth for a tooth."

justification 1. defense; that which is offered as sufficient grounds for an assertion (claim, statement, conclusion) or for one's conduct. **2.** logical proof; in logic, the procedures applied to the premises of an argument that show the proof for the conclusion. Compare with EXPLANATION; PROOF.

K

kakos (Greek, bad, mean, ugly—when applied to persons and when opposed to KALOS; when opposed to AGATHOS, ill-born, ignoble, of mean disposition or temper) *kakos* has a variety of further meanings and interpretations such as: evil, worthless, poor, something to be pitied, wicked, baneful, unlucky. The neuter form *kakon* translates as *evil*.

kalos (Greek, beautiful in outward appearance or in form; excellent) the neuter form *kalon* translates as *moral beauty, virtue, virtuous, excellence*. See AGATHOS.

Kant, Immanuel (1724–1804) German philosopher born in Königsberg. At age 10 he entered the Collegium Fredericianum with the intention of studying theology—he was brought up a Pietist. By the time he entered Könisberg University, in 1740, he had developed a strong interest in mathematics, physical geography, physics, logic, and metaphysics. Later, he taught at the university and in 1770 was appointed to a professorship in logic and metaphysics.

His works prior to 1760 were in the natural sciences, ranging through physical geography, biology, physics, and astronomy. (To Kant, and independently to Laplace, is attributed the *nebular hypothesis* as the origin of the universe.)

Kant's first major philosophic work was his *Critique of Pure Reason* (1781). It was followed by *Prolegomena to Every Future Metaphysics* (1783), basically an attempt to explain in simpler terms the intent and content of *Critique of Pure Reason*. By 1790, Kant's *Critique of Practical Reason* and *Critique of Judgment* had followed. In 1785, *Fundamental Principles of the Metaphysics of Morals* was published, and in 1793, *Religion within the Limits of Reason Alone*.

katharsis (from Greek *katharsis*, a cleansing from guilt or defilement, purification, PURGATION) also transliterated *catharsis*. **1.** the purification, or cleansing, or purgation of emotions by means of the aesthetic experience. **2.** the elimination, sublimation, or transformation of one's emotions, especially destructive emotions.

katharsis (Aristotle) in the *Poetics*, Aristotle used tragedy as an example of katharsis whereby feelings such as pity and fear are gotten rid of (purged) or cleansed (purified) by a vicarious experience of the feelings in a controlled form (the tragedy) and setting (the theater). The emotion of pity is produced when we see an excellence destroyed; when we see a person of noble stature, great promise, and strong character fall from a state of happiness and fortune to a state of unhappiness and misfortune. The feeling of fear is aroused when we recognize that a similar downfall may take place in our own lives. See TRAGEDY (ARISTOTLE).

kathēkon (Greek, duty, that which is fit or proper or one's due) used by the Stoics to refer to that which is the best course of action in accordance with the rational necessity inherent in nature. See STOICS, THE.

kathenotheism see GOD CONCEPTS.

kind 1. a natural CLASS; a group or division whose members have many natural qualities or functions in common, some of which are regarded as the defining characteristic of the class. **2.** a class; that classification which designates a common characteristic among its members, distinguishing those members from other things. Sometimes used synonymously with *species, genus,* a collection, a grouping, a set.

Kierkegaard, Sören Aaby (1813–1855) Danish philosopher and religious writer born in Copenhagen and educated at the University of Copenhagen. After becoming a Lutheran pastor, he developed an antipathy to the Danish Lutheran Church.

He drew a sharp distinction between personal Christian faith and the conformity required to carry out the established Church's needs. Kierkegaard's emphasis in religion was psychological, ethical, and aesthetic—the confronting of emotions such as despair, fear, dread, anxiety, loneliness, and choices—not speculative, dogmatic, or theological. His philosophy was a reaction specifically to Hegelianism and was based on a dualism of thought and reality, faith and knowledge, God and the individual, subjectivity and objectivity, personal truth and institutional truth.

Kierkegaard published his works under pseudonyms. The following are a few of his main publications that have been translated into English: *Philosophical Fragments* (1936); *The Journals of Sören Kierkegaard: A Selection* (1938); *Christian Discourses* (1939); *The Present Age* (1940); *Stages on Life's Way* (1940); *Either/Or* (2 volumes, 1941, 1944); *Fear and Trembling* (1941); *The Concept of Dread* (1944); and *The Attack Upon "Christendom"* (1944).

kinēsis (Greek, change, motion, movement, activity, process, development, any kind of disturbance, dance; from *kinein,* move) in general referring to any kind of change: spatial, temporal, qualitative, biological (such as growth, decay), etc. See CHANGE (ARISTOTLE).

knowledge 1. recognition of something. **2.** familiarity or acquaintance with something from actual experience. **3.** that which is learned. **4.** clear perception of what is regarded as fact, truth, or duty. **5.** information and/or learning that is preserved and continued by civilizations. **6.** things held in CONSCIOUSNESS (beliefs, ideas, facts, images, concepts, notions, opinions) that become justified in some way and thereby are regarded as true.

knowledge (Aristotle) 1. knowledge may be divided into three parts: (a) *theoretical*, knowledge pursued for its own sake as in the study of metaphysics (FIRST PHILOSOPHY), physics, and mathematics; (b) *practical*, knowledge pursued for the sake of actions as in the study of ethics and politics. See *PRAXIS*; (c) *productive*, knowledge pursued in order to make, produce, or create something, as in the study of architecture, engineering, the crafts. See *POIESIS/POIETIKOS* (ARISTOTLE). **2.** only knowledge of the form in things can be directly known by reason (the intellect). Matter that is imbued with form is not as such an object of direct intellectual apprehension. Knowledge is based on a process of uninferred experience or perception (intuitive induction) that grasps the necessary connections among the forms in the particular things experienced. This process provides the self-evident axioms, or first principles, for demonstrative knowledge; the organized deductive system called *science*.

knowledge (Descartes) knowledge (a) must be certain; (b) must be objectively real; and (c) must be necessary, impossible to doubt (if denied, a contradiction ensues). Knowledge is possible only on the condition that there is something (or that there are some things) about which we can never be wrong. All knowledge is derived by a deductive process similar to that in axiomatic geometry from this primitive and absolutely infallible truth. See METHOD (DESCARTES); SUBSTANCE (DESCARTES).

knowledge (Hume) all knowledge comes from **1.** *impressions*, the immediate, sensory, perceptual content of consciousness and **2.** *ideas*, the vague copies of these impressions that linger as content in our memory and imagination. Ideas may be divided into (a) *simple ideas*, every simple idea is a copy of a corresponding impression; and (b) *complex ideas*, simple ideas that are recombined and reorganized into new combinations (for example, ideas of a unicorn or of a human). There are two kinds of relationships among ideas: (1) relations that depend completely on the ideas that are related, such as the necessary truths of logic and mathematics, which when denied involve one in a contradiction, and (2) relations that can be changed without contradiction, and without changing the ideas themselves, such as matters of observed fact or descriptions of actual connections. The first may be called *ideas of reflection* and the second *ideas of sensation*. See IDEAS (HUME); IMPRESSION (HUME); SKEPTICISM (HUME).

knowledge (Kant) all knowledge is related to experience, but not all knowledge is derived from experience. That which is experienced must conform to fundamental structures of thought if it is to be intelligible. (Or, knowledge *is* the conformity of that which we experience with certain fundamental structurings of thought.) *A PRIORI* knowledge makes experience intelligible; it provides the structures with which experiencing must be organized if it is to be objectively real and not merely a product of fancy or imagination. See entries under JUDGMENT with reference to Kant. Also KNOWLEDGE, SYNTHETIC *A PRIORI* (KANT); KNOWLEDGE, TRANSCENDENTAL (KANT); SKEPTICISM (KANT).

knowledge (Locke) all knowledge is the perception of simple and complex ideas and of their relationships (such as of agreement/disagreement, affinity/disaffinity, similarity/dissimilarity). There are three kinds of knowledge:

intuitive, examples: knowledge of our own existence; knowledge that we think; knowledge that a sound is not a color. See INTUITION (LOCKE). *demonstrative*, examples: knowledge of God's existence; knowledge of moral principles; knowledge of mathematics. *sensitive*, examples: knowledge of the existence of specific, particular things external to us. The first two are certain, indubitable kinds of knowledge. See IDEAS (LOCKE); SKEPTICISM (LOCKE).

knowledge (Mill) inductive inference is the major source (if not the only source) of knowledge. See METHODS, MILL'S INDUCTIVE. Mathematical inference itself is based on induction. Abstract thinking such as mathematics is composed of very highly confirmed generalizations based on (or derived from) experience. Mill's theory of knowledge is a form of PHENOMENALISM, whose central theme is that matter is the permanent possibility of sensation and that things (objects) must be considered as phenomenal existents.

knowledge (Plato) there are two general realms of knowledge: **1.** the non-natural realm of eternal ideal forms (ideas) that are transcendent, unchanging, perfect, intelligible with certainty; **2.** the natural realm of ordinary sensations and particular things that are temporal, changing, unstable, unintelligible, and uncertain.

The first is the realm of *true*, being grasped by the intellect. The second is the realm of *becoming*, grasped by our fallible senses. The everyday world of our senses does not give us knowledge, since sense knowledge is erring, uncertain, fallible, imperfect, illusory, changing, imprecise, relative. Knowledge to be true knowledge must be unerring, certain, infallible, perfect, precise, absolute. True knowledge, as opposed to the illusory knowledge of the senses, is derived from an awareness of the eternal forms. See FORMS, PLATO'S THEORY OF IDEAL.

knowledge, analytic see JUDGMENT, ANALYTIC.

knowledge, *a posteriori* knowledge derived from sense experience. To know something *a posteriori* is to know it by experiencing it by one's senses as an aspect of the world, as something existing and found in reality. In principle, the truth or falsity of *a posteriori* knowledge can be checked against sense experience. Since sense experience is relative, inconsistent, variable, and thus not fully reliable, however, *a posteriori* knowledge is not regarded as necessary or certain knowledge; it is rather probable knowledge that can be denied without pain of contradiction. (This is in opposition to *a priori* knowledge, which is regarded as certain knowledge based on reason alone and which cannot be denied without contradiction.) *A posteriori* knowledge is not true in all possible worlds but is true under specific conditions of existence, that is, at particular times and places and for particular types of experiences. *A posteriori* truths are called *truths of fact* or *sense experiences* (as opposed to the *a priori truths of reason*) and are based on the veracity of our experiences of the world around us. Example:

Adam has brown eyes. See *A POSTERIORI*. Compare with CONTINGENT; EMPIRICAL; PROBABLE; INDUCTION. Contrast with *A PRIORI*; CERTAINTY; DEDUCTION; NECESSARY; TAUTOLOGY.

knowledge, *a priori* 1. knowledge derived from the function of reason without reference to sense experience. Nonempirical knowledge. To know something *a priori* is to know it prior to experiencing anything like it in the external world. The truth of *a priori* knowledge (a) is not derived from sense experience, (b) cannot be checked against sense experience, and (c) cannot be refuted by any sense experience. It is regarded as certain knowledge which if denied leads to a contradiction. (This is opposite to *a posteriori* knowledge, which is probable knowledge whose truth is based on sense experience and which can be denied without contradiction.) Since *a priori* knowledge cannot be invalidated, it is true under all conditions and at any time and place: that is, it is true in all possible worlds. *A priori* truths are called *truths of reason* (as opposed to *a posteriori truths of fact* or *sense experience*). *A priori* truths may be regarded as expressing the definitional relationships among ideas (concepts, meanings) such as those found in formal logic and in mathematics. They are truths based on definitionally identical (synonymous, equivalent) statements, which may be correctly substituted for each other. The truth of an *a priori* statement can thus be ascertained by examining the statement itself (or it can be logically deduced from such statements). The statement is true in itself because of its own inherent meanings. Example: All triangles have 180°. **2.** knowledge that is necessary, universal, transcendental to experience, not derived from experience yet applicable to all experiences (Kant's *a priori* judgments). Examples: "There are no uncaused events." "Every cause is followed by an effect." **3.** used synonymously with *self-evident*: innate knowledge, which is not derived from sense experience but which is imposed on reality (such as the categories of understanding) so that reality can be organized and thereby understood and coped with. **4.** sometimes used in the context of innate, self-evident moral truths such as "Killing is wrong." See *A PRIORI*. Compare with CERTAINTY; DEDUCTION; NECESSARY; TAUTOLOGY. Contrast with CONTINGENT; EMPIRICAL; INDUCTION; PROBABLE.

knowledge, explicative see EXPLICATION.

knowledge, private see PRIVACY, EPISTEMIC.

knowledge, public see PUBLICITY, EPISTEMIC.

knowledge, synthetic see JUDGMENT, SYNTHETIC (KANT).

knowledge, synthetic *a priori* (Kant) also *synthetic a priori judgment*. Knowledge (a) that is prior to the experiencing of something, (b) by which that experience is structured and made possible, and (c) into which all experiences can be structured. Examples: "Every event has a cause." "Every cause has an effect." Such statements are not true because of the meanings of the words that are being related (see TAUTOLOGY); they are not true on the grounds of their logical form alone; they are not true because we experience them as true. They are known to be true independently of all empirical evidence. The knowledge contained in such statements is informative but nonempirical, necessary but not tautological (not analytic, not purely definitionally true—its denial does not produce a contradiction according to Kant). Synthetic *a priori* knowledge is found in the physical sciences and in mathematics. See entries under JUDGMENT with reference to Kant. See also REASON (KANT).

knowledge, theory of see EPISTEMOLOGY.

knowledge, transcendental (Kant) 1. the knowledge of those conditions (categories, forms, structures) that make conscious experience possible. For Kant, knowledge of a reality transcending our experience is impossible (see SKEPTICISM (KANT), but transcendental knowledge *is* possible. **2.** that *in* experience, or that *about* experience, which can be ascertained *a priori*. Transcendental knowledge transcends empirical knowledge, but it does not transcend all human knowledge or human experience: that is, it does not become TRANSCENDENT. See KNOWLEDGE (KANT).

knowledge by acquaintance sometimes *immediate knowledge, direct knowledge*. Contrasted with KNOWLEDGE BY DESCRIPTION. **1.** personal knowledge gained through the actual experience of something (as opposed to obtaining it, for example, vicariously by means of its description from someone else). Example: If I have been drunk I have some knowledge of drunkenness by direct acquaintance. If I have never been drunk but I have been told what it feels like to be drunk, then I have knowledge of drunkenness by description. **2.** immediate perception or sensation of an object or event. Example: seeing or touching an eel.

knowledge by description sometimes *indirect knowledge, vicarious knowledge*. Contrasted with KNOWLEDGE BY ACQUAINTANCE. **1.** having an indirect experience or knowledge of something by means of someone relating it in some way such as verbally. Example: never having been drunk but being told how it feels to be drunk. **2.** having knowledge of something based on inference or imagination but not on direct familiarity or experience of that thing. Example: knowing that a person is drunk not because we have experienced drunkenness but because he is swaying, he cannot walk in a straight line, he cannot enunciate properly, he reeks of alcohol, his blood has a high percentage of alcohol.

koinai ennoiai (Greek) a phrase primarily associated with Stoic philosophy (see STOICS, THE) that designates concepts such as good, evil, beauty, the existence of God that are *common (koinai)* to all men (a) as natural tendencies of thought, (b) as innately present as part of the universal LOGOS in man; and (c) as imparted by humanity or civilized society which was a reflection of the Logos.

kosmos see COSMOS.

L

laissez-faire sometimes called *laisser faire* or *laisser passer* (French, allow things to proceed without interference, let [people] do or make [what they wish]) a philosophy of governmental noninterference in the economic activities of individuals (such as in production, marketing, trading, financing, investing, advertising); a philosophy of free enterprise founded on private ownership of goods, property, resources, and services, which asserts that an individual is more efficient and productive when allowed to seek his or her self-interest without governmental regulation or restriction. Principally associated with the philosophy of Adam Smith.

language (from Latin, *lingua*, tongue; hence, speech, language) **1.** that body of words, their standardized meanings, and the forms of speech used as a method of communication. **2.** any means of expressing the contents of consciousness (feelings, emotions, desires, thoughts) in a consistent pattern of meaning.

Language requires *symbols* (such as words, sounds, gestures, signs) that are organized and related in a complex system for the purpose of communicating meanings. This system of symbols can be manipulated in such a way as to be able to construct an indefinite combination to which meanings may be attached and by which meanings can be expressed. Such a system has rules specifying how such combinations can take place and how standardized meanings are to be assigned. Some further elements in a language are: (a) an intelligence producing it; (b) intentionally affecting (communicating with, transmitting something to) some other form of intelligence; (c) hoping for a reaction or a similar response and exchange; (d) having some content (concepts, meanings, ideas) that has some common ground of understanding and/or apprehension. Language is a system of symbols that can be used to express or refer to such things as: (1) external material objects; (2) internal mental existents; (3) qualities; (4) relations; (5) logical-mathematical signs; (6) functions; (7) states; (8) processes; and (9) events.

language, conventionalism in/pragmatism in see CONVENTIONALISM.

language, formal sometimes called *artificial, formalized, symbolic,* or *ideal language,* a language deliberately constructed according to specific conceptual and logical rules and used to accomplish a specific purpose consistently, precisely, and completely. *Formal* languages are contrasted with so-called *natural* languages such as English, Greek, German, etc. (Formal languages are not classified with the *artificial* languages, such as Esperanto, which are languages invented in order to correct and replace what are regarded as inadequate natural languages.)

Formal languages are not primarily intended as substitutes for natural languages. A formal language has characteristics such as: **1.** *symbolism.* **2.** *syntactical rules* (or *formation rules*) that determine how these symbols are to be connected; what grammatical connections (syntax) are possible within the system. Syntactical rules enable the user to transform, replace, and substitute symbols. **3.** *semantical rules* (including any rules of definition) by which the formal language is to be translated. Semantical rules enable the user to assign and interpret the meanings given to the vocabulary (terms) of the language. **4.** *rules of logic,* such as the principles of inference for deductive purposes. **5.** *terms* (vocabulary) that include such items as variables, constants, signs for grouping or punctuation, etc.

Formal languages are used for purposes such as (a) to symbolize scientific theories and laws, and (b) to symbolize languages such as logic and mathematics.

language, functions of language has many functions. Some of the principal functions are given here:

1. *cognitive.* This includes such functions as referring, conveying information, communication of meanings (concepts, ideas, usage), and the construction of symbolic systems to accomplish such functions. Examples: "Marion has black hair" functions to communicate something about a referent, something claimed to be true about an objective world that can be judged to be true or false. "A statement cannot be both true and false at the same time in the same respect" functions to communicate the meanings of a procedural rule used in logic irrespective of whether or not there is a referent for it. **2.** *emotive.* Language functions to express and/or to evoke emotions, feelings, moods, sensations, attitudes, images, values, actions, and prejudices, often in order to influence conduct. Examples: "You are a disgusting person." "That was very embarrassing to me, and you should feel ashamed of yourself." For the most part emotive language does not refer to a referent, does not directly communicate information about a referent, and is not directly concerned with asserting that something is actually true or false. **3.** *imperative (directive).* Language functions to command (advise, exhort, obligate, bind). Examples: "Open the door." "Please do as I say." "Thou shalt not steal." **4.** *evaluative (appraising, judging).* Language functions to analyze the value (worth, merit) of something. Examples: "I believe that our government is the best system of government in the world." "The paintings of Picasso are far more beautiful than those of Cézanne."

Many of these functions are found together in language, and it must be understood that they are not the only functions that can be pointed out. Consider the following: **5.** *questioning.* **6.** *performative* (see LANGUAGE, PERFORMATIVE) **7.** *magical.* **8.** *ceremonial.* **9.** *expressive.* **10.** *interjectional.* See INTERSECTIONS, PURE.

language, object language used to talk about things of which we are conscious, as opposed to METALANGUAGE, which is language used to talk (and/or theorize) about such a language or about other languages. The expressions used in an *object language* have no linguistic or syntactical reference. The expressions used in a *metalanguage* do have linguistic or syntactical reference. Examples: "Doug is a male" is a statement in an object language. "'Doug' is a proper noun with four letters" is a statement in a metalanguage.

To study the structures of a language one must use a language to study it with. The language that is being systematically analyzed is called the *object language*—the object of the analysis, the language being mentioned. The language that is being used in the analysis of this object language is called its *metalanguage*—the language in which the investigation of the language is being carried out, the language being used.

language, ordinary see ORDINARY LANGUAGE PHILOSOPHY.

language, performative sometimes called *performatory language*, language that is used in specific contexts: (a) whose meaning is derived from its being used to act out (perform) the meaning (activity) it is informing us about, or (b) whose meaning consists in the very act of uttering it. Examples: "I promise." "I congratulate you on winning." "I offer you this as a token of my esteem." "With this bottle of champagne, I christen thee SS Elizabeth I." "I apologize for my rude behavior." See TRUTH, PERFORMATIVE THEORY OF.

language, philosophy of the conceptual analysis of language in all its dimensions such as those raised in SEMANTICS, PROBLEMS OF and in such further problems as: **1.** what (if any) are the unique characteristics of religious language, moral language, poetic language, scientific language, mathematical language, computer language, language of gesture, language of body image? **2.** what is the relationship between language and knowledge, language and intuitive understanding? Can we have knowledge without language? **3.** what is the relationship between what our language helps us to conceptualize and that reality which it conceptualizes? **4.** for what purposes and in what ways can language be used? **5.** what are linguistic acts? How do they differ from linguistic uses? **6.** what is a symbol (sign)? **7.** what kinds of symbols are there? How are they invented or constructed? **8.** what is communication? **9.** how is communication of meaning possible? **10.** what are the varieties of ways of communicating? **11.** are there ways of perfecting language? How are (perfect) formal languages constructed? **12.** are there presuppositions that natural, or ordinary, language brings with it that give us an insight into the nature of the mind and/or of reality? See ANALYSIS, LINGUISTIC.

language philosophy, ordinary see ORDINARY LANGUAGE PHILOSOPHY.

Laplace, Pierre Simon, Marquis de (1749–1827) French mathematician and astronomer; born in Normandy; studied in Paris and taught at Beaumont and Paris. Laplace is known for his nebular hypothesis of the origin of the universe and his theory of probability. Laplace is known best in philosophy for a version of determinism (or predeterminism) holding that, if all initial conditions of the universe were known, would enable prediction with certainty of all the events that would subsequently occur in the universe. The universe is necessitated (predetermined) by those original conditions.

His major works are *Exposition du système du monde* (1798); *Traité de la mécanique céleste* (5 volumes, 1799–1826); *Théorie analytique des probabilités* (1812); and *Essai philosophique sur les probabilités* (1814).

latent (from Latin, *latere,* lie hidden) **1.** present but not visible or apparent; hidden; concealed. **2.** POTENTIAL; capable of developing into something. **3.** having possibility; able to be used in some way or for some purpose.

law, natural (ethics) 1. the set of obligations or principles (laws, maxims, duties, codes, commands, etc.) binding upon one's conduct that are obtained by reason from an examination of the universe (nature) in contrast to those obtained by revelation, intuition, innate moral conscience, authority, feelings, or inclinations. **2.** the moral rules of conduct, the sense of fairness and justice, which humans possess by the pure activity of their reason (or moral conscience) and which is obligatory independently of, and in spite of, what other forms of law prescribe. Example: It is a natural law that when a person is using his or her property resourcefully for the community it should not be taken away from him or her. **3.** the universal rules of conduct found in all humans and societies as basic aspects of their nature and activity. **4.** the description of what should be or ought to be binding on all humans discovered by a rational examination of human nature and successful human relationships.

law, natural (Stoics) the universe is a rational whole. All things follow the inexorable necessity of the rational principle in all things (natural law). Humans are unique in that they can either obey or not obey the rational and moral structure of the universe. Morality, justice, and virtue have to do with humanity's accepting and following the direction of this rationality. Common phrases depicting this in Stoicism: "conformity to nature," "adherence to the LOGOS," "following the natural law in all things."

law, natural (theology) a set of codes (rules, precepts) (a) intended by nature and grounded in some *higher* or *transcendent* reality, (b) prescribing what should or should not be done, (c) universally binding on all humans, and (d) found by a rational examination of nature. Example: "It is immoral to have intercourse and mechanically or artificially prevent a sperm from meeting with the ovum. Such a natural union of sperm and ovum is intended by nature, and any deliberate interruption of this process goes against what is intended by nature and by God."

Natural law is contrasted with notions of civil law, secular law, positive law, common law, public law, state law, etc. In theology, natural law supersedes these forms of law and is used to judge them.

law, scientific a general statement describing an invariable order or regularity that exists among phenomena under certain specific conditions. Such a description is regarded as an explanation of how things in fact occur. The description may take the form of:

1. a simple observation of an experience (such as, "Hydrochloric acid dissolves iron filings"). **2.** a complex statement (such as, "Every body perseveres in its state of rest, or of uniform motion in a straight line, unless it is compelled to change that state by forces impressed thereon"). **3.** a highly complex mathematical-deductive statement (such as "If $F = 0$, then $d(mv)/dt = 0$").

Some further characteristics, in most cases, of scientific laws follow:

4. they have a wide range of applicability. **5.** they are expressed in some form of universal statement. **6.** they are expressed in some form of a timeless present tense, whereby they can be considered as true at all times that exemplify their stated conditions or order. **7.** they are subject to confirmation or verification by testing procedures (or there are conditions that can be presented, at least theoretically, under which it would be possible to *falsify* them). **8.** they contain data that can be observed. **9.** they are stated in as precise a definitional and mathematical way as possible relative to the complexity of the situation they are attempting to describe. **10.** they have predictive power. They are able to tell us how things will behave under certain specific conditions. **11.** they assume a hypothetical or conditional stance whereby *if* these conditions occur, *then* such and such will be the case. **12.** they are stated in ideal terms and in highly general and ideal contexts, but can with a margin of error be applied to concrete situations that are empirically examinable. **13.** they are exceptionless (primarily because if any counterinstance is discovered, the law is changed into an exceptionless form, or if there are enough exceptions the law ceases to be regarded as a law). See METHOD, SCIENTIFIC; THEORY, SCIENTIFIC.

law of excluded middle see LAWS OF THOUGHT, THE THREE.

law of identity see LAWS OF THOUGHT, THE THREE.

law of inverse variation (intension/extension) words may be ordered in increasing INTENSION. Example: animal, vertebrate, mammal, canine, dog, poodle. When this is done, their order can be seen to be arranged in decreasing (or at least nonincreasing) extension. EXTENSION and intension vary inversely with each other (or: if the extensions vary at all, they vary inversely with the intensions).

law of noncontradiction see LAWS OF THOUGHT, THE THREE.

law of three stages (Comte) see POSITIVISM (COMTE).

laws, moral (as regulative principles) the view that moral laws are rules or ideals which regulate conduct, by which conduct can be organized and limited, and which remind us of what we are seeking and/or what we ought to do (much as a police officer's uniform reminds us that we should obey the speed limit or a traffic light).

laws, moral and social 1. prohibitions, commands, obligations imposed by authority (or custom, reason, etc.) for the purpose of directing and controlling behavior, as in laws of custom, laws of society, laws of morality, common laws, statute laws, civil laws, and religious laws. **2.** objective, universally applicable and binding rules to be followed in conduct for such purposes as group cohesion, stability, interpersonal relations, protection, expression of sentiments, and standardization of conduct.

laws as conventions the view that scientific laws are conventions which provide explanations of the physical world, and that other conventions could be used to describe it. One convention is accepted over another because it is simpler, more convenient, more useful, and explains a greater variety of phenomena. Laws are not *true* in the sense that they describe the physical world; they are mathematical/logical ways of ordering our perceptions of the world, and the way we describe the world is due to the linguistic conventions our culture has adopted. *Truth* is thus relative to our mathematical/logical and linguistic framework. Many *pictures* or frameworks of a reality can be constructed; some are better than others but none can really be said to be truer. There is no *one* true set of laws describing the universe. Any consistent and highly sophisticated comprehensive system of analysis can be applied to the study of nature. The order (patterns, identities, wholes) we find in the physical world is dependent on how our minds and our mathematical/logical/linguistic systems see it, organize it, and present it. Compare with CONVENTIONALISM.

laws as physical necessities of nature the view that natural laws express the necessary connection among events that irrevocably binds them together and necessitates them to happen as they do happen and in no other way. Physical necessity of this kind is believed to be an irreducible and fundamental aspect of all nature and is what natural law describes.

laws as procedural rules the view that scientific laws are rules that allow inferences from events to events, or from statements about events to other statements about events.

laws as regularities the view that scientific laws describe an order about reality in terms of such basic concepts as (a) the *coexistence* of events (things happening together), (b) the *cosuccession* of events (things happening together in a series), and (c) the *invariant connections* (such as cause and effect relations) among events.

laws of nature (antinecessitarian view) necessity does not exist in nature. Things could have been other than what they are. Nature need not have been as it was; it might have been otherwise. The necessity that is seen in natural (physical) laws is the *logical* necessity stemming from the system of interrelated concepts with which these natural laws are formulated and expressed and the theoretical structure of which they are a part. See ACCIDENTALISM.

laws of nature (descriptive view) the laws of nature are general statements that describe regular sequences of events which are observed to occur. Example: If water is heated at sea level to 100°C, then we also observe that it boils. The law pertaining to this merely points out that as a matter of fact (as a matter of our experience) these connections seem to hold and describe (explain) in a general way what is actually taking place.

laws of nature (necessitarian view) also called the *governance* or *prescriptive view*. The laws of nature are principles (directions, commands, rules) that make things happen, govern or prescribe things to happen in a certain way and necessitate that they happen exactly in that way. Their necessity applies everywhere in the universe and in all possible universes. They are prior in reality and power to what they cause to happen. Example: When water is heated at sea level to 100°C, there is a law that these conditions obey and by which they are governed so that water *must* boil at that temperature and atmospheric pressure. Any water that did not behave in this way would be *violating* a law of nature. In theology, God creates the laws that govern the activity of all things. God's will is expressed by means of the laws of nature, which are signs of God's omnipresence and omnipotence. Compare with PREDETERMINISM.

laws of thought, the three also called *the three principles of thought*, the formulation of what have been called the *Three Laws of Thought* goes back to Plato and Aristotle. These laws have been regarded as *ontologically real* (describing the ultimate features of reality); as *cognitively necessary* (no consistent thinking is possible without their use; all coherent thought, and all logical systems, rely on them for justification; their denial presupposes their use in denying them); and as *uninferred knowledge* (the immediate and direct result of a rational examination of the relations of timeless universals). In modern times, these *Laws of Thought* have been regarded as only three among many *principles,* or *rules, of inference* that can be invented and used in logic; or as definitionally true (tautologous) and hence irrefutable.

1. *the Law of Identity:* If p is true, then p is true. (If p is false, then p is false.) If a thing A is A, then it is A. A is A. Everything is what it is (and cannot, at the time it is what it is, be something else). **2.** *the Law of Noncontradiction* (also called the *Law of Contradiction*): p cannot be both true and false (at the same time and in the same respect). A thing A cannot be both A and not A (at the time it is A). **3.** *the Law of Excluded Middle:* either p is true or p is false; one or the other, but not both at the same time and in the same respect. A thing A is either A or it is not A.

Leibniz (also **Leibnitz), Gottfried Wilhelm** (1642–1716) German philosopher, mathematician, statesman. Educated at the University of Leipsig, where he studied law and philosophy.

He created (independently and at about the same time as Newton) the infinitesimal calculus and invented a calculating machine (more advanced than Pascal's) that not only added and subtracted but also multiplied, divided, and computed the roots of numbers. Leibniz envisaged a universal language for communication and a universal encyclopedia that would bring together all knowledge, from medicine to philosophy, in a unified conceptual whole.

Leibniz, writing in journals and books, produced histories, genealogies of distinguished families, political tracts, practical suggestions to kings about going to war and the conduct of military campaigns, jurisprudence, mathematics and logic, physics, metaphysics, philosophic psychology, epistemology, and theology. In philosophy, Leibniz is known today for works such as *Monadology*; *New Essays Concerning Human Understanding*; *Discourse on Metaphysics*; and *Theodicy*. As a philosopher, Leibniz is known best for his theory of Monads and Pre-established Harmony, his Principle of Indiscernibles, his Principle of Sufficient Reason, his Principle of Identity, and his Principle of the Best (or God Created This Universe as the Best of All Possible Worlds).

Leibniz's law see IDENTITY OF INDISCERNIBLES, PRINCIPLE OF (LEIBNIZ).

Leucippus (fl. c.450 BC) Greek materialistic philosopher, born in Miletus, Ionia; recognized as the founder of Greek atomism. His student, Democritus, elaborated this atomic theory. Epicurus and Lucretius systematized and gave an ethical dimension to atomism. None of his writings survive.

liar paradox see PARADOX, LIAR.

libertarianism 1. in ethics, the view that humans have free will interpreted as an uncaused event. See INDETERMINISM (ETHICS). **2.** in metaphysics, the view that there are uncaused events in the universe.

liberty (from Latin, *liber*, free) **1.** the right of a person to choose from among alternative courses of action or goals without being restricted by authority. **2.** the right of a person not to be interfered with in pursuit or possession of what he or she wills or values. **3.** the right of individuals to express themselves however they wish, without constraint, and to employ the means they wish to obtain their interests. **4.** the absence of (FREEDOM FROM) external restraints, obstructions, constraints, or impediments, and without fear of punishment or reprisal. **5.** the freedom (ability) or opportunity to act in accordance with one's choice.

Liberty has traditionally been thought of in the political and social context of being free to do that (a) for which there is no normal or other good reason against doing it (any interference by authorities must be justified by good reasons, such as a danger to public health or damage to the safety or well-being of others), and (b) which does not infringe on (interfere with, harm, restrain, coerce) the activities of others and their rights. Liberty has been regarded as an inalienable natural right (together with life, property, and the pursuit of happiness). Compare with entries under FREEDOM and RIGHTS.

licentious (from Latin, *licentiosus*, unrestrained) **1.** immoral; deviating from moral principles. **2.** uncurbed; taking excessive liberty, or freedom of action in regard to what is proper, good, or enough. **3.** lawless. Compare with INCONTINENCE.

licentious (Aristotle) of one who feels no conflict between base physical desires (passions, cravings, yearnings) and rational promptings (urges, impulses) toward the attainment of higher values. This is in contrast with the incontinent person (see INCONTINENCE), who does feel the conflict but nevertheless allows the desires to win out.

like causes like, principle of the principle that the qualities in the cause are also qualities present in the effect, and vice versa: cause and effect can never be qualitatively disparate or dichotomous. For example, on the basis of this principle, mind cannot come from something that does not contain mental characteristics; life cannot come from something that does not contain life.

like perceives like, principle of the principle used in Greek philosophy by philosophers such as Empedocles and Plato: (a) that what is perceived resembles (in quality and/or in form) that which is perceived, and (b) that knowledge is possible only if such a resemblance exists. This principle, together with the principle of like causes like (see LIKE CAUSES LIKE, PRINCIPLE OF), is the foundation of the metaphysical assumption that nature *is* as we perceive (and construct) it, and *acts* monistically as an integrated unity.

limit, the see PERAS.

limitless, the see APEIRON.

linguistic analysis/philosophy see ANALYSIS, LINGUISTIC.

Locke, John (1632–1704) English philosopher born in Somersetshire and educated at Oxford. There he lectured in Greek and Latin, rhetoric, and philosophy, but also studied and performed experiments in chemistry and meteorology—he was a friend of the chemist Robert Boyle, and the physician Thomas Sydenham.

Locke has been called a physical REALIST (in contrast to Berkeley's IMMATERIALISM) and is regarded as one of the three leading British Empiricists, together with Berkeley and Hume. Some of Locke's central themes in epistemology center around concepts such as the *tabula rasa*; no innate ideas; sensation and reflection; primary and secondary qualities; the real, objective existence of things, substances, and matter independently of consciousness. Among his many works are *Essays Concerning Toleration* (1666); *Two Treatises on Government* (1685); *Essay Concerning Human Understanding* (1690); *Thoughts on Education* (1693); and *The Reasonableness of Christianity as Delivered in the Scriptures* (1695).

locutionary expression/act (locution) the act of uttering a statement and using a language (or utterance) with a somewhat definite reference and sense and/or meaning; the act of uttering a meaningful statement. Example: "The house is on fire." Compare with ILLOCUTIONARY EXPRESSION/ACT (ILLOCUTION); PERLOCUTIONARY EXPRESSION/ACT (PERLOCUTION).

logic (from Greek, *logikē,* or *logikos,* that which belongs to intellligent speech or to a well-functioning reason, ordered, systematized, intelligible) **1.** the study of the rules of exact reasoning, of the forms of sound or valid thought patterns. **2.** the study and the application of the rules of inference to arguments or to systems of thought.

logic (Aristotle) logic as the science of making correct inferences, regarded by Aristotle as the indispensable foundation for all types of knowledge. Logic is an instrument, or tool, for unlocking the intelligible connections found in concepts and in things. (*To Organon* was the name given by later editors to the compilation of Aristotle's works on logic. *To Organon* means the tool, the instrument, the method for obtaining philosophical and scientific knowledge. Aristotle himself most frequently used a variation of the word *analysis* (from *ana,* up, + *lyein,* loosen) to apply to what we now label his works on logic. For Aristotle, the main part of logic was the categorical syllogism. His syllogistic methods remained the basis for the development of formal logic through the medieval period, when it was studied intensively and considerably enlarged in a systematic way, all the way to the beginning of the twentieth century, when new symbolic techniques and principles for logic were invented.

logic, deductive the systematic attempt (a) to formulate rules of inference that are consistent and complete, (b) to apply them to formally presented arguments, and (c) to determine whether or not their conclusions can be validly inferred from the premises. See DEDUCTION.

logic, deontic logic that deals with and formalizes concepts such as obligation, permissibility and nonpermissibility, ought, should, and could into a coherent system. Some of its basic principles are "If something is obligatory, then it should be permissible"; "if something is not permissible, then it is not obligatory"; "if something is done because it is obligatory, then it itself is something obligatory that should be done"; "it is not true that that which is obligatory is (necessarily) done"; "it is not true that that which is done is permissible"; "it ought to be the case that that which is obligatory should be done"; and "it is the case that for a thing to be obligatory it must be possible for it to be done."

logic, dialectical sometimes called *dialectics* (see entries under DIALECTIC), the general term given to the logic of philosophers such as Hegel, Marx, and Engels, who attempted to refute the *Three Laws of Thought* (see LAWS OF THOUGHT, THE THREE) and develop a logic of *becoming* that attempts to present the ever-changing processes of things. For example, contradiction exists in reality. It is possible for the selfsame thing to be and not to be—the same thing is and is not. It is thought that this process can be seen in the polarities of change (*thesis* and *antithesis*) found in all activity. Contradiction is the driving force in all things. (It would have been more accurate linguistically for them to have used the words *contrast, contrary, opposition,* rather than *contradiction.* The concept of *noncontradiction,* together with the other two Laws of Thought, is definitionally and irrevocably true.)

Hegel viewed logic as a process (the *dialectical process*) and not as an analysis of how form could be applied to content (or of how content could be put into a form). Form and content are inseparably united in a movement that not only describes human thought patterns but also describes the three states by which natural events take place. The movement involves what has been commonly named a *thesis, antithesis,* and *synthesis.* The categories or principles of reason (ideas, notions, concepts) are exemplified in this process of movement from a THESIS to an ANTITHESIS and on to their unity in a SYNTHESIS. The principles of reason, or the categories, cannot be enumerated completely, since the dialectical process has not yet fully actualized itself in reality. See DIALECTIC (HEGEL).

logic, formal logic that constructs valid patterns (forms) of inference as opposed to dealing directly with content (meanings).

logic, inductive the attempt (a) to formulate rules (such as Mill's methods of induction) by which statements can be established as empirically confirmed or probable, (b) to formulate systematic procedures for presenting nondeductive inferences or arguments, and (c) to determine a degree of CONFIRMATION or PROBABILITY for the conclusion based on the degree of confirmation or probability that it is possible to establish for the premises.

logic, informal the study of those inferences that (a) do not follow a precise logical form (and if they do, their truth does not depend on such a form); (b) are based on the meanings rather than the validity of the forms involved in the argument; and (c) may be true or false depending on considerations (such as empirical evidence) other than the form of their argument.

logic, many-valued (multivalued) logic that attempts to employ more than the two (usually three) truth values of *true* and *false* in analyzing some types of arguments. Some values other than true or false: (a) known as true/known as false/not known (or unknown); (b) true/false/undetermined (or undeterminable); (c) true necessarily/false necessarily/possible (contingent); and (d) true certainly/false certainly/true probably/false probably.

logic, modal logic that deals with and formalizes into a coherent symbolic system concepts such as necessity, possibility (and impossibility). Some of its basic principles: "if something is necessary then it should be possible"; "if something is necessary then it is not impossible"; "if something is impossible then it is necessarily false"; "if something is necessarily false then it is impossible"; "if something is necessitated by something necessarily true, then it itself is necessarily true"; and "that which is necessary is both truly actual and possible."

logic, symbolic sometimes called *formalized logic,* logic presented in abstract symbolization consisting of well-defined elements such as (a) symbols, (b) signs, (c) connectives, (d) rules for the combination of symbols, (e) rules for substitution, (f) rules of inference, and (g) rules of derivation.

logic, traditional categorical sometimes called *Aristotelian logic* **1.** the logic of the categorical SYLLOGISM. **2.** the logic of classes. **3.** the study of the rules and procedures by which terms related as subject and predicate lead to conclusions that follow with necessity (certainty).

logic, transcendental see CATEGORIES OF LOGIC, THE (KANT).

logical atomism see ATOMISM, LOGICAL.

logical empiricism see EMPIRICISM, LOGICAL.

logical form see FORM, LOGICAL.

logical implication see IMPLICATION, LOGICAL.

logical independence see STATEMENT, LOGICALLY INDEPENDENT.

logical paradox see PARADOX, LOGICAL.

logical positivism see POSITIVISM, LOGICAL.

logical table of judgments, the (Kant) see CATEGORIES OF LOGIC, THE (KANT).

logicism 1. generally, the theory that mathematics is an extension of logic: (a) mathematics can be deduced from the concepts and the deductive procedures of logic; (b) all mathematical proofs are forms of deductive reasoning; and (c) mathematics can be reduced to logic. **2.** specifically, (a) pure mathematics deals with concepts all of which can be defined in terms of a few fundamental logical concepts; and (b) the statements of mathematics can all be derived from a few logical rules (principles). **3.** the theory that all necessary statements (truths, logical forms) can be seen to be logically analytically true.

lógos (Greek, speech, discourse, thought, reason, word, meaning, study of, the account of, the science of, the underlying reasons for why a thing is what it is, the principles and methods used to explain phenomena in a particular discipline, those features in a thing that make it intelligible to us, the rationale of a thing). In English, *-logy* is used as a combining form in such words as embry*ology* (the study of the embryo), psych*ology* (the science of behavior), ge*ology* (an account of the features of the earth), and phil*ology* (the love of words). In Greek religion, *lógos* referred to the divine word of a god that provided spiritual inspiration, wisdom, and guidance. A prophet (*prophētēs*) was one whose speech (*lógos*) communicated that divine word.

lógos **(Heraclitus) 1.** the immanent cause of the pattern and identity that is evident in the constant flux of all things. Heraclitus may have believed the *lógos* to be a material existence like fire (Greek: *pyr*). **2.** the underlying reason for the existence of any particular thing in the universe. **3.** cosmic necessity, law, fate, or destiny. **4.** that about the universe which remains the same whereas all other things change. Those features about the universe which can be identified, talked about, and named, and remain relatively unchanged.

Humans possess a fragment of the universal *lógos* as exhibited in their reasoning powers and in their continued existence as identities. Compare with CHANGE (HERACLITUS).

lógos **(Stoics) 1.** the underlying, cosmic principle of intelligence or reason (God) that produces the rationally ordered activity in the universe. As in

Heraclitus, it was identified with a material force, and specifically with the eternal fire, which permeates all things as their causal agent. **2.** the active principle of intelligence or reason as exhibited in us, which we can use (a) to understand the rational purpose and direction of the universe; (b) to perceive the necessary way of conducting our lives so as to conform with nature (synonymous for the Stoics with the *rational*); and thereby (c) to cultivate an acceptance and endurance of all things as they happen because they are rationally necessitated (fated) by the *lógos*. The *lógos* was *heimarmenē,* predeterministic, a fating intelligence. **3.** the *lógos* providentially regulated all things (a) toward their own good (insofar as they, being what they were, could express their good), and (b) toward the overall harmony and good of the universe as a whole. The *lógos* was called *pronoia,* which meant divine providence, foreknowledge, premeditation, purposefulness. **4.** the *lógos* was the source of all moral values. Regardless of the physical or cultural differences among individuals, they are all members of humanity because each possesses a part of that eternal *lógos* into which all humans dissolve without distinction at death. **5.** the soul (*lógos*) of humans is immortal, as is the cosmic *lógos* of which the soul is a part.

lógos orthos (Greek, right reason, correct reasoning, straight talk or truth, right argument, validity, soundness of argumentation) *Ortho-* is found in English words such as *ortho*dox, *ortho*genesis, *ortho*pedics, and is a combining form meaning correct, straight, right, upright, regular. **1.** *lógos orthos* was used for example by the SOPHISTS in their development of logic and rhetoric to signify those arguments and logical principles that could be (a) used correctly for proper inferences and (b) used to present correctly the strongest case possible for a point of view. **2.** also used by the Greek Stoics and by Roman Stoics, who used the Latin phrase RECTA RATIO to designate the intelligent and correct (*recta*) rationale (law, necessity, reason, order) in the universe to which human actions and law must conform.

lógos spermatikos (Greek, the life-giving word) the Stoic name for the rational sperm (*spermá*), seed. This was the semen dispersed throughout the universe that was the cause of the generation, development, and change of all things within it. It could be thought of as the forms (Platonic) or the universals (Aristotelian) immanent in nature and giving passive matter the shape and activity that it has. The STOICS looked on the universe as a living organism. The *lógos spermatikos* contains within it an infinite amount of individual sperm (*spermatikoi*), each a rational agent or form creating purposing entities, and all harmoniously interrelated.

Lombard, Peter (c.1095–1160) Italian medieval theologian, born near Novara, in Lombardy; educated in Bologna, Rheims, and Paris. His most influential work was his *Book of Sentences* (1157)—it influenced the thinking of theologians down to the Reformation.

love see AGAPĒ, ĒROS, PHILIA.

love, Platonic commonly understood as a spiritual comradeship or fellow-love without the presence of sexual desire or sexual contact.

Lucretius (Titus Lucretius Carus) (c.98–55 BC) Roman philosophic poet and atomist, following in the philosophic tradition of Leucippus, Democritus, and Epicurus. He is known for his didactic epic *De Rerum Natura* (On the Nature of Things), an espousal in hexameters of the Greek atomism found in Epicurus.

M

Machiavelli, Niccoló (1469–1527) Italian statesman, writer, and political philosopher; born in Florence. He is known for four major works: *The Prince* (1512), advising rulers on how to achieve political success; *The Discourses* (1517), an analysis of republican government; *Art of War* (1520); and his *History of Florence* (1527).

macrocosm (from Greek, *makros,* long, great, + *kósmos,* cosmos, universe, world) **1.** in general, any large complex or whole contrasted with some small part of it (its MICROCOSM). The whole and the part may be contrasted in order to show such things as (a) their similarities, (b) their differences, (c) their interdependence, (d) their fundamental oneness or unity. **2.** specifically, the universe considered in its totality or as an active, structured whole.

maieutic (from Greek, *maieutikos,* one who acts like a midwife; from *maia,* midwife) applied to Socrates' method of serving as the (intellectual) midwife to the birth of ideas from his listeners' pregnant minds; the ideas are there ready to be born, but require someone to assist by asking the proper questions and prodding the intellect. See SOCRATIC METHOD.

Maimonides (Moses ben Maimon) (1135–1204) Jewish philosopher, theologian, physician, master of Hebrew and Rabbinic literature; born in Córdoba, Spain. He lived in Cairo, where he served as physician to Saladin, sultan of Egypt, and became a Rabbinic authority and leader throughout the Jewish community. His best-known work is his *Guide for the Perplexed* (1190).

mania **(Plato)** (Greek, madness, inspiration, frenzy, enthusiasm) possession by a divinity that inspires a poet or artist to a truth, or to an expression of beauty.

manifold, sensory (Kant) 1. the unorganized content presented to our senses which the mind structures into perception by means of concepts. **2.** the sense data of our experience, such as sounds, tastes, or colors, regarded as discrete units before they are organized by the mind.

Marcus Aurelius (121–180) Roman emperor and philosopher, born in Rome; studied Stoic philosophy with Roman Stoics; with tutors, he studied law, rhetoric, poetry, literature, and philosophy. The *Meditations*, his only extant manuscript, was written in Greek. It is a collection of ethical, moral, social, personal, and religious thoughts and feelings.

Marx, Karl (1818–1883) German philosopher, revolutionary, socialist, and journalist; born in Trier; educated at the universities of Bonn, Berlin, and Jena. (His doctoral thesis was on the materialism of Democritus and Epicurus.) After an active career as journalist in Paris, Brussels, and

Cologne, Marx emigrated to London and remained there for the rest of his life. Among his major works are the famous *Communist Manifesto* (1848, written with Friedrich Engels) and *Das Kapital* (first volume, 1867).

material cause see CAUSES, THE FOUR (ARISTOTLE).

material object sometimes called *material body,* or simply BODY, *physical object,* or *physical body.* A thing: **1.** that can be identified as a unity (unit); **2.** that has physical characteristics such as position, size, shape, structure, existence in time and space, mass, inertia, movement, and (sometimes) the sensed qualities of color, hardness, softness, sweetness, heat, weight, solidity, rigidity, etc.; **3.** that exists independently of our perception, although it is our perception of it that brings it to consciousness; **4.** that undergoes physical change; and **5.** that causally interacts and/or interrelates with other independently existing things. Examples: table, chair, plant, animal.

Usually it is admitted that material objects are perceived indirectly by inference from something more immediate and direct such as SENSA. Whereas we are always certain that we are having, or being presented with *sensa,* we do not have that certainty about material objects. Many sensa are associated with particular material objects. Material objects are often thought to persist independently of the sensa and/or persist as the sensa change. See MATTER; OBJECT.

materialism The following are some main views of materialism. **1.** at one extreme, the belief that nothing but matter in motion exists. The mind (spirit, consciousness, soul) *is* matter in motion. At the other extreme, the belief that mind does exist but is caused by material changes (see EPIPHE-NOMENALISM) and is completely dependent on matter; mind has no causal efficacy, nor is it necessary to the functioning of the material universe. **2.** matter and the universe do not in any way possess characteristics of mind such as purpose, awareness, intention, goals, meaning, direction, intelligence, willing, or striving. **3.** there are no nonmaterial entities such as spirits, ghosts, demons, angels. Immaterial agencies do not exist. **4.** there is no God or supernatural (supranatural) realm. The sole reality is matter, and everything is a manifestation of its activity. **5.** every change (event, activity) has a material cause, and material explanations of phenomena are the only correct explanations. Everything in the universe can be explained in terms of material (physical) conditions. **6.** matter, and its activity, is eternal. There is no *first cause* or *prime mover.* **7.** the material configurations of things may be altered, and matter itself may exist in varied and complex dimensions, but matter can neither be created nor destroyed. **8.** no life, no mind, is immortal. All phenomena change, eventually pass out of existence, returning back again to a primordial, eternal material ground in an eternal retransformation of matter. **9.** some materialists are predeterminists (see PREDETERMINISM) and some are determinists (see DETERMINISM). **10.** some materialists are monists in the sense that they regard the universe as being a material unity and/or materially interrelated. Some are monists only in the sense that the sole (*mono*) reality is matter in motion. **11.** Values do not exist in the universe independently of the activities of humans.

materialism, dialectical (Marx-Engels) 1. the theory that (a) social progress occurs through struggle, conflict, interaction, and opposition (in particular of economic classes), and (b) the development (or emergence) of one level of society from another does not happen gradually but by sudden and occasionally catastrophic jumps. **2.** the type of thinking process that attempts (a) to perceive how all things are inexorably interrelated as a whole; (b) to accept the absolute necessity of that interrelated whole (which is the essence of freedom), and (c) to accept the inevitability of struggle, conflict, contradiction, change, and emergence of novelty in the universe.

Dialectical materialism holds to the concept of *struggle* (tension, change, opposite forces) as the most fundamental drive in all things. All things (1) struggle to become other than what they are or were, (2) struggle to avoid being overcome, and (3) struggle to overcome other things. Nothing remains exactly as it is; nothing is self-sufficient; nothing can exist in isolation from other things. Dialectical materialism also holds to the concept of *unity*, the necessary and rational interrelationship of all things in the universe. Complete truth consists in knowing the truths about the existence of any particular thing and knowing how it is related to all other things that exist and have existed in the universe. See DIALECTICS, HISTORICAL (MARXISM).

materialism, mechanistic sometimes called *mechanism*, the theory that the universe is a machine and can be completely explained in terms of the effects of the mechanical operation of its parts upon one another. All phenomena are the outcome of the mechanical motions of matter. The traditional view holds that anything that produces a material (physical) effect must itself be a material object. Material objects can affect one another solely by direct mechanical contact (impact). There is no action at a distance. There are no final causes or purposes in the universe.

materialism, reductive the theory that everything in the universe, including consciousness, can be explained in terms of matter in motion.

materialization sometimes called *particularization, concretization, individuation,* or *actualization.* **1.** prime matter receiving form from a substantial form (see FORM, ESSENTIAL OR SUBSTANTIAL) and thereby becoming secondary matter: a BODY. **2.** the individuation of prime matter into a *this*; the actualization of form into a *this*: this dog, this tree, this cream.

matter the stuff of which something is composed: **1.** the PHYSICAL or material constituent of something; that of which any physical object is composed. **2.** that which occupies space, for the most part is tangible, is empirically observable, and can be acted upon by other matter or forces. Together with ENERGY, matter is regarded as the basis of all natural phenomena. Some of the further characteristics that have been associated with matter: atomic or corpuscular in nature (or a continuity of waves), impenetrable, indivisible (or divisible), having the potential to exhibit physical activity or change, having inertia, being eternal, self-moving (or not self-moving), and having mass (although there are some levels of matter such as light to which mass is not attributed). **3.** the (indeterminate) ground of all reality. **4.** the basic cause of experience. See MATERIAL OBJECT.

matter (Aristotle) see entries under SUBSTANCE with reference to Aristotle.

matter (atomists) see ATOMISM, GREEK.

matter (Descartes) matter (material substance, body) has the essential attribute of *extension,* which undergoes sensible change. Matter fills all space (there is no empty space in the universe) and is incompressible. All properties of matter are quantifiable *modes* of extension that are a necessary part of our conception of any existing material object. These modes are: (a) *duration* (to conceive of a material thing is to conceive of it as continuing to exist from one moment in time to another moment in time), and (b) *time* as a measure of that duration. Our conception of material substance is not in any way derived from our senses but is a product of the ideas of our reason (as are God and mind). See VORTEX THEORY (DESCARTES.)

matter (Stoics) see STOICS, THE.

matter, prime 1. matter in a state of pure potentiality devoid of any properties or characteristics (whose only *property* may be said to be not having any property). **2.** that matter which is in itself the same in all physical things and which is being formed by active principles. **3.** what matter would be like without any form whatever to give it individual, positive qualities. **4.** the common substratum (stuff) that is thought to remain the same, such as when cream becomes butter, or when grapes become wine. See POTENCY, PURE.

matter, principle of the conservation of 1. one of the oldest principles in philosophy, based on the concept that no thing can come from nothing. See ELEATICS, THE. If something comes into existence, it must come from something previously existing. The universe is eternal; its energy is never lost or created. The theory that the matter (energy, mass, force, momentum, motion) in the universe is neither created nor destroyed, but remains quantitatively the same as potential or as actual. In this sense, referred to as the *Principle of the Conservation of Energy* (or *Matter and Energy,* or *Mass and Energy*). **2.** *The First Law of Thermodynamics:* in any closed system—one that is isolated from the rest of the universe—the sum total of matter (mass) and energy remains constant (remains conserved) in any of its changes. This is expressed in the formula $E = mc^2$, where E = energy, m = matter, and c = the velocity of light, or Maxwell's constant.

matter/form (Aristotle) 1. matter is the capacity to receive form, the capacity to be formed. **2.** matter is that permanence (identity) present in anything that changes—that is, is changing in form. Form is that novelty or uniqueness which appears in things that are changing. **3.** every material thing is composed of primary (formless) matter (see MATTER, PRIME) and a form. All material objects are embodied forms. See CHANGE (ARISTOTLE); GENESIS (ARISTOTLE).

mē agan (Greek, nothing in excess).

mean, the (from Latin, *medius*, middle) the moderate, the middle position, or the intermediate position between two points.

Mean, the (Aristotle) also called *Aristotle's Doctrine of the Mean* or the *Aristotelian Mean*; sometimes called *The Golden Mean*; associated with moderation, temperance, the avoidance of extremes; the ethical principle that virtue consists in following a course of action somewhere between the extreme of too much (excess) and that of too little (defect). COURAGE, for example, avoids foolhardiness, recklessness (excess), and cowardice, timidity (defect). Hitting the right balance (moral goodness, virtue) between the extremes of excess and deficiency can be accomplished only through education, training, and experience. The mean is not an absolute center point but is something adjustable and shifting; it is not arithmetical or quantifiable but is relative to the situation at hand and the personality involved. For example, we should in time of war expect the courage mean to be more toward the excess extreme for the soldier and more toward the defect extreme for the grocer. See VIRTUES, MORAL (ARISTOTLE).

meaning 1. signification, that which a thing designates or is intended to express. **2.** explanation, the reason why a thing is what it is.

meaning (behavioristic view) the behavioral responses to stimuli such as symbols, sounds, images, gestures, and body positions.

meaning (sentences) the meaning of a sentence (statement, proposition) is not derivable (a) only from the meanings of its individual components, or (b) only from the pattern given the words, but also from such things as (c) the context, (d) the accent (emphasis) upon certain of its features, (e) the attitudes and emotions conveyed through its utterance, (f) the promptings toward certain types of behavior such as requesting, commanding, promising, suggesting, advising, correcting, praising, and blaming.

meaning, cognitive sometimes called *assertive, informational, descriptive, factual,* or *declarative meaning* **1.** referring to statements that give information and claim that information as true (or false). **2.** the meaning conveyed by statements that assert facts or describe.

meaning, connotative see CONNOTATION.

meaning, definitional sometimes called *lexical meaning,* meaning derived from understanding the definitional meaning of the words themselves and/or how they may be put together in a sentence.

meaning, denotative see DENOTATION.

meaning, descriptive or literal the referents of a word; the variety of things to which a word may be applied.

meaning, emotive 1. the emotions, feelings, attitudes, commands, etc., that things (words, sentences, symbols, images, gestures) communicate, express, or evoke. **2.** our emotional and attitudinal responses to something. **3.** the interpretation of a statement (a) on the level of its intended emotional meaning and/or (b) on the level of the emotional meanings associated with the statement.

meaning, empiricist theory of 1. the theory that words (sentences) get their real meaning from some kind of direct or indirect reference to concrete experiences. See EMPIRICISM. **2.** the theory that words have meaning only if rules about their application and/or VERIFICATION are based on (or derived from) experience. See EMPIRICISM, LOGICAL.

meaning, expressive meaning obtained from contexts that express, and hence elicit, such things as mood, feeling, emotion, values; for example, the meaning derived from poetry, commands, insults, exclamations, pleadings. Expressive meaning may also have cognitive or other kinds of meanings associated with it.

meaning, extensional sometimes called *denotative* or *referential meaning* (see DENOTATION) the collection of *things* referred to by a word; the class of things to which a word may be applied. This concept of meaning stresses the notion that to understand a word is to know how to apply it correctly, to know how to identify its referent. (It is not necessary to know the entire list of all the things to which the word applies.) Criteria are presented to determine whether or not the thing can be subsumed within the extension (list of referents or class) of the word. All things included in the extension of a word have some common characteristics (properties, qualities), which thereby allow us to use the same term to *denote* them. The extensional meaning of a word is determined by its INTENSION. See EXTENSION.

meaning, factual cognitive assertions that purport to be true about the world independently of our statements about them.

meaning, intensional sometimes called *connotative meaning* (see CONNOTATION) **1.** the collection of characteristics (properties, qualities) common to things by which general (class) words are formed and in terms of which they are understood and applied correctly. **2.** the intended meaning of a word; the intensional meaning of a word determines its EXTENSION. See INTENSION.

meaning, linguistic (behavioristic view) the theory that meaning is the tendency of a linguistic expression to produce (elicit, evince, manifest) psychological, cognitive, emotive, sensory effects in the listener by means of a complex conditioning process of learning the use of a language and its associations in the act of communicating.

meaning, logical sometimes called *formal meaning*, meaning derived from the very form of a statement, from the relationships of the components themselves in a statement of logic.

meaning, operational theory of the meaning of a word (concept) as the sum total of operations (procedures, activities, usually of a scientific sort) that must be performed in exemplifying (or understanding) it. See OPERATIONALISM.

meaning, referential theory of the theory that words have meaning only if there is something to which they refer, and that something constitutes their meaning. For example, the statement "Barbara is in the process of finishing her model airplane" must have objectively existing referents for each word in the statement for the statement to be meaningful. Thus, *is, in, process,* and *of* are regarded as objective existents having extralinguistic reference as much as *Barbara, model,* and *airplane.*

meaning, representative theory of also called *correspondence theory of meaning.* Words symbolically represent or correspond to something in the external world, and their meaning is derived from the representation or correspondence.

meaning, verifiability theory of 1. the theory that the meaning of a statement and its method of verification are identical. The conditions that verify a statement constitute its meaning. **2.** a statement is meaningful only if it is possible (at least in principle) to present empirical evidence that could verify it, which would support the factual truth of the statement. **3.** the meaning of a statement is equivalent to the sense experiences we would have to have in order to determine that the statement is true. A statement means nothing more than the collection of sense experiences that taken together constitute the truth of the statement. **4.** a statement has cognitive meaning in direct relation to how it is verified and whether or not it can be verified. If a statement is (a) not verifiable at least in principle, and is (b) not a tautology, then it is cognitively meaningless. Only logic and mathematics, which are tautologous, and the natural sciences, which lead to verifiable empirical statements, can give cognitive meaning. **5.** a statement is meaningful (a) insofar as it can be determined to be true (b) either as an analytic (tautologous) statement or (c) as an empirically verifiable statement. See POSITIVISM, LOGICAL; VERIFIABILITY, PRINCIPLE OF.

meaning as communicating of ideas meaning consists in using symbols to convey our inner and private ideas (thoughts) to others.

meaning as naming the meaning of a statement is the object named by it and/or the act of naming.

meaning as usage the theory that meaning consists in how a language is used by a speaker and how the speaker behaves in that context. Meaning consists in what the speaker does when he or she speaks, what the speaker is doing when he or she uses a language. Meaning has to do with what people do with words and sentences.

mechanism (from Greek, *mēchanē,* an instrument or machine for lifting weights, devices or contrivances for doing a thing; from *mēchos,* the means, the way by which something is expedited) **1.** the view that the interaction of parts with other parts within a whole (or system) unintentionally produces purposive activity and/or functions. The whole is neither ontologically prior to the parts nor causally efficacious upon them but merely the sum total (quantitatively and perceptually) of the interacting parts. Opposite to ANI-

MISM. **2.** the theory that all phenomena can be explained in terms of the principles by which machines (mechanical systems) are explained without recourse to intelligence as an operating cause or principle. Opposed to VITALISM and TELEOLOGY. **3.** the theory that all phenomena (natural, biological, psychological) are physical and can be explained in terms of material changes (matter in motion). See MATERIALISM; MATERIALISM, MECHANISTIC; PHYSICALISM. Opposite to ORGANICISM; SUPERNATURALISM.

meditation see CONTEMPLATION.

Meinong, Alexius von (1853–1920) Austrian philosopher, psychologist, and phenomenologist; born in Lemberg, Galicia (now Lvov, Ukraine); studied under Franz Brentano at the University of Vienna; taught at the University of Graz, where he founded a laboratory of experimental psychology. Meinong is known for his theory of objects and for his studies of the nature and relationships of emotions with the intellect. Most of his extensive writings have not yet been translated into English, even though they have influenced English works in philosophic psychology. J.N. Findley's *Meinong's Theory of Objects and Values* (1963) and *Realism and the Background of Phenomenology* (1960, edited by Roderick M. Chisholm) contain some of Meinong's concepts.

meliorism (from Latin, *melior,* better) **1.** the strong version: the belief (a) that the world tends to become better and better (more harmonious, more creative, more nearly perfect) and (b) that humanity (1) must identify itself as copartner in this creative thrust, and/or (2) *is* a part of this growth of values and betterment. **2.** the weak version: there is evil in the world and there is good in the world. There can be more good in existence than evil. In all probability, evolution is tending toward more good than that which is now present. Humankind can assist in this progress toward more good. If it does not, for some meliorists the universe will do it on its own.

meliorism (theology) the belief that God is omnibenevolent (all-good) but not omnipotent (all-powerful). Humanity must work together with the forces of God in creating a universe with less evil and more good.

Melissus (fl. 5th century BC) Greek philosopher and admiral, born on the island of Samos. He was a defender and disciple of Parmenides.

memory (from Latin, *memoria*; from *memor,* mindful) **1.** the recalling (reproduction, recognition, remembering) of experiences. **2.** the ability to retain the past in the present. **3.** that which is retained of an experience (perception, sensation, conception). **4.** the sum total of the mind's actual and possible experiences which can be remembered. Memory is considered the *SINE QUA NON* of CONSCIOUSNESS. Some of the characteristics ascribed to memory: (a) Memory is immediately given. It can be used in inferential mediate knowledge, but is not itself inferred. (b) Memory involves the concepts of (1) recording of experiences; (2) recalling (reviving, reproducing, remembering) experiences; (3) recognizing experiences as experiences that have occurred in a past (or remembering that they will occur or are occurring); (4) recognizing that the content of the recalled experiences is qualitatively different from immediate experiences; (5) (sometimes) recognizing that some of that content may not be veridical; (6) (sometimes) having a sense of the recalled experiences' temporal-spatial locality—of when and where the experiences took place; (7) inferring from past experience; and (8) extrapolating experiences. See RECOLLECTION.

mentalism the belief that only minds (spirits, souls) and their contents exist. Synonymous with many varieties of IDEALISM.

mentalism, emergent that aspect of the theory of emergent evolution in which mental states (mind, consciousness) are a new quality emerging from a nonmental (physical-chemical-biological) state that does not possess this quality. See EVOLUTION, EMERGENT.

mention see USE/MENTION DISTINCTION.

meta (Greek, after, beyond, between, with, over, over and above) used as a prefix in English implying (in its philosophical use) *transcendence* or *on a higher level*. In most cases, *meta* may be translated as *the study of the characteristics of* whatever it is prefixed to. Example: METALANGUAGE is the study of the characteristics possessed by language; language is that object being studied.

metaethics 1. the study of the characteristics of (the nature of) ethics. **2.** the study of the methods, language, logical structure, reasoning used to arrive at and justify moral decisions and knowledge. **3.** the study of the source, meaning, and justification of ethical inquiry and judgments. **4.** the study of what ethics does and how it does it, as opposed to (a) what might be called *substantive ethics*, such as utilitarianism, hedonism, or stoicism, which designate in a general way what the ethical good is, and (b) *normative ethics*, which studies and prescribes what one *should* do, how one *should* act, based on moral principles.

metalanguage 1. that language in which the theory about a language under study is formulated. **2.** the language used to talk about a language—about what it is and does; a language about a language. A logic language, or syntactical language, is an example of a metalanguage. Contrasted with *object language* (see LANGUAGE, OBJECT), which is the language that is being studied. A *metalinguistic* statement says something about something said or done by the object language. Contrasted with *referential* (nonverbal) *reality* about which a language communicates.

metalinguistic (when not used as a cognate of METALANGUAGE) referring to a source of knowledge that is beyond (META) language, or that is not derived from language.

metaphor (from Greek, *metaphora*; from *metapherein*, carry over, transfer; from *meta*, beyond, over, + *pherein*, bring, bear; in Aristotle's *Rhetoric*, *metaphora* meant *a word used in a changed sense*) a figure of speech by which a word (phrase, statement) that denotes one thing is applied (transferred) to another thing to suggest a likeness between them. Examples: "a sea of troubles." "The destroyer plowed the sea." "Agnes is a sly fox." Opposite to *literal*. Synonymous with *figurative*. Compare with ANALOGY; ANIMISM; PERSONIFICATION.

Metaphors contain a primary and a secondary term. The primary term is the thing being described. The secondary term is the description given to the thing being described. The usefulness or quality of a metaphor is judged by criteria such as (a) the number of similarities (resemblances, correspondences) that exist between the things compared, and (b) the number of similarities brought to awareness that were previously unnoticed.

metaphysics (from Greek, *meta ta physica*, after the physics; from *meta*, after, beyond, + *physikos*, pertaining to nature, or from *physis*, nature, natural, physical; the origin of the word *metaphysics* is uncertain) Aristotle did not use the term, although there is a compilation of his works called *The Metaphysics*. There is no general agreement as to how to define metaphysics. The following are some of the main definitions: **1.** the attempt to present a comprehensive, coherent, and consistent account (picture, view) of reality (being, the universe) as a whole. In this sense it is used interchangeably with most meanings of SYNOPTIC PHILOSOPHY and COSMOLOGY. **2.** the study of being *as* being and not *of* being in the form of a particular being (thing, object, entity, activity). In this sense it is synonymous with ONTOLOGY and with FIRST PHILOSOPHY. **3.** the study of the most general, persistent, and pervasive characteristics of the universe: existence, change, time, cause-effect relationships, space, substance, identity, uniqueness, difference, unity, variety, sameness, and oneness. **4.** the study of ultimate reality—reality as it is constituted in itself apart from the illusory appearances presented in our perceptions. **5.** the study of the underlying, self-sufficient ground (principle, reason, source, cause) of the existence of all things, the nondependent and fully self-determining being upon which all things depend for their existence. **6.** the study of a transcendent reality that is the cause (source) of all existence. In this sense metaphysics becomes synonymous with THEOLOGY. **7.** the study of anything that is spiritual (occult, supernatural, supranatural, immaterial) and which cannot be accounted for by the methods of explanation found in the physical sciences. **8.** the study of that which by its very nature must exist and cannot be otherwise than what it is. **9.** the critical examination of the underlying assumptions (presuppositions, basic beliefs) employed by our systems of knowledge in their claims about what is real. In this sense metaphysics is synonymous with important definitions of PHILOSOPHY and also with EPISTEMOLOGY. All these definitions of metaphysics, with the possible exception of 9, are *rationalistic* (see RATIONALISM). By the process of thinking we can arrive at fundamental, undeniable truths about the universe (reality, the world, existence, God, being). Experimental and scientific methods are not essential in obtaining metaphysical knowledge.

metaphysics (Aristotle) 1. the study of being-as-such (being-in-itself) as distinct from the study of particular beings that exist in the universe. Biology studies the *being* of living organisms; geology studies the *being* of the earth; astronomy studies the *being* of the stars; physics studies the *being* of natural change, movement, and development. But metaphysics studies the properties that all of these *beings* have in common. In this sense of metaphysics the most important questions are: "What is being?" "What is substance?" "What is reality?" **2.** the study of what it means to say that something *is*, what it means to *be*. Metaphysics is the study of those properties (characteristics) a thing must have to be in change and to have an identity. **3.** the study of the eternal first principles (laws) in accordance with which all things act. **4.** the study of the separate realm of eternal, unchanging being. In this sense metaphysics becomes identical with the traditional definition of THEOLOGY. **5.** the study of nonsensible (insensible, not sensed) substance as opposed to the sciences that deal with sensible substances. Aristotle specifically referred to 4. and 5. as FIRST PHILOSOPHY. **6.** the cataloging of (a) the general levels, or realms, of things that exist which are dealt with by the sciences, and (b) the study of how such levels of existence relate to one another and how they provide the framework in which activity occurs and by which it is limited. **7.** (a) the study of the interrelationships of all types of knowledge, (b) the study of how their concepts apply (or can be intelligently applied) to what exists, and (c) the study of their ontological *and* logical status in providing us with truth about reality. Metaphysics as understood in 6. and 7. deals especially with such things as the ontological and logical status of universals, the relationship of particulars to universals and of universals to particulars, the status of the concepts of unity, energy, change, form, mathematical points, lines, geometric forms, etc.

metempsychosis (from Greek, *metempsychōsis*; from *meta,* beyond, + *empsychoun,* animate; from *em,* in, + *psychē,* soul) also called REINCARNATION, TRANSMIGRATION; the passing of an eternal soul at death from its body to another body.

method (Bacon) see BACONIAN METHOD; TABLES OF INVESTIGATION, THE THREE (BACON).

method (Descartes) in his *Discourse on Method,* Descartes presents four rules that provide us with knowledge and are the bases of all philosophic inquiry. **1.** never accept anything as true unless you can recognize it to be self-evidently true. Avoid all preconceptions and include nothing in your conclusions unless it presents itself so clearly and distinctly that there is no circumstance under which you can doubt it. See DOUBT, DESCARTES' METHOD OF. **2.** divide a problem (difficulties) into as many distinct parts as possible or as might be needed to provide an easier solution. **3.** think in an orderly (systematic) manner by beginning with the simplest elements in the problem and the easiest things to understand, and gradually reach toward more complex knowledge (synthesis). In this process you may have to assume an order among the elements that is not really there. **4.** make sure everything has been taken into consideration, and nothing has been omitted from review.

method (Newton) the four *Rules of Reasoning in Philosophy* found in his *Mathematical Principles of Natural Philosophy, Book III*—the foundation of Newton's method: **1.** do not admit any more causes to explain things than are true and sufficient. **2.** assign the same causes to the same effects. **3.** assume that the qualities commonly observed in things are universally present. **4.** consider the statements obtained by inductive procedures as true, or very nearly true, until (a) they are corrected and made more accurate by further observations (or experimentation) or (b) are shown to have exceptions.

method, scientific an empirical, experimental, logicomathematical conceptual system that organizes and interrelates facts within a structure of theories and inferences. In most cases scientific method presupposes that whatever happens has a specific cause followed by a specific effect, that effects can be deduced (predicted) from an empirical knowledge of causes, and that knowledge of causes can be derived from knowledge of effects. Scientific method begins in the formulation of a tentative, working HYPOTHESIS that explains some phenomena. See EXPLANATION, SCIENTIFIC; and entries under LAW.

methodology (from Greek, *methodos,* method, + *lógos,* the study of) **1.** the study of the methods (procedures, principles) employed in an organized discipline, and/or used in organizing it. **2.** the principles themselves of any organized system. **3.** the branch of logic that formulates and/or analyzes the principles involved in making logical inferences and forming concepts. **4.** the procedures used in a discipline by which knowledge is obtained.

methods, Mill's inductive sometimes called *Mill's Canons of Induction* or *Mill's Experimental Methods*, Mill himself used the phrase *eliminative methods of induction.* In his *System of Logic,* Mill propounded five ways for discovering the causal relationship between phenomena: **1.** *the Method of Agreement:* "If two or more instances of the phenomenon under investigation have only one circumstance in common, the circumstance in which alone all the instances agree is the cause (or effect) of the given phenomenon." A cause of phenomena must always be present; is present whenever the phenomena occur. **2.** *the Method of Difference:* "If an instance in which the phenomenon under investigation occurs, and an instance in which it does not occur, have every circumstance in common save one, that one occurring in the former; the circumstance in which alone the two instances differ, is the effect, or the cause, or an indispensable part of the cause, of the phenomenon." Any event that occurs when phenomena of a certain sort do not, cannot be their cause. **3.** *the Joint Method of Agreement and Difference:* "If two or more instances in which the phenomenon occurs have only one circumstance in common, while two or more instances in which it does not occur have nothing in common save the absence of that circumstance, the circumstance in which alone the two sets of instances differ, is the effect, or the cause, or an indispensable part of the cause, of the phenomenon." **4.** *the Method of Concomitant Variations*, also known as *The Method of Isolation by Varying Concomitants*: "Whatever phenomenon varies in any manner whenever another phenomenon varies in some particular manner, is either a cause or an effect of that phenomenon, or is connected with it through some fact of causation." The cause of phenomena must be present to a similar degree as the phenomena. **5.** *the Method of Residues:* "Subduct from any phenomenon such part as is known by previous inductions to be the effect of certain antecedents, and the residue of the phenomenon is the effect of the remaining antecedents." See KNOWLEDGE (MILL).

microcosm (Greek, *mikros*, small, little, + *kósmos*, cosmos, universe, world) generally, any small part of a complex or whole contrasted with the larger complex of which it is a part (its MACROCOSM). The microcosm is often regarded as an epitome or analogue of the greater whole.

Mill, John Stuart (1806–1873) English philosopher, economist, moralist; born in London and educated at home—his father was James Mill, the historian, philosopher, and psychologist. By age 8, young John had read in Greek Aesop's *Fables*, Xenophon's *Anabasis*, all the works of Herodotus, six of Plato's Dialogues, Diogenes Laertius, and others. At age 8 he began the study of Latin, Euclid's geometry, and algebra.

Mill's major works are *The System of Logic*, (2 volumes, 1843); *Principles of Political Economy* (2 volumes, 1848); *On Liberty* (1859); *Utilitarianism* (1861); *An Examination of Sir William Hamilton's Philosophy* (1865); *Auguste Comte and Positivism* (1865); *Subjection of Women* (1869); and *Autobiography* (1873).

mimēsis (Plato) (Greek, imitation, representation by means of art, portrait; some of its cognates in Greek mean *counterfeit*) the name for art that represents (imitates) objects in the sensible world and thereby does not reveal insight into the real and eternal world of forms of which objects are merely imperfect copies. *Mimēsis* is thus a copy of a copy of reality, twice removed from truth. Plato uses *mimēsis* to refer to the imitative relationship of objects in this world that imperfectly copy the ideal form. See IDEAS (PLATO).

mind 1. consciousness; awareness. **2.** human rational powers; thought; the capacity to think. **3.** psyche; self; ego; personal identity. **4.** SOUL; spirit; spiritual substance. **5.** that which endures throughout changes of consciousness (experience, awareness). **6.** the entity that performs such functions as sensing, perceiving, remembering, imagining, conceiving, feeling, emoting, willing, reasoning, extrapolating into a future, or judging. **7.** the name for those functions listed in 6. but not possessing any ontological reality as an entity or substance. **8.** the name for the adaptive responses of an organism to its environment in the struggle for survival. The dynamic, attending, and selective functionings of the organism upon items in its internal and external world that have possible survival value (and in the higher forms of mind have intrinsic interest).

mind, bundle theory of the (Hume) the theory that the mind is "nothing but a bundle or collection of different perceptions, which succeed each other with an inconceivable rapidity, and are in a perpetual flux and movement." The mind is not a mental substance but merely a bundle of experiences that occur in succession from birth to death. The entire series constitutes the bundle, and this bundle may be named *mind* (or *self*). Events in each bundle are related by such features as (a) resemblances of perceptions, (b) contiguity of experiences in time and place, (c) regularity of succession among perceptions, and (d) memory. If these elements are not present, then we cannot be said to have a mind (or a self). The mind does not at any time exist as a self-subsisting entity apart from the above features.

mind, disembodied a mind that continues to possess mental qualities such as feeling, thinking, perceiving, willing, without being in a body. Contrasted with MIND, EMBODIED.

mind, double-aspect theory of 1. the theory that mind and body are distinguishable but inseparable features of one underlying reality (process, substance); two modes of the same substance. Mind and body are separable in abstraction but not in actuality; they ultimately can be reduced to the activities of this one, unitary substance but they cannot be reduced to each other. Example: The head side and the tail side of a coin are distinguishable but inseparable. Looked at from one perspective we can see the coin's head side (*mind*). Looked at from another perspective we can see the coin's tail side (*body*). Yet they are *aspects* of one and the same reality, facets of a common substance, the coin itself. Compare with MIND, DOUBLE-ASPECT THEORY OF (SPINOZA). **2.** mind and body can each be seen as one of the facets or manifestations of a common substance, which itself cannot be known. A variety of neutral monism. See MONISM, NEUTRAL.

mind, double-aspect theory of (Spinoza) a human is composed of two fundamental essences: *mind* (a human as a thinking thing) and *body* (a human as a thing occupying space). These are only two of the infinite aspects of the universe (God), and the only two that humans can know in a direct, immediate way. Many of the other facets of God and of humans can be known, but not in their *essence*. All things in the universe can be explained in terms of the essence of mind. Each essence contains potentially all the universe within it as a reflection of a deductive system. All things in the universe can be explained in terms of the essence of body (*matter*). It makes no difference which aspect of reality we care to use as our basis of explanation. But these two levels of explanation, the mental and the physical, must not be mixed. Looked at from their unique and different perspectives, they appear as being two. But mind and body are attributes of one and the same thing (a manifestation or aspect of a common substance called God, nature, the universe). And for Spinoza: "Thinking substance and extended substance are one and the same thing." Spinoza's double-aspect view of mind/body ends up as a form of extreme MONISM.

mind, embodied 1. in metaphysics, the theory that the universe is imbued with a cosmic mind as its operating principle of order and change; the universal mind IMMANENT in all things. **2.** in the philosophy of mind, the denial of a separate soul or mental agency that produces thought. Consciousness is that activity identified with the whole ordered structure of physiochemical and neurological processes. **3.** body (or matter) imbued with a mind. **4.** mind has mental qualities such as feeling, thinking, perceiving, and willing only while immanent within a body. Contrasted with MIND, DISEMBODIED.

mind, emergent theory of the theory that mind is the quality that emerges from the particular organization (structure, arrangement) of the constituents of living forms. See EVOLUTION, EMERGENT.

mind, types of theories of the theories that attempt to explain the nature of mind fall somewhere along a continuum of *extreme dualism:* mind and body are entirely separate and separable substances (entities) with utterly different characteristics, and *extreme monism:* mind (mental states) and body (physical states) are one and the same thing.

1. *Mind as an Eternal Transmigrating Soul:* The mind is an eternal, immaterial, self-moving, self-activating soul or spirit that uses bodies as the vehicles through which it expresses its functions. The body is regarded as the temple of the soul or as the prison of the soul, depending on the attitude taken toward the body. See METEMPSYCHOSIS; TRANSMIGRATION. **2.** *Mind as a Product of the Action of the Soul upon the Body:* The soul as an eternal and immaterial agent acts upon the body and in so doing mental effects are produced such as perceiving, thinking, feeling, willing, imagining, and remembering. See DUALISM, DESCARTES' SOUL/BODY. **3.** *Mind as Mental* (or *Spiritual*) *Substance:* The mind (or soul) is a substance totally unlike matter or body, which endures throughout the changes of its body and (a) has such nonmaterial functions as: (1) self-direction, (2) thinking, (3) feeling, and (4) willing, and (b) has such nonmaterial characteristics as (1) intangibility, (2) not occupying space, (3) being indestructible (except in some theories by God), (4) being created and placed in a body by God, and (5) being immortal as a disembodied entity in a heaven or hell, etc. **4.** *Mind as a Succession of Mental Events:* The mind is the rapid succession of mental states in continual change and not a self-subsisting entity (soul, spirit, substance, self) in its own right. There are forms of Idealism that view the rapid succession of mental events as caused not by activities of the body but by a spiritual agent. In a form of neutral monism, the cause is something unknown but nevertheless unlike body. **5.** *Mind as the By-product of the*

Body (EPIPHENOMENALISM): The mind is caused by changes of the body (in particular by brain processes). Mental events are effects of the body or the brain. Mind is an appearance, an epiphenomenon completely dependent on body and without causal efficacy of its own even upon subsequent mental events. The body causes the mind, but the mind is a suspended non-causal existence. **6.** *Mind as the Function of the Form of the Body:* Mind is the form of the body, the functioning of the body. Mind is that which a body does and can do in fully expressing (actualizing, realizing, fulfilling) its forms and its capacities, that which it is able to express and by its nature *intends* to express. An analogy taken from Aristotle may be used to illustrate this position: As vision is to (the structures of) the eye, so the mind is to (the structures of) the body. Some of the implications in this analogy: (a) Change the structures and functions of the eye and you change vision. Change the structures and functions of the body and you change the mind. (b) Mind and body are organically interrelated, holistically integrated, and interdependent. One cannot be said to be the main cause affecting the other. (c) Vision as a function of the eye is the expression of the *form* (and matter) of the eye; so too the mind is a function of the body expressing the form (and matter) of the body. **7.** *Mind as a Function of the Organism as a Whole:* Mind is that which an organism (mechanism) does and can do under the influence of internal and external stimuli. Mind is an integrated, self-directing, self-governing organism (mechanism) that has the ability to do such things as store knowledge, learn from this knowledge, prepare hypothetical situations based on this knowledge, adapt to novel situations in the light of this knowledge, predict, develop methods of solving perplexities, etc. See CYBERNETICS. **8.** *Mind as the Behavior Patterns of the Body*: Mind is identical with the physical behavior that a body undergoes. Mental processes are behavioral activities, such as laryngeal movements, muscular responses, bodily movements, skin responses, and eye movements. See BEHAVIORISM. **9.** *Mind as Identical with Brain Processes:* Mental events are one and the same with specific neural processes of the brain. Since they are identical, there is no interaction. See MIND/BODY, IDENTITY THEORY OF; PHYSICALISM (MIND/BODY). **10.** *Mind as Matter, Mind as Material*: Mind is a level of material (physical) manifestation in the universe. All statements that contain references to mental phenomena can be reduced to statements about material (physical) events or processes. Not only is mind caused by physical forces, it is itself a form of energy or matter in motion. See MATERIALISM.

mind/body, God acting on see OCCASIONALISM (MIND/BODY THEORY).

mind/body, identity theory of sometimes called *identity theory* or PHYSICALISM, mind (sensations, perceptions, consciousness in general) is identical with certain brain processes, and certain brain processes are identical with mind. A monistic philosophy.

mind/body dichotomy the differences between statements about mental states (events, qualities) and statements about physical states. The following is a partial list of the fundamental ways in which the characteristics attributed to mind are different from those attributed to body: **1.** mind is private; body is publicly observable. **2.** mind, both as a unity and in its various states, is immediately known, as opposed to body (matter) that is known by inference from perception and memory. **3.** mind is intentional; body has no intentionality. **4.** mind is intangible, nonspatial, and nonlocatable; body is tangible, spatial, and locatable. **5.** mind does not occupy space; body occupies space. **6.** things said about states of mind are INCORRIGIBLE; things said about states of a body are not incorrigible and can be denied without contradiction.

mind/body dualism see DUALISM, MIND/BODY.

mind/body interactionism usually associated with the commonsense theory that mind and body are two separate and distinct realities, each causally affecting the other; mental events can change bodily states and bodily events can affect mental states. Examples: Worry, tension, fear, anxiety (mental events) can affect the body (ulcers, hair standing on end, increase in temperature). Carbon monoxide, too much alcohol in the bloodstream, a blow to the head (bodily events) can affect mental events (headache, unconsciousness, derangement, etc.). Compare with DUALISM, DESCARTES' SOUL/BODY.

mind/body relationships, theories of 1. *Interactionism:* the body acts on the mind; the mind acts on the body. A variety of interactionistic theories exist: (a) The body produces the mind (mental events), but the mind once in existence can cause bodily changes. (b) The mind (as soul, spirit) is prior in existence to the body but interacts with it, being affected by it and affecting it. See MIND/BODY INTERACTIONISM. **2.** *One-Way Causal Action by the Mind:* the mind (as soul, spirit) acts upon body, causing it to perform the functions it does. **3.** *One-Way Causal Action by the Body:* the body produces the mind but then neither acts upon it, nor interacts with it. Mental events are effects of bodily causes. See EPIPHENOMENALISM. **4.** *Parallelism Without Interaction,* also *Psycho-physical Parallelism:* mind and body are correlated but do not affect each other causally or in any other way. They accompany each other in time (are synchronized). Whenever a particular mental event occurs, a particular bodily event occurs which simultaneously and regularly accompanies it. Whenever a particular bodily event occurs, a particular mental event occurs that simultaneously and regularly accompanies it.

mind-stuff theory of mind all things from human beings to the smallest particle are imbued with some amount of *mind-stuff,* or psychic material. The less mind-stuff it possesses, the less its complexity and intelligence. The human mind is the result of the combining together of this psychic matter into a particular continuing unity. A form of materialistic PANPSYCHISM.

miracle (from Latin, *miraculum*, wonder at) theologically, an event in nature produced by God, who suspends God's laws of nature in order to produce a beneficent effect for humans.

misplaced concreteness see CONCRETENESS, FALLACY OF MISPLACED.

modality (Kant) refers to possibility/existence/necessity and to impossibility/nonexistence/contingency in Kant's Table of Categories. See CATEGORIES OF LOGIC (KANT); CATEGORIES OF THE UNDERSTANDING (KANT); MODE (KANT).

modal logic see LOGIC, MODAL.

mode (from Latin, *modus,* a measure, form, the manner in which) **1.** the manner in which relations or qualities are combined. Usually considered as an entity apart from the thing to which it belongs. **2.** the condition (state of being or existence) in which a thing is at a given moment; its form of arrangement as manifested in existence. **3.** the particular form of existence given to (or acquired by) pure being, thereby limiting it and giving it an identity or individuation. See MATERIALIZATION. **4.** the form (way) in which something is understood. **5.** the form by which something is understood and with which a thing is identified as that thing and distinguished from other things. **6.** the way in which a quality (attribute, property) is, or can be, possessed by a thing, as in "Green is a mode (or can be a mode) of the quality color."

mode (Kant) Kant used the word *Modalität,* usually translated as *modality,* which meant the manner—as *actual,* as *possible,* or as *necessary*—in which something existed. These three modes were considered by Kant as A PRIORI and necessary for all experience.

mode (Locke) the manner in which an idea is known. A *simple mode* refers to the compounding of an idea in the same manner. Examples: double, dozen, decade, century. A *mixed mode* is the combining of several different simple modes into a complex idea (usually not representing an entity or substance). Examples: responsibility, loyalty, conniving.

mode (Spinoza) "that which exists in, and is conceived through, something other than itself." Of the substance (God) containing infinite attributes, humans can know only two: mind (thought) and matter (extension). Each of these attributes is infinite when looked at NATURA NATURANS, and finite when looked at NATURA NATURATA. Each attribute has modes by which it can be understood. The principal modes for mind are intelligence (intellect) and volition (will). The principal modes for matter are change (MOTION) and stasis (rest). See MONISM, NEUTRAL.

mode, formal statements that are about words themselves. Examples: "*Cat* is a noun." "*Cat* has three letters." Contrasted with MODE, MATERIAL.

mode, material statements that are about things (entities, objects, relations, qualities) Example: "Tables are hard" is a sentence in the material mode. Contrasted with MODE, FORMAL.

monadology (from Greek, *monas,* unit, + *lógos,* the study of; thus, the study of monads) a term first used by Leibniz to designate his metaphysical system; a speculative analysis of an infinite number of self-determining monads at different levels of actualization operating in a rational PREESTABLISHED HARMONY in accordance with the prime monad (God).

monads (Leibniz) the simple, discrete, irreducible, indestructible units regarded as the fundamental substances of the universe composed of active forces and relationships that mirror the universe as a whole but do not interact with other units. Regarded as analogous to psychic centers of activity. Some further characteristics of a monad: indivisible, impenetrable, teleologically oriented, self-contained, self-sufficient, self-activating, self-directing, having its own source of energy, being the individual center of force (power, energy, process), nonmaterial, unextended, a simple substance without parts, eternal (but can be caused to begin or cease to act by God, the prime monad), and *windowless* (does not *interact* with other monads but contains within itself all the causes of its own activities, in a PREESTABLISHED HARMONY with the self-determining activity of all other monads).

Each monad contains as a part of its inherent nature its own unique program for the rate of its activity and manifestation at any given moment in time; its own unique program for all that has happened to it, is happening to it, and will ever happen to it. All that happens to a monad happens to it because of its nature (*program*). Nothing outside a monad, nothing that is not a part of its internal self-actuating process, affects it. The nature of all monads is programmed by God (the dominant or prime or supreme monad) so that they all express themselves in a preestablished harmony with the activities of all other monads. See ENTELECHY (LEIBNIZ).

Since all things are part of a preestablished harmony, anything that happens anywhere in the universe will (must) have a relationship with everything else in the universe, but not a causal relationship. The relationship is expressed in terms of such metaphors as the monads *mirroring*, *echoing*, and *reflecting* the simple pure monad (God). Since each monad contains all the properties of the universe, it is possible to logically deduce from any monad (a) all of its predicates (all that can ever be said of it) and (b) all that it will ever manifest.

monism (from Greek, *monos*, single) **1.** the theory that all things in the universe can be reduced to (or explained in terms of) the activity of one fundamental constituent (God, matter, mind, energy, form). **2.** the theory that all things are derived from one single ultimate source. **3.** the belief that reality is *one*, and everything else is illusion. Contrasted with DUALISM and PLURALISM.

monism, ethical see ETHICS, MONISTIC.

monism, neutral 1. the theory that none of what we think of as the ultimate constituents of the universe, such as mind, God, or matter, is ultimate. The fundamental reality of all things is a neutral element (*stuff*) to which we can give no definite characteristics. See ENTITY, NEUTRAL. **2.** the theory that mental and material states and processes are the effects of the interrelationships among *neutrally* subsisting entities that are themselves neither mental nor material. See MIND, DOUBLE-ASPECT THEORY OF (2).

monotheism see GOD CONCEPTS.

Moore, George Edward (1873–1958) English philosopher, born in London; educated at Cambridge, where he read classics, philosophy, and moral science. He taught at Cambridge for most of his life and edited the philosophy journal *Mind* for decades. Moore is known for his *Principia Ethica* (1903); *Ethics* (1912); *Philosophical Studies* (1922); and *Some Main Problems of Philosophy* (1953).

moral (from Latin, *moralis*; from *mos, moris,* manner, custom, conduct) **1.** having to do with human activities that are looked upon as good/bad, right/wrong, correct/incorrect. **2.** conforming to the accepted rules of what is considered right (virtuous, just, proper conduct). **3.** having (a) the capacity to be directed by (influenced by) an awareness of right and wrong, and (b) the capacity to direct (influence) others according to rules of conduct judged right or wrong. **4.** pertaining to the manner in which one behaves in relationship with others. Compare with ETHICS. Contrast with AMORAL; IMMORAL.

moral act some of the characteristics involved in a moral act: **1.** a motive or intention to act. **2.** an agent choosing or deciding on some course of action. **3.** the choice must be uncompelled, or self-determined (self-desired). **4.** moral qualities such as good/bad associated with any element in 1., 2., 3. **5.** some consequence, intended or not, that results to oneself or others.

moral postulates, the (Kant) see POSTULATES OF PRACTICAL REASON, THE (KANT).

moral principles 1. principles that indicate what ought to (should) be done; that indicate obligation and responsibility. Examples: "Lying is wrong." "Stealing is wrong." "One ought to be kind." **2.** principles (a) upon which one's moral conduct is consciously or subconsciously based or motivated, or (b) by which it can be explained or interpreted.

morals 1. the manner of behaving of groups or individuals according to what is regarded as good, right, virtuous, proper, correct. **2.** the study of what is to be considered right conduct.

moral sense 1. an innate, intuitive faculty or power (a) that is able to recognize right from wrong, (b) that motivates us toward right and (c) that gives us the standards with which we can make moral judgments. **2.** a *sixth sense* sensitive to qualities of good/bad, virtuous/invirtuous that are found (sensed, responded to) in human activities. See CONSCIENCE.

More, Sir Thomas (1478–1535) English statesman, lawyer, writer; born in London and educated at Oxford; canonized as St. Thomas More. More's interests centered around the law and religious and philosophic themes. His translations from Greek into Latin and his encouragement of the study of the Greek classics, the Greek New Testament, and the early Greek

Church Fathers contributed to what has been termed the English Renaissance.

More's best-known work is his *Utopia* (1516), a description of what More regarded as an ideal society—a form of communal living that stressed a utilitarian and egalitarian goal: the happiness of the community as a whole, therefore, of each community member, which is achieved by means of equality and equal access to the products and services of the community. More's English writings and translations of his Latin writings can be found in R.S. Sylvester (editor), *The Complete Works of St. Thomas More* (1963).

mores (from Latin, *mores,* ways of behaving) customs as determined by usage or practice and not by law; the practices, behavior patterns, customs, attitudes, values held in common by a group.

motion (from Latin, *motio*; from *movere,* move) **1.** generally any CHANGE. (In the classical sense, motion [KINĒSIS] included all forms of change such as change in quality, quantity, position, shape, or potency.) **2.** specifically, movement; change of the spatial location of bodies relative to each other. The process (act or state) of changing place (position). See ENERGY.

Concepts of motion serve as the essential ground for explanation of physical phenomena. (Opposite to rest. Motion has been defined negatively as anything that is not at rest.)

motion (Aristotle) see CHANGE (ARISTOTLE).

motion (atomists) self-movement as the essential characteristic of all atoms. Motion is eternal. All things in the universe can be accounted for in terms of the distribution and redistribution of these self-moving atoms moving within voids (empty spaces). Just as atoms are irreducible and unexplainable in terms of anything more fundamental, so motion is irreducible and needs no further source of explanation. See ATOMISM, GREEK.

motion (Plato) 1. motion externally imparted upon a thing, matter imparting motion to matter by contact. **2.** self-propelling motion, motion originating in the thing itself and not imparted by an outside thing. Only souls (spirits) have their own internal source of motion; only souls originate their own motion. Externally imparted motion is ultimately dependent on the self-propelling eternal motion of souls (spirits). In the final analysis all motion in the universe is dependent on the activity of a world soul.

Plato held that matter of itself is inert. The only thing that can move other nonmoving things is the soul, which can move itself (is eternally self-moving). Because it can move itself it can also move nonmoving things. SOUL is the primary cause of motion (change). The real world of forms is not in motion. The forms are perfect, immutable, and unchanging (see FORMS, PLATO'S THEORY OF IDEAL). The illusory sensible world is in continual motion (flux, change).

motion, continuum of (problems) the problems of continuous motion stemming from conceptualizing motion in terms of an object that is at successively different points (positions, states) at successively different times.

Some of the problems: **1.** how are the two points relatable and/or related in space? **2.** can there be points between these two points? (can there be states of motion between successive states of motion?) **3.** how does the object get from one point to the other—or does it? **4.** what are those points like? **5.** are there gaps between these points? **6.** what is motion doing (what is motion like) at these so-called gaps? **7.** if there are no gaps but only further points (an infinity of points between any two points), then how is motion possible? See ZENO'S PARADOXES.

motion, Newton's three laws of 1. *the Principle of Inertia:* All bodies continue in a state of rest, or of uniform motion in a straight line, unless they are compelled to change that state by other forces acting upon them. **2.** the change of motion of a body is directly proportional to the force acting upon it, and such change occurs in the direction of the straight line from which that force is acting. **3.** to every motion (action) there is an opposed and equal motion (reaction); the mutual motions (actions) of two bodies upon each other are always equal (and are directed to contrary parts).

motion, paradox of a body in motion changes and yet sometimes can be seen to endure as that thing throughout the change. It changes place (position, space) and/or quality but it also retains its identity. See ZENO'S PARADOXES.

motion, relative motion that is understood in terms of reference to some other motion outside itself.

multiplicity, doctrine of (from Latin, *multiplicitas*; from *multiplex*, manifold, multifarious) the universe seen as composed of a variety of existents that can never be reduced to a unity or a *one*. See PLURALISM.

multiplicity, principle of that which causes variety in the universe as opposed to that which causes unity.

mundus intelligibilis (Latin, the intelligible world) usually refers to a Platonic realm of perfect forms or ideas that serve as the models for the imperfect existences in the sensible world. Contrasted with MUNDUS SENSIBILIS.

mundus sensibilis (Latin, the world of sensibles, or the world of existing objects) refers to the things perceived by our senses (as opposed to the abstractions of our intelligence) that are imperfect copies of the realm of perfect forms, or the perfect ideas in God's mind. Contrasted with MUNDUS INTELLIGIBILIS.

mystical experience 1. the enraptured and ineffable state of union with a higher reality (such as the realm of perfect forms) or with God. **2.** the ecstatic identification of the self with the totality of all things, expressed by such phrases as "The All is One and the One is All." See ECSTASY. The mystical experience may be a contemplative union or identification, and/or it may be a state of pure overwhelming feeling. See NUMINOUS EXPERIENCE; RELIGIOUS EXPERIENCE.

mystical experience, characteristics of the some of the characteristics of the mystical experience: **1.** joyous; ecstatic. **2.** indescribably intense and unique. **3.** the most momentous, important, significant experience of one's life. **4.** has a lasting and total effect upon one's life, providing one with *salvation, serenity, light, bliss,* or *blessedness,* which were not there before. **5.** transforms one's moral nature, values, and intuitions. **6.** the experience is transient (yet reveals the eternal and, while one is having it, may seem to last a long time). **7.** the experience is passive; it comes upon one suddenly, at unexpected times and places (although there are forms of mystical experiences that can be induced by such means as rational contemplation, meditation, ascetic practices, drugs). **8.** a feeling, and/or a vision, of an encounter (confrontation) with some unusual reality never felt or seen in any ordinary experience. That reality is a oneness or unity. **9.** a sense of identification (and sometimes communication) with that extraordinary reality (unity) in which the self is dissolved or merged. **10.** the experience is NOETIC; a knowledge is gained about a reality unobtainable by any other means. **11.** that knowledge is ineffable, uncommunicable, and can never be put into language or conceptual schemes of understanding. **12.** the mystical experience itself and the knowledge thereby gained can never be described or conceptualized (nevertheless, attempts are made by means of metaphors, analogies, paradoxes, and poetic imagery that do not hope to communicate the quality of the experience or the content of the knowledge obtained, but seek to evoke, excite, or spark intimations of the experience, an experience latent in all people).

mystical intuition where *mystical intuition* is not used synonymously with MYSTICAL EXPERIENCE, it is used to mean that latent or active faculty of the mind by which, and only by which, a knowledge of a higher reality is disclosed (revealed, perceived).

mysticism (from Greek, *mystērion*; from *mystēs,* one initiated in the mysteries or secrets of a truer reality) **1.** the belief that the ultimate truth about reality can be obtained neither by ordinary experience nor by the intellect, but only by a MYSTICAL EXPERIENCE or by a nonrational MYSTICAL INTUITION. The nature of reality is inexpressible and cannot be experienced in any ordinary experiential and rational way. **2.** the nonrational, nonordinary experience of all-inclusive reality (or often of a transcendent reality), whereby the separateness of the self is merged with that reality usually regarded as the source or ground for the existence of all things. Mysticism asserts that rational knowledge stresses differentiation, distinctions, separation, individuation; it distorts reality and is therefore illusory. See CONTEMPLATION.

mysticism (complete absorption) the experience of total identification or union with all things or with a higher reality in which there is no distinction between the individual having the experience and that which is experienced. The *I* is completely absorbed into the *all* (the *one*), and there is no subject/object separation.

mysticism (partial absorption) the experience of oneness with all things or with a higher reality in which there is an awareness at the time of the experience of a distinction between the self (the individual) having the experience and that which is experienced. The individual stands as a distinct perceiver before the *all*. The *I* encounters (confronts, is in the presence of) the *all*.

myth (from Greek, *mythos,* myth, fable, tale, legend, talk, speech, conversation, rumor, anything delivered by word of mouth) a story whose origin is forgotten and which: **1.** presents a nonscientific history of the thought of a people explaining in an anthropomorphic, animistic form such things as the creation of the universe (COSMOGONY), the structure of the universe (COSMOLOGY), and the source and nature of human and natural phenomena (pride, jealousy, sin, trees, rivers, etc.); **2.** expresses the socially significant events of a people as well as their social consciousness; and **3.** expresses and reinforces, by ritual and other means, the social bonds, customs, and cultural ties of a people. Sympathetic modern interpretations of myths do not regard them as true or false, but as possessing poetic insight into reality (to the extent to which it does so, to that extent it can be called a good, relevant, correct, or proper myth). Also, myths are looked on as expressing archetypal symbolisms that recur because of humankind's collective unconscious. Compare with METAPHOR.

mythical thinking prerational thinking; the human mind casting its perceptions of reality in the form of artistic intuition and imagery.

N

Nagel, Ernest (1901–1985) American philosopher, born in Czechoslovakia; educated at the City College of New York and Columbia University. He was noted for his philosophic naturalism, based on logic and a scientific, empirical methodology and applied to the study of law, history, mathematics, natural sciences, and social sciences. His book *The Structure of Science* (1961) was the culmination of his life's work in the philosophy of sciences. It analyzes the nature of scientific explanation in physics and biology, the logic underlying scientific inquiry, the logical nature of scientific knowledge and its organization, and the use of causality and probability theory in the sciences.

Nagel's other principal writings include *The Logic of Measurement* (1930); *An Introduction to Logic and Scientific Method* (1934, with Morris Raphael Cohen); *Sovereign Reason* (1954); *Logic Without Metaphysics* (1956); and *Godel's Proof* (1958).

naive realism see REALISM, NAIVE.

name, negative see CLASS, COMPLEMENTARY.

name, privative see PRIVATIVE TERM (WORD, NAME).

natura naturans (Latin, nature maturing, nature naturing, nature nurturing) refers to the active, creative processes of nature that are being manifested at any given moment. For Spinoza, nature as a causal agent of modes and attributes. In Scholasticism, a phrase designating God. Compare with *NATURA NATURATA*.

natura naturata (Latin, nature matured, nature natured, nature having been nurtured) refers to the things created by (or in) nature. For Spinoza, the reality created by *NATURA NATURANS*. In Scholasticism, nature as created by God. See MODE (SPINOZA); SUBSTANCE (SPINOZA).

natural (from Latin, *naturalis*) **1.** innate: inborn. **2.** in accordance with the inner nature (essence, predispositions) of a thing. **3.** referring to physical phenomena; in accordance with, or pertaining to, the phenomena of nature and of human nature. **4.** referring to conduct that seems instinctively right. **5.** performed instinctively, without thinking or willing, usually in accordance with ordinary common experience. **6.** normal. **7.** not artificial.

natural law see entries under LAW, NATURAL and NATURE.

natural philosophy originally used to indicate the study of nature in general. With the development of mechanistic systems in early modern science, it referred specifically to the field of physics.

natural rights see RIGHTS, NATURAL.

natural selection (Darwin) the process in nature that brings about the survival of the fittest in a struggle for existence. Those animals and plants survive that are best adjusted to the conditions in which they exist. The process of natural selection depends in large measure on the variability of the forms of life over a long period, gradually resulting in structural changes that are adaptive. Darwin held that in every population of living organisms, there occur random variations that have differing degrees of adaptive value. Variations that increase the chances of survival or the rate of reproduction persist in existence. They are thereby preserved and then genetically transmitted to subsequent generations. Variations that do not have a high survival value decrease or pass out of existence. See DARWINISM, SOCIAL.

naturalism some of the tenets of naturalism: **1.** *Monistic:* the universe (nature) is the only reality. It is eternal, self-activating, self-existent, self-contained, self-dependent, self-operating, and self-explanatory. The universe is not derived from nor dependent on any supernatural or transcendent being or entities. Natural phenomena cannot be interfered with, violated, or suspended. There is no supernatural realm. There are no souls, spirits, disembodied minds, immaterial forces. There is no immortality, reincarnation, transmigration. **2.** *Antisupernaturalistic:* all phenomena can be explained in terms of the inherent interrelationships of natural events without recourse to any supernatural or supernatural explanation. No reality exists other than processes (events, objects, happenings, occurrences) in space and time. There are no nonnatural causes. The universe has its own structure and originates its own structure. Many levels of reality or manifestations of the universe may exist (see PLURALISM), but none are supernaturally caused. **3.** *Proscientific* (put into a progressively stronger version): (a) natural phenomena can be adequately explained by the improving methodology of the sciences; (b) all phenomena are in principle explainable by scientific methods; (c) all phenomena can be explained by scientific methodology; and (d) knowledge can be obtained only by the logical-empirical methodologies of the sciences. Intuition, the mystical experience, faith, revelation are rejected as direct and proper means of arriving at truth about reality. **4.** *Humanistic:* humans are one of the many (natural) manifestations of the universe (and usually regarded as of no special hierarchical importance from the point of view of the universe). Human behavior is to be explained in terms of, and seen to be related to, (a) behavior similar to, but more complex than, the behavior of other animals, and (b) the social and environmental influences creating and conditioning human needs and awareness. The human ethical and aesthetic nature has its ground in natural phenomena. An empirical study of humans' place in nature and of human nature can provide us with ethical and aesthetic values by which humans can live cooperatively and happily. Values are human-made but realistically based on natural conditions. Values do not have a supernatural source or sanction. **5.** *Tendencies toward:* (a) nonteleological explanations, (b) nonanthropomorphic, nonanimistic explanations,

(c) reliance on experience and rational methods of inquiry, (d) individualism (in cooperative endeavor with other individuals), (e) the maximization and realization of human potentials, (f) freedom of inquiry and opportunity, and (g) viewing humans in an organic relationship with their environment, society, and the universe. Opposite to SUPERNATURALISM. Compare with HUMANISM, PHILOSOPHICAL; MATERIALISM.

naturalism, critical a form of naturalism that considers a purely mechanical or materialistic interpretation of reality as insufficient. Mind, life, and values are other significant and efficacious levels of reality that cannot be interpreted purely as matter in motion. Some critical naturalists hold to the notion of a creative thrust in evolution toward the expression of higher and more integrated values. See EVOLUTION, EMERGENT.

naturalism, ethical the view that no sharp demarcation exists between facts about the world and judgments (evaluations) about the world and how humans ought to act in it. Moral evaluations contain facts about natural phenomena. Examples: To determine the rightness or wrongness of an act, one must refer to the facts as to whether or not pleasure will be obtained by such an act, or whether or not specific needs will in fact be achieved, or whether or not it will produce cooperation, unity, harmony. See ETHICS, NATURALISTIC.

naturalistic fallacy used interchangeably with REDUCTIVE FALLACY.

naturalistic fallacy (ethics) 1. the fallacy of reducing ethical statements to factual statements, to statements about natural events. **2.** the fallacy of deriving (deducing) ethical statements from nonethical statements. Compare with ETHICS, IS/OUGHT DICHOTOMY IN. **3.** the fallacy of defining ethical terms in nonethical (descriptive, naturalistic, or factual) terms.

naturalistic fallacy (G.E. Moore) the fallacy of identifying goodness with a natural characteristic (property, attribute) such as pleasantness, being the object of desire, or promoting the general well-being of a community. What *good* means is different from designating which things are good. Moore regarded moral goodness as an indefinable, nonnatural property that cannot be derived from natural properties. See OPEN-QUESTION ARGUMENT (G.E. MOORE).

nature (from Latin, *natura*; from *natus*, born, produced; the past participle of *nasci*, be born) **1.** the universe. The existing system of all that there is in time and space. Everything that happens (good and bad). **2.** the powers (forces) that cause (produce, create) existing phenomena. **3.** the origin (or foundation) of everything. **4.** the ground for the explanation of things. **5.** the essence of a thing; its essential characteristics. **6.** the natural endowments of a thing. **7.** the physical constitution of a thing. **8.** an original, primitive state of things unadulterated and uncultivated by humans; that which happens without human interference.

nature (Aristotle) 1. that which is not made by humans is called *PHYSIS*, *nature*, in contrast to *TECHNĒ*, which refers to all the things made by humans. **2.** nature is a teleological system and makes nothing without a purpose in two senses: (a) natural objects serve purposes other than their own purposes, which interrelate as part of larger purposive schemes, and (b) there exists in the universe an overall pattern or order (purpose or design) that is being imitated throughout nature. **3.** the cause (principle, law, source) of all change (motion, movement). An understanding of nature entails an understanding of the characteristics and kinds of motion. **4.** the innate, immanent impulse for activity in all things (in contrast with TECHNĒ, which is a transcendent or external impulse for activity). This includes the material in which and through which this impulse (active form) expresses itself. See GENESIS (ARISTOTLE).

nature, state of the condition of humanity without (or before) government. Its hypothetical description ranges from Hobbes's portrayal of anarchy with brutal and continual war of *all against all*, to Rousseau's concept of the *noble savage* living in a condition of moral purity, happiness, and health.

necessary (from Latin, *necessarius*; from *necesse*, necessary) **1.** characterized by the impossibility of being otherwise. **2.** indispensable; that without which something cannot be done or cannot exist. **3.** inevitable. **4.** unavoidable. **5.** certain. **6.** involuntary; compelled. **7.** determined. **8.** imperative; must be. Opposite to CONTINGENT.

necessary being (theology) the independent, indestructible, incorruptible, uncaused eternal being (God): **1.** which is the cause of the existence of everything else; **2.** which can never become something other than what it is; and **3.** can never be caused not to be. That being upon which all things depend for their existence and sustenance, but which depends on nothing for its existence and continuance. The self-sufficient being. See entries under ABSOLUTE; COSMOLOGICAL ARGUMENT FOR GOD'S EXISTENCE.

necessary condition see CONDITION, NECESSARY.

necessary existence also called *necessary existent* **1.** that which does not depend for its existence on anything else; that uncaused eternal existence which does not owe its existence to something other than its own being; absolute causal independence in its origin from all other things. **2.** that whose essence is to exist; that existent whose essence cannot be conceived as not existing. The universe, nature, or matter may be thought of as a necessary existence. Opposite to CONTINGENT existence, contingent existent. Compare with CONDITION, NECESSARY; SELF-EXISTENCE.

necessitarianism the theory that all events in the universe are determined (necessitated) by causes, and that these causes themselves are necessitated to happen. Synonymous with PREDETERMINISM. Opposite to ACCIDENTALISM.

necessity, historical see MATERIALISM, DIALECTICAL (MARX-ENGELS).

negation (from Latin, *negatio*; from *negare*, say no, deny) **1.** a contradiction. **2.** a denial or the act of denying. **3.** assertion of the falsehood (unreality, untruthfulness) of something. **4.** a state of being or a making void, empty. **5.** annihilation; obliteration.

In logic, the negation of a term (sentence, statement, proposition) is its contradiction; to negate a term is to contradict it; negating a term is replacing it with its contradictory.

neikos opposite to PHILIA.

neologist (from Greek, *neos,* new, youthful, + *lógos,* the study of) **1.** in general, one who introduces a new word and/or a new meaning into a language or discipline. **2.** in theology, used pejoratively to refer to one (a heretic) who introduces a new doctrine (dogma, decree) that is contrary to the desired and accepted doctrine.

neo-Platonism see BEING, HIERARCHY OF; BEAUTY; EMANATION.

nescience (from Latin, *nescientia*; from *nesciens,* present participle of *nescire,* know not; from *ne,* not, + *scire,* know) **1.** in general, a state of not knowing. **2.** specifically refers to AGNOSTICISM and (a) its suspension of judgment, or (b) its declaration of ignorance about the existence and/or the characteristics of God.

Neurath, Otto (1882–1945) Austrian philosopher, linguist, sociologist, economist; born in Vienna; one of the founders of logical empiricism. Neurath's work encompasses visual education and communication; isotopes, an international language of communication by means of simplified signs and symbols; city planning; and statistical theories applied to economic, scientific, and social issues. His interests included scientific methodology, the history of science, political science, moral theory, economic history and theories, and optics.

Neurath attempted an encyclopedic unity of all the sciences and, with others, developed a world manifesto of science. With other philosophers Neurath founded and edited the *International Encyclopedia of Unified Science*—the first two volumes reached publication. Neurath's major work translated into English is *Foundations of the Social Sciences* (1944), which appears in the second volume of the *Encyclopedia.*

neutral monism see MONISM, NEUTRAL.

Newton's three laws of motion see MOTION, NEWTON'S THREE LAWS OF.

Nietzsche, Friedrich Wilhelm (1844–1900) German philosopher and poet, born in Saxony and educated at the University of Bonn, studying theology and classical philology. Upon reading Schopenhauer's *The World as Will and Idea*, he abandoned his interest in theology and Christianity but retained his interest in philology.

Nietzsche was influenced by Richard Wagner (from whom he later was alienated), Kant, Lange, and his teacher of philology (Ritschl). During his acquaintance with Wagner, Nietzsche wrote *The Birth of Tragedy* (1870), which combined his own research on Greek creativity with Wagner's views of art. During the same period (1873–1876) he wrote four polemical works, mainly to rationalize Germany's defeats and encourage intellectual activity—the last of these was entitled *Richard Wagner in Bayreuth* (1876). By the time these works were completed, Nietzsche had become disillusioned with Wagner and, by 1888, had written the vituperous *Nietzsche contra Wagner*.

A sampling of Nietzsche's other works: *Human, All-too-Human* (published 2 volumes in Germany, 1878); *The Dawn: Reflections on Moral Prejudices* (1880); *The Gay Science* (1881); *Thus Spoke Zarathustra* (1883); *Beyond Good and Evil* (1885); *Genealogy of Morals* (1887); *Ecce Homo* (1888); *Twilight of the Idols* (1889); *The Anti-Christ* (1895); and *The Will to Power* (posthumously published, 1906).

nihil ex nihilo see EX NIHILO NIHIL FIT.

nihilism (from Latin, *nihil*, nothing) nothingness. **1.** in epistemology, the denial of any objective and real ground or state of truth. **2.** the theory that nothing is knowable. All knowledge is illusory, worthless, meaningless, relative, and insignificant. **3.** no knowledge is possible. Nothing can be known. **4.** the psychological and philosophical state in which there is a loss of all ethical, religious, political, and social values. **5.** the skeptical denial of all that is regarded as real/unreal, knowledge/error, being/nonbeing, illusory/nonillusory; the denial of the value of all distinctions.

nihilism (ethics) the theory that moral values cannot be justified in any way—not by reason, by a God, by intuition, by conscience, nor by the authority of the state or law. Moral values are (a) expressions of arbitrary and capricious behavior or (b) expressions of loose feelings and reasonless, social conditioning; and (c) worthless, meaningless, and irrational.

nihilism (Gorgias) see SKEPTICISM (GORGIAS).

nihilism (metaphysics) the theory that (a) the universe is meaningless and without purpose; (b) human life and its activities are of no value or significance; and (c) nothing is worth existing for. See ENNUI.

nihilism (political) the belief that social organization is so corrupt that its destruction is desirable. It is sometimes coupled with a form of ANARCHISM whereby no constructive alternative form of organization is deemed possible, and terrorism, violent revolutionary activities, and assassination are advocated.

nisus (Latin, past participle of *niti*, strive) **1.** a striving; an effort; the conative state of a thing. See CONATION. **2.** a creative tendency in the universe toward the production of qualitatively new emergents. See EVOLUTION, EMERGENT.

noēsis (Greek, intelligence, thought, understanding, mind) in Greek philosophy, the knowledge that results from the operation of NOUS, the mind, reason, intellectual faculty.

noetic (Greek, from *noētikos*, intelligent; from *noein*, perceive, know; and from *noētos*, perceptible to the mind, thinkable; as opposed to visible, *horatos*) **1.** having to do with reason and the intellect. **2.** cognitive; the knowledge that is (a) a consequence of the function of our cognitive faculties or

(b) an innate content of our cognitive faculties. Usually refers to knowledge that is independent of sensation. **3.** ontological cognition; the knowledge of reality had by the pure function of reason alone. Contrasted with ANOETIC.

nomic/nomological 1. lawlike (applied principally to physical occurrences). **2.** having to do with laws; (includes physical, legal, moral laws). See *NÓMOS*.

nominal definition see DEFINITION, TYPES OF (11).

nominalism (from Latin, *nominalis*; from *nomen, nominis*, a name) occasionally called *terminism* **1.** the theory that things do not have essences. **2.** that definitions and languages in general do not refer to things but deal with the names (terms) we attach to things. **3.** that all universal terms, such as those indicating genus/species distinctions, and all general collective terms, are only fictitious names (artificial and arbitrary symbols) and have no objective, real existences that correspond to them. **4.** that only particular existents (particulars) exist. Abstractions, universals, ideas, essences are only products of our language and/or of how our mind understands reality. They do not communicate what reality is like. **5.** that abstractions such as *human* (a) are merely names that can be used to refer to more than one particular, (b) have no objective existence as an entity *human* or *humanhood* shared by all particular humans, and (c) cannot even be present in consciousness as an abstract idea or concept of *human*, *humanhood*. Compare with entries under REALISM. See UNIVERSALS (NOMINALISM).

nómos (Greek, convention, custom, law) contrasted in Greek philosophy with *PHYSIS*, the natural, the necessarily innate. The word *nómos* has had a long history of varied meanings, among them: (a) a feeding place (for example, for cattle); (b) a district or province; (c) the abode assigned to one, a dwelling place; (d) anything assigned; (e) a usage, custom, law; and (f) the law of force or of warring. **1.** in epistemology, the plural, *nómoi*, refers to those qualities of things such as color, smell, and taste, which are only appearances, or secondary qualities, in our mind and do not exist in the external world of objects. This is contrasted with *physis*, which refers to the qualities found in things such as size, shape, figure, and arrangement, which belong to the things themselves. See QUALITIES, PRIMARY/SECONDARY. **2.** in ethics, *nómos* refers to actions performed in accordance with the customs and human-made laws of society as opposed to actions performed according to one's nature or to natural law. See CONVENTION.

nonbeing 1. the nonexistent; nonexistence reified. **2.** the lack (privation, absence) of existence or of an existent. **3.** the nonpresence of a reality essential to the natural activity of a thing and to its identification (or the presence of a reality not natural to the thing). **4.** the lack of any determinate form or order, especially the form or order natural to it. **5.** unreality; nonreality. **6.** matter, the lowest in the hierarchy of reality; complete stasis; the state of no innate potential to be actualized, and no innate tendencies to actualize itself. (In Platonism, identified with evil, darkness, ignorance, ugliness, the furthest removed from the divine ground of being.) Contrast with BEING.

nonbeing (Plato) Plato attempted to strike a compromise between two extremes: (a) the extreme of Heraclitus's philosophy, in which all things are in a state of continual change and in which it is possible for the same thing to be (being) and *not* to be (nonbeing), and (b) the extreme of the Eleatic philosophy, in which nothing changes but is in reality always the selfsame thing (*one*), which cannot help but *be*. For Plato, the sensible world of particular objects, sensations, and perceptions can be thought of as the confused if not illusory realm between the realm of true, eternal, unchanging being (the true reality of the perfect ideal forms) and the realm of nonbeing (which has no existence whatever). See FORMS, PLATO'S THEORY OF IDEAL.

non causa pro causa see FALLACY, TYPES OF INFORMAL (20).

noncognitivism see ETHICS, NONCOGNITIVE.

noncontradiction, principle of see LAWS OF THOUGHT, THE THREE.

nonmoral see AMORAL.

nonnatural property (G.E. Moore) a property **1.** that is not natural (as yellow is), **2.** that is not externally real (as objects are), and **3.** that is not supernatural (as being caused or given by God). A nonnatural property is had: **4.** not by sensation, **5.** not by cognitive faculties, **6.** not by introspection, but **7.** by an intuitive grasp.

Nonnatural intuitive properties are **8.** immediate, **9.** ineffable, indescribable, and **10.** associated with (accompanying) other properties.

A concept used by many ethical intuitionists. See NATURALISTIC FALLACY (G.E. MOORE); OPEN-QUESTION ARGUMENT (G.E. MOORE).

non sequitur (Latin, it does not follow) **1.** used generally to refer to concepts or expressions for which a rational connection is asserted or implied but for which there is none; **2.** used specifically to refer to any conclusion (inference) that does not follow from its premises. See FALLACY.

nonsense see ABSURD; CATEGORY MISTAKE.

normative (from Latin, *norma*, rule, pattern, precept) **1.** referring to that which is (a) regulative of human conduct (according to an ideal, norm, or standard), (b) preferential (expressing felt attitudes, values, biases), and (c) prescriptive (expressing a command or an obligation). **2.** referring to that which should be done, ought to be done; that which one is obliged to do, or responsible for; that which must be done because it ought to be done.

normative ethics see ETHICS, NORMATIVE.

nothing not any thing; the denial of existence or of an existent. Opposite to *something, thing, anything, everything*.

nothing-but fallacy see REDUCTIVE FALLACY.

notion (from Latin, *notio*, from *noscere*, know) **1.** idea; conception; mental apprehension. **2.** view, theory, or opinion. **3.** personal belief or inclination.

4. something existing only in an idea. **5.** state or process of an idea in its being formed into a better idea or concept. **6.** visionary idea. **7.** vague idea.

notion/Begriff (Hegel) the German *Begriff*, translated as *notion*, was used by Hegel in several interrelated senses: **1.** the essence of an object. **2.** the essence of the thought of that object, and **3.** the synthesis of being and essence (basically the synthesis of 1. and 2. as idea).

noumenon (from Greek, *nooúmenon*, the thing perceived; related to *noeîn*, perceive, and to *noûs,* mind) **1.** that which is apprehended as an object by our reason (our understanding, our intellect) without any involvement of our senses, intuition, or other levels of apprehension. **2.** that real but in itself unknowable reality (substance, object) that reason must postulate as the cause (ground, basis) of all phenomena. **3.** a thing as it actually exists in itself apart from how it appears to us, as opposed to PHENOMENON, which refers to how a thing appears to us.

The plural is *noumena. Noumenalism* is the doctrine of the existence of noumena (things-in-themselves) or of a noumenon (a thing-in-itself). *Noumenal* refers to either the singular or plural meaning.

noumenon (Kant) that reality (power, substance) which transcends experience and all rational knowledge. Reason must assume its existence as a beginning point for all science and philosophy (including ethics). Reason can know *that* it exists but not *what* its existence is like. That there is a noumenon is apprehended by reason alone. See KNOWLEDGE (KANT).

noûs (Greek, mind, reason, intellect) in some philosophies used to indicate God as the cosmic or world mind (reason, intelligence). See *DIANOIA, NOĒSIS.*

noûs (Anaxagoras) Anaxagoras used the word *noûs* for the universal intelligence (reason, mind) that arranges the universe into a rational order; that all-pervading mind which imposes (brings about) an intelligible pattern in an intrinsically nonintelligible universe. According to Anaxagoras, *noûs* is not to be found as a constituent (mixture) *in* things. *Noûs* is an intangible being affecting the constituents of all things and patterning them into the order that they have.

noûs (Aristotle) 1. the mind of the eternal divine being in which all the intelligible forms are found and according to which all form actualizes itself. **2.** the single, unitary cosmic intelligence or reason, which can be looked at in two ways (roughly corresponding to Aristotle's form and matter distinction): (a) that which becomes all things (matter) and (b) that which is an active force making all things (form). **3.** the rational part of the human mind, which includes the intellectual and intuitive understanding of the fundamental ideas about reality in contrast to perceptual, sensible understanding. Often divided by Aristotelians into two parts separable only in abstraction: (a) NOÛS PATHETIKOS, and (b) NOÛS POIETIKOS.

noûs pathetikos (Aristotelianism) (Greek) that aspect of the mind (*NOÛS*) able to apprehend and make sense of that which is given in experience.

Passive reason; passive intellection. Contrasted with active reason or active intellection. See REASON, ACTIVE/PASSIVE (ARISTOTLE).

NOûs poietikos (Aristotelianism) (Greek) **1.** that (divine) aspect of the mind (NOûs) able to comprehend the eternal, first principles of all phenomena (the forms or intelligible substances), as opposed to the aspect of the mind that deals with passing phenomena. Compare with SUB SPECIES AETERNITAS. **2.** active reason; active intellection. Contrasted with passive reason or passive intellection. See REASON, ACTIVE/PASSIVE (ARISTOTLE).

now 1. at the present time. Used to refer to that moment of time simultaneous with its utterance: "I exist at this very moment." **2.** at the time immediately to follow, used in expressions such as "Get it done now." **3.** refers to the time immediately preceding a present moment used in expressions such as "Now that I have finished. . . ." *Now* is regarded as an indexical sign (see SIGN, INDEXICAL), such as *this, here,* or *I,* that has no descriptive content.

null (from Latin, *nullus,* not any) **1.** empty; void of. **2.** nonexistent. **3.** equivalent to nothing. Used in English as a prefix in terms such as *null-class* and *null-set.*

numinous experience a sense of some transcendent reality or presence that has qualities associated with it such as awesomeness, the sublime, the terrifying, infinite power, grandeur. This reality is often called God. The experience is of a *total other*, so utterly different from anything in our experience that it is impossible to grasp rationally and impossible to communicate. The numinous experience evokes an inescapable sense of our finiteness, of our complete and total dependence on this transcendent reality, and of our insufficiency as we stand in contrast to the glory and power of that reality. See entries under MYSTICAL; MYSTICISM.

O

object (from Latin, *objectare,* throw before, oppose) **1.** that which is presented to one or more of our senses; something visible, tangible, tactile, etc. **2.** that which is presented to consciousness and of which consciousness becomes aware. *Object* may refer to either (a) the thing in the external world independently existing to which our consciousness or senses have been stimulated to attend (see MATERIAL OBJECT), or (b) the mental content itself being attended to in consciousness. **3.** anything that can be talked about (hence named), and especially as a noun having substantive existence.

object, conative that thing (end, goal, ideal) being desired or willed.

object, epistemological sometimes called *ostensible object*, that which is being known or experienced, whether VERIDICAL or not; anything sensed, perceived, conceived, imagined, etc.

object language see LANGUAGE, OBJECT.

object, material see MATERIAL OBJECT.

object, physical see MATERIAL OBJECT.

objective 1. referring (a) to the ability to make an evaluation of a situation without being affected by feelings, emotions, and preconceived notions, and (b) to the support of a statement (idea, judgment, knowledge, decision) with proof and evidence based on actual events. **2.** that goal, end, ideal, or object sought after by an activity or feeling.

objective existence (reality) existence of an entity or an object in the external world (a) that is known, or (b) that can be known, and (c) that exists independently of our perception, conception, or judgment of it, as opposed to being merely a subjective existence in our mind or to being known in terms of our biases, feelings, and personal judgments.

Often implies something (1) that is publicly observable, or (2) that is the same for all those that experience it, or (3) that is commonly assented to and therefore unlike an individual's own peculiar reaction to it. See EXISTENCE; REALITY, OBJECTIVE AND FORMAL.

objectivism (epistemology) 1. the theory that a world (a) exists in itself independently of and external to our comprehension of it and (b) that it is a world we can come to know about independently of any subjective viewpoint. **2.** the view that knowledge is based on factual evidence that (a) is discovered by objective methods of science and reasoning and (b) describes things as they are. **3.** the view that the only meaningful (true) knowledge is that which is derived from and/or confirmed by sensory experience. Opposite to SOLIPSISM, EPISTEMOLOGICAL.

objectivism (value theory) the view in aesthetics and ethics that (a) values exist in the external world independently of and external to our comprehension of them; (b) they can be found and known; (c) they must be used as principles for human judgments and conduct; (d) objects or activities are valuable or right because of some objectively existing quality in them that, when perceived or experienced, makes them desirable. Opposite to RELATIVISM (VALUE THEORY); SUBJECTIVISM (VALUE THEORY).

obligation (from Latin, *obligare,* bind one to something) **1.** a formal agreement, contract, or bond usually accompanied by the implication of a penalty for not fulfilling it. **2.** a DUTY; a necessity to act in some specified way imposed by law, moral sense, ethical principle, promise, social commitments, etc.

observation (from Latin, *observare,* observe, save, keep) **1.** taking notice; recognizing (and often systematically noting as in science) some feature (fact, occurrence). **2.** the result (conclusion, judgment) of 1.

Observables are those items of reality derived from observation, especially sense perception. *Nonobservables* are items of reality unobservable in principle or at present, but which have observable effects (such as photons).

Occam's Razor see OCKHAM'S RAZOR.

occasion (from Latin, *occasio,* a happening; from *occidare,* fall down) a favorable opportunity for an activity; its timely chance. In this sense an *occasion* is an occurrence or a state of affairs that is a contributory or incidental cause of an event. The specific cause of an event is that which actually brings it about. The *occasion* of an event is the general set of causal conditions that provide an opportunity for the specific causes to act (or sets them going). Example: "The increased level of bacteria caused the milk to sour." The *occasion* was the milk being allowed to stand too long at room temperature.

occasionalism (mind/body theory) an offshoot of the philosophy of Descartes, the view that the apparent reciprocal action of mind and body is caused by an intervention of God, producing on the occasion of a change in one a corresponding change in the other. The main points in this general thesis: **1.** mind and body are two separate and distinct realities so different in kind that they cannot causally interact. **2.** each functions according to its own laws. **3.** God interconnects and synchronizes their activities. An event in one is an occasion for God's making an event happen in the other. For example, when I think, God has produced that thought on the occasion of some corresponding material movement. When I will to lift a weight, God causes me to move my arm to lift the weight on the occasion of my act of willing. When I see a landscape before me, God (and not the external world) has brought that perception into existence on the occasion of the actual existence of that landscape. Compare with entries under MIND/BODY.

occurrent state see STATE, OCCURRENT.

Ockham, William of (c.1285–1349) English philosopher, theologian; born in Ockham, Surrey; educated at Oxford and taught there. He is known today for his OCKHAM'S RAZOR, a principle of economy, or parsimony. Ockham's major work is his *Summa Logicae* (1328). His name is taken as the beginning of a nominalism and empiricism that countered medieval Scholasticism, which saw its task as that of reconciling Christianity with Greek philosophy.

Ockham's (Ockam's or **Occam's) Razor** also called the *principle of parsimony, principle of simplicity,* or *principle of economy,* a methodological principle developed by William of Ockham expressed in Latin as *entia non sunt multiplicanda praeter necessitatem*: "Entities are not to be multiplied beyond necessity," or "The number of entities used to explain phenomena should not be increased unnecessarily." The principle implies: **1.** of two or more possible explanations for phenomena choose the one that (a) explains what is to be explained with the fewest assumptions and explanatory principles; and (b) explains all, or most, of the facts that need explaining as satisfactorily as any of the other theories. **2.** the simplest explanation is the one most likely to be true, to depict reality as it is. See PARSIMONY, PRINCIPLE OF.

omnibenevolent (from Latin, *omnis,* all, + *benevolens,* from *bene,* well, + *volens,* willing) applies to God to indicate that God is all good, a pure moral being capable only of love, mercy, compassion, and charity, and incapable in any way of willing evil. See EVIL, THEOLOGICAL PROBLEM OF.

omnipotence see PARADOX OF GOD'S OMNIPOTENCE.

omnipotent (from Latin, *omnipotens,* all powerful, from *omnis,* all, + *potens,* powerful) usually applied to God to indicate that God is (a) all-powerful and/or (b) of infinite power. (The former need only imply that God is the most powerful, and nothing is more powerful than God. Traditionally, both (a) and (b) are intended.)

Some of the variety of meanings for omnipotent that can be found in theology: **1.** God can do anything, is able to bring about anything God wills or wants. **2.** God can do anything provided that it is logically possible to do; that is, provided it is not self-contradictory. For example, God's power cannot create a squared circle no matter how intensely God wills or wants that to happen, since self-contradictions cannot be brought into existence. **3.** God can do anything provided that it is worthwhile to do and (which amounts to the same thing) provided that it is an expression of God's necessary essence as God.

The focal implication in these definitions is that God is the absolute controller (and in most cases also creator) of all things. See PARADOX OF GOD'S OMNIPOTENCE.

omnipresent (from Latin, *omnis,* all, + *praesens,* that is before one; present participle of *praeesse,* be before) usually applied to God to indicate (a) that God is wholly present in all things at all times or (b) that God's influence is present and may be felt in all things. The main implication in the concept of God's omnipresence is that God is intimately related to all things, as an efficient cause is related to that on which it acts.

omniscience see PARADOX OF GOD'S OMNISCIENCE.

omniscient (from Latin, *omnis*, all, + *sciens*; present participle of *scire*, know) usually applied to God to indicate that God is all-knowing: that God has infinite knowledge. The following are some of the variety of interrelatable interpretations for *omniscient* and *omniscience*: **1.** God perceives all things as they happen, and hence knows of their occurrence. **2.** God knows everything that has happened, is happening, and will happen. **3.** God knows everything that it is possible to know.

The three primary implications in these definitions are: (a) all truths (knowledge) are eternal; (b) they are all known (eternally) by God; and (c) nothing can occur unless it accords with these eternal truths. See PARADOX OF GOD'S OMNISCIENCE.

omnitemporal (from Latin, *omnis*, all, + *temporalis*, from *tempus*, time) something that exists (as itself) at all times: throughout eternity. Usually used to refer to God or to an eternal perfect form, but it can be used to refer to the eternal unchanging atoms of the atomists. See ATOMISM, GREEK.

one, the 1. the eternal perfect form that all things imitate (act according to, participate in). **2.** the absolute (mind, spirit, soul). **3.** the divine being from which all things emanate (see EMANATION). **4.** the universe itself as a self-sufficient being. **5.** God. **6.** the world spirit (soul, psyche, reason, mind).

In all these meanings the following points are emphasized. The *one* is (a) the first principle (the primary being, the underlying ground, the causal and ultimate origin) for the existence of all things; (b) the true reality as opposed to the appearances of phenomena; (c) self-dependent in that its nature is not derived from anything else; (d) a necessary existent; and (e) present in some way throughout its flow of processes. See *HEN*.

one and many, problem of see IDENTITY, PROBLEM OF; UNITY IN VARIETY AND VARIETY IN UNITY, PRINCIPLE OF (METAPHYSICS).

ontological argument for God's existence (Anselm) the following from the *Proslogion* is the main version of the ontological argument for God's existence found in Anselm: **1.** God is "that than which nothing greater can be conceived" (*aliquod quo nihil maius cogitari possit*). **2.** God cannot be "that than which nothing greater can be conceived" only *in intellectu* (in our mind, in the intellect, in our understanding); otherwise, God would not be "that than which nothing greater can be conceived" (since that which exists *both* in reality and in our mind is greater than that which exists only in our mind). **3.** if God as "that than which nothing greater can be conceived" can be thought of as part of our understanding, God must also be conceived to exist in reality, which is something greater; otherwise, that something "that than which nothing greater can be conceived" thought of as existing in reality as well, would be greater than the one conceived only in our understanding—and that conception would thus be God, since God is "that than which nothing greater can be conceived."

ontological argument for God's existence (Descartes) the several ontological arguments for God's existence that can be found in Descartes' writings. Of the three presented here, the first and second are pure forms of the ontological argument (the first being a condensed and simplified version of Anselm's ontological argument), and the third has a tinge of the causal argument mixed with it. (The third argument is presented in two parts.) **1.** God is the completely perfect being. Existence is necessary for anything to be completely perfect. Therefore, God exists as the completely perfect being (for if God did not exist, God would not be the completely perfect being, which God is). **2.** The essence of God is existence, just as the essence of a triangle is a plane figure composed of three straight lines joined together to form three angles equal to 180°. One cannot think of a triangle without thinking of that essence. One cannot think of that essence without thinking of a triangle. The two necessarily go together. So whenever one thinks of God, one thinks of God's existence, and whenever one thinks of existence one thinks of God. The two go together necessarily. Whenever we think of God without existence we contradict ourselves. Therefore, God must exist (any other conclusion leads to a contradiction in terms). **3.** *Part I:* I have an idea of God as a perfect and infinite being. As a finite being, I could not have caused this idea in me. The cause of this idea is greater in reality and power than its effect. Therefore, God exists as this greater reality and power to produce upon my finite mind the idea of an infinite and completely perfect Being. *Part II:* I could not have caused myself. (It requires more reality, power, and perfection to create substance than, for example, to create attributes, qualities, or properties.) If I could have created (caused) myself, I would have given myself perfect attributes (which no finite being has). I have not existed eternally, nor do I have the power to maintain existence from moment to moment. I cannot say that I was caused only by my parents (who were caused by other parents, etc.). It is necessary, therefore, to assume that an eternal, infinitely powerful, perfect God exists who is both the cause of my being and who implants the idea of God in my mind as well as in the minds of my parents, their parents, etc.

ontology (from Latin, *ontologia,* the really existing things, true reality; from Greek, *ont-,* from *eînai,* be, + *lógos,* the study of, the theory that accounts for) **1.** the study of the essential characteristics of being in itself, apart from the study of particular existing things. In studying being in its most abstract form, ontology asks questions such as "What is being-in-itself?" "What is the nature of being-as-being?" **2.** the branch of philosophy that deals with the order and structure of reality in the broadest sense possible, using categories such as being/becoming, actuality/potentiality, real/apparent, change, time, existence/nonexistence, essence, necessity, being-as-being, self-dependency, self-sufficiency, ultimate, and ground. **3.** the branch of philosophy that attempts (a) to describe the nature of ultimate being (the one, the absolute, the perfect eternal form), (b) to show that all things depend upon it for their existence, (c) to indicate how this dependency is manifested in reality, and (d) to relate human thoughts and actions to this reality on an individual and historical basis. **4.** the branch of philosophy (a) that asks the question "What does *to be, to exist* mean?" (the same question is asked of the other categories or concepts used in 2.); and (b) that analyzes the variety of meanings (ways) in which things can be said to *be, exist*. **5.** the branch of philosophy (a) that inquires about the reality status of a thing (for example, "Are the objects of our sensations or perceptions real or illusory?" "Are numbers real?" "Are thoughts real?"); (b) that inquires about what sort of reality (or quality of illusion) things possess (for example, "What kind of reality do numbers have? Perceptions? Thoughts?"); and (c) that inquires about those other realities or about reality, upon which what we call *reality* and/or *illusion* depend (for example, is the reality—or illusory quality—of a thought or object dependent on our mind, or on an independent external source?).

Ontology has been used as a synonym for METAPHYSICS or has been regarded as a branch of metaphysics. But it can be seen to be close to other branches of philosophy as well, such as EPISTEMOLOGY, philosophical analysis, and SEMANTICS. Its similarities to THEOLOGY are also obvious. What Aristotle refers to as FIRST PHILOSOPHY is ontology.

ontology (existential psychology) the study of the inescapable psychic and structural features (predicaments) of life, such as death, fear, dread, suffering, responsibility, anguish, and alienation. For example, the fear of extinction is ontological in the sense that it is possessed by all human beings, it is part of the human condition, it is inescapable and must be faced by all. The anxiety about death can be, and is, repressed, but it remains a part of our unconscious being affecting our behavior in sometimes unaccountable ways. See EXISTENTIALISM.

open-question argument (G.E. Moore) *good* is an immediate, indefinable nonnatural property. See NONNATURAL PROPERTY (G.E. MOORE). Whatever definition of *good* is given, it can always be asked (it remains an *open question*) whether that which the definition refers to *is* good or *does* possess the property *good*. If a set of natural properties can be found for the word *good* such that we can say "Good is (natural properties)," we can ask the question, "Are those natural properties good?" Thus, merely possessing this quality is not what is meant by *good*. See GOOD (G.E. MOORE); NATURALISTIC FALLACY (G.E. MOORE).

operational definition see DEFINITION, TYPES OF (12).

operationalism (from Latin, *operari*, to work; from *opus, operis,* work, labor) sometimes called *operationism*, the theory that the meaning of a scientific idea (concept, term, symbol) is identical with the set of activities (operations) that have to be performed in order to understand it, and to which it refers. See DEFINITION, TYPES OF (12). Compare with INSTRUMENTALISM.

opinion (from Latin, *opinio,* suspicion, belief, conjecture, imagination, notion, thinking, judgment, estimation) **1.** a belief; usually a belief based on personally developed views; that which one thinks about something, but not necessarily implying a definite judgment. **2.** judgment; often a judgment formed by an expert. **3.** a statement (a) backed by rational arguments, and (b) either presented with some doubt as to its truth or (c) presented with the realization that its truth can be doubted. **4.** a belief (idea, statement) that lacks supporting evidence. **5.** used as the translation for Greek words such as DOXA, which imply knowledge that is uncertain, changing, bordering on the illusory.

opposites (metaphysics) (from Latin, *oppositus,* past participle of *opponere,* set or place against, oppose) refers to the fundamental opposing forces in the universe operating to cause change, such as attraction/ repulsion; motion/rest; potential/actual; being/nonbeing; mind/matter; love/hate; good/evil; light/darkness; hot/cold; wet/dry; and fire/water. Opposites imply a difference of kind, a diametrically opposed quality, and an interaction or antagonism. *Opposite* is sometimes loosely used as a synonym for *contradictory* and for *contrary.*

optimism (from Latin, *optimus,* the best) **1.** a disposition to see things from the most promising and hopeful perspective. ("Every cloud has a silver lining"; the pessimist would say, "Every silver lining has a cloud.") **2.** everything is ordered for the best. (An extreme form: This is the BEST OF ALL POSSIBLE WORLDS.) **3.** the world as it stands is not the best possible world, but it possesses much good and so will its future. **4.** the present world is good and will be even better in the future. **5.** humans are able to control evil in themselves and in society. Opposite to PESSIMISM. Compare with MELIORISM. See PERFECTABILITY OF MAN.

order (from Latin, *ordo,* row, series, course, array, rank, class, degree) **1.** a formal or regular arrangement of anything (in contrast to SYSTEM, which implies a definite, methodological or logical plan or order). **2.** a class, type, or level. **3.** the position or rank of a thing in a hierarchy or a series. **4.** command (as in a legal or moral order).

ordinary language philosophy the view that by analyzing ordinary language (its meanings, implications, forms, and functions) and showing how its general philosophic outlook and basic presuppositions reveal a truth about reality, we can better understand the nature of and hence resolve the problems of philosophy. Principal tenets: **1.** the language used in everyday conversation (ordinary language) is adequate for philosophical use. **2.** such a language presupposes a structure or view of reality that is correct. **3.** any departure from ordinary language creates needless philosophical and metaphysical perplexities (puzzles, nonsense). **4.** the solutions to the problems of philosophy are to be found in not misusing ordinary language words and their meanings.

There is little by way of a typical or common set of beliefs among ordinary language philosophers. Some are determinists, some are not. Some are believers in God, some are not. Some are behaviorists, some are not. Some are scientifically oriented, some are not. But in general, ordinary language philosophers are in agreement that philosophical perplexities cannot be resolved by the formal procedures of symbolic logic.

Ordinary language is the key to their solution. Ordinary language is not artificial (formal), nor is it a calculus. It presupposes insights into the structure of reality and everyday experience that cannot be gained by the use of artificial systems. Formal systems are also inapplicable to ethical and psychological problems. John L. Austin, Ludwig Wittgenstein, Gilbert Ryle, and John Wisdom are names that have been associated with ordinary language philosophy. In most cases it is difficult to draw a sharp distinction between ordinary language philosophy and linguistic philosophy or linguistic analysis. See ANALYSIS, LINGUISTIC; ANALYTIC PHILOSOPHY.

organicism. 1. any theory that explains the universe on the basis of an analogy to a living organism. **2.** any theory that explains the universe as the function of a whole causing and coordinating the activities of the parts. Compare with ANIMISM; HOLISM; VITALISM. Opposite to MECHANISM.

organic unity see UNITY, ORGANIC; UNITY, ORGANIC (ARISTOTLE).

organismic explanation any explanation that regards the properties of a whole (a) as being distinct from the properties of the individual parts (or groupings of parts) and (b) as being as necessary to explain something as an analysis of the interaction of the parts is necessary to its explanation. Wholes are considered not merely as the quantitative sums of their parts but as qualitatively different from their sums. Compare with entries under EXPLANATION.

organon (Greek, organ, instrument, tool for making or doing something) Plato used this word to refer to *an organ of sense*. *Organon* is the title given to the logical works of Aristotle, implying that logic is a tool to be used for acquiring philosophic knowledge (for doing philosophy) and is not to be regarded as an end in itself. Francis Bacon titled one of his books *Novum Organum,* referring to his new method or tool of empirical investigation that was to supersede Aristotle's. See LOGIC (ARISTOTLE).

orthodox (from Greek, *orthodoxos*; from *orthos*, right, straight, + *doxa,* opinion, belief) **1.** referring to true or correct belief (opinion, doctrine, creed, idea) as opposed to *heretical* or *heterodox* belief. The doctrine decreed by an institution or group as the true one and the one to be followed. **2.** approved belief. **3.** conventional or traditional belief.

orthos logos see LOGOS ORTHOS.

ostensive (from Latin, *ostendere,* show, stretch out before) showing by pointing to, or exhibiting.

ostensive definition see DEFINITION, TYPES OF (13).

ought implies that (a) something should be done that is not being done and/or (b) something should not be done that is being done. An expression of OBLIGATION, DUTY, or constraint.

ousia (Greek) ESSENCE, the inner essential nature of a thing, the true being of a thing.

P

pacifism (from Latin, *pacificare,* make to be at peace) some basic beliefs of pacifism: **1.** in general, opposition to the use of personal violence in attempting to achieve individual and social aims. **2.** opposition to militarism, military ideals, and war as a means of accomplishing goals or settling disputes. **3.** encouragement of cooperative, supportive relationships among individuals without the type of competition that destroys such relationships. **4.** encouragement of arbitration, diplomacy, appeal to humaneness as means of settling international and political disputes.

pain (from Greek, *poinē,* penalty) bodily suffering and/or mental anguish; regarded as a polar concept to PLEASURE. Attainment of pleasure and avoidance of pain are considered the primary human motivating forces. Pain is regarded as a negative and negating element in human experience and conduct.

Paley, William (1743–1805) English theologian and moralist, born in Peterborough and educated at Cambridge. Paley, an ordained priest, became Archdeacon of Carlisle. He is primarily known for his teleological proof of God's existence, based on the analogy of the order in a watch being created by the intelligence of the watchmaker, and the order in nature stemming from the cosmic intelligence of God. Paley's main writings included *The Principles of Moral and Politics Philosophy* (1785); *A View of the Evidences of Christianity* (2 volumes, 1794); and *Natural Theology; or, Evidences of the Existence and Attributes of the Deity, Collected from the Appearances of Nature* (1802).

panentheism see GOD CONCEPTS.

panlogism (from Greek, *pan,* all, + *lógos,* the study of, reason, the rational) **1.** the theory that the universe is the expression of the LÓGOS (the eternal universal reason or mind). **2.** the *lógos* pervades all things and all activity in the universe.

panpsychism see GOD CONCEPTS.

panpsychism (metaphysics) (from Greek, *pan,* all, + *psychē,* soul, spirit, mind) the view that everything in the universe possesses (a) consciousness (mental life, mind, soul, spirit) or (b) a level of consciousness. All things in existence have inner lives of feeling, willing, thinking, conating. See HYLOZOISM; MIND-STUFF THEORY OF MIND.

pantheism see GOD CONCEPTS.

paradigm (from Greek, *paradeigma,* model, exemplar, archetype, ideal; from *para,* beside, + *dekynai,* to show) **1.** a way of looking at something. **2.** in science, a model, pattern, or ideal theory, from which perspective phenomena are explained. **3.** an ideal situation or exemplification, as in "A *paradigm case* of this disease. . . ."

paradox (from Greek, *paradoxon*; from *para,* contrary to, + *doxa,* opinion) **1.** a statement (tenet, belief, concept, notion) that is contrary to accepted opinion, or opposed to what is regarded as common sense, but may be true. **2.** a statement that on the surface appears absurd or even self-contradictory, but (a) is true or (b) may be true. **3.** an apparent dichotomy (or self-contradiction) that when overcome denies something which is regarded as true. **4.** a situation in which two statements that are incongruent (contrary, exclusive of each other) both appear to be true, and both must be accepted in action. **5.** a statement that when regarded as true leads to its being false, and when regarded as false leads to its truth (or leads to a truth).

paradox, Epimenides' Epimenides, a Cretan, declared that all Cretans without exception were liars. Was Epimenides telling the truth?

paradox, hedonistic see HEDONISTIC PARADOX.

paradox, liar often called the *Megarian Paradox* after the school of Megara, of which Eubulides of Miletus (Euclid's successor), who invented the paradox, was a member; also referred to as *Eubulides' paradox.* The paradox may be stated in a number of ways: **1.** a person says, "I am lying." Is what that person says true or false? (The statement seems to be true if what the person said is false, and false if what the person said is true.) **2.** a person says, "What I am now saying is false." (This statement appears to be false only if true, and true only if false.) **3.** a person says, "If I am lying, is what I have just stated false?" (It would be false if what the person said were true, and true if what the person said were false.)

paradox, logical in general, a paradox composed of two contrary, or contradictory, statements, both of which seem to have good supporting arguments. Compare with ANTINOMY. A logical paradox results when two acceptable lines of argument lead to conclusions that seem contrary or contradictory. Logical paradoxes may be a consequence of: **1.** a misapplication of the rules of logic; **2.** a violation of the rules of logic that cannot be clearly expressed (or is not clearly seen); or **3.** the inapplicability of the rules of logic to the situation. Some reformulation of the logic in 3. is necessary either (a) to avoid the paradox or (b) to resolve it.

paradox of God's omnipotence some of the traditionally stated paradoxes that have to do with God's omnipotence: If God is all-powerful: **1.** Can God create a squared circle? **2.** Can God undo the past? **3.** Can God create a rock big enough so that God cannot move it? **4.** Can God invent problems that God cannot solve? **5.** Can God annihilate God and never come back to life? **6.** Can God deny God's essence? See EVIL, THEOLOGICAL PROBLEM OF; OMNIPOTENT.

paradox of God's omniscience if God is all-knowing (and all-powerful) how is this compatible (a) with human freedom of will and (b) with God's own freedom of will, since presumably such complete foreknowledge entails that an all-powerful God has created things to occur exactly in the way that God knows—and wants—them to occur? See OMNISCIENT.

paradox of self-reference a paradox that arises from statements such as: "All generalizations are false." (Since this is a generalization it must be false, and if false, true; but if true, false.) "No knowledge is possible" (yet claiming this is knowledge). "There are no absolutes." (Is this an absolute?) "Everything is uncertain"; "Nothing-at-all exists"; "I do not exist."

paradox of tragedy see TRAGEDY, AESTHETIC PARADOX OF.

paradox of the ugly see UGLY, PARADOX OF THE.

paradoxes, Socratic see SOCRATIC PARADOXES.

paradoxes, Zeno's see ZENO'S PARADOXES.

parallelism also referred to as *psychophysical parallelism*. See MIND/BODY RELATIONSHIPS, THEORIES OF.

paralogism (from Greek, *paralogismos*; from *para*, beside, + *logizesthai*, to reason) **1.** any reasoning that is false in form. **2.** any error or fallacy in reasoning. **3.** fallacious syllogistic reasoning.

paranormal literally *beyond the normal*, used as a synonym for *extrasensory* or *parapsychological*. See PARAPSYCHOLOGY.

parapsychology (from Greek, *para*, beside, alongside of, against, + *psychē*, mind, soul, spirit, understanding, + *lógos*, the study of) the study of psychological phenomena that deal with PARANORMAL or extrasensory powers (ESP) and events. Classified under this are phenomena such as CLAIRVOYANCE, levitation, mind reading, occult or spiritual presences, PRECOGNITION, PRESCIENCE, EXTRASPECTION, psychokinesis, and TELEPATHY.

Parmenides (fl. 5th century BC) Greek philosopher, born in Elea, Italy; founder of the Eleatic School. He was a follower of Xenophanes, the teacher of Zeno, and influenced Plato's thought. Plato named his dialogue *Parmenides* after him, presenting his main philosophic position. Parmenides wrote *On Nature*, a didactic poem in three parts: an introductory poem; "On the Way of Truth"; and "The Way of Falsehood or Illusion."

parsimony, principle of also called the *principle of simplicity*, refers to the prescription to (a) simplify explanation (see OCKHAM'S RAZOR), and/or (b) economize effort toward a goal.

participation (Plato) see MIMĒSIS.

particular (from Latin, *particularis*; from *pars, partis*, a part) **1.** an INDIVIDUAL member of a class in contrast to the characteristics that describe the members of that class. **2.** *some*, in contradistinction to *all*. **3.** in metaphysics, any individual existing unity interrelating with other unities; a unit.

particulars, egocentric generally synonymous with indexical signs. See SIGN, INDEXICAL.

Pascal, Blaise (1623–1662) French philosopher, mathematician, physicist, inventor (of a calculating machine etc.); born in Clermont-Ferrand. In mathematics he worked, for example, on probability theory; in physics, for example, he experimented with vacuums; and in philosophy he proposed, for example, his wager argument for the existence of God. Pascal's best-known work is his *Pensées*, unfinished and published posthumously in the 18th century.

passion 1. an excessive, intense, or overpowering impulse or emotion such as rage, sexual lust, anger, jealousy. **2.** the overpowering emotion (a) that is the result of such things as antipathy or inordinate desires, and (b) that controls or rules behavior.

Passion is associated in classical philosophy with the irrational, with the tendency toward illicit, irascible, uncontrolled behavior; with the sinful; with lack of discipline and self-direction. In Plato, for example, one has no freedom of the will when one is a slave to passion. Being mastered by passion makes one less than human.

passive intellect/reason, the see REASON, ACTIVE/PASSIVE (ARISTOTLE).

past 1. time gone by; all events that have happened. (All present events and future events will become members of the class *past* at some time. Therefore, this class is not a fixed class, but an ever-growing class.) **2.** something at a former time. **3.** something that has elapsed (gone by).

pathetic (from Greek, *pathētikos*; from *pathētos*, subject to suffering; from *pathein*, suffer) **1.** having to do with feelings or emotions, or with **2.** that which results from feelings or emotions.

In classical philosophy, *pathetic* (sometimes *pathetical*) referred to those things that affected or stimulated the *tender emotions* such as pity, grief, compassion, and sorrow.

pathetic fallacy incorrectly projecting (attributing) human emotions, feelings, intentions, thoughts, traits upon events or objects that do not possess the capacity for such qualities. See ANIMISM, METAPHOR.

pathos (from Greek, *pathos,* a suffering, a passion, anything that befalls one, incident, accident, what one has suffered, misfortune, calamity, EMOTION, FEELING) **1.** that which excites emotions. **2.** the name for emotions, usually specifically for the tender emotions. See PATHETIC. **3.** suffering; the undergoing of distress, grief, or anguish. **4.** that which happens to or affects a human, in contrast with that which a human *does* or how a human *acts*. See *POIĒSES/POIETIKOS* (ARISTOTLE) and PRAXIS. In English usage, *pathos* is contrasted with *ĒTHOS*, in the sense that pathos is a private, individual, personal experience, whereas *ēthos* refers to the feelings in the context of a community. Pathos in Greek also meant *pain, suffering*, as found in the adage *pathei mathos:* "Suffering teaches." See SYMPATHY.

Peirce, Charles Sanders (1839–1914) American philosopher, physicist, chemist, mathematician, logician; born in Cambridge, Massachusetts; educated at Harvard; regarded as the founder of Pragmatism. He worked first as an astronomer and as a physicist; then began to lecture in philosophy, logic, and scientific methodology at Johns Hopkins University. He wrote extensively in all fields of philosophy, mostly for scholarly journals. These writings are collected in six volumes edited by Charles Hartshorne and Paul Weiss (1931–1935) plus two more volumes edited by Arthur Burks (1958).

per accidens (Latin, by accident, accidental, nonessential, by limitation) **1.** referring to a mode of existence that is not essential to the nature of a thing, to a thing's being what it is (and what it should be according to its nature). **2.** referring to a characteristic of a thing acquired by happenstance—without intention and without resulting from its inner nature. **3.** referring to activities or properties of a thing that are not required for its recognition or identification. Compare with PER SE.

peras (Greek, limit, form, end, shape, boundary) used by the Pythagoreans and Plato to refer to that principle (law, power) that forms (shapes, patterns, structures) the infinite or the nonlimited (the APEIRON). They also used *peras* in a moral sense, as the principle that controls (limits) behavior in a rational, ordered way, avoiding disharmony and excesses.

perception (from Latin, *perceptio*; from *percipere*, receive, take) **1.** the bringing of things into awareness by the use of our senses and especially thereby being able to name them and/or identify them as objects in the external world. In general, *perception* is regarded as an interpreting and synthesizing of sensations. **2.** an object of perception is any item present to consciousness, including sense data, an image, an illusion, a vision, an idea, a concept. **3.** an immediate intuitive cognition or evaluation of an idea (or situation) or the ability to have such cognition or evaluation, related in this sense to the concept of insight. Perception is usually regarded as the organization and interpretation of bare sense data. Compare with SENSATION. See CONSCIOUSNESS; EXPERIENCE.

perception, confused (Leibniz) 1. the subconscious or unconscious perceptions that are not clearly apprehended by the intellect but nevertheless affect the tendencies of thought and emotion. **2.** those ideas that are not fully (clearly and distinctly) understood in all their implications to the rational mind. See MONADS (LEIBNIZ).

perception, representative theory of the theory that **1.** objects are independent of (separate from) the ideas we have of them from perception; **2.** our ideas of objects represent, copy, correspond to, or give us a map or diagram of the external world of objects; **3.** these objects cause our ideas of them by physically stimulating our sense organs; **4.** the mind processes these stimuli in the act of perception to form our ideas.

perception, sense see SENSE PERCEPTION.

perception, temporal 1. perception in which the awareness of time is present and often predominates. **2.** the belief in the direct perception of time much as we have a direct perception of colors.

perception, theories of 1. *causal theory:* Perception is of and is caused by externally existing objects stimulating our sense organs. **2.** *creative, constructive,* or *generative theory:* Perceptions are caused by the mind and exist only insofar as the mind is having them. **3.** *selective theory:* Perceptions are those complexes of sensa that the mind consciously or unconsciously selects and puts into an order (cognition).

percepts (from Latin, *percipere,* take, receive) the data of perception; that which appears (or exists) in an act of perception. Contrasted with CONCEPTS (ideas, beliefs, notions, opinions), which refer to abstractions (universals, classes, generalizations). Percepts refer to particulars (individual objects, images, sensations), to concrete items in experience. When not used as a synonym for SENSE DATA, percepts are usually regarded as the mind's first step in organizing undifferentiated sense data.

perfect (from Latin, *perfectus,* past participle of *perficere,* perform, finish) **1.** complete; possessing the essence and/or all the properties that belong to the nature of something. **2.** pure; without qualification, as in 1., but without any properties accruing to it that are accidental or incidental. **3.** faultless; having no potential for defects and having no defects.

perfectibility of man the belief that the human being **1.** is capable of further development and will develop further his or her moral and social sensitivities and behavior; **2.** can eventually actualize all of his or her moral and social potentialities; and **3.** that (sometimes) this process is a continuous onward and upward evolutionary and social process. Compare with OPTIMISM.

perfection (classical) the state of complete fulfillment of a thing whereby all the potentialities inherent in its nature or essence have been actualized to the utmost for its good.

perfectionism (ethics) 1. perfection (a) of our moral character or (b) of all moral character as the highest good to be aimed at in life, as opposed to such ethical ends as pleasure, utilitarianism, and duty. **2.** perfection as the highest virtue of humanity, from which all other virtues necessarily follow.

performative act 1. that act which in fact follows from what is said, and/or **2.** that act done as part of what is being said.

performative (performatory) language see LANGUAGE, PERFORMATIVE.

per genus et differentiam (Latin, by class [kind] and difference [uniqueness]). Example: the human being is a rational animal (species), and its wider class (genus) is that the human being is an animal. Its *differentia* (difference, uniqueness, differentiating/defining characteristic) is that the human being is capable of reasoning, thinking, calculating, using language—all the things presupposed by rationality (and irrationality).

perlocutionary expression/act (perlocution) 1. an act that has a specific effect on feelings, thoughts, or behavior. Examples: frightening someone, inciting someone to anger. **2.** what we do (to ourselves and/or to others) when we say things, when we use language.

In general, a perlocutionary act is the act successfully performed by means of the illocutionary act (such as communication of an image or meaning or evoking a response in someone). Compare with ILLOCUTIONARY

EXPRESSION/ACT (ILLOCUTION); LOCUTIONARY EXPRESSION/ACT (LOCUTION).

per se (Latin, through itself, by itself, intrinsically, innately) **1.** in general, *per se* refers to the essential and indispensable properties that a thing possesses; to its nature. Contrasted with PER ACCIDENS. **2.** if a thing exists *per se* relatively, it can be called a substance (substantial, possessing an essence, an individual entity or unity). **3.** when applied to God (or substance, ultimate being, the universe), *per se* refers to our conceiving this God without having to refer God to any other concept from which God's concept is derived. God is that being who exists *per se* in a complete, totally independent way. God as pure being is *per se* in an absolute sense. See A SE; ASEITY. Nothing except God has the characteristic of being unaffected by anything else. All other things can be said to be *per se* only relatively. See PERSEITY.

per se esse (Latin, exist by its own being, in and for itself out of its own inherent necessity) when predicated of God, eternally existing by God's own being, in and for God out of God's own inherent necessity and inseparably connected with all things as their source and sustainer.

perseity (from Latin, *per se*, by itself, intrinsically, innately) the state in which a thing is *by itself*, acting out of the conditions of its own true inner nature, but (as opposed to ASEITY) always in contrast with or in conjunction with something else. Anything in a state of perseity may be regarded as a substance, and to the degree to which it fully manifests its essential inner nature, it possesses purity of perseity. No matter how perfect a state of perseity is reached, it falls short of aseity (which is reserved for God) since it cannot attain complete independence from God as the efficient cause of its nature and activity.

per se notum (Latin, known by means of itself) used to refer to statements or concepts that are self-evident. See TAUTOLOGY.

per se subsistere Latin, subsist by itself, of its own nature, and require no other thing for its continued existence.

person (from Latin, *persona,* mask used by actors, part, role, person, personage) **1.** that to which we can ascribe both (a) mental characteristics and (b) bodily characteristics. **2.** the unity of bodily and mental actions in activity. **3.** the bodily form, or outward appearance, of a human being. **4** the real, true self of a human being.

personal identity 1. sameness of self (consciousness, mind). The awareness of being the same conscious unity at different times and places. **2.** the identification of a persistent or enduring unity of activity (personality, individuality, character) throughout change of activity or behavior.

Among other things, personal identity implies: (a) existence of a memory; (b) bodily activities; (c) ability to identify oneself (one's *sameness*); (d) ability never to fail to know something that has happened or is happening to one. Compare with entries under EGO; SELF.

personalism a philosophy having the following basic beliefs: **1.** the characteristics possessed by the *person* and *personality* are the keys to understanding the universe and all things in it. **2.** the whole of existence is an expression of a universal personal consciousness and can be analyzed in terms of the forms of human personality. **3.** reality is a system of persons (selves, personalities, egos). **4.** *persons* are irreducible elements of all existence and cannot be explained by anything else. **5.** *person* and *personality* are the highest levels attainable in the universe and are to be esteemed as being the highest values attainable in the universe.

Personalism has taken many forms in the history of philosophy, such as absolutistic, idealistic, realistic, theistic, critical, teleological, pantheistic, panpsychistic, phenomenological, monadistic, and monistic. Personalism is almost indistinguishable from most forms of IDEALISM. See ANIMISM.

personalism, realistic see REALISM, PERSONAL.

personality 1. individuality; the distinguishing traits of a person that stand out in one's awareness of him or her. **2.** the recurrent basic and general mental and behavioral patterns exhibited by a person. **3.** the sum total of the mental and behavioral actions ascribed to a person.

personification 1. attribution of personal qualities or form to external reality, in particular to the inanimate world. See ANIMISM. **2.** a way of thinking such as that in mythology, children's fiction, etc., in which abstract ideas or inanimate objects are endowed with personal (or personality) traits. **3.** the depicting of a person or creature as representing a force, abstract quality, or thing. See HYPOSTATIZATION; REIFICATION/REISM. Example: The goddess *Moira* was the personification of the concept of fate. **4.** the embodiment of some characteristic, as in "He was the personification of greed."

perspective (from Latin, *perspicere,* look through) **1.** the point of view from which something is seen. **2.** the basic presuppositions consciously or unconsciously assumed by which a conclusion is reached or an analysis made. **3.** delineation of that which is possible or significant in the process of organizing and resolving a problem.

pessimism (from Latin, *pessimus,* worst) **1.** the tendency to take the worst, or least hopeful, view of things. Opposite to OPTIMISM. **2.** viewing things from the emotions of sorrow, pity, gloom, despondency, hopelessness, meaninglessness, absurdity, pain, or death, and believing that those states are the basic and inescapable ingredients of life.

pessimism (metaphysics) the view **1.** that all things are ordered for, or tend toward, the worst. Opposite to BEST, PRINCIPLE OF THE. **2.** the world is essentially evil and will remain so in spite of human effort. Opposite to MELIORISM. **3.** this is the worst of all possible worlds. Opposite to BEST OF ALL POSSIBLE WORLDS, THE.

pessimism (Schopenhauer) 1. we ought not to take joy in being alive but ought rather to bemoan that fact. Nonexistence is preferable to existence. Life is something that ought not to be. **2.** if the individual had a choice, he or she would have declined life, had he or she first understood its hopelessness. **3.** all states in life end up as frustrated, unhappy, illusory, or painful. **4.** life is fraught with suffering, disappointment, uncertainty, disillusionment, helplessness, despair, and death. **5.** the world is the worst possible, than which nothing worse can be created or conceived. **6.** the world is the expression of a blind, irrational will. Everything possesses the will to live, and the necessary consequence is an existence of suffering. **7.** individuals can overcome the world and their suffering by such means as philosophic contemplation, transcendence through the aesthetic experience, and compassion.

petitio principii sometimes called *petitio* or *circular reasoning* (Latin, begging of the question), the informal fallacy of already assuming in an argument what is to be proved as a conclusion. See CIRCULARITY; FALLACY, TYPES OF INFORMAL (13); VICIOUS CIRCLE ARGUMENT. Sometimes used to refer generally to deductive arguments, since their conclusions are implicitly or explicitly included in their premises.

phantasia (Greek, imagination) the faculty or power by which an object is given or appears, used in Plato to mean a mere image, a fantasy, an unreality.

phantasma (Greek, the object presented to the mind, sensation, sense representation, an appearance, phantasm) used to mean an apparent likeness, a semblance of the original upon which it is modeled and (sometimes) from which it emanates as a film. Occasionally it is used to mean a vision or dream. See entries under *EIDŌLA*.

phenomenalism a view some of whose principal tenets are: **1.** only phenomena (SENSE DATA) can be known as they appear to our consciousness. **2.** we cannot know the ultimate nature of a reality in itself. **3.** what we know is dependent on the activity of consciousness. The reality of an external, physical object is based on its being perceived by someone. **4.** knowledge is limited to what can be perceived (observed) in consciousness about the external world and what can be perceived by introspection about our mental activities and states. **5.** reality is the totality of all possible conscious experiences. **6.** MATTER is the permanent possibility of sensation. Material objects are sequences or groups of actual or possible sensa. The physical world cannot be said to exist apart from the actual or possible sensa. The physical world cannot be said to exist apart from the actual or possible sense data of some perceiver. **7.** physical (material) objects are logical constructions based on perception (sense data). The meanings of statements about physical objects can be fully analyzed in terms of, can be fully reduced to, statements about patterns of sense data (phenomena). See KNOWLEDGE (MILL).

phenomenology (Husserl) a descriptive, introspective analysis in depth of all forms of consciousness and immediate experiences: religious, moral, aesthetic, conceptual, sensuous. The true focus of philosophy should be the exploration of the life-world (*Lebenswelt*) or the subjective, inner life

(*Erlebnisse*), emphasizing the intentional character of consciousness, and without assuming the conceptual presuppositions of the empirical sciences. Philosophy is not, and cannot be, a factual science. Philosophy has its own unique methods and findings, which are essentially different from those of the natural sciences and from those of the formal systems of logic and mathematics. Phenomenology studies and describes the intrinsic traits of phenomena as they reveal themselves to consciousness. The aspect of Husserl's phenomenology that seeks to unearth the essential, interrelated set of laws of human consciousness is called *transcendental phenomenology*. See BRACKETING (HUSSERL).

phenomenon (from Greek, *phainomenon,* from *phainesthai,* appear; from *phainein,* show, appear) **1.** object of perception; that which is perceived. **2.** what appears to our consciousness. **3.** object of sense experience; what appears to our senses. **4.** any observable fact or event. The plural is *phenomena.* Contrasted with NOUMENON.

philia (Greek, friendly love, attraction, personal affection, fondness, appealing, affinity toward) contrasted with EROS, which refers to sexual love, and AGAPE, which refers to moral or spiritual love and, in Christianity, the love of God by humans and the love of humans by God. The term *philia* was used to refer to the force of attraction/love in nature as opposed to *neikos,* the force of repulsion/hate, both forces being a necessary cause for all change in nature.

philosopher, the eulogistic term referring to Aristotle used by the medievalists from the early 13th century, when his works were being translated into Latin from Arabic and Greek sources; used especially in veneration by Thomas Aquinas.

philosopher-king (Plato) the concept of a supreme, completely rational and righteous ruler(s) of a utopia as envisaged in Plato's *Republic.*

philosophes (French) the term applied to the 18th-century French philosophers, including Condorcet, Condillac, Rousseau, Diderot, and Voltaire.

philosophy (from Greek, *philosophia;* from *philos,* love; or *philia,* friendship, affection, affinity for, attraction toward, + *sophos,* a sage, a wise one; or *sophia,* wisdom, knowledge, skill, practical wisdom or experience, intelligence) a term with as many meanings as there have been philosophers engaging in it. Some basic definitions: **1.** the speculative attempt to present a systematic and complete view of all reality. **2.** the attempt to describe the ultimate and real nature of reality. **3.** the attempt to determine the limits and scope of our knowledge: its source, nature, validity, and value. **4.** the critical inquiry into the presuppositions and claims made by the various fields of knowledge. **5.** the discipline that tries to help you *see* what you say and *say* what you see. Pythagoras was the first to call himself a *philosophos,* a philosopher. *Sophia* meant for him the knowledge of the underlying reasons or causes for things as they appear to us, knowing the reasons why a thing is what it is. This entails an esoteric knowledge of mathematical forms that constitutes true reality as opposed to knowledge of everyday appearances.

philosophy, first see FIRST PHILOSOPHY.

philosophy, Gestalt see GESTALT PHILOSOPHY.

philosophy, ordinary language see ORDINARY LANGUAGE PHILOSOPHY.

philosophy, political see POLITICAL PHILOSOPHY.

philosophy, speculative see SPECULATIVE PHILOSOPHY.

philosophy, synoptic see SYNOPTIC PHILOSOPHY.

philosophy, synthetic see SYNTHETIC PHILOSOPHY.

phronēsis (Greek, prudence, practical wisdom, thoughtfulness, a minding or intending to do something) **1.** knowing how and when to act in the appropriate (proper, acceptable, mannerly, rational) manner relative to the given circumstances. **2.** knowing (a) the right goals to seek, and (b) the proper and most efficient ways of achieving them. **3.** the wisdom that comes from experiencing and learning from life. Compare with entries under SOPHIA.

phronēsis (Aristotle) 1. knowledge wisely applied to everyday living. Practical wisdom. **2.** the faculty (power, ability, capacity) in humans that (a) enables them to discover what the correct (proper, right) action is in a given situation and (b) makes human desires conform to reason (or allows reason to control such desires). *Phronēsis* entails knowledge of the goods (ends, goals) of rational human conduct, and knowledge of the means and their proper application in achieving those desirable rational goods. See *DIANOIA*.

physical referring to: **1.** anything that is a part of nature or the universe. **2.** any material thing. **3.** that which (a) can be analyzed as existing in time and space, (b) is believed to be externally real, and (c) is potentially publicly verifiable.

A *physical thing* is regarded as a three-dimensional object (entity, being, existent, etc.) that can move (or change), or can be moved, or has movement. A *physical event* is regarded as a change (process, movement, alteration, activity) in or upon a physical thing (or among physical things). *Physical causation* is the causal relation existing between or among physical events. See entries under MATTER.

physical object see MATERIAL OBJECT.

physicalism the theory that the language of any science is (should be) translatable into a language containing terms and concepts that refer only to empirically observable and testable characteristics of events.

physicalism (mind/body) the theory that mental events (states, processes) are identical with brain events. Sensations, for example, are one and the same as specific neurological and bodily changes occurring in an individual. See MIND/BODY, IDENTITY THEORY OF.

physis (Greek, origin, natural form of a thing) **1.** in general, *physis* means nature, or whatever exists outside of humankind. **2.** specifically, when applied to humans it means the *nature of a human* (the natural qualities, powers, condition of a person); and when applied to things it means a *natural object, the constituents of a physical entity*. Usually contrasted with NÓMOS. A further metaphysical use for *physis* in Greek philosophy was to refer to the ultimate reality or realities of things as opposed to their appearances; to refer to the real, essential nature of reality, or the true nature of things.

Four other common meanings for the word *physis:* (a) the origin (source, beginning, foundation) of a thing; (b) the physical constitution and structure of a thing; (c) the stuff (substance, substratum, composition) out of which things are made, or used to make things; and (d) the natural kind (genera, species, class, type) of a thing, its classification.

physis (Aristotle) some meanings: **1.** NATURE; all that occurs in the natural order of things, in contrast to TECHNĒ, which encompasses all that is created by humans. (But even *technē* is ultimately a subcategory of *physis*.) **2.** the inner impulse possessed by things that is the cause of their development (change, processes, activities). **3.** the essence or form of a thing that is in process of becoming, of making a thing into something other than what it was. **4.** the study of anything that changes in any of the varieties of change. See CHANGE (ARISTOTLE). Compare with NOMÓS.

physis (Plato) often used by him to refer (a) to the intrinsic and essential realities of things: their natures, powers, inherent qualities, and (b) to the realm of the perfect and eternal ideas. The emphasis in this use was on the *true* perspective on nature and reality as opposed to an illusory or inadequate one.

physis (Stoics) used to express their pantheistic and panpsychistic tendencies. *Physis* meant (a) all of nature, but (b) a nature that is a living rational organism, (c) imbued with a universal mind (see LÓGOS), and (d) of which humans and all things were a necessary part. In effect *physis* was identical with God viewed as the whole of nature itself, or as the active, guiding, rational force in nature. The principal characteristics of *physis* for the Stoics were rationality, necessity (fate), and goodness. It is *physis* that gives the individual knowledge of what is good and rational, and what is to be accepted in life. (The Stoics divided philosophy into three areas: logic, ethics, and physics. This restricted use of *physis* referred to the study of natural phenomena.)

pity (from Latin, *pietas,* piety, kindness, pity) **1.** a feeling of compassion for the suffering of another or of others. **2.** a feeling of grief. **3.** a feeling of mercy. **4.** a feeling of sorrow or commiseration.

Pity in one or more of the above senses has served as a motivating force for ethical conduct. See EMPATHY; KATHARSIS (ARISTOTLE); PASSION; PATHOS; SYMPATHY.

Plato (c.428–c.348 BC) Greek philosopher born to a distinguished family—his father, Ariston, was said to have been descended from the god

Poseidon. It is evident from Plato's writings that Socrates' life and thought served as the inspiration and foundation for Plato's philosophy. About 387 BC, about twelve years after Socrates' execution, Plato founded his Academy in Athens for the study of philosophy, mathematics and logic, the sciences, and ethical, political, and legislative ideas. The academy lasted for several centuries after his death and is regarded by many to have been the first university.

Plato's Dialogues have been organized—perhaps correctly—by scholars into early, middle, and later Dialogues, of which there were more than 24.

Early Dialogues: *Hippias Major.* The central question is What do we mean when we say that something—morally or aesthetically—is beautiful, fine, good? *Hippias Minor.* The central idea is No one does wrong voluntarily; one who knows the good will do the good. *Menexenos.* A funeral oration learned from the goddess Aspasia, but in the form of a satire on patriotism.

Ion. A conscious artistry, science, or know-how is not the source of poetry; is not possessed by poets. Poetry stems from some kind of inspiration—poets are overtaken by some nonrational power and are unable to explain the source of their poetry.

Charmides. The virtue of moderation, temperance, self-control, discipline.

Laches. What is courage? What is to be feared and not feared?

Lysis. What is friendship? What attracts our devotion to others?

Cratylus. What are names, words? What are their origin and philosophic status? Are they derived from natural essences, or from customary usage based on arbitrary human standards? (Some scholars classify *Cratylus* as a middle Dialogue.)

Euthydemus. (A brief and limited discussion of some linguistic fallacies.) Happiness is not a matter of possessing worldly goods, but of using worldly goods toward the attainment of a spiritual life. In tending to our souls, we use our mind, body, and circumstances to gain knowledge of the true good.

Gorgias. A discussion of topics such as rhetoric, its nature, worth, and use; the will to power; and happiness as the gratification of one's passions.

Meno. What is virtue? Can virtue be learned? Knowledge is a recollection or reminiscence.

Protegoras. Can goodness be taught—like a language, craft, or trade?

Euthyphro. What is piety, or holiness? What is religion?

Apology. The defense Socrates made at his trial in the presence of his accusers and the Athenian jury against charges such as that he was corrupting the youth of Athens, that he believed in false gods, and that he broke the laws of Athens.

Crito. This Dialogue takes place in prison. Crito tries to persuade Socrates to make his escape. Socrates presents his reasons for not escaping, for obeying the decision of the jury that he be put to death.

Phaedo. Socrates gives arguments in support of the immortality of the soul. The *Phaedo* takes place in prison and ends with Socrates taking hemlock.

Middle Dialogues: *Symposium*, sometimes translated as the *Banquet*, a discussion by several speakers of the many meanings and kinds of love, ending with Socrates' discourse on the origin, nature, and values of love.

Phaedrus, a dialogue centering on such themes as the principles of composition; a description of the passions and pleasures and their relationship to reason; and the mystical contemplation of the eternal, perfect, ideal forms that all the universe is aspiring to imitate.

Republic. What is justice? What the perfect State? Can a human be happy without being moral?

Theaetetus. What is knowledge? What are the kinds of knowledge?

Philebus. What is pleasure, or the pleasurable? The *good* as a pleasurable feeling. The use of intelligence, reason, is a pleasurable feeling. Pleasures derived from wisdom and virtue; pleasures not preceded by any craving; pleasures preceded by cravings. A discussion of the Doctrine of the Mean.

Timaeus. A presentation of cosmology—the origin and nature of the universe—a presentation that is mathematical and theological.

Later Dialogues: *Parmenides*, a discussion of the problem of one and many, unity and variety, similarity and difference; of how things in the real world participate in or imitate the ideal form.

Politicus. The nature and purpose of law for the individual and society; rule by persons, rule by constitution.

Sophistes. What is a negative predication? What is the logical nature of false statements?

Laws. A description of a practical State, one that could become a reality with a constitution and less than perfect humans?

Epinomis. A somewhat mathematical and Pythagorean account of the planets, sun, circle of the heavens, etc. Some concepts: the earth is a planet that revolves around an unseen center; the sun too is a planet; the earth is not a satellite of the sun; the earth revolves around a central point, but does not rotate.

Platonism the philosophy of Plato and/or the philosophy of those who have based their approach on that of Plato. The following are some of its general beliefs: **1.** this world as it appears to our senses, not the real world. There are two realms: (a) the real realm of perfect unchanging eternal ideas (forms) known only by our intellect, and (b) the illusory, or the less real, realm of concrete, individual, changing objects known by our senses and existing as imperfect copies of the perfect ideas. The real world is nonspatial and nontemporal. The actual world is spatial and temporal. **2.** abstract entities such as universals, souls, forms, and essences, existing in the real world independently of our conception of them, and more real than sensible objects. **3.** humans, through the use of reason, can control their base emotions and their irrational nature and thereby develop morally and spiritually. Humans do evil because they lack knowledge of the good. **4.** philosophic knowledge of the true, good, and beautiful as essential to the development of righteousness and the proper guidance of oneself and of others. Philosophic knowledge can be attained by the rigorous application of reason through a process of dialectic. **5.** humans possess a soul and it is immortal. **6.** there is a spirituality and a rationality that pervades all the universe. See BEAUTY; BECOMING; BEING; BEST, PRINCIPLE OF THE.

pleasure 1. state or feeling of delight, joy. **2.** gratification. **3.** the feeling that results from the satisfaction of a drive, desire, need. **4.** the feeling of enjoyment resulting from activity. **5.** the feeling that is a consequence of the exercise and fulfilling of an act of will. Contrasted with PAIN.

pleasure principle see UTILITY, PRINCIPLE OF.

plenitude, principle of (metaphysics) a conception of a perfect universe as (a) one that is as full of as many diverse existences as possible, and (b) one in which given an infinite amount of time all the possible combinations of existence that can be expressed will be expressed.

plenitude, principle of (methodology) an explanation of any kind should take into consideration the plethora of qualities found in existence and not reduce them either (a) to one form of explanation or (b) to the simplest theory. Contrasted with OCKHAM'S RAZOR; PARSIMONY, THE PRINCIPLE OF.

plenum (from Latin, *plenus,* full, fullness) **1.** an occupied space. **2.** all space, every part of which is filled with matter. Space without void or emptiness. (Opposite to empty space, or vacuum.) *Plenum* is often used to refer to Parmenides' one, eternal, indivisible, unmoving, immovable, unchanging reality.

Plotinus (c.205–270) Greek philosopher, born in Lycopolis, Egypt; founder of the Neoplatonist School. He studied philosophy under Ammonius Saccas in Alexandria and at age 40 went to Rome to teach. He founded a philosophic community there, which he governed in accordance with the principles expounded in Plato's *Laws.* After the death of Plotinus, his student Porphyry organized the writings of Plotinus in six sets, thus called the *Enneads,* with each set containing nine treatises. Porphyry's introduction to the *Enneads* constitutes a short biography of Plotinus.

pluralism (from Latin, *pluralis,* from *plus, pluris,* more than one) characterized by beliefs such as the following: **1.** there are more than one and more than two kinds of fundamental realities. Contrasted with DUALISM; MONISM. **2.** there are many separate, irreducible, and independent levels of things in the universe. **3.** the universe is basically indeterminate in form; it has no basic harmonious unity or continuity, no fundamental rational and coherent order.

pluralism, ethical see ETHICS, PLURALISTIC.

plurality of causes see CAUSES, THE PRINCIPLE OF THE PLURALITY OF.

pneuma (Stoics) (Greek) in Stoic philosophy, spirit, soul, the agency of life and rationality; used somewhat interchangeably with *LÓGOS*. All things possess a *pneuma*. These *pneumata* are incorporeal (immaterial) forces that enter and leave objects. Some STOICS regarded them as very fine material entities such as they believed were contained in fire. There is an overall universal *pneuma* that is the cause of the eternal cyclical pattern of all things and the cause of their return into the material substratum, from which they are again organized into definite objects. This creative force brings matter together into patterns and sustains for a time the unity and continued existence of objects.

poiēsis (Greek, poetry, the art of poetry) referred to anything made either by poets or craftspeople, or to the activity of making something.

poiēsis/poietikos (Aristotle) Aristotle classified knowledge into three general groups: **1.** *THEŌRIA*, abstract or cognitive knowing; **2.** PRAXIS, practical knowledge that comes by doing, from activity or development of a manual skill; and **3.** *poiēsis* or *poetikos,* knowledge that is involved in making, producing, or creating something. See KNOWLEDGE (ARISTOTLE); ACT/ACTION.

poietikos (Greek, capable of making something, one who is creative or productive) applied to both craftspeople and poets.

polar concepts see POLARITIES.

polarities (from Greek, *polos*, pivot, pole, axis, hinge) **1.** the extremes in a range of degrees. **2.** OPPOSITES or contraries. **3.** ideas that contrast in almost every respect, such as good/evil, love/hate, right/wrong, moral/ immoral, just/unjust, beautiful/ugly, light/dark, odd/even, and hot/cold.

When one member of a polarity is thought to exist, ontological status is usually also affirmed for its contrasting member. Examples: Light cannot exist without the existence of darkness. Love cannot exist without hate existing. If good did not exist in reality, then there would be no evil.

political philosophy the area of philosophy that studies the characteristics and problems of people as, in Aristotle's phrase, *political animals*. Some of the issues it focuses on: **1.** the origin, nature, purpose, and importance of government (states, ruling bodies) in human development. **2.** the classification of governments that have existed and their philosophies. **3.** the structure of utopias and their possible attainment. **4.** the relationship between the individual and government, obedience and freedom, control, suppression, censorship, and the power of government. **5.** the area of freedom from governing bodies. **6.** the extent to which one can, or should, disobey the law. **7.** the rights and protection of minorities. **8.** the right of nations to wage war. **9.** the analysis of value concepts such as justice, equality, freedom, liberty, rights, and possession and use of property.

politics (from Greek, *politikos*, of, for, or pertaining to citizens; *politēs*, citizen, member of a city or state; *polis*, city or state; one's country, city, or state; a body of citizens; *politeia*, citizenship, the rights of a citizen) **1.** that which has to do with governing. **2.** managing, directing, and enforcing the affairs of public policy and decisions or of political parties. **3.** the field of study that deals with civil-social problems and develops approaches to their solution.

politics (Aristotle) Aristotle wrote a treatise titled *Politeia*, translated as *Politics*. Politics is for Aristotle a brand of practical knowledge. See PRAXIS. Politics is the part of ethics that deals with people in group activity. Humans are animals of the *polis* (the city-state). The natural tendency of humans is to form into groups, to act within groups, and to act as groups. The purpose (end, goal) of politics is the same as that of ethics, and the same as that of human life in general: to attain EUDAIMONIA, the vital well-being (happiness) of the individual.

polla (Greek, many, very many, much, too much) used in many senses. The two principal senses in philosophy: **1.** to contrast with HEN (one, oneness), and **2.** to refer in the expression *hoi polloi*, to *the many, the commonality of the people,* what *the majority* think.

polydaemonism see SPIRITISM.

polytheism see GOD CONCEPTS.

polytypic concept a concept which if any of its major characteristics is claimed to be logically necessary, it is then possible to present a case that does not have that characteristic, but nevertheless would be accepted as an example of the concept. Examples: species, life, animal, insect, human, house. Most of our definitions and concepts have this polytypic character. Our understanding of words is generally based on whether they have a number of characteristics presented in their definition, not on their having all these characteristics. See DEFINITION, FAMILY RESEMBLANCE (WITTGENSTEIN).

positivism (Comte) some of its main tenets: **1.** the *Law of Three Stages*. The history of thought can be seen as an unavoidable evolution composed of three main stages: (a) the *theological* stage, during which anthropomorphic and animistic explanations of reality in terms of wills (egos, spirits, souls) possessing drives, desires, needs predominate; (b) the *metaphysical* stage, during which the *wills* of the first stage are depersonalized, made into abstractions, and reified as entities such as forces, causes, essences; and (c) the *positive* stage, in which the highest form of knowledge is reached by describing relationships among phenomena in such terms as succession, resemblance, coexistence. The positive stage is characterized in its explanation by the use of mathematics, logic, observation, experimentation, and control.

Each of these stages of mental development has corresponding social, economic, and cultural correlates. The theological stage is essentially authoritarian and militaristic. The metaphysical stage is basically legal and ecclesiastical. The positive stage is characterized by technological and industrial activity. As these stages change, so do the features of their correlates.

2. progress, the fulfillment of the evolutionary cycle of the Three Stages, is inevitable. **3.** the sciences are one unified whole, but in differing stages of development. They are also related in a hierarchical order of dependency; for example, astronomy must develop before physics can become a field in its own right; biology must reach a given point of sophistication before chemistry can begin its development. **4.** reality can be understood by means of basic concepts such as organic unity, order, progression, succession, resemblance, relation, utility, reality, movement, and direction. **5.** the highest form of religion in its evolution is the religion of universal humanity or reason (devoid of references to God).

positivism, logical sometimes called *positivism, logical empiricism* (see EMPIRICISM, LOGICAL), *scientific empiricism,* or *scientific positivism.* Some of the tenets of logical positivism: **1.** the acceptance of the verifiability principle (see VERIFIABILITY, PRINCIPLE OF), a criterion for determining that a statement has cognitive meaning. The cognitive meaning of a statement (as opposed to its emotive or other levels of meaning) is dependent on its being verified. A statement is meaningful if and only if it is, at least in principle, empirically verifiable. Some rock-bottom sense experience (positive knowledge) must be reached before a statement can have cognitive meaning. **2.** all statements in mathematics and logic are analytic (tautologies) and true by definition. They are necessarily true statements useful in organizing cognitively meaningful statements. Their concepts are not verified (discovered by examining reality) but are definitional conventions applied to reality. **3.** scientific method is the only source of correct knowledge about reality. (There have been attempts to construct a unified system of all the sciences under one logico-mathematical-experiential methodology.) **4.** philosophy is the analysis and clarification of meaning with the use of logic and scientific method. (Some logical positivists attempt to eliminate all philosophies that are not constructed as the logico-mathematical sciences are.) **5.** language is in essence a CALCULUS. With formalization it can be handled as a calculus (a) in solving philosophical problems (or showing which of them are pseudo-problems), and (b) in clarifying the foundations of science. Logical positivists and empiricists have tried to construct artificial, formally perfect languages for philosophy in order to gain efficiency, precision, and completeness of the physical sciences. **6.** metaphysical statements are meaningless. They are not empirically verifiable and they are not fruitful tautologies. There is no possible way to determine their truth (or their falsity) by appeal to experience. No possible experience could ever support metaphysical statements such as "The nothing itself nothings" (*Das Nichts selbst nichtet*—Martin Heidegger), "The absolute is beyond time," "God is perfect," "Pure being has no characteristics." Metaphysical questions are pseudo-questions. Metaphysics is to be relegated to nonsensical utterances. **7.** in an extreme version of positivism, statements about the existence of the external world, and of external minds independent of our own minds, are considered meaningless because there are no empirical ways of verifying them. **8.** the acceptance of an emotive theory in axiology. Values do not exist independently of the human ability to place values. Values are not objects in the world. They cannot be found by experimentation, testing, or experiencing them as we experience or verify the existence of objects. Values are not absolute. Values are statements, but not empirical statements. "Killing is evil," "Abortion is wrong," "Thou shalt not steal," and "That sculpture is beautiful" are statements that have no empirical or descriptive content at all. They do not reflect, or refer as a standard, to a transcendent perfect realm (such as Plato's archetypes), nor is their source a supernatural God. Statements of that sort express our attitudes, preferences, feelings, convictions, or conditioning *about* such activities as killing, abortion, stealing, and beauty. They do not directly communicate facts or information or cognitive knowledge. They indicate such things as our approval, disapproval, acceptance, nonacceptance, and affinity or nonaffinity for certain things. Some of the names associated with logical positivism: Herbert Fiegl, Philipp Frank, Moritz Schlick, Rudolph Carnap, and A.J. Ayer. See MEANING, VERIFIABILITY THEORY OF.

possible/possibility 1. capable of existing (occurring, being, happening). **2.** capable of becoming. Capable of coming into existence. Having the POTENTIAL to exist. **3.** that which usually happens, but does not *have* to happen. **4.** that which might happen. Not contrary to what could happen, or to what might happen, or to what has happened, or to what is happening. **5.** that which will happen given enough time. **6.** free (at liberty) to happen or not to happen. **7.** true insofar as our knowledge indicates. **8.** thinkable. **9.** not a self-contradiction. **10.** anything that is not self-contradictory and not (empirically or logically) necessary. Anything that is not impossible. Contrasted with ACTUALITY; CERTAIN. Compare with NECESSARY.

post hoc, ergo propter hoc see FALLACY, TYPES OF INFORMAL (21).

post res (Latin, after reality, after things) used by medieval philosophers in the context of NOMINALISM, wherein universals were regarded as existing only as abstract names after the fact of experiencing things and were not prior to, and not a causal agent for, the existence of material objects. See *ANTE RES* and *IN RES*.

postulate (from Latin, *postulatum*, request; from *postulare*, to demand) **1.** a statement (a) needed as an assumption and/or (b) asserted (c) without proof and/or (d) as self-evident, usually in the context of a formal system of logic or mathematics. **2.** a statement (a) accepted as true without itself having a logical proof given for it and (b) used to derive other statements that form a coherent system of logical or logico-empirical analysis. **3.** an assumption, presupposition, or hypothesis (essential preliminary assertion or condition) granted or posited so that a study (inquiry, investigation) may be carried out in a systematic way.

Related to concepts such as ASSUMPTION, AXIOM, primitives of a system.

postulates of practical reason, the (Kant) also *the moral postulates*, the unprovable but necessary and practical presuppositions (ground) for morality: **1.** the existence of a God; **2.** immortality; **3.** free will. See ETHICS (KANT).

postulates of pure reason, the (Kant) also *the postulates of thought*. See CATEGORIES OF THE UNDERSTANDING, THE (KANT).

potency (from Latin, *potentia*) **1.** the quality of possessing power. **2.** the ability to exercise power, to act. **3.** the capability (capacity) to become something of a definite sort. Opposite to ACTUALITY.

potency, active the innate capacity and tendency of a thing to become or to do something specific to its nature. Example: a rosebud becoming a flower. Contrasted with POTENCY, PASSIVE.

potency, passive the capability of a thing to become or to do something that is not specific to its nature as a necessary, innate capacity or tendency. Example: using a rosebud to make perfume. Contrasted with POTENCY, ACTIVE.

potency, pure that which has not in any way manifested any actual form in existence and which therefore cannot be identified—does not possess a *whatness* (see QUIDDITY) about it but only a *thatness*. See MATTER, PRIME.

potential/potentiality 1. latent. **2.** existing as a possibility. **3.** existing as a necessary possibility, one that must and will express itself. **4.** POTENCY. **5.** power. **6.** ability; that which is possible and can be done by something. **7.** the innate CAPACITY (and tendency) of a thing to actualize its inherent nature (form, essence). **8.** that which has the possibility of achieving its form, or a form. See ACTUALIZATION and DYNAMIS.

potential/potentiality (Aristotle) for Aristotle: **1.** a potential can be actualized only by something already actualized which acts as a cause in the potential's actualization. **2.** also, potential exists in some way to be actualized and in this sense has a level of being that is itself actual, that is actually present, for example, as an inherent capacity or form. See PRIME MOVER (ARISTOTLE); UNMOVED MOVER (ARISTOTLE).

***pour soi* (Sartre)** (French, for itself, for oneself). a phrase used by Sartre to refer to that type of personal existence in which one acts as an aware, pure subject initiating free choices and responsibly assuming the consequences of actions for oneself and others in a process of self-direction of one's life. These qualities of *être* (being) *pour soi* belong only to humans as individuals. Sartre contrasts *pour soi* with EN SOI. Opposite to inauthentic existence, ALIENATION; ESTRANGEMENT. See EXISTENTIALISM; BAD FAITH (SARTRE).

power (from Latin, *posse, potesse,* be able) **1.** the ability to act, or to make something. **2.** the ability to respond and/or resist. **3.** the FORCE (ENERGY), effort, strength exerted in 1. and 2. See DYNAMIS.

power (Aristotle) the three general categories of power: **1.** that which is the agent or cause of change in something; **2.** that capability (CAPACITY; POTENTIAL) in things enabling them to act and/or to do things; and **3.** that ability or tendency of a thing to remain itself, to retain its substantial form in spite of efforts to change it.

practical reason see REASON, PRACTICAL (ARISTOTLE).

praedicabilia (Latin, those things that can be attributed to any subject whatever; in English called *predicables*) refers to the categories or modes by which anything can be classified, defined, or understood. Usually the list contains five such classes: **1.** genus. **2.** species. **3.** DIFFERENTIA. **4.** QUALITY (attribute, characteristic, property), and **5.** ACCIDENT.

praedicamenta (Latin, the things that can be attributed [predicated of] a thing) understood by medieval philosophers to be identical with ten of Aristotle's categories: **1.** substance, **2.** quantity, **3.** quality, **4.** time, **5.** place, **6.** relation, **7.** position (state, condition), **8.** activity, **9.** passivity, **10.** possession.

See CATEGORIES (ARISTOTLE).

pragmatic fallacy see FALLACY, TYPES OF INFORMAL (40).

pragmatic theory of truth see TRUTH, PRAGMATIC THEORY OF.

pragmatics a branch of SEMIOTICS. The study of what we *do* to and with symbols apart from their meanings. Pragmatics deals not with what symbols mean or designate or how they are related to other symbols, but with how those who invent symbols, and/or those who interpret symbols are related to, are affected by, and use those symbols.

pragmatism (from Greek, *pragma*, thing done, act, work, thing of consequence; from *prassein*, do) Some of the main views in pragmatism: **1.** knowledge is derived from experience, experimental methods, and practical efforts. Pragmatism is critical of metaphysical speculation in arriving at truth. **2.** knowledge must be used to solve the problems of everyday, practical affairs; to help us adapt to our environment. Thinking must relate to practice and action. **3.** ideas must be referred to their consequences (results, uses) for their truth and meaning. Ideas are guides to positive action and to the creative reconstruction of experience in confronting and adjusting to new experiences. **4.** truth is that which has practical value in our experience of life. It serves as an instrument, or means, (a) in the attainment of our goals and (b) in our ability to predict and arrange the future for our use. **5.** truth is changing, tentative, and asymptotic. **6.** the meaning of an idea (theory, concept, belief) is the same as (a) the practical uses to which that idea may be put and (b) the practical consequences stemming from it. Compare with CONVENTIONALISM; INSTRUMENTALISM; OPERATIONALISM.

praxis (Greek, doing, an activity, an action or act, practical ability or manual skill) usually refers to practical human conduct, including ethical and political activity. Contrasted with *POIĒSIS/POIETIKOS* (ARISTOTLE), *THEORIA*. See

KNOWLEDGE (ARISTOTLE); VIRTUES, DIANOETIC (ARISTOTLE). Marx used *praxis* to refer to the synthesis of theory and practice.

precept (from Latin, *praeceptum,* from *praecipere,* take beforehand, teach) **1.** that which is given and intended as a rule (maxim, principle) of action or conduct, especially moral or religious conduct. **2.** that which is accepted as a regulative or working principle in the organization and direction of conduct.

precognition (from Latin, *praecognoscere,* foreknow) **1.** strong version: Foreknowledge; knowing what is to occur before it happens. **2.** weak version: Foresight; foreseeing what is going to occur, or might occur. From the point of view of paranormal phenomena, precognition is thought to have a *nonsensory* and noninferential source. See PARAPSYCHOLOGY; PREDICTION; PRESCIENCE.

preconscious that aspect of the mind *prior* to consciousness, which can be brought to consciousness by such acts as attention, concentration, stimulation. Example: I may not be presently conscious of my teacher's name but when asked, I become conscious of it; it was in a preconscious state. *Preconscious* is contrasted with *subconscious* and *unconscious*. Compare with ANOETIC.

predestination (theology) (from Latin, *praedestinatus,* past participle of *praedestinare,* predestine), also called *foreordination* and *preordination.* the doctrine that (a) all events that have happened, are happening, and will happen have been predetermined to happen (and are being caused to happen) by God and (b) that whether one's soul is to go to heaven or hell has already been decreed by the will of God. See FATE; FATALISM.

predeterminism 1. the theory that every event has a cause which is necessitated to be that cause at the exact time it is that cause and at no other time, in accordance with the designs of some operating principle (God, natural necessity, eternal forms). **2.** all things in the universe are governed by, or operate in accordance with, fixed causal laws that compel things to happen the way they do happen without exception and according to a necessitated sequence in time. See FATALISM.

Most predeterminists hold that if humans were omniscient, they would be able to perceive the necessitated scheme and interconnections of all events in the universe and thereby be able to predict what would happen, and what has happened, at any point in eternity.

predicament 1. a state (condition, situation, problem) that is unpleasant, unfortunate, especially with reference to good/bad, right/wrong, proper/improper. **2.** a problem that cannot be avoided and for which there is no solution. Example: The fear of death is a human predicament. It may be handled with courage or intelligence, fear or irrationality, but it cannot be eliminated. Compare with DILEMMA.

predicament, egocentric see EGOCENTRIC PREDICAMENT.

predicate (from Latin, *praedicatus,* past participle of *praedicare,* proclaim;

from *prae,* before, + *dicere,* say, speak) **1.** to assert or affirm something about something else. **2.** that which is affirmed or denied of a subject. Example: Grass is green. Snow is not green. Green is the predicate affirmed of (is predicated of) grass and denied of snow. In a categorical statement (proposition), the predicate appears as the term after the copula. See ATTRIBUTE; QUALITY.

predicate, simple a property such as *red* **1.** that is not reducible to any other property, **2.** that cannot be further analyzed, and **3.** that must be defined, or can only be known ostensively, that is, by pointing.

prediction 1. foretelling; declaration that something will happen before it happens, as in prophecy, augury, divination, or precognition. **2.** inferential knowledge asserted prior to an event about something that actually comes about and/or is expected to come about, made on the basis of regularities found in past experiences.

preestablished harmony (Leibniz) the view that mind and body do not interact. God has established a noncausal perfect harmony of activity between them analogous to the noncausal harmony of activity existing between two clocks whose ticking is synchronized perfectly. God has fore-knowledge of all the possible harmonious parallel relationships that could exist between mind and body. God chooses to bring into existence all those possible minds whose ideas fit perfectly with the activities of human bodies, each expressing in a proper sequence the representation of the other. See MIND/BODY RELATIONSHIPS, THEORIES OF (4); MONADS (LEIBNIZ).

prehension (from Latin, *prehensus,* from *prehendere,* grasp, seize) **1.** mental grasp; mental APPREHENSION. **2.** the process of perception (thought or feeling) whereby one takes something into one's level of attention and relates accordingly.

prehension span the maximum number of things the mind can grasp at any given moment of attending.

premise also *premiss* **1.** a statement that is in fact true or which is assumed to be true, employed (usually together with at least one other such statement) to argue toward a conclusion. **2.** in traditional categorical logic, one of the two statements that in a syllogism follow the standard categorical form from which a conclusion is reached. **3.** any statement that serves as a, or the, basis for an argument or inference.

preordination see PREDESTINATION (THEOLOGY).

prescience (from Latin, *praesciens,* present participle of *praescire,* fore-know) **1.** foreknowledge. **2.** foresight; knowledge of what will happen. Generally used in the context of an immediate, noninferential knowledge. See PARAPSYCHOLOGY.

prescriptivism (from Latin, *prescribere,* write (order) beforehand) **1.** in ethics and religion, the view that moral rules of action are commanded and necessitated by an authority that is their only source of justification. Example: "Thou shalt not kill," prescribed by the authority of God.

Contrast with ETHICS, DESCRIPTIVISM IN. **2.** in science, when a law is given a prescriptive status, it becomes a reified principle that *makes* things happen the way they do; things must act in accordance with its decree. Thus, the prescriptive, as opposed to the descriptive, interpretation of natural law would maintain that the *law* of falling bodies necessities bodies to fall as they do and in no other way, and bodies must so conform; otherwise they *violate* the law. Compare with entries under LAW, NATURAL.

present, the that immediate, instantaneous, momentary, and transient part of time (or durationless instant) at which any given experience takes place. Any given point in consciousness that can be declared a NOW. Existing not as a past or a future.

Present time is often thought of as in the analogy of a point on a line taking place immediately or instantaneously at the moment when the point is recognized. Metaphorically, it is often thought of as the *cutting* or *knife* or *boundary* that invisibly separates the past from the future.

present, the timeless the grammatical use of a verb such as *is* in the present tense without intending any reference to the present as distinct from the future or the past; the tenseless use of verbs whereby they do not relate to any specific time period, but may be said to relate to any and all time periods. Example: If *A* is larger than *B*, and *B* is larger than *C*, then *A* is larger than *C*.

presentment/presentational immediacy (from Latin, *praesentatio*, a showing or appearance of something) that which is directly perceived in consciousness from any source such as sensation, reason, memory, or imagination, singly or in combination. Often used interchangeably with DATUM.

presuppose 1. to require something antecedently if something else is to be what it is. Examples: For something to be a rock presupposes that a rock is hard. To hit a ball presupposes that there is someone who can hit it. **2.** to assume that something is logically or definitionally dependent. Examples: A cause presupposes an effect. Being a husband presupposes the existence of a woman.

presupposition 1. an implicit or explicit ASSUMPTION made in the act of viewing something or in the process of inference. **2.** that which must be assumed in order to arrive at a desired conclusion. **3.** a conjecture; that which can be reasonably assumed on examination of the circumstances or evidence.

preternatural also *praeternatural*, that which is beyond and/or different (irregular, abnormal) from what is natural (ordinary, explicable) but which is not supernatural and/or miraculous.

prevarication (from Latin, *praevaricatus*, past participle of *prevaricari*, walk crookedly) **1.** deviation from the truth or fact. **2.** evasive tactics in an argument. **3.** committing an equivocation in discourse for the purpose of misleading. **4.** a quibble or logical shuffle in order (a) to avoid the truth or reality of a situation, and/or (b) to avoid the impending or stated conclusion of a good argument. See EQUIVOCATION and SOPHISM.

prima facie (Latin) at first view, so far as appears on the surface, on the first appearance.

prima facie duties (Ross) duties (a) that are regarded as morally self-evident, (b) that tend to be absolute duties, and (c) that are to be regarded as absolute duties if no other PRIMA FACIE duty conflicts with them. A modified version of Kant's notion of absolute or unconditional duties: those moral actions one must always, without exception, perform. See ETHICS (KANT).

William David Ross is the leading exponent of *prima facie* duties. A list of such duties: **1.** the duty that arises because of *my* previous acts: (a) the duty of *fidelity* to promises made and (b) the duty of *reparation* for wrongful acts. **2.** the duty that arises out of the previous acts of *others,* such as gratitude. **3.** the duty of *beneficence,* of promoting the greatest amount of good. **4.** the duty of *nonmaleficence,* of refraining from harming other people. **5.** the duty of *justice,* the equitable distribution to others of goods. **6.** the duty of *self-improvement* in respect to intelligence, abilities, virtue, compassion.

primary and secondary substance see SUBSTANCE, PRIMARY AND SECONDARY (ARISTOTLE).

primary qualities see entries under QUALITIES, PRIMARY/SECONDARY.

prime matter see MATTER, PRIME.

prime mover 1. in the sense of first mover: that self-moving being (God) that gave the initial impetus to put the universe in motion. (Before this event no motion existed in the universe.) The beginning cause of all activity. Compare with UNMOVED MOVER. **2.** in the sense of a sustainer of motion: that being (God) which at any given moment is the cause of and which maintains all motion in the universe, and without which there would be no motion in the universe. The ground of all activity. (This second meaning of *prime mover* can maintain that motion in the universe has existed infinitely, that is, coinfinitely with God.) See COSMOLOGICAL ARGUMENT FOR GOD'S EXISTENCE; FIRST CAUSE.

prime mover (Aristotle) 1. that being (god) which moves the world by serving as an inspiration to the activity of its form in structuring matter. **2.** the perfect and unchanging ultimate goal (end, purpose, reality) of the world which itself does not move but which is the occasion of love and affinity toward it by self-moving, intelligent agents in the world that attempt to actualize it. See UNMOVED MOVER, THE (ARISTOTLE).

principle 1. the source or origin of something. **2.** the ultimate cause of something. **3.** a faculty or original endowment. In these first three senses, a principle is usually thought of as (a) innate, (b) immanent, and (c) found as an agent in a number of things. **4.** the rule or ground for a person's action. **5.** a general statement (law, rule, or truth) that serves as a basis for explaining phenomena. In 4. and 5., the words *rule* and *law* are often used in place of the word *principle*.

principle, regulative a principle used to guide our conduct or inquiry. It may be regarded as ideal only, as actually true, or as unprovable, nevertheless having practical and/or theoretical success. Examples: In science, some have considered the causal principle as only a regulative principle in scientific inquiry. In ethics, the CATEGORICAL IMPERATIVE has been considered a regulative principle for practical living.

principle of causation see CAUSAL PRINCIPLE, THE.

principle of difference in identity see DIFFERENCE IN IDENTITY, PRINCIPLE OF.

principle of excluded middle see LAWS OF THOUGHT, THE THREE.

principle of identity see LAWS OF THOUGHT, THE THREE.

principle of identity in difference see IDENTITY IN DIFFERENCE, PRINCIPLE OF.

principle of indifference see INDIFFERENCE, PRINCIPLE OF (PROBABILITY THEORY).

principle of individuation see INDIVIDUATION (METAPHYSICS).

principle of induction see INDUCTION, PRINCIPLE OF (METAPHYSICS).

principle of noncontradiction see LAWS OF THOUGHT, THE THREE.

principle of nonsufficient reason see REASON, PRINCIPLE OF NONSUFFICIENT.

principle of parsimony/simplicity/economy see OCKHAM'S RAZOR.

principle of sufficient reason see REASON, PRINCIPLE OF SUFFICIENT.

principle of uncertainty see UNCERTAINTY, HEISENBERG'S PRINCIPLE OF.

principle of uniformity of nature see UNIFORMITY OF NATURE, PRINCIPLE OF.

principle of universal causation see CAUSAL PRINCIPLE, THE.

principle of universality see UNIVERSALITY, PRINCIPLE OF (MORALITY).

principle of utility see UTILITY, PRINCIPLE OF.

prior (from Latin, *prior,* former, previous) **1.** antecedent; preceding in the order of time. **2.** preceding in order of (a) knowledge, (b) classification, (c) hierarchy (rank, order), (d) source (origin), (e) cause, or (f) privilege. Opposite to *posterior.* See A POSTERIORI; A PRIORI.

privacy, epistemic also called *private knowledge,* **1.** the content of consciousness that is inaccessible to anyone except the person having it. See EGOCENTRIC PREDICAMENT. **2.** that knowledge a person has, such as of his or her pains, pleasures, feelings, or emotions that cannot be known by others, cannot be made available to public knowledge, and cannot be directly verified by public knowledge. Opposite to PUBLICITY, EPISTEMIC. See PRIVILEGED ACCESS.

privation 1. negation. **2.** state of lack; the absence of.

privation (Aristotle) 1. a lack of form where it can be (or should be) present. **2.** a lack of some attribute that a thing (a) usually possesses, (b) is capable of possessing, and (c) ought to possess.

privative term/word/name a term denoting negation (lack, absence of).

privileged access refers to the brute fact that a person has direct and immediate knowledge of the contents of his or her consciousness (as opposed to the inferential knowledge based on overt behavior that others have of that person's consciousness).

probabilism 1. the theory that certainty about reality is utterly unattainable, since reality is not a completely rational system. Probable knowledge of things and of human conduct is the only kind of knowledge we can have. A rational person is one who, faced with the lack of certainty, is directed by probabilities. See entries under SKEPTICISM. **2.** empirical science must assign probability values to hypotheses (theories) and in this way show their degree of confirmation or disconfirmation. Compare with IMPROBABILISM.

probability 1. a determination of the rational expectation for the occurrence of an event. **2.** chance. **3.** a theory or calculus of chance such as the measurement of the likelihood of the occurrence of a particular event by determining the rate of its frequency. **4.** possibility. See EXPLANATION, SCIENTIFIC.

probability, classical theory of the ratio of the occurrence of an event to all the other possible alternatives. Example: Two dice can be thrown in thirty-six possible combinations (assuming that it is equally probable for each to occur). Eleven of the throws include at least one six. The probability of getting at least one six is 11/36.

probability, relative frequency theory of sometimes called the *actuarial theory of probability*, determines the rate of frequency at which something will occur, expressed as empirical statistical statements of the ratio of the number of times a thing happens to the number of times it *can* happen. Examples: (a) The probability that a given person will be bald is calculated as the number of bald persons divided by the total number of persons (bald and with hair). (b) In determining the chances that a given individual X will die in the next twenty years, personal knowledge about X, such as age, sex, occupation, years of marriage, and number of children, is obtained. The probability of survival of X to any given age is estimated on the basis of a class of persons that comes close to having characteristics such as those possessed by X. The characteristics of this class and their actual relationship to longevity are derived from statistical analyses and applied relative to X.

probability, subjective 1. the determination of (a) the degree to which one believes something or (b) the intensity of one's inclination to believe something (as opposed to not believing it). Example: Calculating (a) or (b) in terms of the odds or bets a believer would be willing to take about the possible occurrence or truth of something. **2.** the expression in an utterance (as opposed to a determination or description) of 1.

probable (from Latin, *probabilis*; from *probare*, try, prove) **1.** likely to be the case; that which is supported by good grounds (arguments, observation, inference) which incline one to believe but leave room for some doubt. **2.** likely to happen; that which is not demonstrably certain to occur, but which has some evidence in its favor for occurring. **3.** the area of knowledge between complete disbelief and complete CERTAINTY. **4.** a close approximation to what is the case or is believed to be the case.

problem of evil, the see EVIL, THE THEOLOGICAL PROBLEM OF.

problem of induction. See INDUCTION, PROBLEM OF.

problematic/problematical 1. doubtful. **2.** uncertain. **3.** possible. **4.** probable.

process, dialectical see LOGIC, DIALECTICAL.

process philosophy Alfred North Whitehead was the leading exponent of process philosophy, a theory that emphasizes the creative and novel advance of nature. Some of its tenets: **1.** nature is a continuously changing but progressing series of events. **2.** the fundamental ground of reality is not substance in which properties inhere, but process: directional and unified change. **3.** there are no durationless instants except as abstract concepts. **4.** language and its concepts cannot without creating paradoxes express (a) the continuous (no instants, no discrete units) nature of processes (change, becoming) or (b) the identity (individuality, unity, wholeness) of events in process. See CONCRETENESS, THE FALLACY OF MISPLACED; CONCRETION; CONCRETION, THE PRINCIPLE OF (WHITEHEAD); INGRESSION; SIMPLE LOCATION, FALLACY OF.

projectionism (epistemology) the theory that sensations exist as external qualities independently of consciousness. Sensations are had as the subjective content of consciousness and also are externally focused upon (projected) by such acts as localizing, positioning, and distancing.

prolegomenon (from Greek, from *prolegein,* say beforehand, foretell, state publicly) a preliminary statement serving as a preface or as a general introduction to something that is to follow. The plural is *prolegomena.*

prolēpsis (Greek, conception; from *prolambanein,* receive or take beforehand; anticipate an event, action, or truth) an innate, preconceived idea that comes to consciousness without deliberate rational effort, considered as (a) potentially present in all rational beings but expressed only by some, or as (b) universally expressed by all rational beings. Sometimes a *prolēpsis* is regarded as derived not from an innate source but from the sense experiences common to all humans.

proof 1. demonstration; a process that establishes (provides firm evidence or complete JUSTIFICATION for) a truth or a fact. **2.** in logic, the series of arguments based on the rules of INFERENCE of that logic which are used to derive the conclusion from the premises. Compare with EXPLANATION.

proof, transcendental (Kant) proof that shows that what is proved is a necessary condition for all possible human experience and hence applicable to all phenomena; without it, experience would be impossible and phenomena of a certain kind could not be known. See KNOWLEDGE (KANT).

propensity (from Latin, *propensio,* inclination, disposition, proneness) **1.** a natural innate tendency, inclination, disposition, bent, or bias. **2.** same as 1. but as a mental set which also includes desires, urges, appetition, cravings. **3.** the tendency or predisposition of conscious states to interrelate or to be associated due to conditioning or to the nature of our mental operations.

proper 1. correct; conforming to usage, convention, or conduct. **2.** belonging to a thing's natural constitution or essence. **3.** befitting one's nature, endowments, or inclinations. **4.** designating one individual only as in *proper noun.* See SENSIBLES, PROPER (ARISTOTLE).

property that which is PROPER to a thing; the attribute or quality (characteristic, feature, etc.) which a thing is said to possess. Usually a property is something that can be possessed by other members of the class in which it is found and also by members of other classes.

proposition 1. a SENTENCE or STATEMENT that asserts or denies something (a) that has two possible truth values, true or false; has two possible relations to fact, truth or falsity; or (b) that can be, at least in theory, verified or confirmed as true. **2.** the meanings that statements have; that which statements *propose* or express. In this sense, a distinction is made between sentences and propositions (statements). Example: "Adam loves Jane" and "Jane is loved by Adam" are two different sentences, but they express the same proposition (statement). See SENTENCE/STATEMENT DISTINCTION. For a more complete listing, see entries under SENTENCE and STATEMENT.

proprium (Latin, property, proper to a thing) **1.** that quality which is unique to a class but not essential to its identification or definition. Example: The ability to be humorous is a quality that only the class *human* can have, but it is not essential that a human have that quality to be known as human or to be defined as human. **2.** also used to refer to *essence,* or *that which is properly and indispensably a part (property) of the nature of a thing.*

prosyllogism a syllogism whose conclusion has become a premise of another syllogism in an argument.

Protagoras (c.485—c.420 BC) Greek philosopher and teacher, born at Abdera; an early Sophist. In Athens, Euripides and Pericles were his friends, and Plato named the dialogue *Protagoras* after him. Protagoras's treatise *On the Gods* begins: "In regard to the gods, I cannot know that they exist, nor yet that they do not exist; for many things hinder such knowledge—the obscurity of the matter, and the shortness of human life." Protagoras is known best for his statement, known as the *homo mensura* theory, "Man is the measure of all things, of those that are, that they are; of those that are not, that they are not."

Protagorean relativism see RELATIVISM, PROTAGOREAN.

protocols (from Greek, *prōtokollon,* which referred to the first leaf glued to the rolls of papyrus and documents; from *prōtos,* first, + *kolla,* glue) the basic, irreducible content of immediate experience on the basis of which empirical statements are formulated. See GIVEN, THE.

psi often used as a synonym for *extrasensory powers, phenomena,* or *perception*; see ESP. From the transliteration of the Greek letter ψ (psi), used as an abbreviation for parapsychological or PARANORMAL functions or phenomena. See PARAPSYCHOLOGY.

psychē (Greek, soul, mind, breath, breath of life, spirit, life) used originally to refer to the state of being alive; then to the principle of life (a breath, an invisible vapor, a spirit, a soul in things that causes life); then to the source of consciousness and also of conscience; then to the WORLD SOUL.

psychological atomism see ATOMISTIC PSYCHOLOGY.

psychological behaviorism see BEHAVIORISM.

psychological egoism see EGOISM, PSYCHOLOGICAL.

psychological hedonism see HEDONISM, PSYCHOLOGICAL.

psychologism 1. the nonpejorative meaning: (a) all philosophical concepts and problems can be reduced to some form of psychological analysis; (b) all the fields of philosophy can be explained on the basis of psychological principles, and fields such as ethics can be seen to be nothing more than applied psychology; and (c) the essential characteristics of psychological analysis are: (1) introspection and (2) observation. **2.** the pejorative meaning: the mistake of assuming that philosophical concepts and problems can be reduced to and resolved by psychological analysis; the failure to distinguish between the psychological treatment of the origin of our knowledge in an activity of thinking and the nonpsychological structure, quality, and veracity of the content of that knowledge.

psychology, association see ASSOCIATIONISM.

psychology, atomistic see ATOMISTIC PSYCHOLOGY.

psychology, behavioristic see BEHAVIORISM.

psychology, faculty see FACULTY PSYCHOLOGY.

psychology, functional see FUNCTIONAL PSYCHOLOGY.

publicity, epistemic also called *public knowledge* (*Epistemic* comes from the Greek *epistēme,* knowledge) **1.** knowledge that (a) is communicated and (b) shared and (c) made accessible to others. **2.** knowledge as in 1. but in addition tested or verified by a number of people. **3.** knowledge such as about the size or shape of objects, which can be directly known by many people or inferred by many people. Opposite to PRIVACY, EPISTEMIC.

punishment the infliction on a person of pain, suffering, loss, deprivation, or penalty for a crime or fault that has been committed intentionally and in disobedience, usually as a violation of a law.

punishment, rehabilitative theory of some of the main views: **1.** the purpose of punishment is to change, remold, the behavior of the offender. **2.** punishment for the sake of punishment, or for revenge, is evil and unjust. The only occasion for the infliction of punishment is when it will benefit the person being punished.

punishment, retributive theory of sometimes called *retaliative theory of* *punishment.* Commonly understood as "an eye for an eye, and a tooth for a tooth," or more appropriately as "the punishment must fit the crime." Some of the main tenets: **1.** the purpose of punishment is revenge and/or to extract from the offender something equal to the wrong he or she has committed. **2.** this is done not necessarily to rehabilitate the offender but to correct an inequity or moral imbalance that the offense has created. **3.** injustice consists in permitting someone to injure others without being injured proportionately in return. **4.** punishment is a deterrent.

punishment, utilitarian theory of some of the main views: **1.** the purpose of punishment is to assist in producing good: the greatest good of the greatest number. **2.** punishment is intrinsically evil but can be justified by the good results it produces. If punishment does not produce good consequences, it should not be administered.

pure act sometimes called *pure actuality* **1.** the completely actualized being, God, in whom there can never be any POTENCY. **2.** that state or process in which everything is actualized, without in any way being dependent on something else for its ACTUALIZATION and activity.

pure experience 1. the immediately given mental states such as sensations, feelings, images prior to (or devoid of) interpretation, judgment, conceptualization, and structuring. **2.** those mental states such as sensations, feelings, images that remain when purged of interpretation, judgment, conceptualization, and structuring. Compare with EXPERIENCE.

purgation (from Latin, *purgare,* purge, purify, cleanse; from *purus,* pure, + *agere,* make, do) **1.** the act of purifying, cleansing, or exculpating (a) emotions, (b) guilt, or (c) moral defilement or sin. **2.** the state of being cleansed of such things listed in 1. See KATHARSIS.

purism the insistence on purity (nicety, singleness of taste, etc.) in things, for example, in the use of words or in strict adherence to the letter of the law or to a sacred text.

puritan ethic some of the views associated with the Puritan ethic: **1.** the highest human values to be got out of life are through hard physical work that has definite practical results for oneself and the community in which one lives. **2.** living is a dedication to work, which produces, and is pervaded by, moral values such as industriousness, discipline, honesty, moderation, temperance, devotion, humility before God, frugality, thrift, simplicity, acceptance of toil, hardship, and pain; self-sufficiency, dedication to family life and to others in developing a sense of community, and awareness of the purpose and presence of God, from whom these values stem and for whom these values are expressed.

purpose 1. INTENTION. **2.** design. **3.** that which one sets before oneself as an object (result, END, aim, plan) to be reached or attained. See TELEOLOGY.

putative (from Latin, *putare,* reckon, suppose) **1.** supposed. **2.** deemed or reputed to be the case. **3.** disputable.

Used in phrases such as *putative entities* and *putative truth.*

Pyrrhonism generally connotes extreme SKEPTICISM; refers to the doctrines of the Greek philosopher Pyrrho and his followers. Some of its main tenets: **1.** one must suspend judgment (*EPOCHĒ*) about the true nature of reality since all one can know are one's sensations, and they are relative and inconsistent. **2.** arguments can be given for any position one wishes to defend. **3.** one must accept the fact that one's knowledge is limited and be content not to inquire into more than can be known or comprehended. **4.** one must strive for *ATARAXIA*, an imperturbability of mind and body, an indifference (*APATHEIA*) stemming from the acceptance of whatever happens. **5.** the highest values in life are calmness, independence, and self-sufficiency.

Pythagoras (6th century BC) Greek mathematician and philosopher, born on the island of Samos. He settled in Croton, where he founded an ascetic brotherhood stressing the religious transformation of humankind and transmigration (reincarnation) and purification of the soul. Based on the belief that the soul migrates from human to human, and human to animal, Pythagoras and his followers were vegetarians. Pythagoreanism persisted as a religious sect until the 4th century AD, but mathematically and philosophically it influenced Plato and subsequent philosophers to the present day. No writings by Pythagoras are extant.

Q

Q.E.D. abbreviation for the Latin *quod erat demonstrandum,* that which was to be demonstrated. Q.E.D. sometimes is used immediately before (or after) a conclusion much as we use the word *therefore.*

qua (Latin, as, as far as, insofar as).

quadrivium (Latin, a place where four ways [roads] meet) the four mathematical studies of the medieval educational system: geometry, arithmetic, astronomy, and music. Together with the TRIVIUM—grammar, rhetoric, and logic—this made up the seven liberal arts of education in medieval times.

qualia (Latin, quality, property, nature, state, kind, condition) sometimes used as a synonym for SENSA, often called *SENSE QUALIA. Qualia* is a Latin plural but is used in English with either a singular or plural meaning. *Quale* or *qualis* is the Latin singular, with the meaning *of what kind or property* a thing is or has.

qualities, primary/secondary 1. *primary qualities* are (a) qualities such as motion, rest, size (extension), shape (figure), solidity (impenetrability), number, and structure, (b) which are believed to be inherent characteristics of matter in itself and not to depend for their existence on consciousness. **2.** *secondary qualities* are those (a) sensed qualities, such as of color, smell, taste, sound, heat, and cold, (b) which are believed to be caused in us by the primary qualities inherent in matter, and (c) which depend for their existence on the operations of the mind. Primary qualities exist in reality independently of an observer. Secondary qualities exist only as content in consciousness. This distinction has in general been made since the time of Leucippus and Democritus (see ATOMISM, GREEK), and was commonly accepted during the rise of modern science by thinkers such as Galileo, Boyle, and Newton. The distinction in philosophy is mainly associated with Locke. See *NOMÓS.*

qualities, tertiary sometimes called *tertiary values* (from Latin, *tertiarus,* containing a third part, + *qualis,* the constitution of a thing) **1.** qualities added by the mind to the primary and secondary qualities, thus constituting a third quality; those qualities (or values) produced by the presence of a mind capable of appreciation, interest, selectivity, judgment, and concentration, for example, goodness, truth, and beauty. **2.** those interpretive and evaluative responses and reactions of consciousness (to the primary and secondary qualities) that are regarded as essential to human experience and to reality as are the primary and secondary qualities.

quality (from Latin, *qualitas;* from *qualis,* how constituted, as a thing is) **1.** that characteristic (a) which is possessed by a thing and (b) by which the thing is recognizable. For example, sweetness is a quality of honey. **2.** that content of consciousness usually associated with external objects produced by physical stimuli. For example, sweetness is not a quality of honey but a quality of consciousness produced by physical processes.

PROPERTY, ATTRIBUTE, and CHARACTERISTIC are a few of the words used as synonyms for *quality*. In many respects, quality may be regarded as having the most general meaning. A *property* is often thought of as a special or particular quality. An *attribute* is often used in the context of an inherent, essential, or necessary quality. A *characteristic* usually refers to a distinctive (distinguishing) quality or property or to a typical quality or property.

quality (Kant) see CATEGORIES OF LOGIC, THE (KANT); CATEGORIES OF THE UNDERSTANDING, THE (KANT).

quality (logic) in traditional categorical logic, *quality* refers to whether a categorical statement is affirmative or negative.

quality, accidental a nonessential, incidental, or fortuitous quality. See ACCIDENTAL ATTRIBUTE.

quality, emergent see EMERGENT, AN.

quantification, suppressed a form of ambiguity in which, in ordinary conversation, we do not know whether a word or sentence refers to all members of a class or only to some. Example: "Children are naughty." It is unclear whether "all children are naughty" or "some children are naughty" is meant. See entries under AMBIGUITY.

quantifier (logic) a word (symbol, sign) that indicates *all, some,* or *no*.

quantifier shift fallacy the fallacy of confusing universal and particular (existential) quantities in an argument or inference. Example: Inferring the statement "All those who don't mind taking exams are good students" from the statement "All good students don't mind taking exams." See entries under FALLACY.

quantity (Kant) see CATEGORIES OF LOGIC, THE (KANT); CATEGORIES OF THE UNDERSTANDING, THE (KANT).

quantity (logic) in traditional categorical logic, *quantity* refers to whether a categorical statement is universal or particular.

quiddity (from Latin, *quidditas,* the whatness of a thing; from *quid,* what) **1.** the essence (whatness) of a thing; that which answers the question "*Quid est?*" ("What is it?") and therefore serves as the essential distinguishing characteristic in its definition. **2.** often used in ordinary English to mean a *trivial nicety* or a *quibble*.

quintessence (from Latin, the fifth essence; from *quinta,* fifth, + *essentia,* essence) **1.** used by the Scholastics to name the eternal and immutable celestial objects in Aristole's superlunary world. In Aristotelianism the purest and highest essence found anywhere is possessed by celestial bodies, which were regarded as a fifth element following the traditional four: earth, air, fire, and water. See ELEMENTS, THE FOUR. **2.** also used by the Scholastics to refer to the highest and most nearly perfect essence or power possessed by a natural body. **3.** used in English to mean *the finest* or *the most nearly perfect example* of something.

R

random 1. aimless; without a definite direction, order, purpose, system, method, or aim. **2.** happening by CHANCE or haphazardly. Related words: *casual, fortuitous, accidental,* and *spontaneous.*

ratio (Latin, reason; from *reri, ratus,* reckon, think) used in a general philosophic sense to refer to the human ability to discriminate, to identify, and to relate things.

In medieval philosophy, *ratio* (reason) was usually distinguished from *intellectus* (intelligence). *Ratio* leads one to practical action and to a commonsense view of the world and exists prior to the development or activity of human intelligence. *Intellectus* is the foundation for theorizing, speculating, abstracting, inferring, and contemplating. See entries under *INTELLECTUS.*

ratiocination (from Latin, *ratiocinatus,* past participle of *ratiocinari,* to reason) **1.** reasoning; the mental process of logical or exact thinking. **2.** proof; the specific logical demonstration of the reasoning leading to a conclusion.

rational (from Latin, *rationalis,* rational) **1.** containing, or possessing REASON or characterized by reason. **2.** capable of functioning rationally or participating in rational inquiry. **3.** capable of being understood. **4.** in conformity with reason; intelligible; sensible; reasonable. **5.** adhering to qualities of thought such as consistency, coherence, simplicity, abstractness, completeness, order, or logical structure.

rational self-interest also *enlightened self-interest.* See EGOISM, ALTRUISTIC; EGOISM, ETHICAL.

rationale (from Latin, neuter form of *rationalis,* rational) **1.** an explanation of the basic principles used in support of an idea, hypothesis, opinion, theory, etc., or **2.** the basic principles themselves.

rationalism in general, the philosophic approach that emphasizes reason as the primary source of knowledge, prior or superior to, and independent of, sense perceptions. Some main tenets: **1.** by the process of abstract reasoning (thinking) we can arrive at fundamental, undeniable truths (a) about what exists and about its structure, and (b) about the universe in general. **2.** reality is knowable—or some truths about reality are knowable—independently of observation, experience, and the use of empirical methods. **3.** the mind is capable of knowing some truths about reality that are prior to any experience (but are not analytic truths). These truths are innate ideas and isomorphically conform with reality. **4.** reason is the principal origin of knowledge, and science is basically a rationally conceived deductive system only indirectly connected with sense experience. **5.** truth is not tested by sense-verification procedures, but by such criteria as logical consistency. See TRUTH, COHERENCE THEORY OF. **6.** there is a rational (deductive, logicomathematical, inferential) method that can be applied to any subject matter whatsoever and can provide us with adequate explanations. **7.** absolute certainty about things is the ideal of knowledge and is attainable to some extent by finite minds. Absolute certainty (and necessity) is the essential characteristic both of reality and of all true knowledge. **8.** only those necessary and self-evident truths derived from reason alone can be known as true, real, and certain; all else is subject to falsification, illusion, and uncertainty. **9.** the universe (reality) follows the laws and rationality (form) of logic. The universe is a rationally (logically) designed system whose order conforms to logic. **10.** once this logic is mastered, all things in the universe can be seen to be deducible from its principles or laws. Contrasted with schools of thought such as EMPIRICISM; POSITIVISM, LOGICAL; INTUITIONISM; revelationism.

Rationalists, Continental (European) notably René Descartes, Benedict Baruch Spinoza, and Gottfried Wilhelm Leibniz.

rationalize 1. the positive sense: to make rational or to endow something with reason or reasonableness. **2.** the pejorative sense: to present what one wants to appear as a good rational justification for a belief or action that in truth (a) has no good justification, and/or (b) has another more plausible but embarrassing justification. The reasons given in such a rationalization are usually untruthful inventions that are more acceptable to one's ego than the truth. See ETHICS, CASUISTIC.

rationes seminales/causales (Latin, seminal reasons or causal reasons) a term referring to the physical powers (tendencies or _seeds_) potentially present in matter. Material things are analogous to seeds. Seeds contain within themselves the potential (the potency) to become fully matured plants. So material things are in a latent state, ready to receive the right conditions for their full development. The Latin equivalent of _LÓGOS SPERMATIKOS._

real 1. actually existing apart from our perception; true; having substantive or objective existence. Opposite to fictitious, false, erroneous, imaginary, illusory, unreal, seeming, apparent, appearance, phantasm, fantasy, artificial. **2.** existing inherently in the thing itself, for example, as an ESSENCE or as a structure, and not as we see it in appearance. **3.** actuality; an actual situation; that which is now occurring, not a past, future, or theoretical occurrence. Opposite to IDEAL; HYPOTHETICAL; POTENTIAL; POSSIBLE. Related to positive, actual, authentic, verifiable, veritable, genuine, factual, external.

real definition see DEFINITION, TYPES OF (5 and 16).

real dispute see VERBAL DISPUTE.

realism 1. the attempt to see things as they are without idealization, speculation, or idolization. **2.** the dedication to facts regardless of how unpleasant they may be.

Realism can be interested in how things _ought_ to be, but only after an honest and objective assessment of how things _are_ in fact. See also UNIVERSALS (REALISM).

realism, Aristotelian the theory that universals (essences, abstractions, general terms) **1.** exist only within objects in the external world (as opposed to a world or realm of ideas); **2.** exist independently of our perception of them; **3.** our intellect abstracts them from our sense perceptions of the objects in which they inhere; and **4.** this resulting abstraction is the foundation for our knowledge of reality. See UNIVERSALS (ARISTOTLE).

realism, common-sense 1. the attempt to provide a justification for the (realistic) beliefs of an ordinary (common) person that are derived from his or her everyday experiences of the world. **2.** the view that the external world is as it appears to us. Often referred to as *direct realism* or *natural realism*. Both meanings are associated with Thomas Reid's Scottish school of common-sense philosophy.

realism, epistemological 1. the theory that universals (essences, abstract concepts, general terms, relations) exist in reality independently of our consciousness—or of any consciousness. Universals exist in the external world even when not perceived. Opposite to NOMINALISM. For most realists, these externally, objectively existing universals have more reality than the concrete, particular objects in which they are seen, or from which they are abstracted. **2.** the theory that that which is known *about* a thing exists (in essential respects the same way) *in* the thing known, and would exist without the knower. Compare with CONCEPTUALISM.

realism, naive the belief that the world is as we perceive it. No distinction exists between what the world appears to be like (appearance) and what the world is really like (reality). Sense data impart correct (accurate, true) information about things. See MONISM, EPISTEMOLOGICAL. Often used in a pejorative sense.

realism, personal the theory that personality (a) is the real ground for the sustenance of all existing things, (b) is present as an active presence in all things, and (c) can be known directly in an intuitive apprehension or identification with things in nature. See PERSONALISM.

realism, Platonic universals (forms, essences, ideas, abstractions, general terms) such as *humanity, redness, circularity, beauty* **1.** exist in the external world (or in a realm of perfect forms) independently of our perception of them; **2.** are unchanging and eternal; **3.** have a greater reality than our sense perceptions or external material objects; **4.** are the causal agents (or the models for) the existence of particular objects (are the reasons why objects are as they are rather than being some other way); and **5.** are the means by which reason recognizes contrasts, and identifies things and thereby gains knowledge. See UNIVERSALS (PLATO).

reality 1. that which is. Opposite to APPEARANCE. **2.** everything that is; the sum total of all that exists; the UNIVERSE. **3.** all that which exists apart from CONSCIOUSNESS.

reality, objective and formal objective reality is the external reality to which our language and perceptions refer and is contrasted with formal reality, which refers to the modes of thought employed in understanding reality and/or to the logical interrelationships of ideas as ideas. See OBJECTIVE EXISTENCE (REALITY).

reason 1. the intellect; the capacity to abstract, comprehend, relate, reflect, notice similarities and differences, etc. **2.** the ability to infer.

Reason, when thought of as a FACULTY, is contrasted with the faculty of the will, the faculty of appetition, the faculty of sentience, the faculty of intuition, etc. and is usually believed to be a characteristic of humans and not of lower animals. Reason is regarded as distinct from FAITH, REVELATION, INTUITION, EMOTION, FEELING, sentiments, sensations, perceptions, experience. See INTELLECT; UNDERSTANDING.

reason (Kant) 1. reason is one of two intellectual faculties; understanding is the other. See UNDERSTANDING (KANT). Understanding innately possesses A PRIORI ideas by which it structures experience (or reality). These ideas cannot be derived from our experience, nor are they found in pure experience. See KNOWLEDGE, SYNTHETIC A PRIORI (KANT). **2.** reason, in contrast with understanding, is an active principle driven by an impossible demand to transcend the limitations of all human experience and arrive at a comprehension of an absolutely unconditional and all-inclusive reality. **3.** reason must be content (a) to be the overseer of what is possible and what is impossible for the understanding to know, and (b) to examine and apply all the possible ways by which experience can be structured and made empirical.

reason, active/passive (Aristotle) also called *active/passive intellect*. The active reason enables the passive reason to acquire the sensible form or image (*PHANTASMA*) of the object being sensed or perceived. The active reason must make the phantasm explicit to awareness by abstracting it from sense experience. See *NOÛS PATHETIKOS* (ARISTOTELIANISM); UNIVERSALS (ARISTOTLE); VIRTUES, DIANOETIC (ARISTOTLE).

reason, insufficient see INDIFFERENCE, PRINCIPLE OF (PROBABILITY THEORY).

reason, postulates of practical (Kant) see POSTULATES OF PRACTICAL REASON, THE (KANT).

reason, practical (Aristotle) 1. the faculty with which we perceive (a) what means are available to us in order to achieve a goal, (b) which among these means is the most efficient and/or the most appropriate, and (c) how to employ these means in actual conduct. **2.** deliberation (reasoning, thinking) about (a) what we will do and (b) what we will not do, which results in a decision (choice, action, resolution). See KNOWLEDGE (ARISTOTLE); *PRAXIS*.

reason, practical (Kant) 1. reason that originates knowledge about moral conduct (and is also the source of religious feelings and intuitions). **2.** reason that reflects on the possibilities provided us by freedom of the will. Contrast with REASON, THEORETICAL (KANT); REASON, PURE (KANT).

reason, principle of nonsufficient the chances (probability) of two things happening can be regarded as being the same if there are no good (sufficient) reasons for saying that they are not the same, that one will happen rather than the other. See INDIFFERENCE, PRINCIPLE OF (PROBABILITY THEORY).

reason, principle of sufficient 1. all things (objects, events, changes, causes) are (a) related to each other in a necessary relationship (by necessity); (b) require each other in that relationship; and (c) cannot be other than what they are. And (d) there is a reason for all this. **2.** all things are what they are because that is the best rational way for them to be. **3.** all things occur for a reason and (a) would not occur unless that reason existed and (b) would be different if their reason for being were different. See *AITIA*.

reason, principle of sufficient (Leibniz) Leibniz held to three principles: The *Principle of the Best* or of *Perfection* (see BEST OF ALL POSSIBLE WORLDS, THE [LEIBNIZ]), which he applied to all actuality as opposed to possibility; the *Principle of Noncontradiction,* which he regarded as the foundation of all necessary truths (the truths of logic or reason); and the *Principle of Sufficient Reason,* the basis of all contingent events in the universe, of all matters of fact.

The Principle of Sufficient Reason asserts that nothing happens in the universe without a reason for its happening that way rather than another way. There is a reason why an object is that object and not another. (Humans are not able to comprehend all such sufficient reasons for the occurrence of events, but if they knew all things sufficiently they could give a reason why things are as they are and not otherwise, why the universe is the way it is rather than its being some other kind of universe.)

The main arguments for the Principle of Sufficient Reason: Since no two things can ever be identical (see IDENTITY OF INDISCERNIBLES, PRINCIPLE OF [LEIBNIZ]), there must be a reason for this, and that reason must exist in (and have been put into) the very being of things. For Leibniz, the sufficient reason for things and for the universe exists (must exist) outside the infinite series of contingent events. The ultimate sufficient reason subsists in a necessary substance, or MONAD (God), the source of all the (rational) activity of the universe and of its necessitation.

reason, pure (Kant) reason functioning on its own without relationship with other faculties of consciousness, such as will or appetition. Contrast with REASON, PRACTICAL (KANT); REASON, THEORETICAL (KANT).

reason, theoretical (Aristotle) sometimes called *contemplation* **1.** reasoning or thinking in order to arrive at knowledge (a) of what is the case, (b) of what inevitably or necessarily must be the case, and (c) of what may possibly be the case (*if* certain conditions occur). This activity results in a conclusion (statement, knowledge, action) of some sort. **2.** the faculty with which 1. is accomplished. See KNOWLEDGE (ARISTOTLE).

reason, theoretical (Kant) reason that constructs intellectual knowledge,

such as scientific knowledge. Contrast with REASON, PRACTICAL (KANT); REA-
SON, PURE (KANT).

reason, universal see *LÓGOS*.

reasoning 1. the process of inferring conclusions from statements. **2.** the
use of logic and/or abstract thought patterns in the solution of problems or
in the act of planning. **3.** the ability to know some things without direct
recourse to sense perceptions or immediate experience.

Reasoning is a kind of thinking (or state of consciousness) that can be
contrasted with others, such as daydreaming, dreaming, imagining, remembering, intuiting, imaging, perceiving, sensing, doubting, suppressing,
inhibiting, controlling, selecting, and deceiving. It is possible that some element or form of reasoning can be involved in any of these. Reasoning can
be used for a variety of purposes: to deceive, to argue, to debate, to doubt,
to persuade, to express, to explain, to apologize, to rationalize, etc. It seems
that any form of conscious activity can be affected and structured by the
reasoning process.

reasoning, analogical see ANALOGICAL REASONING.

reasoning, discursive the process of proceeding from premises to a conclusion.

reasons 1. statements used in support of a conclusion, or an idea, or a fact;
the rational JUSTIFICATION that makes something intelligible. **2.** statements
made to explain purposive actions, or goal-oriented activity. **3.** sometimes
used as a synonym for *causes* (see CAUSE), as in the statement "The reasons
for the rain are ..." but *reasons* may be distinguished from *causes* in two
principal ways: (a) The time at which reasons are offered is not necessarily
synchronous with the actually operating cause. Reasons can be provided
before, after, or during the operation of the cause. (b) Reasons are explanatory and are not physically or causally relevant to the occurrence of a causal
series.

receptivity (from Latin, *recipere*, take back) **1.** in general, the passive process of COGNITION, ranging anywhere from sense experience to abstract
thought. Usually contrasted with creativity, physical activity, intentional
actions. **2.** specifically, receiving sensations (impressions, ideas, images) in
the act of knowing, as opposed to (a) forming those sensations into concepts
and/or (b) formulating abstract concepts.

reciprocity (ethics) the giving in return of equal good (rights, benefits) for
the good received.

recognition (from Latin, *recognitio*; and from *recognoscere*, know once
again) **1.** the acknowledgment of the knowledge and/or identity of something. **2.** the acknowledgment that something known and/or identified has
been part of one's previous awareness.

recollection (from Latin, *recollectus*, past participle of *recolligere*, collect
again) **1.** remembrance; the ability to remember, to use one's memory or to
recall something. **2.** that which is remembered.

Recollection is often used interchangeably with remembrance, REMINIS-CENCE, or MEMORY. *Recollection* implies a deliberate conscious effort to remember or to recall something to consciousness. *Remembrance* often connotes the condition of being kept in consciousness. *Reminiscence,* used more in the plural, now suggests a retrospective recall of items in our consciousness about the past and usually ones that have some significance or sentimental attachments. *Memory* is a general term for anything brought to consciousness about the past and is believed by common sense to be a mental reproduction of past experiences. See *ANAMNĒSIS.*

recta ratio (Latin, right *or* correct reason) referring to the Law (Necessity) of Nature; the Latin equivalent of *LÓGOS ORTHOS.* See entries under LAW, NATURAL.

recurrence, eternal also called *eternal return* or *eternal reemergence* **1.** the belief that all events in the universe (a) have occurred an infinite number of times in the past in their exact details and order, and (b) will so occur again an infinite number of times in the future. **2.** the repetition of general cyclic patterns in the universe: the seasons; day and night; birth and death; plant growth and decay; order out of chaos. **3.** the unending emergence of an ordered universe out of a state of chaos into which the ordered universe continually dissolves to reemerge. See CONFLAGRATION (STOICS); STOICS, THE.

recursive (from Latin, *recurrere,* run back) referring to a procedure that can be continued without end unless something is specified to terminate it.

recursive definition see DEFINITION, TYPES OF (17).

reductio ad absurdum (Latin, reduction to absurdity *or* reducing to absurdity) a method of arguing in which a statement is established as true because its falsity leads to absurd, unacceptable, or contradictory conclusions. In formal deductive reasoning, the procedure is as follows: (a) Negate the conclusion of the argument. (b) Add this negated conclusion to the premises (which are accepted as true). (c) Deduce a contradiction from these premises that includes the negated conclusion. (d) If such a contradiction can be derived, then the initial argument is valid, and the original conclusion logically follows from the original premises. We have in effect shown that the negation of the conclusion leads to something that is necessarily false or absurd. See DIALECTIC (ZENO).

reductio ad absurdum, principle of that which implies its own denial is always false.

reductio ad impossibile (Latin, reduction to an impossibility *or* reducing to the impossible) a method of arguing for the truth of a statement by proving that its negation (or nonacceptance) leads to impossible statements and unacceptable consequences.

reductionism/reductivism 1. in the philosophy of science, the belief that all fields of knowledge can be reduced to one type of methodology, or to one science, which encompasses principles applicable to all phenomena. (Physics has been considered the basic science to which all other sciences can be reduced and of which they are extensions.) **2.** in metaphysics, the belief that all things can be reduced to one kind of thing (substance, process, matter, God, form, idea) that is ultimate, necessary, and the most real.

reductive fallacy also called the *"nothing but" fallacy* and sometimes referred to as the *naturalistic fallacy*. **1.** erroneously believing (a) that a complex whole is nothing but or is identical with its parts or causes, and/or (b) that a complex whole can be entirely explained in terms of the description of its parts or causes. Example: Mental states are caused by neural processes. Neural processes can exist without the occurrence of mental states. Therefore, mental states are nothing but neural processes. **2.** the error of explaining a phenomenon and regarding its explanation as being real rather than the phenomenon being explained. Compare with the *genetic fallacy* in FALLACY, TYPES OF INFORMAL (39).

reductive materialism see MATERIALISM, REDUCTIVE.

reductive mechanism see MECHANISM.

reference (from Latin, *referre,* bear again) **1.** the relation to something. **2.** REFERENT; that which is referred to. **3.** designation; that which is indicated or signified by a word.

reference, transsubjective also called *objective reference* and *transcendental reference* the reference of an idea to some independently existing external object.

referent that to which something refers.

reflect 1. consider; think seriously about; ponder. **2.** contemplate or think about. **3.** concentrate one's thoughts back upon a problem or idea.

reflection (Locke) used interchangeably with most meanings of INTROSPECTION. Reflection is the source of our awareness of our existence and mental states and activities such as perceiving, reasoning, thinking, believing, willing, hearing, touching, and seeing. Reflection coupled with sensation provides us with complex ideas such as active tendencies, powers, identity, unity, solidity, extension, pleasure, pain, substance, infinity, and cause and effect. See IDEAS OF REFLECTION (LOCKE) and other entries under IDEAS with reference to Locke.

reflexive (from Latin, *reflectere,* bend back) **1.** referring to that which is, or can be directed (reflected) back to, the subject or to a thing. **2.** referring to any expression whose meaning can be applied to any of its terms.

refutation a denial; usually a formal disproof of an argument or statement showing its falsity or error; sometimes, showing that some assertion has not been supported correctly or proved true. See COUNTEREXAMPLE, METHOD OF.

regulative principle see PRINCIPLE, REGULATIVE.

rehabilitative theory of punishment see PUNISHMENT, REHABILITATIVE THEORY OF.

Reichenbach, Hans (1891–1953) German philosopher, born in Hamburg; educated at the universities of Stuttgart, Berlin, Munich, Göttingen, and

Erlangen; taught at Stuttgart, Berlin, Istanbul, University of California, and Columbia. With Rudolph Carnap he founded and edited the *Journal of Unified Science*, originally called *Erkenntnis*.

Reichenbach has been labeled a logical positivist, but called himself a logical empiricist. His work was primarily in the philosophy of science and logic, ranging over such subjects as probability, induction, deduction, space, time, relativity, quantum mechanics, scientific methodology, verifiability criteria, confirmation, geometry, physical laws, semantics, and logical relations. His major translated works include *Experience and Prediction* (1938); *The Theory of Probability* (1939); *Philosophical Foundations of Quantum Mechanics* (1944); *Elements of Symbolic Logic* (1947); *The Direction of Time* (1956); *Modern Philosophy of Science* (1958); and *The Philosophy of Space and Time* (1958).

reification/reism (from Latin, *res,* a thing) sometimes called *concretism,* the fallacy of considering abstractions as actually existing entities that are causally efficacious and ontologically prior and superior to their referents. Example: taking the noun *good* to refer to an actually existing entity (much as the word *table* refers to an actual individual entity) that exists objectively as a cause for good things or that exists as an ideal standard in another realm to be imitated. Often used interchangeably with HYPOSTATIZATION. See CONCRETENESS, FALLACY OF MISPLACED (WHITEHEAD).

reincarnation (from Latin, from *re,* again, + *incarnare,* make into flesh) literally, to again become flesh. Synonymous with METEMPSYCHOSIS and TRANSMIGRATION.

relation 1. connection. **2.** qualities predicable of two or more things taken together. **3.** an ordering of two or more things.

relation (Kant) see CATEGORIES OF LOGIC, THE (KANT); CATEGORIES OF THE UNDERSTANDING, THE (KANT).

relations, doctrine of internal 1. the theory that (a) a thing is what it is because its relations with other things (and especially the whole of which it is a part) are what they are. (No thing or no part of a thing would be what it is unless its relations to other things were exactly what they are); (b) a thing is what it is because its relations with other things (and especially the whole of which it is a part) are not different from what they are and have been. (No thing, or no part of a thing, would be what it is if its relations to other things were different from what they in fact are and have been.) **2.** the view that all events in the universe are causally related to all other events. To know the truth of any event in the universe, one must know all the causes operating on it, hence all that is happening in the universe. **3.** all relations are inherent in the nature (essence) of the things being related.

relations, external things are said to be related externally if the relationship expressed about them is not essential to, or does not directly affect, their natures (or our understanding of the terms involved). Example: "The car is near the house." Contrasted with RELATIONS, INTERNAL.

relations, internal things are said to be related internally if the relationship expressed about them is essential to, or directly affects, their natures (or our understanding of the terms involved). Example: "Human beings are rational animals." Contrasted with RELATIONS, EXTERNAL.

relativism (value theory) the theory that values: **1.** differ from society to society, from person to person, **2.** are conditioned by the peculiarities of the society in which they arise, **3.** are not universally applicable at all times or in all places, **4.** are correct or incorrect, desirable or undesirable only relative to whether or not they conform to a common norm or to common acceptance. Opposite to ABSOLUTISM. See SUBJECTIVISM (VALUE THEORY). Contrast with OBJECTIVISM (VALUE THEORY).

relativism, Protagorean a theory about the relativity of knowledge and the RELATIVITY OF SENSE PERCEPTION. Often referred to as the *homo mensura* (man is the measure) theory, based on a saying attributed to Protagoras the Sophist: "Man is the measure of all things; of things that are that they are, and of things that are not that they are not."

Some of the beliefs in Protagorean relativism: **1.** what is perceived is as it is perceived by the perceiver. **2.** what is perceived is true to the perceiver. **3.** truth is identical to what is perceived and relative to the physical condition of the perceiver. **4.** given different organs of sense, what is perceived will be different and what is regarded as true will be different. **5.** truth does not exist independently of a perceiver and the perceiver's assertion that something is true. **6.** it is erroneous to say that one person is right (has the truth) and another person is wrong (does not have the truth) about sense perception. **7.** whenever truth is not related to perception and people agree about it, then it can be seen to be based upon a common agreement or consent to call that thing true and not upon any descriptive state of affairs.

Examples of some of the above points: *X* says "The wind is cold." *Y* says "The wind is warm." Neither statement is incorrect. Neither *X* nor *Y* is uttering false statements. Both statements are true relative to how *X* and *Y* perceive (feel) the wind. No method or standard exists that transcends those perceptions and that can be used to determine which statement is true and which is false. See APPEARANCE/REALITY and SOPHISTS.

relativity of sense perception supported by arguments such as the following (which are also used to support the distinction between APPEARANCE/REALITY): **1.** the same thing sometimes appears different to the same person. Example: A raincoat appears black in the closet. The same raincoat appears purple in the moonlight on a rainy night. **2.** the same thing sometimes appears different to different persons. The raincoat appears black to me but yellow to my neighbor, who is color blind. **3.** sensed qualities such as color, odor, and heat are not qualities that inhere in the objects we are perceiving, but are qualities (appearances) relative to the structures of our sense organs. What we sense or is produced in us is thus contrasted with what is really out there in reality, such as atoms in motion, empty space. See

QUALITIES, PRIMARY/SECONDARY. **4.** what we perceive cannot be what a thing is like at the moment we are perceiving it, since it takes time for perception to occur and the reality of the thing has in the meantime changed. Example: The sun as we *perceive* it now is not the sun as it *is* now, but is merely an appearance of what it was eight minutes ago, or more accurately, an appearance caused by an unknown (and unknowable) reality that existed eight minutes ago. See RELATIVISM, PROTAGOREAN.

relatum of a relation (Latin, suppletive past participle of *referre*, carry back) the term to which a relation goes. In the statement "Jane is the wife of Ralph," *Ralph* is the *relatum*.

relevancy 1. the relationship that exists among (a) terms (ideas, concepts, words) such that they can be related to each other to form meaningful statements (or further meaningful ideas, concepts, words) and/or (b) terms that are classified as members within the same class of meanings. **2.** in inductive logic, the degree (probability) of reasonable expectation that one thing will be or is empirically (or causally) related with another thing.

religion, philosophy of the central questions studied in the philosophy of religion: **1.** the definitions of religion. **2.** the varieties of God concepts. **3.** the definitions of God and God's characteristics. **4.** the arguments for God's existence; their variety and validity. **5.** the meanings and the interrelationship of faith, reason, revelation, and dogma. **6.** the nature, value, and validity of mysticism and the religious experience. **7.** the meaning and use of religious language. **8.** the existence of immortality. **9.** the source and sanction of morality in religious thought. **10.** the relationship between church and state, philosophy and religion, science and religion. **11.** the question "Is there a divine cosmic purpose?"

religion, types of definitions of a subject that varies between two poles: *total reference to supernaturalism* (religion is the belief in and worship of a divine transcendent reality that creates and controls all things without deviation from its will); *total reference to humanistic ideals* (religion is any attempt to construct ideals and values toward which one can enthusiastically strive and with which one can regulate one's conduct).

religious experience a characterization that takes a variety of forms from **1.** the view that the experience is of an object, that one directly confronts a divine being (see MYSTICISM) to **2.** the view that the religious experience refers not to an object but to a *quality* of experience, to a consummatory or peak experience in which one feels actualized or in which one becomes ecstatically aware of one's highest ideals and aspirations. See MYSTICAL EXPERIENCE.

reminiscence (from Latin, *reminisci*, recollect) **1.** remembrance; the act of recalling experiences. **2.** recollection; that which is remembered. **3.** ANAMNĒSIS.

reminiscence (recollection/remembrance), Plato's doctrine of see ANAMNĒSIS (2).

reportive definition see DEFINITION, TYPES OF (9).

representation a likeness of; a picture, copy, or model of.

representative perception, theory of see PERCEPTION, REPRESENTATIVE THEORY OF.

representative theory of meaning see MEANING, REPRESENTATIVE THEORY OF.

res cogitans (Latin, a thinking thing, a thinking being, a thinking self) a phrase principally used by Descartes to signify *thinking substance* in contradistinction to RES EXTENSA, which signified *extended (material) substance*. This thinking substance for Descartes referred to both the individual mind or thinking self and to that spiritual thing or soul that served as the underlying pervading ground for all individual minds or thinking selves. See ENS.

resemblance, family see FAMILY RESEMBLANCE.

res extensa (Latin, an extended thing, a material thing, material being) a phrase principally used by Descartes to signify *material (physical) substance* in contradistinction to RES COGITANS, which signified *thinking substance*. This material substance for Descartes referred to the underlying ground for all material (mechanical) change in the universe and possessed no characteristics of mind or life.

residues, method of see METHODS, MILL'S INDUCTIVE.

responsibility a concept grounded on notions such as the following: **1.** OBLIGATION. There are actions that a rational being must and can perform. **2.** liability. Neglect of these actions is punishable. **3.** observance of these actions is subject to reward (honor, praise).

All three notions are based on the view (a) that human motives are causes of behavior; (b) that they can be conditioned (controlled, affected, modified) by such things as reward and punishment; and (possibly) (c) such motives must and should be conditioned. Related to the concepts of *answerability, accountability,* and *self-control.*

retributive justice see JUSTICE, RETRIBUTIVE.

retributive theory of punishment see PUNISHMENT, RETRIBUTIVE THEORY OF.

retrospection 1. the ability to reflect, or the act of reflecting (looking back) on things past and/or on past items or operations of consciousness. **2.** the remembering of past mental states and functions in an attempt to describe them; an act of INTROSPECTION but not on what are regarded as presently occurring mental events. See EXTRASPECTION; REFLECTION.

return, eternal see RECURRENCE, ETERNAL.

rhetoric (from Latin, *rhetorica,* from Greek, *rhetorikē,* rhetorical art) **1.** the art of expressive, persuasive speech and argumentation. **2.** the art of using eloquent (elegant) language to impress as well as to persuade. See SOPHISTES.

right 1. that which a person has due to him or her. **2.** that upon which one has a just demand. **3.** that to which one has a proper claim. **4.** the privilege (freedom or power) given to one, sanctioned and safeguarded by what is regarded as an authoritative source such as God, a ruler, law, a social group, custom, tradition, or conscience.

right, moral the right to perform certain activities (a) because they conform to the accepted standards or ideas of a community (or of a law, or of God, or of conscience), or (b) because they will not harm, coerce, restrain, or infringe on the interests of others, or (c) because there are good rational arguments in support of the value of such activities.

right, political the power (right) to perform certain activities in a politically organized society, such as run for office, vote, petition, lobby, communicate with and criticize public officials, speak out and not be censured, express and defend one's beliefs, and protect one's property.

right reason see LOGOS ORTHOS.

rights, civil rights granted to citizens of a community by the power of its legal and legislative authorities.

rights, human rights (claims, needs, ideals) to be achieved by individuals and/or provided by society, such as a good education, decent housing, health care, a secure job, an adequate standard of living, freedom from interference in the pursuit of goals, freedom from oppression, and equality of opportunity.

rights, inalienable rights that are natural, innate, incapable of being denied. Their source and inviolability are considered beyond civil, political, legal, or other forms of rights, and universally possessed by all humans. Example: the right to protect one's life or property.

rights, legal 1. the power (right) to use the legal system for things such as (a) defense against charges, (b) claims against others, (c) protection against others, and (d) the change and/or correction of laws. **2.** the right to equality of treatment under law with respect to 1.

rights, natural freedoms (privileges, prerogatives, powers, claims) possessed innately (see RIGHTS, INALIENABLE) and/or assumed by the very fact of being a human being. Contrasted with RIGHTS, CIVIL. Lists of natural rights usually include life, liberty, equality, the pursuit of happiness, ownership of property, the right to work, equality of opportunity, and equality of treatment under law.

It is generally held that both natural rights and civil rights constitute the foundation of social justice. It is sometimes held that natural rights and inalienable rights are really forms of civil rights. In either case governments are the principal means of protecting and maintaining any system of rights.

romanticism an expression of a romantic temperament, or the product of that temperament, in the history of art and of philosophy (and in other fields). Some of the qualities and characteristics associated with romanticism: **1.** a stress on immediate sensation and the intense feelings aroused by nature and by events in it. **2.** a tendency to personify nature (*Mother Earth, World Spirit*) and to identify emotionally with its processes and forces. **3.** an emphasis on the uniqueness, the importance, and ultimate sacredness of the individual and his or her powers. **4.** a distaste for the orderly, rational, intellectual, and moderate. A lust for spontaneity, disorder, variety, unpredictability, uncertainty, rebellion, the wild, the fanciful, the extravagant, the strange, the atypical, the novel, and the eccentric. Compare with DIONYSIAN SPIRIT. **5.** a drive for freedom: freedom from restraint as an individual and as an artist, freedom of the artist to treat his or her subject matter as openly, honestly, and candidly as desired, freedom to rebel against anything an artist regards as a suffocating hold of the past. Contrasted with CLASSICISM.

Rousseau, Jean Jacques (1712–1778) French philosopher and man of letters, born in Geneva, Switzerland; converted to Catholicism in 1728 and reconverted to Protestantism in 1755. His works include *Discourse on Sciences and the Arts* (1750); *Discourse on the Origin of Inequality* (1753); *Political Economy* (an article in the *Encyclopédie* of 1755); *The Social Contract* (his masterpiece, 1762); *Emile* (a novel of a child brought up apart from other children, 1762); *Dictionary of Music* (1767); *Rousseau, Judge of Jean Jacques* (1782); and *Confessions* (published posthumously, 1782–1789).

The *Social Contract* begins: "Man is born free, and everywhere he is in chains." Rousseau espoused a social contract in which all people surrender their rights to the collective will. The book became the popular justification for the French Revolution.

Royce, Josiah (1855–1916) American philosopher, born in California; known both as an Absolute Idealist and a Pragmatist; educated in Germany and at Harvard and Johns Hopkins University; taught at Harvard. His main works are *The Religious Aspect of Philosophy* (1885); *Philosophy of Loyalty* (1908); *The Problem of Christianity* (1913); and *The World and the Individual* (2 volumes, 1900 and 1901).

rule, semantical a METALINGUISTIC rule that deals with the meaning of symbols (words, expressions) used in an object language.

Russell, Bertrand Arthur William (1872–1970) British mathematician, logician, philosopher, moralist, social reformer born in Wales and educated at Cambridge, where he studied mathematics, logic, and philosophy. He became a Fellow of Trinity Collge, Cambridge; later, Lecturer in Philosophy, until his dismissal in 1916 because of his agnosticism and pacificism. He was reinstated three years later but did not accept the position. At Cambridge his mathematics professor was Albert North Whitehead, with whom he later collaborated on mathematical-logical works, such as *Principia Mathematica.*

Russell studied social democratic thought in Berlin, where he wrote his *German Social Democracy* (1896). After attending the Mathematical Congress in Paris in 1900, he wrote his first important book, *The Principles of Mathematics* (1903) and, with Whitehead, *Principia Mathematica* (1910).

From 1910 to 1949, Russell was also occupied with moral, ethical, political, and social issues and wrote many books, among them: *Political Ideas* (1918); *Introduction to Mathematical Philosophy* (1919); *The Practice and Theory of Bolshevism* (1920); *The Analysis of Mind* (1921); *The A.B.C. of Relativity* (1925); *The Analysis of Matter* (1927); *Why I Am Not a Christian* (1927); *Outline of Philosophy* (1928); *Marriage and Morals* (1929); *The Scientific Outlook* (1931); *Religion and Science* (1935); and *A History of Western Philosophy* (1944).

In 1949, Russell received the Nobel Prize for Literature.

Ryle, Gilbert (1900–1976) English philosopher, born in Brighton, Sussex; educated and taught at Oxford, where he succeeded G.E. Moore as editor of the scholarly journal *Mind*. Most of Ryle's extensive writings are journal articles and reviews, and he has exerted a strong influence on the philosophy of mind and on philosophic methodology. His important books are *Philosophical Arguments* (1945); *The Concept of Mind* (1949); and *Dilemmas* (1954).

S

same and other, problem of the see IDENTITY, PROBLEM OF.

sameness 1. IDENTITY. **2.** SIMILARITY. **3.** UNIFORMITY OF KIND.

sanction (from Latin, *sanctio*; from *sancire*, make sacred, fix unalterably) **1.** that which obligates and hence motivates someone to act or not to act in accordance with a precept or rule. **2.** a binding force (influence, power) that induces conformity to, or observance of, such things as a law, moral command, custom, or mode of behavior. A *sanction* may refer to, or be given by, an authority, peer or social pressure, institutions, God, conscience, or sense of duty.

Santayana, George (1863–1952) Spanish philosopher, novelist, poet, critic; born in Madrid; lived in Spain until age 8, when he was taken to Boston; educated at Harvard and in Germany; taught at Harvard until 1912; from then on, devoted himself to writing, living at various times in England, France, and Italy. His principal writings include *The Sense of Beauty* (1896); *Interpretations of Poetry and Religion* (1900); *The Life of Reason; or the Phases of Human Progress* (1906; in five volumes: *Reason in Common Sense, Reason in Society, Reason in Religion, Reason in Art,* and *Reason in Science*); *Three Philosophical Poets* (1910); *Winds of Doctrine* (1913); *Skepticism and Animal Faith* (1923); *Realms of Being* (1927–1940, 4 volumes); *Platonism and the Spiritual Life* (1927); *Some Turns of Thought in Modern Philosophy* (1933); and *The Idea of Christ in the Gospels* (1946).

Sartre, Jean-Paul (1905–1980) French existentialist, writer, political activist; born in Paris; educated at the Ecole Normale Supérieure in Paris, the Institut Français in Berlin, and the University of Freiburg; taught in a number of lycées. With Simone de Beauvoir he founded the review *Les Temps modernes*, devoted to political, literary, and philosophic themes. His major writings include *La Nausée* (1938, a novel: *Nausea*); *Le Mur* (1938, short stories: *The Wall*); *Esquisse d'une théorie des emotions* (1939, *The Emotions: Outline of a Theory*); *L'Etre et le néant* (1943, *Being and Nothingness*); and *Existentialisme est un humanisme* (1946, *Existentialism and Humanism*).

satire (from Latin, *satira*; from *satura,* a medley) some form of artistic expression that ridicules in a cutting way what is considered to be abuse, vice, or foolishness. See SOCRATIC IRONY.

schema (from Greek, *schema*, form, shape, figure, outline, plan) the plural is *schemata* **1.** in traditional categorical logic, the figure of a syllogism. **2.** in metaphysics, the application upon our experiences of the forms (categories, intuitions, innate ideas, etc.) by which things are understood. **3.** in epistemology, the application of concepts according to rules in order to organize and/or formulate the content of our experience.

schism (from Greek, *schisma,* a division of opinion; from *schizein,* split, cleave, separate) **1.** a division of belief within a group or institution that leads to factions and possible separation. **2.** the actual separation (secession) of a faction.

Schlick, Moritz (1882–1936) German philosopher born in Berlin; educated at the university of Berlin, where he studied under the physicist Max Planck; taught at the universities of Rostock, Kiel, and Vienna. At the last named, he was assassinated by a deranged student. Schlick was one of the founders and leaders of the Vienna Circle of logical positivists and a proponent of logical, analytical methods in philosophy. His major works in translation (with their dates of publication in translation) include *Space and Time in Contemporary Physics, An Introduction to the Theory of Relativity and Gravitation* (1920); *Problems of Ethics* (1939); *The Future of Philosophy* (1939); and *Philosophy of Nature* (1949).

Scholasticism (from Greek, *scholastikós,* enjoying leisure, devoting one's leisure time to learning, scholar) used historically to refer to **1.** the entire medieval Christian movement in Western philosophy, beginning as early as the 5th century with St. Augustine and lasting until the mid-17th century, or **2.** medieval Christian philosophy between AD 1000, about the time of St. Anselm, and about AD 1300, shortly after St. Thomas Aquinas.

Some other important figures of the latter period were Peter Abelard, Peter Lombard, Bernard of Clairvaux, John of Salisbury, Alexander of Hales, St. Bonaventure, Albertus Magnus, Duns Scotus, and William of Ockham. During this time there was a resurgence of interest in logical and rational inquiry, stemming from new translations of Greek texts, especially those of Plato and Aristotle, that were being introduced through Arabic sources.

Scholasticism was characterized by (a) an intense interest in logical and linguistic analysis, in order to (b) create a systematic presentation and defense of Christian belief based on (c) the Bible as the revealed word of God; (d) the Church's authoritative interpretation and extension of the Bible; and (e) the accepted knowledge of past Christian writers. Some of the principal trends in Scholasticism were (1) to reconstruct Greek thought so that it was consistent with, and supported, Christian faith; (2) to subordinate philosophy to faith (and faith to revelation as seen and interpreted by the Church); and (3) to use reason and the deductive techniques of logic to systematize and defend the Christian faith.

Schopenhauer, Arthur (1788–1860) German philosopher noted for his pessimism; born in Danzig; educated at the University of Göttingen and the University of Berlin. His readings in Plato and Kant at Göttingen led him to philosophy, and the lectures of Fichte and Schleiermacher renewed his early interest in the classics. Schopenhauer's principal works include *On the Fourfold Root of the Principle of Sufficient Reason* (1813, *Über die* *vierfache Wurzel des Satzes vom zureichenden Grunde*); *The World as Will and Idea* (1819, *Die Welt als Wille und Vorstellung*); *On the Will in Nature* (1819, *Uber den Willen in der Natur*); and *The Basis of Morality* (1841, *Die beiden Grundprobleme der Ethik*).

science, philosophy of some of its main areas of concentration: **1.** the study of (a) the concepts, presuppositions, and methodology of science; (b) their conceptual and linguistic analysis; and (c) their extension and reconstruction for more consistent and precise application in obtaining knowledge. **2.** the study and justification of the reasoning processes used in science and its symbolic structure. **3.** the study of how the various sciences are related, similar, or different and the degree to which they exemplify a PARADIGM of scientific method. **4.** the study of the consequences of scientific knowledge for such matters as our perception of reality, our understanding of the processes of reality or the universe, the relationship of logic and mathematics to reality, the status of theoretical entities, our sources of knowledge and their validity, and the nature of humanity—its values and place in the processes around it. All the above studies entail discussions of concepts such as explanation, verification, confirmation, probability, control, experimentation, prediction, measurement, facts, evidence, classification, models, hypotheses, theories, laws, deduction, induction, causation, definitional systems (axioms, theorems, postulates), and artificial languages. See METHOD, SCIENTIFIC.

scientific empiricism see EMPIRICISM; POSITIVISM, LOGICAL.

scientific explanation see EXPLANATION, SCIENTIFIC.

scientific method see METHOD, SCIENTIFIC.

scientism 1. strong version: science is the *only* method for obtaining knowledge. **2.** weak version: science is the only method we presently have that is a reliable source of knowledge.

The pejorative connotation of scientism: the unwarranted idolization of science as the sole authority of truth and source of knowledge.

secondary qualities see entries under QUALITIES, PRIMARY/SECONDARY.

secular (from Latin, *saeculum,* a race, the world, an age) temporal, earthly, or worldly. Contrasted with sacred, spiritual, religious, holy.

self 1. same; identical. **2.** the identity of anything regarded abstractly. **3.** an individual considered as an entity or as an identical person. **4.** an agent acting of its own nature. **5.** that which is the object of an action. **6.** the unity (ego, subject, memory, mind, *I*, awareness, consciousness-knower) that endures throughout change and is aware of its unity, its endurance, and the change. **7.** the entire sequence of mental events of which one can be aware at any given moment. See entries under EGO. Compare with PERSONAL IDENTITY.

self-alienation 1. the state of awareness in which the *self* becomes foreign, or strange to itself, with the accompanying feelings of knowing the actions (and their results) of the *self* objectively, as one knows an object produced by an artist. **2.** the act of keeping one's *self* or mental states at an emotional distance. See ALIENATION; ESTRANGEMENT. That self-alienation which is not total has as its counterpart moments of DEALIENATION, in which an affinity for social engagement and individual commitment is felt.

self-consciousness (self-awareness) 1. the experience of the items and activities of one's CONSCIOUSNESS, such as sensations, images, thoughts, feelings, emotions, and desires. **2.** the AWARENESS that one has consciousness or is conscious. (The consciousness that one has awareness or is aware.) **3.** the ability to treat one's consciousness as an object of knowledge. **4.** the ability of a subject (consciousness) to become an object to itself, or to become objective about itself. **5.** the ability to see oneself as others might.

self-contradiction see CONTRADICTION, SELF-.

self-determination the belief that a human being is able to cause or control his or her choices in opposition to external and internal forces compelling the human to do otherwise. See entries under FREE WILL.

self-evident obvious (evident) without needing proof. Sometimes called *A PRIORI*.

self-existence also called *self-sufficient existence*, an existence needing nothing else for its existence, but upon which other things depend for their existence. See NECESSARY EXISTENCE.

self-identity 1. the way in which one imagines, characterizes, or views oneself. **2.** the *self* one believes oneself to be, and with which one identifies or is involved.

self-interest see EGOISM, ETHICAL.

selfishness 1. acting in order to procure one's own benefit (interest, satisfaction), and (usually) only one's own benefit and (usually) at the exclusion or expense of someone else's benefit. **2.** showing a concern only for oneself. See entries under EGOISM.

self-realization theories also called *self-actualization* or *eudaimonistic theories,* theories that emphasize that the highest good of human beings is the development of their emotional and intellectual potentials. See EUDAIMONIA.

self-reference, paradoxes of see PARADOXES OF SELF-REFERENCE.

self-transcendence 1. the view that the self (or thought, consciousness, mind) involves an awareness of itself that goes beyond any of its immediate states, acts, or processes. **2.** the state of 1.

semantical rule see RULE, SEMANTICAL.

semantics (from Greek, *sēmantikos,* significant; from *sēmainein,* signify, and *sēma,* sign, token of identity; *sēma* also meant a grave that had a sign to indicate something about the dead person) the study of the relationship of linguistic symbols to things other than themselves with reference (a) to what they mean (see INTENSION), and (b) to what they refer to (see EXTENSION). Compare with SYNTAX; PRAGMATICS.

semantics (linguistics) the study of: **1.** the meanings of symbols and how these meanings change, **2.** the variety of symbols (signs, gestures, words) and speech forms used to communicate meanings, **3.** the relationship of these symbols to each other, and **4.** their effect on human behavior.

semantics, descriptive the scientific study of, or the description of, natural languages. Often synonymous with *linguistics*.

semantics, formal the analysis of such things as (a) the connections between a given theory and the logical calculus by which it is formulated, and (b) the relationships between the syntactical and semantical levels of logic.

semantics, problems of questions such as the following asked in the study of semantics: **1.** what does *meaning* mean? **2.** what kinds of meaning are there? **3.** how is meaning communicated? **4.** what is a language? **5.** what is the relationship of language and meaning—how is meaning formed by language? **6.** what type of meaning is conveyed by proper names, singular terms, general terms, descriptions, definitions? **7.** what determines that two linguistic expressions have the same meaning? **8.** in what way does the context of a linguistic expression create and/or affect meaning? **9.** what is the distinction between literal meaning and figurative meaning? (How and what meaning is communicated by metaphor, simile, irony, analogy, etc.?) **10.** under what conditions can we say that a meaning is ambiguous, vague, imprecise, inconsistent, etc.? See LANGUAGE, PHILOSOPHY OF.

semantics, pure the analysis of formal or artificial languages.

semasiology (from Greek, *sēmasía*, signification, meaning) the study of (a) the meanings of words, (b) the development of these meanings, and (c) the senses in which words may be understood.

seminal reasons see *LÓGOS SPERMATIKOS; RATIONES SEMINALES/CAUSALES*; STOICS, THE.

semiosis (from Greek, *semeîon*, sign, signal to act, mark of proof) refers to both (a) the process of functioning as a symbol (sign, linguistic expression, speech form) and (b) the state of understanding (behavior, response) the symbol produces.

semiotics 1. the study of (a) the nature and kinds of signs, (b) what they mean, (c) how they are used, and (d) how they produce the intended effect or communicate the intended meaning. **2.** sometimes the term *semiotics* refers to the analysis of the language used in scientific method.

sempiternal (from Latin, *sempiternus*, everlasting) always ETERNAL; everlasting.

sensa (plural; the singular is *sensum*) **1.** the private content (data, items) of our immediate consciousness or awareness, such as smells, colors, shapes, sounds, and tactile qualities. **2.** the private, immediate, and directly GIVEN content of our perceptions; that upon which our perceptions are based and out of which they are formed. **3.** the private, immediate, and directly given object of our sensing or of our sensation.

Sensa are usually distinguished from external physical objects; they are conceived as numerically distinct from physical objects. Physical (material) objects such as tables, chairs, animals, and plants are regarded as externally real, locatable in space and time, publicly observable at the same time by more than one perceiver, and existing in the same publicly defined space. Physical objects persist independently of sensa associated with them, and persist during the process of changing sensa. See QUALIA.

Material objects (see OBJECTS, MATERIAL) are often thought to be known (perceived) indirectly by inference from something more immediate and direct, such as sensa. We feel a certainty about having, or being presented with, sensa, but we do not feel that same certainty about perceiving material objects.

Sensa may or may not be considered to be caused by external sources. They may or may not be considered to resemble the physical objects that cause them or with which they are associated. Sensa are generally regarded as transitory, lasting only during the time in which they are sensed. They are not usually considered as efficacious; they cannot produce effects on other things, nor can they act on them in any way. Sensa are indubitable, incorrigible, and certain. The word *sensa* is often used with a connotation closely akin to *image*. Often used interchangeably with SENSE DATA.

sensation (from Latin, *sensatus,* gifted with sense [or intellect]) **1.** the immediate and direct mental product of neural activity that results from the activation of sense organs by external stimuli and/or internal brain stimuli. **2.** the CONSCIOUSNESS (awareness, experience) itself of items such as sounds, colors, or smells that are produced by the senses. See SENSES, THE FIVE. **3.** the simplest specific items of consciousness produced by our senses, such as a high C, green, a chocolate taste.

A sensation is regarded as private and a spontaneous ultimate content or object of consciousness. It is often distinguished from PERCEPTION, which involves judgment, inference, interpretation, bias, or preconceptualization, and is thus subject to error; sensation is regarded as incorrigible, a rock-bottom *given,* a raw sensum, or brute fact. For many, sensation connotes more of a relationship with FEELING (but not with EMOTION) and perception more of a relationship with cognition.

Sensation is often used synonymously with *sense impression, sense datum, sensum,* and *sensibilium.*

sensationalism (epistemology) sometimes called *radical empiricism* (see EMPIRICISM, RADICAL) some of the main views of sensationalism: **1.** perception is the association of sensations (sensa, sense data). **2.** all knowledge has its source in sensations. **3.** all knowledge can be reduced to sensations; all empirical (hence meaningful) statements can be analyzed into statements that have as their content the interrelationship of sensations. **4.** knowledge can be verified (confirmed, validated) only with reference to sensations.

sense, internal the innate ability of the mind (consciousness, self) to introspect—to become aware of its inner states and activities.

sense, internal and external (Kant) internal sense: the A PRIORI awareness (intuition, knowledge) of TIME or the form of time; external sense: the *a priori* awareness of spatial attributes or the form of SPACE. See KNOWLEDGE (KANT).

sense, manifold of see MANIFOLD, SENSORY (KANT).

sense, moral see MORAL SENSE.

sense data 1. the specific, immediate, incorrigible, and irreducible qualities or content of sensations. **2.** that which is given to us directly and immediately, such as color, shapes, and smells, without identification of them as specific material objects, such as a green ball or an onion. Sense data are usually thought to be devoid of judgment, interpretation, bias, and preconception. The singular is *sense datum.* Often used interchangeably with SENSA.

sense perception an unanalyzable mental state, or act, that is related to, and dependent upon, the functions of sensory organs.

sense perception, relativity of see RELATIVITY OF SENSE PERCEPTION.

sense *qualia* 1. the qualities of sensations considered in abstraction, such as whiteness or sourness. **2.** the qualities sensed in association with specific objects such as a white rose, a sour grape. See QUALIA; SENSIBLE.

senses, the five the common classification: sight (visual), hearing (auditory), touch (tactile), taste (gustatory), smell (olfactory).

sensibile (Latin, a sensible, that which can be perceived by a sense) that which impresses a sense, an object of sense. Words often used as synonyms: *sensum,* sense datum, sense *quale* (or *qualis*). The plural form is *sensibilia.* See QUALIA.

sensibility (Kant) the power (ability, faculty) by means of which we have sensations. This power is passive or receptive, as opposed to reason or understanding, which are active and structuring. See INTUITION (KANT).

sensibles, common (Aristotle) qualities of objects that are (can be) grasped by different senses. Examples: motion, rest, shape, size, and number. Contrasted with *proper sensibles.*

sensibles, proper (Aristotle) qualities of objects that are grasped by only one sense; if that sense functions, it cannot but perceive that quality (sensible) unique to it. Examples: taste, smell, color, and sound. Contrasted by Aristotle with *common sensibles.* According to Aristotle our senses are not in error about the fact that they have sensibles unique to them: vision is unique to our sense of sight, sound to our sense of hearing, touch to our sense of touch, etc.

sentence (from Latin, *sententia*; from *sentire,* think, feel, perceive) a grouping of words (symbols, signs) according to a SYNTAX, expressing an idea or thought, and used for a variety of purposes such as declaring, asserting, pleading, requesting, commanding, interrogating, and persuading. Often used interchangeably with *statement* and sometimes with *proposition,* but see SENTENCE/STATEMENT DISTINCTION.

sentence, categorical a sentence that has a subject-predicate form and that affirms or denies a property or membership in a class.

sentence connectives 1. the words used to connect or relate sentences or statements such as *and* in "Bill is a bachelor *and* Sally is married." **2.** the symbols used in logic to connect sentences or statements.

sentence/statement distinction the distinction between a SENTENCE and a STATEMENT, based on points such as the following: **1.** *different sentences may make the same statement.* Examples: (a) "Beth loves Jon" and "Jon is loved by Beth" are two different sentences, but both make the same statement. (b) *"Sebestyen hazament ennui"* is a sentence, and its translation, "Sebastian has gone home to eat," is a sentence. They may be regarded as two sentences that make the same statement, that have the same meaning. (c) The declarative sentence "All reasonable persons believe in the existence of free will" and the rhetorical question "How can any reasonable person deny the existence of free will?" are different sentences, but they say the same thing—make the same statement. **2.** *the same sentence may be used to make different statements.* Examples: (a) The sentence "He has black hair" is a true statement when applied to Adam, but that same sentence when applied to John is a false statement. (b) The sentence "Grass is green" is a sentence that makes a true statement about the grass on Marian's lawn during June, but it makes a false statement about that same grass during August. Therefore, a sentence is called a true or false sentence whenever the statement it makes is a true or false statement. See PROPOSITION.

sentience (from Latin, *sentiens*; from *sentire,* feel) elementary, incipient (inchoate or just beginning) consciousness at the level of sensuousness or primal sensations. Animals are presumed to be sentient creatures.

sentiment 1. feeling; emotion. **2.** sensibility toward something. **3.** a mental attitude (judgment, thought) permeated with and/or predisposed by a feeling or an emotion, as in the phrases "the moral sentiment of sympathy" and "the religious sentiment of compassion." In Hume, sentiment and SYMPATHY served as the ground of all moral action.

set any collection regarded as a whole (totality) of individual things (members) that can be clearly distinguished in some way. See CLASS, *GENUS.*

Sextus Empiricus (fl. last half of the second century, first quarter of the third century) Greek philosopher and physician. Little is known of his life. It is known that he headed a school of Skepticism. His extant works include *Outlines of Pyrrhonism* and *Against the Dogmatists,* both of which synthesize and organize the leading points of view of the Skeptical schools of thought.

sign 1. anything that stands for something else. **2.** anything that represents (stands for, signifies, indicates) an object (or a relation or an activity) to someone who understands it or responds to it. Examples: "Clouds of certain kinds are signs of snow." See SIGN, NATURAL. "The mark > is a sign for the relation *greater than*. "The mark ∞ is a sign for the concept of infinity." "A written musical note is a sign for a certain tone to be played." "The ringing of the doorbell is a sign that someone is at the door." "The cat's hair standing on end is a sign to a dog not to attack."

sign, conventional a sign devised and/or stipulated to mean a specific thing, such as a gesture meaning *go away*, or a buzzing sound meaning the end of a round, or a color meaning to stop. X is a conventional sign of Y when human beings designate it as such. A word signifies, or is a sign of, a meaning or of a thing. Conventional signs are conventional in the sense that human beings chose them and could have used different signs to indicate or stand for the same meanings or things. Compare with SIGN, NATURAL.

sign, iconic 1. sometimes called *representational sign*, a sign that resembles, or has an apparent resemblance to, that which it signifies. The word *curve* on a road sign does not resemble that which it signifies, but a curve drawn on the road sign as a line curving in a direction similar to the one that the road takes does resemble that which it signifies and is classified as an iconic sign. (That one thing resembles another does not make them signs of each other.) **2.** a sign that signifies an attribute (characteristic, property, quality) by exhibiting it. See ICON.

sign, indexical a sign whose meaning is dependent on, and relative to, the characteristics of the user (speaker) and the context in which these characteristics and signs are found. Despite the fact that the reference changes from one context to another, indexical signs (for example, *now, I*) continue to mean the same thing. Indexical signs are not verbally descriptive but disclose their referents in as direct a way as possible. Some words that are regarded as indexical signs (sometimes referred to as *demonstratives*): *this, that, he, she, you, I, them, now, then, here,* and *there*. Gestures such as pointing, nodding the head toward something, raising the eyebrows to indicate a referent, etc., are also regarded as indexical signs. Often referred to as *egocentric particulars*.

sign, indicative see *endeiktikon*.

sign, natural implicit in saying that X is a natural sign of Y is their factual (causal) association together in a number of instances, which enables one to anticipate, predict, or infer that Y will be followed by X. X is a natural sign of Y when a certain relation is assigned between X and Y: clouds of a certain sort are a *sign* of snow; smoke is a *sign* of fire; fever is a *sign* of illness. The relationship is not one that has been created by human convention (see SIGN, CONVENTIONAL), nor is there necessarily a resemblance between X and Y (see SIGN, ICONIC). The relationship is a description of a nonlinguistic, natural, or causal order that can be observed and from which observations we have constructed the notion that X is a (natural) sign of Y.

signal 1. a sign (a) used to give notice of something, such as of a danger, and/or (b) used to give notice to something, such as a cough giving notice to one's spouse not to be so indiscreet. **2.** a previously agreed upon sign used to initiate action.

signification 1. the meaning of something. **2.** the act of giving meaning to something. **3.** making a meaning known by the use of symbols, signs, gestures, etc. See CONNOTATION.

simple location, fallacy of a phrase coined by Whitehead to refer to what he regarded as fallacious: the belief that reality consists of bits of matter isolated from each other at given locations in space and time. See PROCESS PHILOSOPHY.

simple predicate see PREDICATE, SIMPLE.

simpliciter (Latin) simply, absolutely, without qualifications.

simpliciter **(God)** not subject in any way to differentiation, classification, or analysis. In medieval philosophy ultimately applicable only to God. God does not exist as a *this* or a *that*. God is *simpliciter* and not *compositum*.

simplicity, principle of see OCKHAM'S RAZOR.

sine qua non (Latin, without which not) (referring to) the indispensable and necessary characteristic an idea or thing must possess to be what it is.

skeptic (from Greek, *skeptikos,* thoughtful, reflective, curious; from *skeptesthai,* consider, examine, look carefully about) **1.** one who suspends judgment about something because of doubt and/or because he or she is waiting for more or better evidence. See *EPOCHĒ*; AGNOSTIC. **2.** one whose attitude is critical and usually destructively so. Compare with CYNICISM, PESSIMISM. **3.** one whose attitude is critical and inquiring. **4.** a disbeliever; one who has doubt about or does not believe in a doctrine. **5.** one who believes in SKEPTICISM or uses it as a philosophic method.

skepticism 1. a state of doubting. **2.** a state of suspension of judgment. **3.** a state of unbelief or nonbelief. Skepticism ranges from complete, total disbelief in everything, to a tentative doubt in a process of reaching certainty.

skepticism (Carneades) the main points in the skepticism of the Greek philosopher Carneades: **1.** knowledge of what is correct information about reality, and what is incorrect information, is impossible. All we can ever have are images (representations, copies, PHANTASIA) of an external world, but we are never sure which images are accurate and which are inaccurate, since the human mental set contributes to the interpretation and understanding of those images. **2.** truth does not exist; only degrees of probability exist. **3.** probability is the only guide to life. The individual does not need the certainty of truth in order to act and to understand. (If one waited for the certainty of truth before acting or understanding, one would be able neither to act nor to understand.) The individual must—and in reality does—act and understand only on the basis of what is probable. **4.** some beliefs can be rated as more probable than other beliefs. (This rating is subjective and relative to the individual and depends on the context in which the individual finds himself or herself.) **5.** the highest degree of probability of a belief is related to its intensity and immediacy in our experience, and to its relationship to other intense and immediate experiences. The lowest degree of probability of a belief is related to its not having any ground in our experience. **6.** the more probable we feel a belief is, the greater should be our *tendency* to accept it, but we should never allow this tendency to be so overwhelming that it forces us to acquiesce or to assent. Life is a continual and never-ending quest.

skepticism (Cratylus) no knowledge can be had of reality; one cannot say anything about anything. The communication of knowledge or of anything at all is impossible because all things are in perpetual change. The language that is used to communicate itself changes in the process of communication; the speaker is in a process of change; the meanings and ideas change even as one is thinking and uttering them; the recipient of the communication is in change; and the total environment is in continual change without anything ever remaining the same. Cratylus concluded that one cannot say anything about anything and that one should not try. He refused to talk, since talking appeared to him senseless, meaningless, a waste of effort. He merely wiggled his finger to indicate he was fleetingly responding to stimuli. See CHANGE (CRATYLUS).

skepticism (Descartes) Descartes' skepticism, sometimes called *provisional* or *methodological skepticism,* consisting of doubting all things until something is reached that cannot be doubted. Descartes' skepticism is based on two fundamental questions: **1.** what do I in fact know clearly and distinctly that is so absolutely certain as to be beyond any doubt whatever? **2.** what further knowledge is it possible to derive from this certainty?

Descartes was never really skeptical about there being such an indubitable truth and he was not skeptical about there being a definite procedure for attaining a complete deductive knowledge based on this indubitable truth. Descartes believed it is possible to rise above skeptical doubt and find knowledge that is absolute, certain, necessary, and self-evident, which knowledge serves as the ground for all other knowledge and for knowledge of all reality.

For the sake of argument, Descartes doubts the existence of everything. He denies the existence of the external world, external minds, God, etc. Perhaps everything is a dream. Perhaps a powerful, malicious daimon is deceiving him. But there is one fundamental thing that cannot be doubted: that he exists to be deceived; that he exists to be having a dream; that he exists in the very act of denying. One can doubt even that one is doubting, but one must exist to be doing the doubting. See *COGITO ERGO SUM.*

Thus, by means of a provisional and methodical skepticism one can clearly and distinctly grasp an indubitable truth. According to Descartes all true ideas must be known this clearly and distinctly, and ideas that are thus known are true. Among these ideas are: the existence of an external world and of other minds; the existence of God and God's characteristics; that God can never be a deceiver (it can be clearly and distinctly perceived that

God is not liable to any errors or defects since if God were, God would not be God, and deception necessarily follows from a defect); that God supports the principle that all ideas which are clearly and distinctly perceived are true (since God is completely benevolent, God would not lead us into error). See IDEAS, CLEAR AND DISTINCT (DESCARTES).

skepticism (Gorgias) the Greek philosopher Gorgias propounded an extreme form of skepticism, sometimes referred to as NIHILISM, which denied the possibility of knowledge and doubted whether anything existed at all. The main argument was: No thing can be said to exist. (The stronger nihilistic version: Nothing exists.) If anything did exist, we would not be able to know it, and if we were able to know it, we would not be able to communicate it.

skepticism (Hume) the main points in Hume's skepticism: **1.** the individual cannot ever obtain knowledge about any subject matter beyond the relationships of his ideas. The only knowledge an individual can have is of what he or she can directly experience (observe, perceive, have an impression of). **2.** no knowledge can be had of anything existing behind our impressions, such as that of substance or God. Any knowledge claimed to be of something beyond our sense impressions is the consequence of speculative reasoning from immediate sense impressions to their supposed source or cause. **3.** no good rational justification can ever be given for believing anything that is not an immediate sense impression. Anything that can be imagined or conceived is possible; therefore, there can never be any definite evidence (a) to refute anything (since anything is possible), or (b) to assert anything (to assert that either something *is* the case or *must be* the case). **4.** no factual truths about the external world or about reality can ever be arrived at by either induction or deduction. *Inductive reasoning* rests on an unjustifiable assumption that natural events will occur in the future as they have occurred in the past, that the future will be similar to the past. No possible experience can ever indicate that similar past (or present) connections between natural events will apply to future events. Such connections are based on psychological states such as habit, custom, convention, expectation, or hope. *Deductive reasoning* deals with the necessary connections among statements; it can never show us that such necessity exists in the external world. Nothing in our experience indicates a necessary connection, a necessary tie or bond, between impressions or between a cause and its effect. It is impossible to know that any particular state of affairs is necessarily connected with another state of affairs. Such necessity does not exist. **5.** thus, no empirical or rational justification can ever be given for such things as the belief in substance, the belief in the existence of an external world, the belief in the existence of a God, the belief in the existence of a *self*. These beliefs can have only psychological defenses and explanations based on things such as custom, habit, convention, constancy, and coherence among our impressions and their ideas, and the principles of the association of our ideas. See CAUSE AND EFFECT RELATIONSHIP (HUME); KNOWLEDGE (HUME); SKEPTICISM, MITIGATED (HUME).

skepticism (Kant) Kant's skepticism represents a middle point between extreme skepticism and complete dogmatism. Kant was skeptical about speculative metaphysical claims to knowledge of true reality, reality as it is in itself. See DING AN SICH, DAS; ILLUSION, TRANSCENDENTAL (KANT). Yet, there is a specific kind of knowledge that is both universal and necessary. Such knowledge has to do with the conditions any experiencing process must satisfy before it can be recognizable as experience. These conditions are the conditions for all possible experiences.

The main points in Kant's skepticism: **1.** knowledge is initiated in an experience (in the process of experiencing), but knowledge (a) cannot be reduced to experience and (b) does not come directly from (pure) experience. Knowledge comes from the structuring of experience that is involved in the process of experiencing. **2.** space and time are the necessary intuitions (structurings, forms) of all possible experiences. No experience is possible without its being imbued with, or structured by, the intuitions of space and time. **3.** the categories (see entries under CATEGORIES [KANT]) are the necessary and universal conditions for having any knowledge at all about what we are experiencing. **4.** space and time and the categories (including the logical forms for making inferences and judgments) are the modes in which what comes from the world around us must be shaped if experience is to exist at all. The world cannot be experienced except in these modes. **5.** by transcendental analysis we can reveal the universal, necessary, and innate conditions that are impressed on all experiencing and on all knowledge. (But we can never know whether or not reality-in-itself or things-in-themselves are in space and time, or operate according to these categories of our understanding.) **6.** the knowledge derived from transcendental analysis does not and cannot give us further knowledge (a) about any realm that transcends our actual or possible experiences (such as of a supernatural realm, or of a self-identity that is the source of our perceptions and knowledge, or of a reality distinct from the phenomenal world), or (b) about any specific content to experience. **7.** speculative metaphysical knowledge that goes beyond the limits of all possible experiencing cannot be had because there is no method (a) for determining *if* and *how* the conditions for our possible experiencing are applicable and (b) for determining what conditions are and what are not applicable. See KNOWLEDGE (KANT).

skepticism (Locke) some of the main points in Locke's skepticism: **1.** the external world (as distinct from substance) exists and can be known only to a limited extent. **2.** we can never know the essence of substance. Substance is *a something we know not what*. **3.** knowledge of the external world may be thought of as somewhere between the truly existing but unknowable reality of substance and the ideas by which we understand things. **4.** we can have a clearly formed idea of things such as God, matter, personal identity, spirit, but we cannot know the essence of any of them. (Though we can know *that* they exist.) **5.** knowledge cannot be extended further than our sensations and the reasoning powers applied to them. **6.** a great deal about the universe will always be unknown because of the limitations of human knowing. See KNOWLEDGE (LOCKE).

skepticism (Sextus Empiricus) the version of skepticism held by the Greek philosopher Sextus Empiricus is characterized by the following views: **1.** we should suspend judgment (see EPOCHĒ) about whether knowledge is possible or impossible. **2.** no belief can be said to be probable or improbable, more probable or less probable. **3.** one should not attach oneself to or accept any belief. **4.** no belief and no disbelief can ever be proved correct or false. (No method for proving or disproving any belief can ever exist.) **5.** believing and disbelieving should be avoided because they bring with them emotional and mental turmoil, and the aim of life should be ATARAXIA, serenity of mind and spirit.

skepticism, mitigated (Hume) beliefs have neither rational nor empirical justification; nevertheless, there are some that we are bound to accept in the everyday course of affairs, such as the existence of the external world, the existence of other minds, the existence of a *self*, and the possible existence of some general intelligence pervading the universe.

skepticism, mitigated or limited the denial of, or the suspension of, judgment about (a) certain means for attaining knowledge, such as speculation, revelation, intuition, faith, sense perception, or reason, and/or (b) certain kinds of knowledge (for example, of a self, of other selves, of an external world, of a supernatural world). Usually, any knowledge that is accepted is not granted certainty, but only a high degree of probability or possibility. Mitigated or limited skepticism is opposed to claims to unique and esoteric knowledge.

skepticism, Platonic no knowledge is possible by means of sense perception (but knowledge and ultimate truth can be reached by the use of reason).

skepticism, Socratic a general form of skepticism found in Socrates' remark "All I know is that I know nothing." In an important sense Socratic skepticism is a provisional and voluntary suspension of all knowledge in order to reach knowledge or certainty with the use of a definite method from, so to speak, *a clean slate*. See SOCRATIC IRONY; SOCRATIC METHOD.

skepticism, solipsistic the theory that one can know (a) that one exists and (b) that one is having certain ideas. All else is subject to denial or to suspension of judgment.

slave morality (Nietzsche) the name given by Nietzsche to any system of thought (a) that controls and convinces the oppressed, suppressed (defeated, downtrodden) that they are actually better off and superior to those who are oppressing them; (b) that creates fear of change and creative assertion; and (c) that idolizes passivity, duty, control of emotions, and acceptance of authority and tradition. See SUPERMAN, TRANSVALUATION OF VALUES (NIETZSCHE).

social contract theory (Hobbes) natural existence without a social contract means a state of war of one against all, and all against all; no one would have property, rights, or claims. One must submit oneself to a contract for self-preservation and protection (guaranteed by a being, or other source of military and legal power, to which allegiance and financial support are given).

social Darwinism see DARWINISM, SOCIAL.

Socrates (c.470—399 BC) was closely associated with the leading ruling and political figures of Athens but took little part in politics. (He served as a member of the jury of 500 for a year and supported some unpopular positions, which may have had a bearing on the verdict in his own trial.) Socrates says in the *Apology* (see PLATO) that he sought no public office because he did not want to compromise his philosophic principles.

Late in life Socrates married Xantippe, with whom he had three sons. He felt himself charged with a mission to help people tend to their souls—to find that special knowledge of what is good for the soul. A side effect of this mission was Socrates' life of poverty and austerity.

Socrates wrote nothing. Our knowledge of his life comes principally from Plato's Dialogues, in which Socrates is the leading character. Other sources are Ameipsias, Ion of Chios, Aristophanes, Xenophon, Aristotle, Isocrates, Aeschines, Diogenes Laertius, and Athenaeus.

Although Socrates was versed in geometry, mathematics, astronomy, and the natural sciences, such as physics, his main interest throughout his life focused on (a) the nature of human nature—its needs, goals, and values; (b) the nature of language—thinking, meanings, logic, and definitions; (c) the nature of true reality as found in the perfect ideal forms of which this world is an imperfect imitation or copy; and (d) the nature of universal values, such as goodness, truth, beauty, justice, righteousness, courage, and temperance. Socrates can be said to have brought philosophy to what many consider its proper purpose: the study of man in his relationship to himself, others, society, and the universe. Whereas philosophers before Socrates stressed the natural sciences, he emphasized the personal, ethical, and social aspects of life, thus bringing out the insights, values, and methodology needed in any attempt to attain a happy life.

Socrates was put on trial, convicted, and sentenced to death by the Athenian jury on two principal counts: (1) impiety—believing in novel gods, not the gods of Athens—and (2) corrupting the youth of Athens. Those condemned to death by the Athenian jury drank poisonous hemlock within 24 hours after the verdict. At the time of Socrates' case, the sacred ship sent to Delos each year had not yet returned, and no execution could be carried out until it did. During the month-long wait for its return, Socrates carried on conversations in prison with his friends, with the result that Plato's

SOCRATES' *DAIMŌN*

Dialogues, the *Crito* and the *Phaedo*, detail the last days of Socrates' life.

Socrates' *daimōn* (The Greek word *daimōn* is also transliterated as *daemon*.) Socrates used *daimōn* (and *daimonion*) to refer to an inner voice pictured as a genie or spirit sitting on the lobe of his ear, which warned him about, or forbade, certain actions. See CONSCIENCE; *DAIMŌN*.

Socratic irony refers to: **1.** Socrates' habit of pretending humility and ignorance, and by a series of questions and answers, leading his listeners to knowledge—knowledge that could only be prodded by someone with a great deal of skill and wisdom. **2.** Socrates' declaration that the oracle at Delphi, in saying Socrates was the wisest of human beings, must have meant that Socrates was wisest because he knew he knew nothing. **3.** Socrates' assumed willingness to learn by means of questioning others since he said he did not possess knowledge, and in the process exposing their errors and lack of knowledge.

Socratic irony connotes a paradoxical mixture of humbleness on the one hand and arrogance on the other. It refers basically to declaring one's ignorance about a topic on which one in reality is extremely knowledgeable.

Socratic method the method of instruction whereby a series of questions and answers are asked and given, eliciting (a) points of view, meanings, attitudes, concessions, opinions, moral feelings, etc., that eventually establish, or lead to a sense of, a general truth or ideal, and (b) unrealized knowledge (as Socrates elicits a theorem in geometry from the ignorant slave boy in the *Meno*) that one does not know one possesses. Socrates regarded himself as a midwife (*maieutria*) using this method to assist in the birth of ideas—ideas already formed and carried (impregnated) in the mind and the nature of human beings. See MAIEUTIC.

Some of the main features in Socrates' distinctive use of this method: **1.** a highly critical and analytic discussion leading to an intense self-examination on the meanings and implications of one's ideas and on the ground for one's beliefs, usually in a conversation (dialogue) with another person who is part of a group. (Members of the group ask and answer questions and may occasionally take the leading parts.) **2.** it is wrong to accept beliefs merely on the ground that they are accepted by one's group, are handed down by tradition, or are part of a body of knowledge. The only foundation of knowledge is that which can withstand the scrutiny of rational inquiry. **3.** the leader (Socrates) serves as the gadfly. With Socrates' probing examination of another person's beliefs it becomes evident (a) that the meanings of the concepts being discussed (such as piety, justice, beauty, virtue, good, or courage) are unclear, confused, and untrue; (b) that these meanings have no rational justification or consistency; and (c) that the beliefs and conduct based on them lead to irrational thought and to irrational behavior. **4.** the main person in the conversation (discussion, dialogue) claims expert knowledge of the subject matter to be discussed. Socrates asks questions, initially short and simple, to which he prefers short and simple answers.

These answers present a series of interrelated statements from which Socrates draws absurdities, inconsistencies, and conclusions that are in opposition to the original confident assertions and that serve to indicate the conceit of the person who has dogmatically asserted dogmatic knowledge of the topic being discussed. (It appears that the result, if not the aim, of Socratic dialectic is not only to show that the person cannot rationally justify his knowledge claims, but that he really does not know what he is talking about, that he does not know truth, that he is—if he will only stop to admit it—intellectually conceited and overly confident about something he thinks he knows but really does not.) **5.** once the embarrassment is resolved about not having a real grasp of the concepts being discussed—once humility is established—then the serious task is undertaken of beginning to philosophically construct an adequate and acceptable rational foundation for the concept by means of asking and answering a series of questions, and by means of denying and assenting to ideas as they are presented, until better knowledge is reached. **6.** the principal controlling pattern of this process of question/answer, denial/acceptance to points as they are brought up is that the knowledge obtained must conform to the general categories (forms, values) of good, beauty and truth—none of which for Socrates could ever exist alone. **7.** thus, Socratic method or dialectic is a continuing quest for truth by constant critical analysis, interrogation, self-examination and further analysis, questioning, and self-examination. The concern is to uncover truth no matter how hurtful it might appear to us in the beginning. Socratic method is the persistent tendency to follow a rational argument through to its conclusion regardless of what that conclusion is. Of course, the Socratic assumption is that if that conclusion were completely rational it would conform to the good, beautiful, and true, since the good, beautiful, and true are truly rational. See DIALECTIC (SOCRATES); SKEPTICISM, SOCRATIC.

Socratic paradoxes a few: **1.** no one does evil of his or her own free will. **2.** if one knew the good, one would not hesitate to do it. **3.** one commits evil only from ignorance of what the good is. (Evil is caused by ignorance.)

These are regarded as paradoxical statements because it is presumed to be obvious (a) that one does, and can do, evil, of one's own free will; (b) that one often does know the good yet does evil; and (c) that one can commit evil not out of ignorance but in full knowledge that what he or she is doing is evil.

Socratic quest, the 1. to find the ESSENCES (universals, ideal forms) that make things what they are and according to which they must (should) behave, and **2.** to organize the individual's conduct in accordance with these essences, which are necessary and rational and operate everywhere for the best. **3.** to examine life and know oneself. See GNOTHI SE AUTON.

Socratic skepticism see SKEPTICISM, SOCRATIC.

Socratic theory of definition 1. an ideal definition gives us the ESSENCE (that without which a thing would not be what it is) of that to which a word refers. See DEFINITION, TYPES OF (5) and (16). **2.** this essence will be seen to be single and simple. **3.** it will answer the question "What is the central and essential element that makes that thing what it is?" **4.** in answering this question we will come to know (a) that which actually makes all courageous things courageous (beautiful things beautiful, good things good, or true things true, etc.) and (b) that in terms of which we recognize and are able to name a courageous thing courageous (a beautiful thing beautiful, etc.). **5.** with this knowledge as a standard, we can then rationally, methodically become courageous (or become beautiful, good, or truthful, etc.). See DIALECTIC (SOCRATES).

solipsism, epistemological (from Latin, *solus*, alone, single, sole, + *ipse*, self) **1.** the theory that one's consciousness (self, mind) cannot know anything other than its own content. See EGOCENTRIC PREDICAMENT. **2.** one's consciousness alone is the underlying justification for, and cause of, any knowledge of the existence or nonexistence of anything at all. Contrasted with OBJECTIVISM (EPISTEMOLOGY).

solipsism, metaphysical literally, "I myself only exist"; the theory that no reality exists other than one's self. The self (mind, consciousness) constitutes the totality of existence. All things are creations of one's consciousness at the moment one is conscious of them. *Other* things do not have any independent existence; they are states of, and are reducible to, one's consciousness.

***sophia* (Aristotle)** *sophia*, translated as theoretical wisdom, was regarded by Aristotle as the highest intellectual virtue, thus the highest of all the virtues. Aristotle distinguished *sophia* from PHRONĒSIS, practical wisdom. See VIRTUES, DIANOETIC (ARISTOTLE).

A human is capable of *sophia* because there is in human nature something unique and divine; humans come close to the intellectual activities of God. The highest function possible for God and for humans is thinking, reasoning, using intelligence. The highest form of thinking is about objects (first principles of all things), which are eternal, unchanging, necessary, and certain—those objects that cannot be other than what they are. The study of FIRST PHILOSOPHY gives us *sophia*.

sophism (from Greek, *sophisma*, a skillful act, a clever device, a sly trick, a captious argument, a quibble, a FALLACY) a specious and subtle argument, usually presented as a formal argument, that is intended to deceive and/or mislead. See PREVARICATION.

sophistēs (Greek) a master of one's craft or art, one adept at doing (or teaching) something; used synonymously with the Greek word *phronimos*, one who is clever in matters of life, and with *sophos*, a wise man; in Athens, *sophistēs* was used specifically to refer to a *Sophist* (professor, teacher) who taught grammar, RHETORIC, political affairs, logic, law, mathematics, literary criticism, and linguistic analysis. At first the Sophists were held in high respect. For a variety of reasons they fell into ill repute and the word *sophist* came to mean a cheat, a quibbler, or both. See SOPHISTS.

sophistic 1. referring to an argument (a) that is fallaciously subtle and clever and (b) that is intended to deceive and/or mislead. **2.** sometimes used synonymously with ERISTIC. Aristotle distinguished between sophistic and eristic arguments on the basis that sophistic arguments are engaged in for a fee, and eristic arguments merely for the victory.

sophistry 1. showy and intentionally fallacious reasoning in order to deceive, mislead, persuade, or defend a point regardless of its value or truth. **2.** disputation for the sake of disputation. **3.** the techniques, teachings, and practices of the SOPHISTS, especially as they engaged in 1. and 2.

Sophists itinerant professors (teachers, philosophers) of Ancient Greece who lived during the 4th and 5th centuries BC. Among the most important names: Protagoras of Abdera (c.481 to c.411 BC), Gorgias of Leontini (c.485 to c.380 BC), Prodicus of Ceos (probably born before 460 BC, death date unknown but probably after 399 BC), Hippias of Elis (probably born before 460 BC, death date unknown), Antiphon of Athens (c.480 to 411 BC), Thrasymachus of Chalcedon (dates unknown but alive during the time of Socrates), and Callicles (dates unknown but alive during the time of Socrates).

The Sophists (see SOPHISTĒS) are said to have taught for a fee (which in the opinion of Socrates was an evil thing to do, since if anyone had something good and true to teach people he should feel it his duty to communicate it without pay). They taught a variety of subjects: grammar, rhetoric, the art of persuasion, the art of defending oneself in court, political affairs, moral conduct, logic, legal principles, mathematics, natural sciences, literary criticism, and linguistic analysis. They taught whatever their students wanted to learn. They generally seemed to be interested in teaching the art (TECHNĒ) of how to improve oneself and succeed in life.

The Sophists fell into ill repute in the eyes of other philosophers. They were regarded as eloquent but captious and fallacious reasoners, as adroit at specious reasoning, as logic choppers, as appealing to and taking advantage of popular trends and wishes for their own monetary gain, as telling people what they wanted to hear, as teachers of persuasion and verbal manipulation of others, as being interested not in attainment of truth but in how to refute an argument merely for the sake of refuting it, and in how to defend any argument whatever, as teaching that victory in argumentation at whatever cost, outwitting opponents, is the sole aim of disputation no matter how bad the argument, as being able to make the worse appear the better and the better appear the worse.

Some of the main ideas of the Sophists: **1.** the *relativity of sense perception*. The individual is the measure of all things. Things are as one says they are and sees them as being. See RELATIVISM, PROTAGOREAN. **2.** the *relativity of knowledge*. Knowledge and truth are relative to the social, cultural, and unique personal predispositions of the individual. There is no absolute truth. **3.** the *denial of knowledge of any ultimate reality behind our sensations*. The natural world can only be known in terms of those sensations that appear to our consciousness. There is no reality such as a WORLD SOUL or universal mind behind phenomena as they appear to and are interpreted by our sensations and perceptions. **4.** EMPIRICISM. All knowledge is ultimately based on our direct and immediate experiences as they occur to us in consciousness. **5.** laws are the product of humans living in society. Laws are made by those who have power in order to keep the weak in control, or laws are made by the weak in order to keep the strong from asserting themselves and taking over. **6.** the state of society is a progressive state from a state of primitive nature out of which humans came and in which it was a battle of each with everyone else. **7.** morality is a product of humans. Wherever humans group together, especially to act in a concerted way, rules of conduct emerge to regulate behavior. Morality not only originates in human activities and institutions, it is also sanctioned and maintained by them. God has nothing to do with morality. **8.** if humans could do evil and get away with it without being punished, they would do so. Humans do good only because they are afraid of the repercussions of doing otherwise. **9.** the basic motivating force in humans is egoism (self-interest, selfishness). **10.** humans are not born innately virtuous. If humans are virtuous they have become that way through social and intellectual conditioning. **11.** virtue can be taught. Virtuous conduct is something that can be developed. **12.** respect of others must not be based on heritage, tradition, privileged status, class, or birth, but on what excellences an individual has perfected. **13.** there is a distinction between NÓMOS, those things that are true and necessary and are given or devised by convention (law, society, our own perceptions); and PHYSIS, those things that are true and necessary and are given by nature.

sophocracy (from Greek, *sophos,* wise, + *kratein,* rule) a state governed by wise individuals and/or by wisdom.

sophos (Greek) originally one skilled in any handicraft or art, or one who has excellence of skill, it was also applied to one clever in matters of common life, prudent, shrewd, cunning, wise, and to one skilled in profound learning and knowledge. The term was used to mean sage, seer, prophet, wise person who encompasses all the ideal virtues and commands utter respect. (Sometimes used interchangeably with SOPHISTĒS.)

sōphrosynē (Greek, soundness of mind, moderation, discretion, self-control, temperance) used in Greek philosophy in a variety of meanings. **1.** the state of harmony or serenity reached when rational faculties control one's desires and emotions. *Sōphrosynē* is not to be thought of only as a state but also as the power (ability) to achieve such a state. **2.** the state of contentment felt when the mean between pleasures and pains is attained. **3.** the ability to know and choose the good and to recognize and avoid evil. **4.** temperance, one of the four virtues. See VIRTUES, CARDINAL.

soul the following characteristics, or combinations of them, have been ascribed to the soul: **1.** eternality. **2.** an immaterial or spiritual entity (substance, being, agent). **3.** something separable and entirely different from the body and matter that persists throughout the changes of the body. **4.** the activating cause of life and consciousness (although in CREATIONISM it is held that God creates the soul as God creates matter at an instant in eternal time). **5.** immortality. **6.** the ability to enter the body at birth and leave the body at death (and in some cases during life). **7.** the ability to transmigrate or reincarnate (see METEMPSYCHOSIS), or to pass on to heaven or hell, or into *nirvana*. **8.** inexplicability; the soul is not in any way subject to a materialistic or mechanistic explanation, not even in terms of very fine material particles believed in by the Greek atomists (see ATOMISM, GREEK) and by the STOICS. Compare with entries under EGO and SPIRIT.

soul (Plato) the soul is a disembodied spiritual being that: **1.** can exist independently of matter and all things (except God), **2.** is (or is the source of) the real person, self, or consciousness, **3.** moves itself (is self-moving), **4.** is the cause of the motion of matter, which cannot move itself, **5.** is eternal (ungenerated by anything else), **6.** is simple, **7.** is self-sufficient, **8.** is incorruptible, and **9.** is the source of all the best and good.

One's body and all matter are corporeal (material) composites. The soul is not a composite. The soul has no parts. (The soul is simple and irreducible to any other elements.) The soul is not corporeal. It is incorporeal (immaterial). The soul is entombed in (imprisoned by or attached to) a body. The incorruptible soul does its best to fight against the corrupting influence of the body. See FACULTIES OF THE SOUL (PLATO); MOTION (PLATO).

soul, concept of the (Aristotle) the following is one of several accounts that can be given of Aristotle's concept of the soul: The soul is the FORM, or functioning excellence, of a particular living body. The soul is the capacity of the organism to act in certain ways. The soul is to the body as vision is to the eye. The soul is inseparable from the body physically (functionally) as well as logically. It is inconsistent to say that the act of seeing can exist without the functioning of an eye, or that the functioning of an eye can exist without the act of seeing. So is it inconsistent to say that certain functions (soul) of the body can exist without a living organism, or that a living organism can exist without certain functions (soul).

soul, functions of the (Aristotle) the main functions of activities of the soul: **1.** the *nutritive* or *vegetative,* having to do with growth, nourishment, and survival. (Plant life has only this level of soul.) **2.** the *sensate* (sensitive, perceptive), having to do with receiving and reacting to sensations and feeling. (All animal life has this level as well as the previous level.) **3.** the *volitional,* self-motion (and self-direction in the higher animals) and the power of causing motion. **4.** the *rational* or *intellectual,* related especially to the ability to reason and use symbols, and which is the essential characteristic only of humans. These functions are related in a hierarchy of emerging qualities, each level incorporating qualities of the previous level. Living organisms can be classified according to the number of faculties they possess (related to the degree of complexity possessed by the organism).

soul, rational and nonrational parts of the (Aristotle) the soul, according to Aristotle, has a rational part and a nonrational part (which may be thought of as including all the parts of the soul that are not rational). The rational part is itself divided into two parts: (a) the *completely rational*, which deals with eternal objects and pure theory (see FIRST PHILOSOPHY [ARISTOTLE]); and (b) the *not so completely rational*, which deals with the mundane affairs of everyday living and bodily needs such as our appetites, cravings, and desires. See REASON, PRACTICAL (ARISTOTLE). Insofar as these appetites and desires are controlled by reason (or insofar as they conform in their own way to reason), then they are classified as rational. Insofar as they do not, then they are irrational. Moral virtue (see VIRTUES, MORAL [ARISTOTLE]) is the rational control of our desires and appetites (or the conformity of our desires and appetites to reason). Moral virtue involves a choice as to the way the desire or appetite is to be handled—by means of reason or not.

soul/body dualism see DUALISM, DESCARTES' SOUL/BODY; MIND, TYPES OF THEORIES OF.

sound (logic) referring to a deductive argument that is formally valid and whose premises are all (empirically) true, hence its conclusion must be true as well, is said to be sound. Example:

Premise 1: All animals are mortal.
Premise 2: All dogs are animals.
Conclusion: Therefore, all dogs are mortal.

space 1. that which can be characterized by a dimension. **2.** linear distance. **3.** time distance; interval; duration. **4.** extension; that which has area or volume as determined by the three dimensions: length, width, and height. **5.** boundary; that area in which something exists (moves, changes). **6.** receptacle; that in which all things are found. **7.** a void; empty or devoid of something. **8.** the void; nothingness.

space (Aristotle) for Aristotle the principal meaning of space must be sought in the concept of *place*, thought of as that absolute location (in a place or at a place in the cosmic space) of a thing (or the boundary of a figure). Things tend to seek their natural places in the universe. Their not being in their natural places is one source of motion.

space (atomists) the Greek atomists (see ATOMISM, GREEK) regarded space as a void (pure empty space) that existed between atoms and in which atoms moved. No motion would be possible without this empty space. All things in the universe are composed of atoms and empty space.

space (Descartes) space and MATTER (material substance) are one and the same thing. Anything that occupies space is extended, and that extension *is* space. Space is the volume physical things take up. There is no VOID or empty space.

space (Kant) Kant did not regard space as identical with matter, or as a receptacle, or as a void, or as absolute, or as the relationship of external real objects. Kant attempted to present a consistent subjectivistic view of space. The mind organizes and orders pure (nonspatial) experience by means of the intuition of space, by means of the subjective projection of the concept of space upon pure experience. See SENSE, INTERNAL AND EXTERNAL (KANT); SPACE/TIME (KANT).

space (Leibniz) space has two aspects: the objective or ontological, and the subjective or psychological. In both, external space is not real. Only the MONADS are real: **1.** space is the relationships among the internal properties of monads. **2.** space is that which makes many diverse perceptions cohere among themselves (or is that sense of coherence). See SPACE/TIME (LEIBNIZ).

space (Plato) space is a receptacle that (a) contains or receives the (basically mathematical) activity of matter, and (b) restrains that activity by providing the structures and limits in which that activity can take place.

space, absolute (Newton) Newton held a metaphysical view of space (and time) as being absolute and unchanging: **1.** motion (movement) can be explained by reference to this framework of absolute and unchanging space (and time). **2.** there is no need to refer motion to other motions. **3.** the three-dimensionality of space is an intrinsic, essential, and necessary attribute of space (and space of reality). **4.** space is separable from time. **5.** these truths about space are *contingent truths*.

space-time a structure consisting of, or a four-dimensional analysis in terms of, three perpendicular and linear dimensions (length, width, and height) and a fourth of an interval or duration (time).

space/time (Kant) according to Kant: **1.** we do not derive our ideas of space and time by abstracting them from experience. **2.** we do not derive our ideas of space and time from experience of succession, precedence, simultaneity, concurrence, coexistence, proximity, etc. These experiences themselves presuppose our having the ideas of space and time. **3.** space and time are A PRIORI intuitions. They are pure, intuitive, nonconceptual ideas. **4.** knowledge of space and time is (a) clearly, immediately, intuitively possessed and (b) not framed or given by concepts; (c) all experiences presuppose this intuition and depend upon it for a form. **5.** space and time are pure intuitions in the sense that their essence is known *prior* to experience and is not an outcome *of* experience. **6.** space and time are the *form* of experience—the form that all experience takes—and are *not* the *content* of experience. **7.** space and time structure experience (sensation) in the very act of its being experienced (sensed) and known. **8.** space and time apply to anything we know through our experience (senses). **9.** time applies to anything we experience as an inner flow of consciousness (and since consciousness cannot be consciousness unless it is a flow, then time is constantly an aspect of consciousness). See SPACE (KANT).

space/time (Leibniz) Leibniz's theory of space/time has two aspects, the objective or ontological, and the subjective or epistemological: **1.** space and time are not absolute and are not independently real as entities but are the order (relationship) of succession and coexistence in which real entities (the MONADS) are related to the coexistence of things. Time is relative to the cosuccession of things. **2.** space and time are systems of relations abstracted by the mind from particular contingent experiences (and not clearly perceived). In this sense space and time are logical constructs expressing relations based on experience and are not substances, or real entities. See SPACE (LEIBNIZ).

space-time continuum some of the main concepts: **1.** all physical (material) things are part of a four-dimensional framework. See SPACE-TIME. **2.** nothing can exist or be conceived to exist except in a space-time continuum. **3.** any location and description of a thing must be given in terms of the four space-time coordinates. **4.** the universe, thus any object within it, can be interpreted as changeless (immutable, motionless) only insofar as it is said to exist in space (three dimensions) without being related to time. **5.** all things are in a space-time continuum, and space cannot be separated from time (except in abstraction). All things are in a state of process. **6.** changing events regarded in abstraction from the time dimension are the source of our concept of physical *objects*, which exist substantially and endure without change. **7.** the space-time continuum that is the universe can be analyzed as a very general structure determined by the configurations and relationships of four-dimensional events represented by such concepts as mathematical points in four-dimensional geometric patternings (for example, by using non-Euclidean geometries, such as the elliptic geometry of G.F.B. Riemann, in which space is regarded as positively curved [curving] as in a sphere, or the hyperbolic geometry of N.L. Lobachevsky, in which space is regarded as negatively curved [curving] as in a saddleback). **8.** specific events within this space-time continuum can be analyzed in the same way. For example, gravity is to be thought of as a characteristic of space-time configurations (*fields*) or relationships rather than as a property of matter. The same can be done with concepts such as force, mass, and power.

species (from Latin, *species,* outward appearance, kind, type, shape, form, idea, sort) **1.** the subclass of a large class (GENUS). **2.** one of the subclasses into which a class may be divided.

speculative philosophy 1. in the nonpejorative sense: philosophy that constructs a synthesis of knowledge from many fields (the sciences, the arts, religion, ethics, social sciences) and theorizes (reflects) about such things as its significance to humankind, and about what it indicates about reality as a whole. **2.** in the pejorative sense: philosophy that constructs idle thoughts about idle subjects.

speech acts any of the variety of things done and affected in the act of speaking, such as describing, informing, commanding, persuading, altering another's opinion, and expressing feelings. See PERFORMATIVE ACT.

speech situation the name given to the following set of conditions: **1.** a speaker makes an utterance using symbols (or signs) in order to communicate. **2.** that utterance is understood, interpreted, and judged by the one to whom it has intentionally been addressed. **3.** a behavioral response of some sort (such as an answer or an action) is generated in the receiver of the utterance. **4.** (a) some information (a meaning, a fact, a reference to an object, etc.) has been conveyed and/or (b) some change has been initiated. See entries under LANGUAGE.

Spinoza, Benedict (Baruch) (1632–1677) Dutch philosopher born a Jew in Amsterdam. In 1656, he was expelled from the synagogue for what were considered heretical views. He earned his living by grinding lenses.

As a philosopher Spinoza based his rational thinking on the deductive method found in geometry, the ideal method for all thought. His general aim was to become aware of the unity and wholeness of the universe, and to find an acceptance and tolerance of the necessary and inevitable activity of all things.

Spinoza's major works are an exposition of Descartes' *Principia Philosophiae*, with Spinoza's own *Cogitata Metaphysica* appended (1663); the *Tractatus Theologico-Politicus* (1670); and his final work, collected in *Opera Posthuma*, which included his *Ethica Ordine Geometrico Demonstrata* and *Tractatus de Emendatione Intellectus* (found and published after his death, in the late 18th century).

spirit (from Latin, *spiritus,* spirit, breath) **1.** the breath of life; the cause of life conceived as a fine vapor or air that animates the organism. In human beings it has sometimes been conceived as mediating between body and soul. It has also often been viewed as a gift of God (or the gods) and/or even as part of the very breath of God. **2.** the SOUL; the immaterial agent in humans that causes consciousness (including willing) and the life functions such as growth, appetition, and feeling; in some views, the cause also of CONSCIENCE. **3.** the WORLD SOUL. **4.** a disembodied soul such as a ghost. This disembodiment may take several forms: (a) a soul without a body inhabiting an unseen world such as Hades, Heaven, Hell; (b) a soul without a body but appearing to the living in the likeness of a body; (c) a soul without the physical body to which it was attached during life but attached to its spiritual body such as at resurrection after death.

Spirit is regarded as having characteristics similar to those of soul, such as immateriality, intangibility, (sometimes) eternality, and (sometimes) immortality.

spiritism the belief (a) in the existence of spirits affecting the real world and/or humanity and (b) that human beings can, by specific means such as propitiation, ritual, or initiations, come into contact with spirits in order to (c) receive their powers, alter their activity, or communicate with them.

SPIRITUAL

The acts, service, or works produced by a spirit are called *spiriting*. The belief in and worship of many spirits is often called *polydaimonism*. These spirits may take a variety of forms, from disembodied nature spirits, to manes, to deities. In most instances spiritism is used interchangeably with SPIRITUALISM.

spiritual 1. immaterial; incorporeal; consisting of SPIRIT. **2.** referring to the higher faculties (mental, intellectual, aesthetic, religious) and values of the mind. **3.** referring to nonmaterial human values such as beauty, goodness, love, truth, compassion, honesty, and holiness. **4.** referring to moral, religious, and aesthetic feelings and emotions. Contrast with CARNAL.

spiritualism (metaphysics) 1. the view that the underlying, ultimate reality (or foundation of reality) is spirit or a WORLD SOUL that (a) *is* the universe or pervades the universe at all its levels of activity; (b) is the cause of its activity, order, and direction; and (c) stands as the only completed and rational explanation for the existence of the universe. See *LÓGOS, PNEUMA, NOÛS*. **2.** the view that only the absolute spirit exists (and its consequent finite spirits such as humans), and all else is a product of the absolute spirit.

square of opposition, the a square diagram used in logic texts and derived from the medieval studies of Aristotelian categorical or syllogistic logic that places the four standard form statements of Aristotelian logic into logical relationships.

The four standard form categorical statements of Aristotelian logic are:

A = All S are P.
E = No S are P.
I = Some S are P.
O = Some S are not P.

All concepts and ordinary language statements must be translated into one of these four forms in order to fit into a syllogistic form. The labeling of A, E, I, O is derived from the Latin *AffirmO* (A and O) and from the Latin *nEgatIo* (I and O).

Contraries A and E *cannot* both be true, but both *can* be false.

Subcontraries I and O *can* both be true, but both *cannot* be false.

Contradictories A and O, and E and I, can never be false together. If one is declared to be true, the other *must* be declared to be false automatically. They can *never both be true*. One of the two contradictories must be true, and the other false.

In subalteration, A to I, and E to O, if the superaltern is declared to be true, then automatically its corresponding subaltern *must* be true also. And if the superaltern is declared to be false, then its corresponding subaltern *must* be left undecided—it can be either true or false.

In superalteration, I to A, and O to E, if the subaltern is declared to be true, the truth-value of its corresponding superaltern *must* be left undecided—it can be either true or false. And if the subaltern is

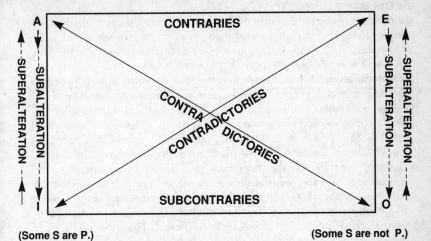

Superaltern
(All S are P.)

Superaltern
(No S are P.)

A — CONTRARIES — E

CONTRADICTORIES

SUBCONTRARIES

I — O

SUPERALTERATION — SUBALTERATION — SUPERALTERATION

SUBALTERATION — SUPERALTERATION

(Some S are P.)

(Some S are not P.)

declared to be false, then the truth-value of its corresponding superaltern *must* be false.

state 1. condition; the mode or state of being of something. **2.** the level, rank, standing of something, especially in a hierarchical order. **3.** quality of living and/or position in life. **4.** a situation (a) seen in terms of its actual relationships to other things and/or (b) seen from the point of view of its potential relationships to other things.

state, disposition sometimes called *dispositional state* **1.** a state of mind such as a mood, want, emotion, or inclination that tends to lead to certain kinds of behavior whenever certain conditions are present. Examples: (a) "I am frustrated" discloses a state of mind in which if an annoyance occurs, then some expression of irritability will follow. That state of frustration predisposes one to certain kinds of behavior. (b) "She is a charitable person" indicates that in specific situations she will tend to act with compassion, help, tolerance, or sacrifice. **2.** a physical state such as malleability, solubility, rigidity, or fluidity that describes (a) what the object can be made to do—or does—under given conditions and/or (b) what behavior it tends to engage in. Example of (a): "Buttermilk is nutritious" implies a *disposition* toward a specific activity—what buttermilk will do—if certain conditions are satisfied. Example of (b): "Helium expands" suggests a *disposition* to behave in a certain way unless prevented. All disposition states may be classified as occurrent states (see STATE, OCCURRENT), but not all occurrent states can be classified as disposition states. See DISPOSITION.

state, occurrent a state of consciousness at any given moment, for example, a feeling. Examples: "I feel morose." "I feel excited." Contrasted with STATE, DISPOSITION.

state of nature see NATURE, STATE OF.

statement any sentence or group of sentences used to assert or deny something. Often used interchangeably with *sentence* and *proposition*. To *make a statement* is to write or utter a sentence or sentences so that something true or false is said. See SENTENCE/STATEMENT DISTINCTION.

statement, analytic 1. a statement that is true by definition—true due to the meanings assigned to the words in the statement—and needs no verification in experience to be true. Example: "A triangle is a three-sided figure." "Matter occupies space and exists in time." "A thing cannot be both true and false at the same time and in the same respect." **2.** a statement that contains the meaning of the predicate in the meaning of the subject. Example: the subject of the statement "All bachelors are unmarried males" is *bachelors*, and the predicate is *are unmarried males*. The predicate is merely repeating what is already understood as the meaning of the subject. By definition, it could never be the case that a bachelor is married. (If he were married, we would not call him a bachelor.) Thus, the meanings of the words themselves make the statement true—true under any and all sets of conditions (even if there were no unmarried males), at any place or time in the universe (on Mars, at the edge of our galaxy, or in any galaxy).

Analytic statements have the following characteristics: (a) If they are denied, a self-contradiction ensues. (If I deny that bachelors are unmarried males, yet still accept the meaning of *bachelor*, I contradict myself.) (b) They need no verification in experience. (I do not need to find an actual bachelor to know the truth of the statement. It would still be true if there were no bachelors.) (c) They cannot be empirically disproved. (I cannot go out in the world and find a bachelor who is married.) (d) They are true by definition, true by their linguistic and logical structures, and thus do not as such provide information about the real world (although they can be applied to the real world). The information they provide us is contained in their linguistic meanings and logical form. They help us construct and clarify concepts but they do not necessarily point to specific referents beyond themselves. Contrast with STATEMENT, SYNTHETIC.

statement, logically impossible see IMPOSSIBLE, LOGICALLY.

statement, logically independent 1. a statement that does not logically follow from another statement. **2.** a statement that cannot be derived by the rules of inference of a logical system. **3.** a statement whose truth or falsity has no effect on the truth or falsity of another.

statement, metalinguistic see METALANGUAGE.

statement, synthetic sometimes called *synthetic proposition* or *synthetic sentence*, an empirical statement that describes a state of affairs; a statement that is informative—whose predicate adds something not definitionally contained in the subject. For example, the subject of the statement

"The table is red" is *table*, and the predicate is *is red*. The predicate states something more than what is contained in the meaning of *table*. The content of the predicate is not definitionally (not linguistically or logically) derived or derivable from the meaning of the subject. To discover whether or not it is true that the table is red, one must go beyond the statement itself and find an existing state of affairs that will indicate the truth or falsity of the statement. Unlike analytic statements (see STATEMENT, ANALYTIC), synthetic statements are not true under any and all sets of conditions, nor are they true at any place or time in the universe, but depend for their truth (or falsity) on specific conditions, places, and times in the universe.

Synthetic statements have characteristics such as: **1.** if you deny their truth, you are not involved in contradiction. (If I deny that the table is red, and say that it is gray, I am not involved in a contradiction, for it could well be true that it is gray rather than red, or it could be true that it is gray in appearance to me, since I am color-blind, but red in appearance to other people.) **2.** synthetic statements, at least in principle, can be falsified (or verified). (Theoretically, there must be conditions under which their falsity would be accepted; otherwise, they would not be classified under the heading of synthetic statements. They would be true by their linguistic and logical form.) **3.** synthetic statements are informative. They tell us about the world and refer to things in the world.

statement/sentence distinction see SENTENCE/STATEMENT DISTINCTION.

stoa (from Greek, *stóa*) a roofed colonnade or a portico; the STOICS may have received their name from this word, because it is thought that they taught and gathered at a *stóa* in Athens.

Stoics, the a school of philosophy founded in Athens about 305 BC by Zeno of Citium, a city in Cyprus. Zeno and his disciples were called Stoics possibly because Zeno lectured at a STOA. The Stoic philosophy lasted as an influential system of belief for over 500 years during the Hellenistic, Roman, and Christian periods. It drew its inspiration primarily from Socrates and Heraclitus. The principal Stoic philosophers were Zeno of Citium (c.336 to c.264 BC), Cleanthes of Assos (c.331 to c.232 BC), Chrysippus of Soli (c.280 to c.206 BC), Posidonius (c.135 to 51 BC), Cicero (106 to 43 BC), Seneca (c.4 BC to c.AD 65), Epictetus (c.50 to c.138), and Marcus Aurelius (c.121 to c.180).

Some of Stoicism's leading beliefs: **1.** the universe is a rational whole. The universe is pervaded by the LÓGOS. **2.** knowledge of the functioning of the universe as a whole (as a MACROCOSM) provides us with knowledge, and of how each individual thing (the MICROCOSM) must behave. **3.** everyone must follow the rational will of the universe and live in conformity with the divine laws of nature, just as people must follow and live in conformity with the laws of their country. **4.** everyone must accept with equanimity his or her rightful place in the scheme of things and fulfill its necessary purposes of. **5.** duty (see KATHĒKON) is doing the most rational thing possible in accordance with the rational necessity fated by the world soul. **6.** all virtues are forms of knowledge. See VIRTUES (STOICS). No one can be virtuous without knowledge. **7.** the cardinal virtues of reason, courage, justice, and self-discipline are ends in themselves. Virtuous living is the only good and the ultimate aim of life. **8.** study of philosophy leads one to the virtuous life. **9.** concomitant with the attainment of the virtuous life is the attainment of (a) KATHĒKON, (b) APATHEIA, and (c) AUTARKEIA. **10.** *apatheia* is the psychological state of insensitivity or indifference to pleasures and pains, emotions and passions, joys and grief, anxieties and mental elation. *Apatheia* is a state of tranquility of mind and body—a psychic detachment from mental and physical disturbances. **11.** *autarkeia* is a state of self-sufficiency—a state of nondependence on anyone else for survival and the satisfaction of physical and emotional needs. **12.** all people are related as common, cooperating, rational members fulfilling the design of the *world reason* (LÓGOS or PNEUMA). **13.** everyone possesses a part of the eternal *world reason*. **14.** morality is a rational system transcending nationality, race, and class differences. **15.** all things are predestined. **16.** all things recur eternally. See ADIAPHORA; CONFLAGRATION (STOICS); LÓGOS ORTHOS; LÓGOS SPERMATIKOS; PHYSIS (STOICS); RECURRENCE, ETERNAL.

struggle for existence see NATURAL SELECTION (DARWIN).

stuff, neutral a nonmental and nonphysical substance usually regarded as unknown and unknowable, considered by some philosophers to be the underlying ground for the existence of both mental and physical events.

subject 1. that of which something (a quality, relation, characteristic, attribute, property) may be affirmed (or denied). **2.** that in which something may be said to inhere. Used in a metaphysical sense, *subject* is interchangeable with words such as SUBSTANCE, SUBSTRATUM, *ground*, BEING, the REAL, REALITY, and the ABSOLUTE. **3.** the thinking agent; the being that supports or is the cause of mental functions and events. **4.** the MIND. **5.** the EGO.

subjective referring to **1.** that which is derived from the mind (the consciousness, the ego, the self, our perceptions, our personal judgments) and not from external, objective sources. **2.** that which exists in consciousness but has no external, objective reference or possible confirmation. **3.** that which is relative to the knower's own individual experiences (sensations, perceptions, personal reactions, history, idiosyncrasies).

Subjective is contrasted with OBJECTIVE and with *public* (see PUBLICITY). It is also used to refer to the experiencing modes and processes of the experiencer (subject) in contrast with the things (objects) in the real world that he or she is experiencing. *Subjective* is often used pejoratively to connote privately arrived at judgments based on emotional or prejudiced grounds without the support of objective, logical analysis.

subjectivism (epistemology) 1. the theory that all knowledge (a) has its source and validity in the knower's subjective mental states, and (b) knowledge of anything objective or externally real is hypothesized or based on inference from these subjective mental states. **2.** everything that is known is (a) a product selectively structured and created by the knower, and (b) it cannot be said that there is an externally real world to which it corresponds.

subjectivism (ethics) see ETHICS, SUBJECTIVISM IN.

subjectivism (value theory) the theory, especially in aesthetics and ethics, that (a) values are entirely dependent on and relative to the modes of human experiencing; (b) values are reflections of the feelings, attitudes, and responses of the individual, and have no independent objective or external reality or source; and (c) objects or activities are valuable or good insofar as they produce desired or desirable pleasurable states of consciousness, feelings, subjective experiences. Opposite to OBJECTIVISM (VALUE THEORY). Compare with RELATIVISM (VALUE THEORY).

sublimation (from Latin, *sublimatus,* past participle of *sublimare,* elevate) **1.** transference of a suppressed desire to a new object. **2.** substitution of another object and/or activity for one aimed at by an instinct, impulse, feeling, drive, or desire. Example: channeling the sex drive toward artistic expression.

sublime, the (from Latin, *sublimis,* high, lifted up, exalted) the feeling or experience of, or an object that produces a feeling of, (a) grandeur, nobility, majesty, elevated beauty, amazement, awfulness, horror, terror, impending doom, the terrible, that is (b) mingled with pleasure and awe, and that (c) captivates and completely involves the mind.

The sublime can include feelings (emotions) of pain, danger, power, emptiness, obscurity, privation, loneliness, vastness, the infinite, God, the universe. When these emotions stand out by themselves as only ugly, threatening, and undesirable, they cannot be labeled *sublime.* The sublime is associated with the beautiful, with the fascinating, with the appealing, with that which is exhilarating and which attracts.

sublime, the (Kant) 1. the feeling stemming from the power and greatness of our reason. Though our imagination staggers at the vast complexity of the universe, our finite reason produces ideas that reach out to grasp the intricacy, the totality, and the infinity of things. **2.** the feeling stemming from our awareness of a moral sense and destiny. We recognize our weaknesses as finite selves, yet we can also recognize our duty to each other, and we can strive to transcend our mortal condition and become aware of our worth as moral creatures. **3.** the feeling stemming from being confronted with a terrifying power that can utterly destroy us at any moment, yet at the same time having a sense of safety and being aware of a pleasurable attraction to that power.

subliminal (from Latin, *sub,* under, + *limen,* threshold) sometimes synonymous with *subnoetic* and ANOETIC; existing below the threshold of consciousness; not yet strong enough to be recognized by consciousness.

subset any given set such that all its members are members of another given set.

subsistent (from Latin, *subsistere*, stand still, stay, remain alive) **1.** having being or existence. **2.** characterizing that thing (entity, object, being, existence) which does not exist in time or space but is nevertheless real, such as a relation, number, universal, value, ideal, spirit, soul, God. Subsistents in the last three senses are usually thought of as eternal and immaterial and in many cases also as nonmental.

subsistent forms forms that are not in any way corporeal (material). They are free from all matter and from the necessity to relate to matter in order to act and to exist. Each subsistent form is its own species. It can have no individuation or particularization. Example: angels. Contrasted with SUBSTANTIAL FORMS.

sub specie aeternitas (Latin, under the view or aspect of eternity) the phrase used to signify the attempt to see all things at once in one thought without any past or future as a species of eternity—as God might grasp them. The term is commonly associated with Spinoza.

substance (from Latin, *substantia*; from *substare*, be under, be present, be firm, support) **1.** that which is the underlying ground (support, substratum) of all phenomena. **2.** that upon which everything else depends for its existence and (usually) which itself does not depend for its existence on anything else. **3.** that which is real; real existence as opposed to appearance or illusion; that which exists in and of itself. **4.** that without which a thing would not exist, would not be what it is. **5.** that in which properties inhere; that which possesses properties but which itself is not a property. **6.** that which endures throughout the changes of its properties. **7.** the real ESSENCE of a thing; that without which a thing could not be what it is and would be something else. **8.** the primary and the most important aspect of a thing; the essential nature of a thing in terms of which a thing is recognized and defined and without which it could not exist as that thing. **9.** MATTER; the material of a thing. **10.** BODY; the body of a thing.

substance (Aristotle) 1. the definition of anything always involves reference to a substance. **2.** a definition of the substance of a thing is present in any definition of a thing. **3.** knowledge of substance is always prior to our knowledge of a particular thing. We must know *what* a thing is (its *whatness*) before we can know its categories, such as quantity, quality, and position. See CATEGORIES (ARISTOTLE) and further entries for Aristotle under SUBSTANCE.

substance (Descartes) there are three kinds of substances in Descartes' philosophy: **1.** *God substance:* the infinite, uncreated being that depends on nothing other than itself in order to exist. The completely perfect *necessary existence* upon which all things depend for their creation and continued existence. Substance is eternal, spiritual, immaterial, immutable, indivisible, not spatial, not temporal, omnipresent, omnipotent, omnibenevolent, creator of the universe, creator of all the other kinds of substances, and its essence is innately known to us. **2.** *created finite spiritual substance,* such as the immaterial soul of each individual. The essence of human spiritual substance is to think and have thoughts. It is not extended; hence, it is intangible, invisible, nonspatial, and nontemporal. It occupies and uses material bodies but is not confined to bodies, since it may enter heaven bodiless. By means of the pineal gland at the base of the brain, it interacts with bodies to produce consciousness, mind, ideas, willing, imagination, etc. **3.** *created finite material substance*, such as bodies, material objects, matter, and the universe. The essence of physical, bodily substance is extension. It occupies space, exists in time, is tangible, visible, locatable, changing, divisible, and has shape and can be moved from place to place.

The following are some of the assumptions involved in Descartes' concept of substance: (a) Substance is that which can be conceived alone by itself without needing something else in terms of which it is known, and without depending on something else for its existence. (This would in effect leave only one true substance—God substance.) (b) Each substance has a distinct essence that it never loses. If substance did lose essence, it could no longer exist, it could no longer function, and it would no longer be known or knowable. (The essence of spiritual substance is *thinking*; the essence of material substance is *extension*.) The other properties possessed by substances are called modes of these essences, or essential attributes. For example, all the properties of spiritual substance, such as imagining, doubting, and willing, are modes (expressions, exemplifications, manifestations) of its essence—thinking. (c) Substances interact. (d) They oppose each other. (e) They logically and ontologically exclude each other. (They can be conceived and can exist without each other.) (f) Substances must exist; otherwise, attributes (properties, qualities, etc.) would not have anything in which they inhered (the attribute *thinking* would not be an attribute of anything). Both the concept of thinking and that of extension would be meaningless. It is contradictory to say that thinking occurs but there is nothing that is doing the thinking. It is contradictory to say that a spatial dimension exists but there is nothing that is extended or that has that dimension. See KNOWLEDGE (DESCARTES).

substance (Kant) 1. the word *substance* does not, and cannot, refer to something independent of our consciousness. (If it did, it would have no possible meaning.) **2.** the qualities such as unity in variety, endurance, permanence, and persistence that we attribute to *substance* are modes of our perceiving, structuring, and understanding the phenomena of experience. See CATEGORIES OF THE UNDERSTANDING, THE (KANT).

substance (Locke) 1. the word *substance* refers to an unknown, and unknowable, something that is the underlying base for the appearance of all natural phenomena. Substance is *something we know not what*, which would be left if all the properties or qualities of a thing were taken away. **2.** our idea of there being a *substance* is derived from, and composed of (a) our complex ideas of the powers (forces, tendencies) that things have to affect one another and to affect us and (b) the associations of qualities that happen together in time and space and which we group together. We cannot conceive of these powers or qualities as subsisting by themselves; therefore, we assume the existence of a substance that is their cause and in which they inhere. Substance is their *supposed but unknown support*. See QUALITIES, PRIMARY/SECONDARY (LOCKE).

substance (logical positivism) metaphysical concepts such as substance and attributes (qualities, properties, etc.) can be reduced to statements about language. The difference between *substance* and *attribute* is the linguistic difference between noun (substance) and adjective (attribute). Substance is not an entity-thing but a *thing-word*. Attribute is not a quality-thing but a *quality-word*. Words such as *good, beauty, badness,* and *ugliness* are not actually existing entities. They have been so regarded because, as thing-words, they have been hypostatized or reified. See HYPOSTATIZATION; REIFICATION/REISM.

substance (Plato) Plato presents a variety of meanings for substance. Three principal ones: **1.** that which (a) is the primary cause of the existence of things, (b) maintains their continuing order, thereby sustaining their intelligibility, and (c) makes things intelligible to us. Compare with DEMIURGE. **2.** the universal form or idea that is present in each class of things. See IDEAS (PLATO). **3.** *OUSIA*, the essential being or nature of things that differentiates them from other things and makes them what they are.

substance (Spinoza) 1. God (the universe) and substance are one and the same thing. **2.** substance is one, infinite, eternal, absolutely independent and self-sustaining. **3.** substance is that which exists in and of itself, needing nothing else in order to exist. **4.** substance is that on which all things depend for their existence but which depends on nothing other than itself for its own existence. **5.** substance is that which is conceived without the assistance of any further concepts to make it intelligible.

Substance (God, the universe) has infinite *attributes,* two of which we know; mind (thought) and matter (extension). The principal MODES of mind are intelligence and volition. The principal modes of matter are change (motion) and stasis (rest). These two attributes are infinite from the *NATURA NATURANS*; from *NATURA NATURATA* they are finite.

substance, primary and secondary (Aristotle) sometimes translated as *first and second substance*. Primary substance refers to particular, concrete, individual things such as an individual human, or that particular horse, or that specific house (things that are designated by nouns or noun phrases and serve as the subjects of sentences). A primary substance exists only as a subject and never as a predicate. (It conveys a *thisness* and *thatness* about it, as opposed to a secondary substance, which conveys a *whatness* about it.) Primary substances are individual existents that exist in a relatively nondependent ontological and logical relationship to other things. Their existence does not entirely depend on something else, and understanding of them is not derived from the knowledge of some prior concept.

Whereas *primary substance* refers, for example, to the individual man *Socrates*, *secondary substance* refers to that which can be predicated of a primary substance (and by which a primary substance is identified). For example, *man* can be predicated of *Socrates*, as in the sentence "Socrates is a man." A secondary substance exists because of something else. Secondary substances are those things within which the primary substances are included as species and genera. For example, the individual man *Socrates* is included in the species *human*, and the genus for this species is *animal*. Thus, the species *human* and the genus *animal* are said to be secondary substances. The genera and species to which individual things belong are secondary in the sense that (a) they would not exist and (b) they would not be recognized without the existence of the primary substance to which they are applied (and in which they inhere).

Primary substance has to do with particulars (*this*), and secondary substance has to do with universals (with the differing *kinds* of things, the *whatness* of things). Whereas qualities such as redness, roundness, or softness can be had in degrees, substances cannot. For example, Adam is the particular, concrete, individual thing *that* he is because of *what* he is; Adam's body has taken on the form of *human* (as opposed to, say, *horse*), which form is the cause of Adam's having the characteristics of the human that he is.

The more actual concrete properties that secondary substance can be seen to have, the more substantial or real it is. A species is more truly a substance than its genus, and the individual member of that species is even closer to a true substance. Example: The actual dog Pooch is more substantial than its species (domesticated canine) and more substantial than its genus *Canidae* (which includes dogs, foxes, jackals, and wolves).

As primary substance, the single, concrete thing (object, unit, whole) possesses attributes from all the categories. The same attributes applicable to the primary substance are also applicable to every genus and species. In this sense, *genus* and *species* can be considered as subjects, as substances in their own right. The substance of any one member of the genus or species is not a different substance from the substance of any other member of the genus or species. For example, in the statement "Socrates is a human," the substance of *human* is the substance of *Socrates* and not a transcendent or independent substance. *Human* stands for an entity. This entity (human) is the subject (in this case, Socrates) of which it is predicated.

Using Aristotle's metaphysical writings, one can interpret secondary substance as that form (essence, idea, universal) which causes primary substance to be what it is and which maintains its continued existence.

substance as a category (Aristotle) the category that, alone of all the categories, (a) has no opposite or contrary to which it can be contrasted; (b) has none of the qualities of the other categories; (c) includes within it reference to all the other categories; (d) is prior in existence and in our knowledge to the other categories; (e) is independent of them (but they are not independent of substance); and (f) whose meaning is not obtained by specific reference to the other categories. See CATEGORIES (ARISTOTLE).

substance as a particular subject (Aristotle) any subject (noun) of a sentence that cannot be predicated of another subject and is not included in another individual thing can be termed a *substance*.

substance as substratum (Aristotle) 1. that to which qualities attach; that in which qualities inhere. **2.** that which endures (persists, subsists) as itself throughout its changing qualities and in which 1. takes place. **3.** that which can possess or receive contrary qualities. Since substance in this sense has no opposite, and change is from opposite to opposite, substance itself does not undergo change, does not either as matter or form come into existence or pass out of existence. What does come into existence is a particular, concrete object that is a combination of form and matter: a *this-such-of-a-kind*. Both matter and form are already in potential existence before the existence of the particular, concrete *this-such-of-a-kind*. The origin of this particular involves the development of both matter and form from a potential existence to an actual existence.

Substance as substratum or substrate is not in itself a particular thing and therefore must be distinguished from Aristotle's other meanings of *substance*. Substance as a substratum lacks characteristics such as separability, specific unity, particularization, a *thisness* or *thatness*. A substratum that has a *thisness* or particularity about it and thereby can be recognized as having assignable properties is then *a substance* of some sort. See GENESIS (ARISTOTLE).

substance as a universal term (Aristotle) any subject (noun) of a sentence that cannot be included as part of an individual thing but can be used to predicate something of it, can be termed a *substance*. Thus, any universal can be regarded as a substance. See UNIVERSALS (ARISTOTLE).

substance theory of the mind see MIND, TYPES OF THEORIES OF.

substantia (Latin, that of which a thing consists, a being, an essence, material, contents) post-Augustinian Latin word sometimes used as a replacement and synonym for the English word *substance*. The Latin *substantia* was probably created out of the literal meaning of the Greek word HYPOSTASIS, meaning *standing under*.

substantial (from Latin, *substantialis,* of or belonging to the essence of something or to substance, essential) **1.** material. **2.** of or pertaining to SUBSTANCE. **3.** REAL.

substantial forms forms that imbue themselves into matter, thereby giving it a particular being. Examples: vegetative souls, animal or sensating souls. Substantial forms are not material. Substantial forms need to enter matter in order to manifest themselves and reveal their potential, whereas SUBSISTENT FORMS do not. In all members of the same species or class, the substantial forms are all of the same kind, and it is in terms of the class to which they belong that they are identified and known.

substantialism the belief that constant, unchanging realities or substances underlie all changing phenomena.

substitutivity, Leibniz's principle of stated in Latin: *eadem sunt, quae sibi mutuo substitui possunt, salva veritate,* which may be translated as: "Those things that can (at any time) be mutually substituted one for the other, without changing their truth, are identical."

substratum (substrate) (from Latin, *substratum,* a spreading or laying under) **1.** that (a) which underlies, maintains, causes, or supports a thing and (b) in which the qualities of the thing inhere. **2.** that permanent, unchanging subject, structure, or cause of phenomena and its properties. **3.** that (a) which remains identical as the selfsame thing despite the changes of its properties and (b) which remains when all the properties are taken away from the object. **4.** the ground of all being. See entries under SUBSTANCE.

subsumption (from Latin, *sub,* under, + *sumere,* take, put) **1.** the act of subsuming or the state of being subsumed under something else. **2.** in logic, the act or the state of including (a) the species under its genus and the individual under the species, or (b) the particular instance under a generalization, rule, or law.

sufficient reason, principle of see REASON, PRINCIPLE OF SUFFICIENT; REASON, PRINCIPLE OF SUFFICIENT (LEIBNIZ).

sui generis (Latin, of its own kind, alone of its kind, unique) when regarded in an absolute sense, referring to the universe or to God.

summum bonum (Latin, the highest good, the ultimate good, the supreme good, the final good) **1.** that ultimate final goal (aim, end, purpose, value) of human life for the sake of which everything else is done. **2.** that which is (or should be) desired or valued as the most cherished and most sought after experience or object. The following are some things that have been regarded as the *summum bonum* of life: pleasure, happiness, the greatest happiness of the greatest number, virtue, self-actualization, fulfillment of duty or conscience or the voice of God, perfection, self-mastery, contemplation, a good will, love of humankind, love of God, ecstasy, beatitude, salvation, power, and money. **3.** in metaphysics and theology, the highest value or good in a hierarchy of values or goods that cannot be subordinated to any other. (The other values mentioned above (a) are listed in a subordinate and descending order of preference and/or (b) are seen to be ontologically related to that highest good which is their source, inspiration, cause. All goods in the case of (b) derive their value from the power of the *summum bonum* to impart value to the other dependent goods.)

summum genus see GENUS, SUMMUM.

superman the term usually employed in translating, and associated with, Nietzsche's ÜBERMENSCH, literally *overman*; the level of humanity far superior to the present one, toward which we must aspire and which is the aim of evolution. See SLAVE MORALITY (NIETZSCHE).

supernatural, the a realm of being that: **1.** is superior in power and reality to the universe; **2.** exists beyond the universe; **3.** transcends the powers and laws of the universe; **4.** is in some manner and to some degree in control of the universe; **5.** (usually) is able to suspend the laws of the universe in order to produce miracles; and **6.** (usually) is thought to create the universe out of nothing. Compare with PRETERNATURAL.

supernaturalism sometimes called *supranaturalism* **1.** the belief in a realm of existence over and above the material realm of existence. **2.** the belief that there are powers (forces, agencies, energies) beyond the universe which affect the course of events in the universe. **3.** the belief in a transcendent God: a God that exists in another realm and as a totally different existent from the universe. Opposite to MATERIALISM; NATURALISM.

supposition (from Latin, *suppositio,* a placing under, a substitution; from *supponere,* put or set under) the act of positing, supposing, assuming something tentatively or hypothetically without its being given in experience, for the sake of the development of an argument that may lead to something capable of being experienced.

supranaturalism see SUPERNATURALISM.

suspension of disbelief sometimes called *suspension of belief,* the interruption of a disbelieving attitude so that one may imaginatively and perhaps sympathetically enter into the perspective of another system of thought (a religion, a philosophy, a play, a ritual) in order to see the interconnections of, and experience the feelings of, that system.

suspension of judgment see *EPOCHĒ.*

syllogism (from Latin, *syllogismus,* from Greek, *syllogismós,* a reckoning all together, a reasoning, a syllogism) any valid deductive argument having two premises and a conclusion. The premises are so related to the conclusion that they imply it; the conclusion must follow.

syllogism, categorical 1. a valid deductive argument (a) expressed in categorical statements; (b) composed of two premises (a major and a minor premise) and a conclusion; (c) containing three and only three terms, of which (d) one is found only in the premises and once only in each premise, and (e) the other two are found once each in the conclusion and once each in each premise; and (f) the premises of which taken together necessarily imply the conclusion. Example:

> Major Premise: All humans are mortal.
> Minor Premise: Adam is a human.
> Conclusion: Therefore, Adam is mortal.

2. a valid deductive inference (a) stated in categorical statements (b) in which a conclusion connecting two terms (a major term, which is the predicate of the conclusion, and a minor term, which is the subject of the conclusion) is (c) deduced from two premises that connect those two terms to a third term (the middle term).

symbol (from Greek, *symbolon,* a sign by which one knows or infers a thing, an outward sign representing a hidden meaning or an abstract idea) **1.** something (usually a visible sign) that stands for an idea or object. **2.** that (a word, a mark, a gesture) which is used to represent something else (a meaning, a quality, an abstraction, an idea, an object). **3.** that which is given meaning by means of common agreement and/or by convention or custom. (This may range anywhere from a flashing light that means an emergency, to a gesture that means boredom, or to a musical notation that means a high C.)

The meaning of *symbol* is often limited to a conventional sign (see SIGN, CONVENTIONAL): something constructed by society or by individuals and given a more or less standard meaning that members of that society agree upon or share. This restricted sense of *symbol* is contrasted with *natural sign*. See SIGN, NATURAL.

sympathy (from Greek, *sympátheia*, fellow feeling, sympathy) **1.** feeling something believed to be that which another person (or living creature) is also feeling. **2.** having feelings that correspond to or duplicate those that another person (or creature) is experiencing. **3.** partaking of, sharing, or participating in the feelings of others. **4.** fellow feeling toward another person or toward others, especially in sorrow, grief, affliction, or TRAGEDY. **5.** the feeling of sorrow for the suffering of another creature or creatures and/or of another person or persons. **6.** the conscious or nonconscious shared feelings, inclinations, or emotions of people that induce further common feelings, conformity, harmony, or mutual understanding. **7.** the formal or informal expression of any of the above feelings.

Sometimes used loosely as a synonym for EMPATHY; sometimes called or included in SYNAESTHESIA. Related words: PATHOS, PITY; *commiseration*, which implies a profound pity, sorrow, or grief about another person's suffering; *compassion*, which is a deeply felt tenderness for another person or living creature, especially in reference to severe or inevitable distress, misfortune, pain, anguish, or suffering.

sympathy (ethics) 1. (a) the feeling of unity and emotional involvement with and resemblance to fellow humans whereby (b) one has a desire to live in harmony with and cooperate with them. (This may be extended to all living things and/or creatures.) **2.** the tendency in human nature to identify with the feelings of humanity in general and of individual persons, in order to promote such things as harmony, cooperation, respect, love, order, and peace in society. In Hume, sympathy and SENTIMENT were the foundations of morality.

synaesthesia also given as *synaesthesis* (the latter a Greek term, composed of *syn*, with, + *aesthēsis*, sensation) **1.** concomitant sensation; the experience of one kind of sensation but apprehended as another sensation, as when a sound is felt to have a characteristic color. **2.** EMPATHY and SYMPATHY.

syncretism (ultimately from Greek, *synkretízein*, form a union of) the bringing together of, or the attempt to bring together, conflicting ideologies into a unity of thought and/or into a cooperating, harmonious social relationship.

synoptic philosophy the attempt to envision in an abstract way an all-inclusive world view and to see the relationships of all things with one another in accordance with basic principles of change and activity. See entries under METAPHYSICS.

syntactics the study of the grammatical structures into which the symbols (words) of a language can be put in order to convey meaning. Synonymous with most meanings of SYNTAX.

syntax (from Greek, *syntaxis,* a putting together, an order, an arrangement, a structure, a grammatical construction) **1.** the grammatical structure of sentences. **2.** the grammatical construction of sentences. **3.** the proper structuring (arranging, constructing) of words into sentences according to grammatical rules and to usage. **4.** the study of (a) the structural or grammatical relationships among symbols and (b) the ways in which these symbols can be arranged in order to communicate meaning.

Syntax focuses mainly on the grammatical interrelationships of the structures of a language and their systematic organization, in comparison with SEMANTICS, which deals with the meaning level of language and its components.

synthesis (from Greek, *synthesis;* from *syn,* with, + *tithenai,* put, place) **1.** the bringing together of separate ideas or differing ideologies into a whole. **2.** the result of 1. **3.** the combining of things (ideas, concepts, qualities) into more complex wholes from simpler things. **4.** the result of 3. **5.** the third phase in the dialectical process of thesis, antithesis, synthesis. See DIALECTIC (HEGEL).

synthetic (from Greek, *synthetikós,* one skilled in putting together) referring to a statement (sentence, proposition, judgment) that asserts something about the real world (and not about how words are used or about the meaning of words). *Synthetic* is contrasted with *analytic, tautological, definitional,* A PRIORI, *certain, necessary,* APODEICTIC, and used interchangeably with *contingent, empirical, probable,* A POSTERIORI, and *descriptive.*

synthetic philosophy 1. in general, the attempt to combine all the fields of knowledge into a coherent, consistent unity. **2.** specifically, the philosophy of Herbert Spencer, which attempted to combine all the sciences into a connected whole.

system 1. an assemblage of things unified into a consistent whole by a regular interrelationship (interaction, interdependence, interconnection) of its parts. **2.** an assemblage of things (objects, ideas, rules, axioms, etc.) arranged in a coherent order (of subordination, or of inference, or of generality, etc.) according to some rational or intelligible principle (or plan, or scheme, or method). **3.** the principle or method of operation by which 1. and 2. are achieved and/or explained (as in the phrases "the system of logic," "the system of physical laws," "the system of classification"). See ORDER.

T

table of categories see CATEGORIES OF THE UNDERSTANDING, THE (KANT).

table of judgments, logical (Kant) see CATEGORIES OF LOGIC, THE (KANT).

tables of investigation, the three (Bacon) Francis Bacon propounded a procedure for scientific research that he named Tables (or Rules) of Investigation (or Presentation): **1.** *The Table of Affirmation* or *The Rule of Presence.* Enumerate and examine all the varied positive examples of the phenomena under investigation that have the same characteristics. Bacon cited as an example the study of heat. All the variety of instances having heat present in them must be listed and studied—the sun, light, fire, friction, the human body. **2.** *The Table of Negation* or *The Rule of Counterexample.* Cite all the negative cases in which, for example, heat is not present but where one might think it should be, as in things such as the skin of dead persons, and some reflections of light. **3.** *The Table of Comparison* or *The Rule of Differing Degrees.* Examine and compare the differences among phenomena in order to find any correlations that exist among their differences. See BACONIAN METHOD.

***tabula rasa* (Locke)** (Latin, a smoothed or blank tablet) used by Locke as a metaphor in describing his concept of the mind. Some of the main points: **1.** the mind before birth (or a specific experience) is like a blank tablet (or slate or piece of white paper). **2.** by means of stimuli from the external world, sensations (simple ideas) are imprinted on that tablet. **3.** such an activity is the source and the ground of all knowledge and thinking. **4.** there are no innate ideas or principles. **5.** the mind is a passive entity: a receptacle that can receive stimuli, sensations, ideas, knowledge, but cannot create them on its own.

taste personal preference.

tautology (from Greek, *tautologia*; from *tauto,* the selfsame, + *lógos,* word, meaning) **1.** the repetition of the same meaning but using different words. Example: "audible to the ear." **2.** restating the same idea but in different words. Example: "That bachelor is unmarried." **3.** in categorical logic, expressing a quality or meaning in the predicate that is already contained implicitly or explicitly in the subject. Examples: "All women are human." "All bachelors are unmarried males." "All colored objects are colored." "All causes have effects." "All subjects have predicates." **4.** any statement that is necessarily true because of its meaning. Examples: "All black horses are black." "Bachelors are unmarried males." "Every effect has a cause." "If she is a mother, then she is a parent." "That which is green is colored." "Today is tomorrow's yesterday, and today is yesterday's tomorrow." "If today is Saturday, then tomorrow is Sunday." **5.** any compound sentence (statement) that is necessarily true because of its logical form. Examples: "If all *X*'s are *Y*'s, then no *X*'s are non-*Y*'s."

Of tautologies the following can be said: (a) their truth cannot be, need not be, and is not established by relating them to sense experience or empirical testing. Their truth is known merely by understanding the meanings of the statements and/or their logical form (and also by logically inferring their truth from statements so understood); (b) they are always necessarily true under all conditions, true by definition. If they are denied, a self-contradiction results. (c) they cannot be falsified by experience. The rules of inference in logic and mathematics are tautologies. See A PRIORI; STATEMENT, ANALYTIC. Contrasted with CONTINGENT (LOGIC).

technē (Greek, art, skill, craft, cunning of hand, technique, a trade, handiwork, a system or method of making or doing something) a term found in English words such as *technic, technical, technicality, technician, technique, technology, technological,* and *technosophy.* **1.** the very general meaning of *technē,* especially as found in Aristotle, refers to anything deliberately created by humans in contrast to anything not humanly created. (The latter is a product of PHYSIS, or nature.) This sense of *technē* includes houses, shoes, paintings, songs, vases, toys, and bombs, and excludes things found in nature, such as lakes, mountains, people, and stars. **2.** a less general meaning of *technē* refers to a handiwork, a craft, a technique, or a skill. This includes any skill (a) in *making* things (sculpture, clothes, shoes, poems, vases); (b) in *doing* things (teaching, healing, managing, diplomacy); (c) in *acting* (reciting poetry, dramatizing an event on stage); (d) *dancing;* and (e) *singing.* **3.** specifically, *technē* refers to the knowledge of *how* to do or make things (as opposed to *why* things are the way they are); *how* to achieve a desired end or *how* to produce something. **4.** *technē* also refers to the rational, professional knowledge of the *rules of procedure* involved in making or doing things. The Greeks included a variety of sciences and arts under the heading of *technē,* such as all the crafts we regard as the fine arts, the industrial-vocational arts, the applied sciences (technology), the medical arts, and the medical sciences. In the class of *technē* that we call fine arts, Plato had three general categories: (a) the *musical arts* (songs, dances, instrumental performances, and combinations of these); (b) the *visual arts* (sculpture, architecture, painting, pottery making, mosaics); and (c) the *literary arts* (lyric, epic, and dramatic poetry; drama; the dialogue). See entries under POIĒSIS.

For the Greeks an aesthetic response or attitude is possible both to *technē* in any sense of that term (fine art, useful art, productive art, action) and to *physis* (nature) in any of its aspects. We can have an aesthetic relationship as much to a sunset or to a piece of driftwood as we can to a sculpture. Compare with FINE ARTS.

teleological animism see ANIMISM, TELEOLOGICAL.

teleological argument for the existence of God embodied in a variety of forms, among them the following: **1.** order (purpose, design, pattern) exists in the universe. Order cannot exist without an orderer. Therefore, God exists as the source of that order. **2.** things move toward goals; they struggle to complete themselves. God exists as the intelligent being that (a) impels things toward their goals, (b) sets up the goals, and (c) designs the means by which these goals are to be attained. **3.** the universe as a whole has a purpose toward which it is struggling. God exists as the creator and the sustainer of that purpose. See DESIGN, ARGUMENT FROM.

teleological causation see CAUSES, ARISTOTLE'S FOUR.

teleological ethics see ETHICS, TELEOLOGICAL.

teleological explanation see EXPLANATION, TELEOLOGICAL.

teleology (from Greek, *telos*, end, purpose, completed state, + *lógos*, the study of, the rational principles of) the study of phenomena exhibiting order, design, purposes, ends, goals, tendencies, aims, and direction, and how these are achieved in a process of development. See EXPLANATION, TELEOLOGICAL. Contrast with DYSTELEOLOGICAL.

telepathy (from Greek, *tēle*, far, far off, at a distance, + *pathos*, emotion, feeling, passion, suffering) **1.** the communication of information (ideas, feelings) from one person to another without the use of the five senses, and without any physical contact or known physical means of transferring that information. **2.** the ability to obtain information as in 1. **3.** mental states and processes of one person directly affecting the bodily and/or the mental states and processes of another person whether known to that other person or not. Telepathy is characterized as being nonsensory, noninferential, immediate, and a direct transfer of information. See CLAIRVOYANCE, EXTRASPECTION, PARAPSYCHOLOGY.

telos (Greek) the completion or fulfillment of something, the completed stage of an activity, end, result, purpose, goal, aim, that final point toward the achievement of which a process is directed.

temperament the general bodily or mental character or predisposition of the personality. Temperaments were classified as sanguine, phlegmatic, bilious (or choleric), melancholic, etc.

temporal 1. characterized by or referring to time. **2.** temporary; limited by or in time. **3.** transitory (as opposed to eternal). **4.** material, pertaining to matter. **5.** secular; earthly; concerning that which has to do with this life or world as opposed to the supernatural, heavenly, sacred, or eternal world. **6.** pertaining to that which is political, civil, earthly, common (as in *temporal power* versus *clerical power*).

term 1. any word or phrase that can be applied to some thing. **2.** any word or phrase that has a meaning, as in, "Please define your terms." **3.** any of the things being related in a statement. Example: In the statement "Emma loves karate," *Emma* and *karate* are the terms being related by the relationship *loves*. **4.** any member of a function, series, or sum, as in "the terms of this sequence," "the terms of this binomial equation."

term (categorical logic) the SUBJECT or PREDICATE of a categorical statement. Example: In the categorical statement "Adam is strong," *Adam* is the subject term and *is strong* is the predicate term.

term, distributed a term is distributed whenever it is preceded explicitly or implicitly by a universal quantifier, whenever it refers to all the items it can mean, whenever it refers to all of its EXTENSION, and whenever what it says is applicable to every instance of it. Otherwise it is an *undistributed term*. See DISTRIBUTIVELY.

term, empty see EXTENSION, EMPTY.

term, privative see PRIVATIVE TERM/WORD/NAME.

tertiary qualities see QUALITIES, TERTIARY.

Tertullian's dictum see *CREDO QUIA ABSURDUM EST*.

testability principle see CONFIRMATION, PRINCIPLE OF; VERIFIABILITY, PRINCIPLE OF.

Thales (c.640—c.546 BC) Greek philosopher, mathematician, astronomer, and statesman, born in Miletus, Ionia, and considered one of the seven wise men of ancient Greece. He is listed as the first of the group of three Milesian Naturalists, the others being his students Anaximander and Anaximenes, and founder of the Ionian or Milesian school of natural philosophy.

For Thales, water is the ultimate, fundamental stuff of all things in the universe. All things arise from water into what they are, and then go back into water. Water is the agent of all change, all motion. All the rhythms of physical processes are cyclical.

He accurately predicted an eclipse of the sun on May 28, 585 BC. He provided geometric arguments for showing, for example, that a circle is bisected by its diameter; that the angles at the base of an isosceles triangle are equal; that two intersecting straight lines form two equal opposite angles at the intersection; and that two triangles are of identical shape whenever they have one side and their corresponding angles equal. In a nongeometric way he calculated the height of a pyramid by measuring the shadow it made at the exact time when a man's shadow was the same length as the man, and in this way counting off the number of such units in the pyramid's shadow. Using trigonometric concepts he measured the distance of ships at sea. He also measured the cycles of the solstices, correctly explained the source of the moon's light, and calculated five celestial areas: arctic, antarctic, equator, tropic, etc.

Thales' philosophic contribution rests on his belief that explanations of phenomena in the universe are not to be found in mythology, poetry, imagination, or fantasy, but in observation (looking, perceiving), the use of rational methods (geometry, logic, reason), and reference to such concepts as cause and effect, regularity, unity, variety, change, self-motion, and substance.

thanatism (from Greek, *thánatos*, death) the belief in the complete cessation and annihilation of consciousness (soul, mind, self, ego) at death. Opposite to ATHANATISM.

thanatology (from Greek, *thánatos,* death, + *lógos,* the study of) the study of death and dying in all its aspects.

theism (from Greek, *theos,* divine, god) **1.** belief in divine things, gods, or a God. Opposite to ATHEISM. **2.** belief in one God (monotheism) transcending but yet in some way IMMANENT in the universe. Contrasted with DEISM. Other characteristics are usually associated with this monotheistic deity of theism: God is personal, the creator, the sustainer of existence; omnipotent, omnibenevolent, omniscient; supreme in power, reality, and value; the source and sanction of all values; and accessible to human communication. See GOD CONCEPTS.

theodicy (from Greek, *theos,* god, + *dikē,* justice, right) **1.** the discipline that attempts to justify the ways of God to humanity. **2.** the attempt to vindicate the goodness and justice of God in ordaining or allowing moral and natural evil and human suffering. **3.** the attempt to make God's omnipotence and omnibenevolence compatible with the existence of evil. **4.** the attempt to defend the belief that this is the best of all possible worlds.

theology (from Greek, *theología*; from *theos,* god, + *lógos,* the study of) **1.** the study of the relation of the divine (or ideal, or eternally unchanging) world to the physical world. **2.** the study of the nature, being, and will of God (or the gods). **3.** the doctrines or beliefs about God (or gods) of particular religious groups or of individual thinkers. **4.** any coherently organized body of doctrine concerning the nature of God and God's relationship with humans and the universe. **5.** the systematic attempt to present, interpret, and justify in a consistent and meaningful way the belief in gods and/or God. See FIRST PHILOSOPHY (ARISTOTLE).

theology, negative sometimes called *via negativa* **1.** theology based on the belief that God's being so vastly exceeds our human finite being that none of God's characteristics can be known in any real or full sense. None of the attributes of God reveal God's true nature. We can know *that* God is (*quod sit*) but not *what* God is (*quid sit*). **2.** theology that holds we can only know what God is by knowing what God is not.

theorem (from Greek, *theōrēma,* theory, sight, view, rule, principle) **1.** that which is regarded and established as a principle (rule, law, necessary truth). **2.** that formula in a logical calculus for which there is a proof and which is used to deduce other statements.

theoretical 1. depending on, or confined to, speculation and/or theory. Opposite to actual, real, applied. **2.** not practical; having no applicability. **3.** obscure and/or abstract. **4.** having to do with issues concerning generalities and/or general principles about things rather than about what exactly is to be done or should be done.

theoretical construct see CONSTRUCT, THEORETICAL.

theoretical reason (Kant) see REASON, THEORETICAL (KANT).

theōria (Greek, a looking at, viewing, beholding, rational contemplation, knowing) used by Plato to mean *contemplation* or *the intuitive grasp of the intelligible eternal forms*; used by Aristotle to refer to abstract, intellectual knowledge and contrasted with PRAXIS and POIĒSIS. See DIANOIA; POIĒSIS/POIETIKOS (ARISTOTLE).

theories of perception see PERCEPTION, THEORIES OF.

theory 1. an apprehension of things in their universal and ideal relationships to one another. Opposite to practice and/or to factual existence. **2.** an abstract or general principle within a body of knowledge that presents a clear and systematic view of some of its subject matter, as in a *theory* of art or the atomic *theory*. **3.** a general, abstract, and idealized principle or model used to explain phenomena, as in the *theory* of natural selection. **4.** a hypothesis, supposition, or construct assumed to be true and on the basis of which phenomena can be predicted and/or explained and from which further empirical knowledge can be deduced.

theory, scientific although the distinctions among concepts such as THEORY, LAW, and HYPOTHESIS are not finely drawn, a few things can be said about scientific theory: **1.** a theory contains many terms that are not directly observable—direct experience does not give us a *meson*, *neutrino*, *photon*, etc. A theory is based on indirect evidence and is assumed for pragmatic reasons as being useful in systematizing, simplifying, and explaining phenomena. **2.** there is no direct and definite empirical procedure for identifying and verifying the terms and models of a theory—experimental tests can be conducted that seem indirectly to indicate the existence of the concepts and referents of the theory, such as traces on photographic film indicating the existence of radiation. **3.** the terms in a theory are not defined as precisely as the terms found in scientific laws. **4.** a theory depends on the confirmation or verification of laws for its usefulness, logical support, and acceptance. **5.** a theory is a part of a system of interrelated concepts that imply the existence of phenomena that can be described by laws. Some laws may be deduced from theories. **6.** theories are used to support or explain a law—laws usually are not thought of as dependent on the theories sometimes used to explain them. Theories may change, or contrasting theories may be used to support, explain, or describe a law. **7.** a theory is often more abstract, less concrete, than a law. **8.** a theory often has the capability of predicting phenomena, extrapolating to new phenomena, and suggesting further applications, and is considered as valuable or correct to the extent to which it can do these things. **9.** a theory can apply to new experimental observations without itself undergoing many conceptual alterations. **10.** theories are often not formalized, and one of the main aims of science is to construct more formalized systems of theories.

theory of types see TYPES, THEORY OF.

thesis (metaphysics) see MATERIALISM, DIALECTICAL (MARX-ENGELS).

thing-in-itself, the see DING AN SICH, DAS.

thinking 1. a mental activity whereby a person uses concepts acquired in the process of learning and directs them toward some goal and/or object. **2.** any of the mental activities of which we are conscious, such as reflecting, inferring, remembering, introspecting, retrospecting, doubting, willing, feeling, understanding, apprehending, perceiving, meditating, imagining, and pondering.

thinking, black-and-white see BLACK-AND-WHITE THINKING.

this an indexical sign (see SIGN, INDEXICAL) such as *not, that, I,* or *here* that (a) attempts to disclose the meaning of its referent directly (usually ostensively) by such maneuvers as pointing, (b) on its own contains no descriptive dimensions until amplified further, (c) when applied has in each case a different referent, and (d) attempts to select or discriminate features of reality, thereby focusing attention on specific items in our consciousness.

thought, a that of which we are conscious (ideas, willing, imagining, understanding, perceiving, sensing, feeling) at any given moment.

thought, the three laws of see LAWS OF THOUGHT, THE THREE.

time 1. that in which events are distinguishable in terms of the relations of before and after, beginning and end. (Sometimes *time* is thought of as a *nonspatial medium [realm, order]* in which things change and events take place.) **2.** that which is distinguished by the relationships of *before* and *after, beginning* and *end,* and which is inseparable from change. **3.** the measurable aspect of duration (instants, intervals)—a particular point, moment, period, portion, or part of duration or of what endures. **4.** the irreversible succession of instants (events, segments, points, intervals, durations) conceived of as a linear progression or only as a directional line. **5.** a measure of change, or change itself observed, as in the positional change of the sun or the hands of a clock, or the qualitative change of the color of an object or sharpness of a sound or sight. Such changes are often used as a reference for comparison to other changes; for example, the cycle of the moon is called a *month*, and is used as a measure of time to compare to the cycle of light and darkness we call a *day*.

time (Kant) 1. the intuited infinite continuum (of all present and possible experience) and **2.** the immediately given innate *a priori* form by which the given is experienced as a flow. See SENSE, INTERNAL AND EXTERNAL (KANT); SPACE (KANT), SPACE/TIME (KANT).

time (Plato) considered "the moving image of perfect eternity." By this, Plato meant that *time* is an imperfect imitation of the timeless unchanging realm of perfect ideal forms. Change, succession, and hence *time* are merely the results of the mind's inability to grasp things all at once (SUB SPECIE AETERNITAS) in their entirety. *Time* is a product peculiar to the mind and dependent on its functions.

time, absolute (Newton) some of the basic points in Newton's concept of absolute time: **1.** absolute time is independent of natural (physical) events and is prior in existence to natural events. **2.** absolute time is mathematical time, a homogeneous mathematical order. **3.** its essential nature is to flow uniformly without regard and without relation to any external thing. **4.** absolute time is eternal. It flowed before the creation of the universe. **5.** absolute time is directional. It has an absolute direction and movement.

Newton's concept of *absolute time* was opposed to the concept of *relative time*, which held that time and space were sets of relations among objects and were never independent of objects and of change.

time, subjective 1. positive meaning: Time is the sense of a *now*, or a present, which implies also a sense of a past and a future. Subjective time is usually regarded as a continuous but heterogeneous flow of an irreversible series of successive states that cannot be sharply divided. Subjective time is not a passive but an active sense of a process directed into a future, or being taken into a future. It is something experienced intuitively, immediately, concretely as an ongoing activity. Subjective time as immediately felt is not quantified (but it can be quantified). **2.** negative meaning: Time is unreal and only a product of the operations of our consciousness and/or imagination. Time as something existing independently of consciousness is an illusion. What we regard as the *past* is merely a part of a memory-state. The *future* is merely an expectation in consciousness at any given moment of its operation.

timeless 1. not in time. **2.** not describable in terms of tenses, or time.

timeless present see PRESENT, THE TIMELESS.

timocracy (timarchy) (from Greek, *timē,* esteem, honor, dignity, worship, + *kratein,* control, rule, govern) **1.** Plato: a state in which the love of honor, glory, esteem is the highest ideal and the ruling principle of government. **2.** Aristotle: a state in which honors are distributed according to the evaluation of property held. **3.** a state ruled by leaders of honor, worth, competence, and esteem as opposed to class, heredity, power, privilege.

timology (from Greek, *timē,* honor, worth, valuation, esteem, + *lógos,* the study of) **1.** the study of value or what makes a thing valued. See AXIOLOGY. **2.** the belief that values are intrinsically worthwhile without regard to external justifications. Opposite to RELATIVISM.

token 1. a particular and individual sign such as a word, an utterance, a gesture. **2.** an instance or replica of a written or spoken word.

Contrasted with TYPE, which is an instance of a particular kind of token. Example: In the statement "The color was not the one I wanted," there are eight instances (tokens) of *words* and two instances (tokens) of the type *the*. The former may be called *word-tokens* and the latter *word-types* (or *type-tokens*). See AMBIGUITY; TYPE-TOKEN; TYPE/TOKEN DISTINCTION.

tragedy (Aristotle) (from Greek, *tragōdia,* tragedy—originally meaning *goat song*) the term stems from early times, when either a goat was given as a prize for the best lyric tragedy, dance, or song, or the actors clothed themselves in goat skins; the main elements of tragedy are a work: (a) of dramatic art (as opposed to narrative art); (b) that depicts serious action, character, and thought; (c) structured with a beginning, middle, and end that is a complete story in itself; (d) of appropriate length, not too long, yet not too short; (e) with a plot; (f) in which a great person of noble stature is seen inexorably to fall from a state of happiness to a state of undeserved suffering or misery; (g) presented in an artistic setting of fine language, diction, song, and spectacle; and (h) that is an interconnected whole which produces feelings such as awe and relief and the purgation of the emotions of pity and fear. See KATHARSIS (ARISTOTLE). Compare with COMEDY (ARISTOTLE).

tragedy, aesthetic paradox of like other works of art, tragedy provides us with aesthetic beauty and pleasure. But tragedy depicts happenings that are not pleasurable to perceive; rather, they are painful, traumatic, and in some cases border on the ugly. Compare with UGLY, THE PARADOX OF THE.

transcendence of the ego see EGO, TRANSCENDENTAL (KANT).

transcendent (from Latin, *transcendere*; from *trans*, across, over, beyond, + *scandere*, climb) **1.** superior, supreme, surpassing, exalted, of superlative quality. **2.** beyond what is given to our experience. **3.** referring to that which is forever beyond the grasp of ordinary experience and scientific explanation. **4.** independent and separate.

transcendental analytic (Kant) refers to Kant's attempt to analyze all A PRIORI knowledge in terms of the concepts found in the ideal and pure cognition of the understanding. See CATEGORIES OF LOGIC, THE (KANT), CATEGORIES OF THE UNDERSTANDING, THE (KANT).

transcendental deduction see DEDUCTION, TRANSCENDENTAL (KANT).

transcendental dialectic (Kant) see DIALECTIC, TRANSCENDENTAL (KANT).

transcendental ego of apperception see APPERCEPTION, TRANSCENDENTAL.

transcendentalia/transcendentia (Latin, transcendentals) both terms used in medieval philosophy to refer to any idea (concept, notion) that applies to all existence of whatever kind. The list includes *res* (thing), *ens* (being), *aliquid* (something), *unum* (one, unity, whole), *verum* (true), and *bonum* (good, perfect). These ideas were believed to go beyond (transcend) Aristotle's categories (see CATEGORIES [ARISTOTLE]) because it was believed they could not be subsumed under them.

transcendentalism 1. the belief in the superiority of the intuitive or spiritual over the empirical and scientific. Holds that there is an ideal, spiritual reality beyond the space-time world of our experience that can be grasped and with which all things are infused. Associated especially with Ralph Waldo Emerson and his followers, who have been called transcendentalists. (The name was erroneously applied to them because of an incorrectly supposed relationship to Kant's philosophy—see TRANSCENDENTAL PHILOSOPHY [KANT].) **2.** that in philosophy which goes beyond (transcends) empiricism or what is experienced in order to ascertain the A PRIORI fundamental principles or structuring processes of all knowledge.

transcendental idealism see IDEALISM, TRANSCENDENTAL (KANT).

transcendental illusion see ILLUSION, TRANSCENDENTAL (KANT).

transcendental knowledge (Kant) see KNOWLEDGE, TRANSCENDENTAL (KANT).

transcendental logic see CATEGORIES OF LOGIC, THE (KANT).

transcendental philosophy (Kant) 1. in general, the name given to the philosophy of Kant. **2.** specifically, the A PRIORI analysis of pure reason that Kant proposed, which would present and analyze the basic concepts of pure reason and trace out all its implicit concepts and assumptions.

transcendental table of the pure concepts of the understanding see CATEGORIES OF THE UNDERSTANDING, THE (KANT).

transcendental proof (Kant) see PROOF, TRANSCENDENTAL (KANT).

transmigration also REINCARNATION, METEMPSYCHOSIS the passage, at death of a body, of a spirit or soul into another body.

transsubjective reference see REFERENCE, TRANSSUBJECTIVE.

transvaluation of values (Nietzsche) sometimes called *reevaluation of values*, the phrase used by Nietzsche to indicate that humans must revolt against and transcend the customary values and narrow-mindedness of society. See SLAVE MORALITY (NIETZSCHE).

triad (from Greek, *tria,* three) a relation or group of three.

triad, inconsistent see ANTILOGISM.

trichotomy/trichotomizing (from Greek, *tricha,* threefold, in three parts, + *temnein,* cut) the division of things into three basic parts that are regarded as fundamentally and/or irreducibly different. Examples: "A human is composed of body, mind, and soul." "Three realities exist: the realm of God, the realm of spirits, and the realm of nature."

trivium (from Latin, *trivium,* a place where three ways [roads] meet) the three philosophic or linguistic studies of the medieval educational system: grammar, rhetoric, and logic (including dialectic). Together with the QUADRIVIUM (geometry, arithmetic, astronomy, and music), these studies made up the seven liberal arts of education in medieval times.

truth the quality of being true or correct according to some ground or test for establishing the reality of a statement (proposition, idea, thought, belief, or opinion). There are a number of such grounds or tests for justifying truth: the approximation, conformity, or correspondence to facts; the COHERENCE among ideas; the pragmatic usefulness of ideas; EXPERIENCE, FAITH, AUTHORITY, INTUITION, self-evidency; revelation; tradition. *Truth* assumes that what it applies to does depict fact or reality and appeals for support to all of these methods or a mixture of these methods. Not all statements can be labeled by the word *truth* (or by the word *falsity*). Examples: *proposals* (accepted or rejected, not true or false); *resolutions* (followed or violated); *promises* (kept or not kept); *suggestions* (heeded or unheeded); and *commands* (obeyed or disobeyed).

truth, coherence theory of the view that a statement (proposition, idea, thought, belief, opinion) is true if it can be put logically, consistently, systematically into a coherent body of knowledge whose every member entails and is entailed by every other member. The truth of the entire body of knowledge is relative to the degree to which it represents a complete picture of absolute reality. Some further views of the coherence theory of truth: **1.** one cannot establish a correspondence between an idea and something that is not an idea (such as a fact or an objective referent); only logical relationships among ideas can be established. **2.** a statement (idea, concept, etc.) is true if it is logically consistent with other statements accepted as true. **3.** knowledge is a system of logically (conceptually) interrelated truths (statements, ideas) and a (partial) truth is any member of that system. (Individual truths are only partly true with respect to other truths in the system.) **4.** the collection of all the coherent truths constitutes the truth (admittedly unattainable). **5.** the ABSOLUTE is the all-inclusive truth from which all other truths derive their being, and from which they may be logically deduced. **6.** all phenomena in the universe are connected by logical necessity and flow necessarily from the absolute. The coherence theory of truth is associated with the rationalistic and/or idealistic metaphysics of philosophers such as Leibniz, Spinoza, Hegel, and Bradley, in whose mathematics (geometries in particular) are taken as the model for truth. Contrasted with TRUTH, CORRESPONDENCE THEORY OF.

truth, correspondence theory of the view that a statement (proposition, idea, thought, belief, opinion) is true if what it refers to (corresponds to) exists. That to which a statement truly corresponds is called a fact. The process of finding such a correspondence or conformity is called VERIFICATION or CONFIRMATION. Example: The statement "Tina is sitting at her desk" is true if it corresponds to the observed fact of her sitting at her desk. The statement otherwise is false. Contrasted with TRUTH, COHERENCE THEORY OF.

truth, performative theory of calling something *true* is merely performing an act of concession (assent, acceptance, agreement) with what has been stated. *Truth* is not a quality or property of anything but is a SPEECH ACT (a performative act); it has nothing to do with the true or false description of a state of affairs. Sometimes referred to as the *ditto theory*. See LANGUAGE; PERFORMATIVE; PERFORMATIVE ACT.

truth, pragmatic theory of a statement (proposition, idea, thought, belief, opinion) is *true* if it works or has practical results such as control or predictive value, or if it stimulates creative inquiry, resolves problems in science and everyday life, makes us happy.

truth, relativity of (Sophists) whatever seems to be true, or is declared to be true by someone, is true for that person and since it is true for that person, it *is* true. See RELATIVISM, PROTAGOREAN.

truth frequency see PROBABILITY.

truths of fact (Leibniz) statements (propositions, assertions) that are not necessarily true, since they may be denied without contradiction; they just happen to be true of something about this particular real world or might happen to be true of something about a particular possible world. Statements that are not true of all objects in the universe but only about some of them.

truths of reason (Leibniz) statements (propositions, meanings, ideas, concepts) that are true everywhere and in all possible worlds. *Truths of reason* are not true only by definition, but apply descriptively to the real, external world. No amount of power, not even God's, can change *truths of reason*, since they are the very formal structures (limitations) in which events must take place. *Truths of reason* cannot be denied without contradiction. The prime example of a truth of reason for Leibniz was the Law of Noncontradiction: A thing cannot be both A and not A. The other principal ones: the law of identity, the law of excluded middle, and the law of sufficient reason. See LAWS OF THOUGHT, THE THREE; REASON, PRINCIPLE OF SUFFICIENT (LEIBNIZ).

tychē (Aristotle) (Greek, luck, fortunate coincidence) that which occurs unexpectedly, was not necessitated to happen, but which serves a purpose or can be taken advantage of to achieve some desired goal; an event unintended yet fulfilling a plan or wish one might have had. Example: You happen to meet a friend at a supermarket; you ask her to pay you the five dollars she borrowed a few weeks ago; it was *tychē* (luck) that you bumped into her; it was *tychē* that she had enough money with her to pay you back; you use the money to buy a ticket to the latest tragedy; you had not intended to go because you didn't have enough money; that lucky occurrence *(tychē)* of meeting your friend and getting your money back makes possible your seeing the tragedy which you had wanted to see but couldn't afford; the final *tychē* was that it was the last day for the tragedy's showing. Aristotle distinguished an accident *(autómaton)* from *tychē*, in that the former is an unexpected, out-of-the-ordinary event that does not and cannot serve any possible intention or goal.

tychē (Plato) CHANCE; one of the three causes for events in the universe. The other two are nature *(PHYSIS)* and human purposiveness *(TECHNĒ)*.

tychism (from Greek, *tychē,* luck, chance, fortune) **1.** the view that chance is objectively real and is one of the conditions for the occurrence of events in the universe. **2.** the belief that much if not all of evolution happens according to chance variations and events.

type 1. a class of things, all of whose members can be regarded as members of the same class—the same type of thing. **2.** an instance of a particular kind of TOKEN (word, utterance, gesture). Example: In the statement "The color was not the one I wanted" there are eight words *(word-tokens)* and one *word-type,* namely *the,* found twice. The word-type may be regarded as one word but as two word-tokens. See TYPE/TOKEN DISTINCTION.

types, theory of developed by Russell and Whitehead, with these basic concepts: (a) predicate (or class) and (b) predicate of a predicate.

A predicate applies to individual things (instances). A predicate of a predicate applies to predicates of individual things but cannot be said to apply to the individual things themselves that possess the predicate. Predicates can be analyzed on different levels. Example: The property *red* in the statement "The apple is red" is a first-order type. The property *red* in the statement "Red is a property of apples" is a second-order type.

type-token ambiguity see AMBIGUITY, TYPE-TOKEN.

type/token distinction the distinction between a TYPE and a TOKEN, which distinguishes between two senses of referring to something. Example: If I ask, "How many words are there in the sentence *The color was not the one I wanted*?" the response may be "Eight" or it may be "Seven." In a sense both answers are correct. There are eight different words regarded as *tokens*, but only seven different words regarded as *types*, since two of the eight words (tokens) (*the* and *the*) are of the same type. See AMBIGUITY, TYPE-TOKEN; TOKEN.

U

ugly, paradox of the the ugly, whether found in works of art or in ordinary experience, is supposed to be distasteful and unappealing yet, under certain circumstances, the ugly has an appealing aesthetic fascination and pleasure associated with it. See TRAGEDY, AESTHETIC PARADOX OF.

uncaused cause a cause that has no cause; a cause that causes things to happen but which itself has no cause to cause things to happen. Applied to an eternal God or to an eternal universe and to human free will. See FIRST CAUSE; PRIME MOVER; UNMOVED MOVER, THE.

uncertainty, Heisenberg's principle of for subatomic particles, both the exact position and the exact momentum (motion, velocity) cannot be known at the same time. If the position is known, then a determination of its motion will be uncertain; when the motion of the subatomic particle is known, the determination of its position will be uncertain. (A corollary of this principle is that the process of investigating subatomic phenomena affects what is being investigated, so the phenomena as observed do not depict true reality.) Heisenberg and others have used this principle to defend the concepts of (a) uncaused events and (b) free will. In these respects it is referred to as the *Principle of Indeterminancy* or the *Principle of Indeterminance*. See INDETERMINISM (ETHICS); INDETERMINISM (METAPHYSICS).

understanding 1. the ability to have knowledge and thereby to comprehend, discern, judge, interpret, or explain. See COMPREHENSION. **2.** reason; the faculty of knowing. In *faculty* conceptions of the mind, the understanding is regarded as a faculty of the mind by which reality is grasped and adjusted to. In Cartesianism, for example, it is the purpose of the faculty of the understanding to present reality to us clearly and distinctly. Occasionally, it falls short of this aim and presents it obscurely or confusedly, and sometimes falsely as in the case of hallucinations, mirages, illusions, and deceptions.

Understanding is usually contrasted with the will. See INTELLECT.

understanding (Kant) the aspect of thinking that deals (a) with concepts, judgments, and principles and (b) with the categories in terms of which pure sensation is synthesized and thereby brought into our unity of consciousness. See CATEGORIES OF THE UNDERSTANDING, THE (KANT); REASON (KANT).

understanding, pure concepts of the (Kant) see CATEGORIES OF THE UNDERSTANDING (KANT).

understanding and the will see entries under WILL AND THE UNDERSTANDING.

undetermined referring to the inability of assigning (a) truth values to a statement, or (b) causes to an event.

unextended without spatial dimension.

unhappiness (Mill) identical with (a) pain and (b) the privation of pleasure. Contrast with HAPPINESS (MILL).

uniformitarianism, physical the belief that (a) the universe exhibits the same order (laws) throughout and (b) what exists now is the product of physical activity taking place over an extremely long period of time.

uniformity of nature, principle of the 1. the theory that what has happened once will happen again, provided the circumstances for its happening are similar, and it will happen as often as those same circumstances recur. **2.** the theory that events occur in repeated patterns throughout the universe. This is based on the assumption that since events have been seen and can be seen to occur in repeated patterns and in a general regularity, all events will continue to occur in such repeated patterns. See INDUCTION, PRINCIPLE OF (METAPHYSICS). **3.** the theory that nature is uniform throughout. Given a set of conditions X followed by a set of conditions Y, upon repetition of the same set of conditions X, the same set of conditions Y that followed X will occur. Compare with CAUSAL UNIFORMITY, THE PRINCIPLE OF.

unity, functional see FUNCTIONAL UNITY.

unity, organic the unity of a whole whereby the functions of the parts are interrelated with the functions of other parts within the whole. The human body is usually given as a typical example of an organic unity: The workings of the lungs depend on the workings of the heart, blood vessels, brain, kidneys, and other organs, and the workings of each of these organs to some extent are interrelated with the workings of the lungs. See FUNCTIONAL UNITY.

unity, organic (Aristotle) a unity such that its parts are integrated to fulfill a primary activity; all parts serve as means to the accomplishment of ends and ultimately *an end*. No part of an organic unity acts independently or in isolation from any other part. Any change occurring in a part makes a difference in the functions of the other parts and in the whole. In a truly perfect organic unity, everything necessary for the performance of its function would be there, and anything not necessary for the performance of its function would not be there.

unity, principle of organic the intrinsic value of a unity is not equal to the sum total of the intrinsic values of its parts.

unity in variety and variety in unity, principle of (metaphysics) variety exists in nature, yet a recognizable form or unity can be discerned. Example: A large variety of trees exist, but there is unity of structure and function within that variety. Varieties exist even within these unities, which varieties themselves have a unity. Example: Avocado trees are a unity among the variety of trees, but among this unity of avocados are a variety of avocado trees, etc. See IDENTITY, PROBLEM OF.

universal 1. that which pertains to the whole or to all of a class either COLLECTIVELY or DISTRIBUTIVELY. **2.** general; a general statement, or generalization about a large number of things, as opposed to a statement about only a few of them. **3.** unlimited; all-encompassing or all-reaching. **4.** total; entire.

universal (epistemology) 1. a general concept common to a number of things; a feature (characteristic, quality, property) that particular things share, or have in common, with other particular things. **2.** that which is predicable of many individual things and by which we then classify them into a class. Examples: *Female* (or *femaleness*) is predicable of *Simone, Anne, Lori, Barbara,* and *Diana*; hence, it may be regarded as a universal. *Red* (or *redness*) is common to a number of things such as *red apple, red table,* and *red lips*; hence, it may be regarded as a universal. Universals are usually common nouns or adjectives, and are contrasted with proper nouns, which are regarded as individuals and not as universals. **3.** an abstract or general word (term, idea, class, concept) such as *beauty, goodness, truth, redness, justice,* or *equality,* which indicates something common that is repeated in a number of things or names and thereby can be recognized, identified, named, and classified according to kinds, classes, genera/species, properties, unities, and wholes.

universal (logic) 1. affirmation or denial of the whole of a class. Opposite to PARTICULAR. **2.** any of the five most general relations in the traditional logic of classification: GENUS, SPECIES, *DIFFERENTIA*, PROPERTY, and ACCIDENT.

universal, absolute concrete see ABSOLUTE, THE (HEGEL).

universal causation, the principle of see CAUSAL PRINCIPLE, THE.

universal reason see *LÓGOS*.

universalia ante res (Latin, universals before reality, universals independent of things, universals as existing apart from particulars) applied to the Platonic view of universals. See UNIVERSALS (PLATO).

universalia in rebus (Latin, universals in reality, universals in things, universals as existing within particulars; sometimes given as *universalis in re*) applied to the Aristotelian view of universals. See UNIVERSALS (ARISTOTLE).

universalia post res (Latin, universals after reality, universals derived from particulars; sometimes given as *universalia post rem*) applied to NOMINALISM and CONCEPTUALISM.

universality, principle of (morality) the principle that what is considered right (good, correct) for one individual must also be considered right for any other individual in the same situation. Example: Saying that Richard ought not to steal in a given situation implies that Lauri and any other individual in a similar situation ought not to steal.

universalizability, principle of (ethics) 1. the theory that a moral principle or judgment must apply universally in the same way under the same circumstances to all individuals; otherwise, it cannot be regarded as a moral principle or judgment. **2.** the theory that moral principles must be such that they can be practiced by anyone at any time without immoral consequences.

universals (Aristotle) the main points in Aristotle's theory of universals: **1.** universals exist independently of the mind. **2.** universals do not exist independently of the things in which they are recognized. **3.** universals are externally real but are not separable from their particulars except in abstraction as concepts. They are real entities existing *in* particulars. **4.** a universal exists as that feature of a particular which is common to or shared by other particulars. A universal is a property predicated of an individual thing, which is one among many about which this property may be predicated. **5.** the mind becomes aware of universals by a process of abstracting the concept of this common property from the particulars in experience, from the concrete things which contain this common property. Apprehension of a universal is the same as the formation of a concept. Aristotle calls this *intuitive induction*. **6.** a general outline of intuitive induction: Sense perception and experiencing lead to memory. Memory serves as a means of recognizing what is common in any present experience and identifying it with something in past experience. By being fixed in the mind and abstracted in thought, what is common becomes a concept recognized as a universal. See REALISM, ARISTOTELIAN; REASON, ACTIVE/PASSIVE (ARISTOTLE).

universals (conceptualism) 1. universals are concepts (thoughts, ideas) that are constructed by the mind after experiencing particulars and recognizing the common quality they share. **2.** universals exist as concepts put into an abstract language after our experience of particular things. We can never have knowledge of universals prior to an experience that has been conceptualized. **3.** universals as concepts predicate something that correctly describes reality. See CONCEPTUALISM.

universals (nominalism) universals are not objects or entities. They exist neither *in* particulars nor *in* another realm. Universals exist only as general words or names, such as *man, manness*; *red, redness*; *cow, cowness*, which have linguistic functions and can be applied in conventional usage to things. There is no correspondence possible between the universal *red* or *redness* and a particular red thing. See NOMINALISM.

universals (Plato) the main points in Plato's theory of universals: **1.** universals exist independently of minds. **2.** universals as ideal, perfect entities exist in another unchanging realm (see FORMS, PLATO'S THEORY OF IDEAL) that is separate from this world and the particular things within it. **3.** universals as ideal entities are never perfectly exemplified (copied, imitated, participated in) by things in this world; nevertheless, vague emulations of them can be seen by the intellect in the world of sense experience. **4.** universals are apprehended in a process of ANAMNĒSIS, a recollection, reminiscence, or recovery of knowledge that is with us from a previous existence. With the proper stimuli, our ordinary sense experiences revive this latent innate knowledge. **5.** knowledge of all universals is prior to experience, and experience is formed, shaped, and structured by this knowledge. See REALISM, PLATONIC.

universals (realism) universals exist in reality independently of our awareness of them. Platonic realism holds that universals are separate entities distinct from the particular things in which they may be found. Aristotelian realism holds that universals are externally real concepts that are not separable from the particulars in which they are found.

universe, a any distinct field or system of reality or thought conceived as complete and closed, usually for the purpose of analysis, as in *universe of discourse*. Compare with CLASS.

universe, the (from Latin, *universus,* universal; from *unus,* one, + *vertere,* turn; thus, turned or combined into one) everything that is, was, and will be; the totality of existence in all its forms; the whole of space and time and all that is subsumed under them. See COSMOS.

universe of discourse sometimes referred to as *the* or *a realm of discourse,* the area of things being talked about (communicated, discussed, presented, reasoned about, etc.) whether implied or explicitly stated.

univocal 1. a statement that is neither equivocal (see EQUIVOCATION) nor ambiguous. **2.** the application of a term to things with exactly the same meaning. Example: "I am applying the word *good* in a univocal sense to both God and humans."

unknowable, the see AGNOSTICISM.

unlimited, the see APEIRON.

unmoved mover, the (Aristotle) sometimes referred to as *the prime mover*. See PRIME MOVER (ARISTOTLE). **1.** two main interpretations can be given of Aristotle's unmoved mover: (a) The *unmoved mover* is a perfect, unchanging ideal, transcendent to nature or the universe. (b) The outermost heaven is the first source of motion for the universe; it causes or initiates the motion of the universe by its own self-originating motion. The motion of the heavens is an eternal, cyclical (circular), and perfect motion. **2.** ignoring for the most part the distinction between the two interpretations, the following are the principal points in Aristotle's view of an *unmoved mover*, most of which can be applied to either interpretation. The unmoved mover is (a) eternal; (b) self-moving (although there are portions of Aristotle's writings that imply that the unmoved mover is an unchanging, nonmoving ideal that moves the universe by just being there as a beloved object moves the lover); (c) self-sufficient, nondependent on anything else for its existence or for its nature; (d) one, a unity; (e) a substance—the *primary substance* that is the source of all other things; (f) completely actualized—no latency or potentiality is part of its essence; (g) immaterial; (h) good; (i) unchanging; (j) immutable (cannot be changed);

and (k) divine thought or mind. **3.** for Aristotle, there can be an infinite regress of material movements but only in a special sense. Material motion is not a brute fact, not an ultimate in the nature of things. Material motion needs a causal explanation. Motion in the universe is not self-activating but needs accounting for. Matter is not self-activating. Aristotle believed that organisms have *self-motion*, but that this self-motion requires a motion or a cause outside itself to initiate its self-movement. All material motion has its source in an *eternal mover* that is itself unmoved. **4.** the unmoved mover did not cause movement in any physical way, such as by physical contact or physical action. Ordinarily, that which is moved is acted upon or reacts with that which does the moving. The unmoved mover is not an actively engaged principle of order—planning, purposing, directing, affecting the material universe—as was Plato's DEMIURGE. The unmoved mover moves things as an ideal moves or motivates a human being: by being the perfect object of desire or aspiration. The unmoved mover does not make motion, does not impart motion, does not sustain or maintain motion; it *elicits* motion. **6.** the unmoved mover moves things without itself being moved. It itself is not moved by anything else. Where the unmoved mover is regarded as pure self-motion as in 1.(b), it passes its motion on to all other things, but its own motion is not passed on to it from any other source. **7.** the unmoved mover is *pure actuality* without any potential for change, without any matter. It must exist solely as actuality because it actualizes all the potential motions in the universe. The unmoved mover is not actualized by anything else. It is self-actualized just as it is self-activated. Everything else is actualized by it. The unmoved mover is not in any way in a state of potential. Matter is always in some degree of potential for change and motion. **8.** as pure actuality, the unmoved mover is substantial and a primary substance, since it is able to move all other kinds of substances and is their ultimate source. **9.** the unmoved mover is immaterial, noncorporeal. It is spatially unextended. **10.** the unmoved mover is eternal. Material motion, physical change, is eternal so the actualized existence that is its cause must also be eternal. **11.** as the object of desire for all things the unmoved mover is good. **12.** the unmoved mover is unchanging and immutable, as is pure thought. **13.** the unmoved mover is an eternal, divine mind or thought and is the object of its own thinking and activity. Consider Aristotle's famous passage from the *Metaphysics:* "Thought thinks itself as object, in virtue of its participation in that which is being thought." See entries under SUBSTANCE referring to Aristotle.

use/mention distinction the *use* of a linguistic expression (term, word, symbol, etc.) refers to its occurrence in language in order to speak or communicate about something to which the expression refers or which it means. The *mention* of a linguistic expression (which can be indicated by using italics, or by supplying quotation marks around its written form) has to do with communicating something *about* the linguistic expression itself, and it therefore has a metalinguistic reference. Example: In the statement "*Virginia is strong* is a sentence with sixteen letters," reference is not being made to something beyond the sentence but *to the sentence itself;* mention is being made *of the sentence itself.*

utilitarian theory of punishment see PUNISHMENT, UTILITARIAN THEORY OF.

utilitarianism sometimes referred to as the *greatest happiness theory*, a systematic ethical theory first propounded by Jeremy Bentham (see HEDONISTIC CALCULUS [BENTHAM]) and his student John Stuart Mill. Its main tenets are: **1.** one should so act as to promote the greatest happiness (pleasure) of the greatest number of people. **2.** pleasure is the only intrinsic good, and pain is the only intrinsic evil. **3.** an act is morally right (a) if it brings about a greater balance of good over evil than any other action that could have been taken, or (b) if it produces as much good in the world, or no less good in the world, as would any other act possible under the circumstances. **4.** in general, the moral worth of an act is judged according to the goodness and badness of its consequences.

utilitarianism, act two central ideas: **1.** the moral worth of an act is judged according to the good (pleasant) or bad (unpleasant) consequences that are produced by each individual act judged in itself. **2.** at any given moment, act in such a way that your act will promote the greatest good of the greatest number.

utilitarianism, rule 1. the moral worth of an act is judged according to the good (pleasant) or bad (unpleasant) consequences that ensue from following a general moral rule of conduct, such as *Never lie*, *Never steal*, *Never murder*. **2.** act in accordance with the moral rule that brings more good (pleasurable) consequences than would another rule, or than would no rule at all. **3.** obey those moral rules that produce the greatest happiness of the greatest number of people.

utility, principle of sometimes referred to as the *pleasure principle* **1.** the doctrine that holds (a) pleasure and the absence of pain are in fact desired by all human beings, and (b) each person seeks his or her own pleasure. **2.** the doctrine that one ought to do that which brings about the greatest happiness (pleasure) to the greatest number of people, or to the community as a whole.

The *proof* for the principle of utility is founded on what is believed to be the undeniable, universal, empirical observation that everyone in fact desires pleasure, and since this is the case, it has to be admitted that pleasure is desirable and of paramount worth. UTILITARIANISM is based on the principle of utility in the following way: It is a fact that pleasure is desired and hence desirable. Every individual should strive to produce as much pleasure as possible for the greatest number of people (based on the implied assumption that in procuring the greatest amount of pleasure for the greatest number, one thereby procures pleasure, or the greatest amount of pleasure, for oneself).

utility calculus see HEDONISTIC CALCULUS (BENTHAM).

utopia (from Greek, *ou*, not, + *tópos*, place; literally, a land of no place, a never-never land) **1.** an ideal or perfect society. Plato's *Republic* and *Laws*, in describing the perfect or ideal state, present utopias. The word *utopia* was first used by Sir Thomas More in his book *Utopia* (1516), describing an imaginary island that had an ideal political, economic, religious, legal, and social structure. Others, since More's time, who have written utopias: Tommaso Campanella, *The City of the Sun* (1612); Francis Bacon, *New Atlantis* (1627); Morelly, *Code de la Nature* (1755); Etienne Cabet, *Voyage en Icaria* (1888); Edward Bellamy, *Looking Backward* (1888); William Morris, *News from Nowhere* (1890); and H.G. Wells, *A Modern Utopia* (1905).

Three distinct attitudes can be taken toward utopias: (a) they are visionary and ideal, but they can be approximated, if not fully achieved, in reality; (b) they are visionary and ideal, and they cannot be approximated in reality, although they may serve as standards for evaluation of existing societies; and (c) they are totally unrealistic visionary and idealistic schemes with no value whatever. See UTOPIAN. Contrast with DYSTOPIA.

2. the pejorative sense of *utopia*: a naive description of an unrealizable and impractical ideal state.

utopian 1. in the positive sense, referring to (a) a perfect or ideal society or to features of a perfect or ideal society, or (b) to a person who is a visionary or an idealist about a perfect society. **2.** in a negative sense, referring to an impractical, chimerical scheme of social regeneration that involves imaginary and unattainable perfections.

V

vague/vagueness not definite; not clearly defined or expressed, such as a *vague* word, concept, idea, or statement. A word may be said to be vague or to exhibit vagueness under any of the following conditions: **1.** when no agreement can be reached whether the word or its contradictory applies to a given situation, especially even when more factual information is obtained. Example: The word *bald* is vague in those contexts in which a decision cannot be reached as to whether or not to apply the word to a specific person. No rules are specified as to how many hairs a person must have on his head not to be called *bald*. More factual information as to the exact number of hairs on the person's head will not resolve the vagueness, since vagueness has to do with the imprecision and indefiniteness of the meaning of the word itself. When vague words are made more nearly exact, they lose the import of their ordinary language usage. **2.** when a word has borderline cases in its application and no determination can be made as to whether or not in that instance it should, or can, be applied. Examples: *bald, hairy, crowded, happy, race.* **3.** when the denotation of a word is not precisely known or ascertainable from its meaning or common usage and there is no definite way of delimiting or determining its application. Examples: *elderly, young, stiff, difficult.*

Vagueness is distinct from AMBIGUITY. In ambiguity, the two or more meanings a word has may be quite precise and definite. Ambiguity is not a problem of meaning but a problem of which meaning is being used in a given context. In general, vagueness applies to both concepts and words; ambiguity, mostly to words. Vagueness is also to be distinguished from *generality*. General statements need not be vague, and vagueness need not be associated with general words or terms. Vagueness is sometimes thought to be associated with the subjective meanings attached to a word and the unwillingness to admit an application for it. What one might call *warm*, another might prefer to call *hot*. But this is of secondary significance to a definition of *vagueness*.

valid (from Latin, *validus*, strong) **1.** justified; supported. **2.** not defective but correct. **3.** founded on truth or fact.

In general, a set of concepts or beliefs is said to be valid in the above three senses whenever it is coherent within itself, consistent with known and significant evidence, and fits in with other accepted concepts or beliefs. Contrast with INVALID.

valid (logic) a deductive argument is valid whenever its conclusion necessarily follows from the premises; *if* the premises of the argument are true, then its conclusion cannot be false; the conclusion too must be true.

valid inference see INFERENCE.

value (from Latin, *valere,* be worth, be strong) **1.** worth; the quality of a thing that makes it desirable, desired, useful, or an object of interest. **2.** of excellence; that which is esteemed, prized, or regarded highly, or as a good. The opposite of a positive value is *disvalue* (sometimes *dysvalue*) or *negative value. Good* would be a value and its opposite, *evil*, would be a negative value or a disvalue.

value, instrumental sometimes called *pragmatic value* **1.** the value a thing has in producing desired consequences or results. **2.** a value put on something that is used as a means of acquiring something that is desired or desirable. Instrumental values need not be of intrinsic value, but may be neutral or even intrinsically of disvalue.

value, intrinsic see GOOD, INTRINSIC.

value, theory of see AXIOLOGY.

value, utilitarian 1. the value a thing has in being useful for the accomplishment of some purpose. **2.** the value a thing has in promoting the greatest good of the greatest number.

values, objectivity theory of 1. the theory that values such as good, right, truth, and beauty exist in the real world and can be found as real subsisting entities, qualities, or relations much in the same fashion as we can find objects, qualities, or relations, such as *tables, red, bigger than.* **2.** the view that values are objective in the sense that they can be supported by careful and consistent rational argumentation as being the best under the circumstances.

values, relativity of the belief that (a) values are relative to social and personal preferences (attitudes, likes, dislikes, feelings, tastes, predispositions, etc.) conditioned by one's environment, culture, and genetic makeup; (b) values differ (radically in many cases) from culture to culture; (c) judgments such as right/wrong, good/bad, correct/incorrect, cannot be (and should not be) applied to them; and (d) there are not, and cannot be, any universal, absolute, and objective values applicable to all people at all times.

values, subjectivity of the view that values such as good, right, truth, and beauty do not exist in the real objective world but are personal feelings, attitudes, or interpretations of reality.

variable (logic) 1. any one of a class without the specification of any particular instance of that class. Example: p may stand for any statement, such as "Henry is a male." **2.** the symbol symbolizing 1. **3.** a symbol used as a substitute for statements, predicates, terms, objects, meanings.

variations, methods of concomitant see METHODS, MILL'S INDUCTIVE.

variety in unity refers to the qualitatively diverse or disparate parts of a whole, yet all of which contribute in their unique ways to the total unification or integration of the whole.

The lack of variety in unity is said to lead to such states as monotony and boredom. Continued repetition leads to lack of attention and interest. The lack of unity in variety leads to chaos and confusion. Compare with UNITY IN VARIETY AND VARIETY IN UNITY, PRINCIPLE OF (METAPHYSICS).

Venn, John (1834–1923) English logician and philosopher, born in Drypool, Hull; educated and taught at Cambridge. During the last 20 years of his life, he was President of Caius College, Cambridge; as Hulsean lecturer there, he published a moral, religious work entitled *On Some Characteristics of Belief* (1870).

Venn's work was chiefly in technical and philosophic logic, which is sympathetic to the writings of George Boole and John Stuart Mill. Some of his views: recognition of the problem of *existential import*—universal statements do not imply the existence of members for that class; stress on a variety of logics, each with its own systematic correctness and chosen because of criteria such as convenience, simplicity, correctness, and utility; emphasis on the empirical use of theories of probability, whereby the rational *belief* element is replaced by a concept of statistical frequency of occurrences logically related to their class of happenings and their properties, over a period of regularity and irregularity of their occurrence, and related to a series of tendencies within the parameters of small, running into large, numbers; and skepticism regarding the inductive method as being capable of arriving at precise knowledge—the inductive method is only approximate and not predictive in character.

Venn's major works include *The Logic of Chance* (1866); *Symbolic Logic* (1881); and *The Principles of Empirical or Inductive Logic* (1889).

verbal (from Latin, *verbum*, word) **1.** that which has to do with words. **2.** used in a pejorative sense: that which has to do only with words rather than with the issues or ideas that are involved. In ordinary language sometimes referred to as *verbalism*. See VERBAL DISPUTE. **3.** that which is expressed in written or spoken words. **4.** in ordinary usage *verbal* often refers to that which is expressed only orally and not written, as in *a verbal agreement*. **5.** sometimes used in ordinary language as a synonym for *literal* or *word-for-word*, as in *the verbal translation of the Greek phrase*.

verbal dispute sometimes called *definitional dispute, semantical dispute,* or *verbal problem,* a dispute caused by the meanings of the words or concepts being applied. Contrasted with *real dispute,* which is a disagreement regarding the facts or real issues of a situation. Example: The verbal dispute engendered by the question "If a tree fell in the forest and no consciousness existed to perceive its falling, would its falling produce a sound?" No real dispute exists about the facts of the situation. Any dispute refers to the meaning of the word *sound*. The answer to the question can be *yes* in terms of one meaning of the word *sound* (defined as the presence of physical vibrations whether or not humans are present) and *no* in terms of another meaning of the word *sound* (defined as the auditory sensation produced in a human). In order to resolve a verbal dispute, agreement has to be reached about the meanings of words to be used and not about the facts to which the words are to be applied.

veridical (from Latin, *veridicus*; from *verus*, true, + *dicere*, speak) **1.** truthful. **2.** characterized by truth. **3.** truth-indicating or truth-telling, as in *a veridical experience*.

Nonveridical experiences include hallucinations, illusions, delusions, and mirages. Such experiences are not used, and cannot be used, as sources of true statements about reality.

verifiability, principle of sometimes called *verifiability principle*, *verification principle*, or *principle of verification* **1.** strong version: A statement is meaningful if-and-only-if it is empirically verified. Compare CONFIRMATION, PRINCIPLE OF. **2.** weak version: A statement is meaningful if-and-only-if it is at least in principle empirically verifiable. Identified with logical positivism and logical empiricism. See MEANING, VERIFIABILITY THEORY OF; POSITIVISM, LOGICAL.

verifiability theory of meaning see MEANING, VERIFIABILITY THEORY OF.

verification 1. the process of determining the truth of a statement by empirical methods. **2.** the scientific testing of a statement to ascertain its truth. **3.** CONFIRMATION of a statement.

verity (from Latin, *veritas*, truth, reality, true nature of something) **1.** that which is true or real. **2.** the quality of being true or real. **3.** the conformity of a statement with fact, a truth or reality.

Eternal verities are truths (ideas) that are true, have been true forever in the past, and will remain true everlastingly. Usually they are known *A PRIORI*.

vicious circle argument sometimes called *PETITIO PRINCIPII* or *vicious circle proof* (in Latin, *circulus in probando*) a fallacious and/or inane method of arguing. An argument or proof that uses a statement (or a series of statements) S^1 to justify another statement S^2, which in turn is used to prove S^3 etc., until a last member in the series of logically connected statements is used to provide evidence for the initial statement S^1, and thereby the entire series is believed to have been completely proved.

vicious circle principle (Russell) the main principle in Bertrand Russell's theory of types, originally presented in his *Principia Mathematica*: Whatever involves all the members of a collection of things must not be considered as a member of that collection. Examples: "All generalizations are false"; that is, generalization about all other generalizations is not to be included as a member of those generalizations but is to be considered a higher type, or order, of generalization. "All red things are red"; that is, the class of all red things includes all red objects but cannot itself be considered as being red (as being a red thing or as a red class).

It is a fallacy to generalize about the type of all of whatever it is that we say are the types we are generalizing about. Thus, no whole or totality can contain members that are defined in terms of itself. See TYPES, THEORY OF.

virtues (Stoics) the principal or cardinal virtues in Stoicism are: reason, courage, justice, and self-discipline. **1.** reason, or intelligence, consists of (a) knowing what is good (the best, the correct, the proper, the most rational under the circumstances) and (b) knowing how to attain the good and/or avoid evil. **2.** courage consists of (a) knowing what to fear and what not to fear and (b) being able to control one's fear in the presence of a crisis. **3.** justice is (a) knowing how to be righteous, knowing how to give to others what is rightly due to them as individual human persons and members of a universal brotherhood and (b) knowing how to get from them in return what is rightly due to oneself. **4.** self-discipline (which incorporates both the notions of self-sufficiency and self-control) is (a) knowing which desires or drives to give in to and which to resist and (b) knowing one's reality without deception and illusion.

For the Stoics, the virtuous life is the only good but is unattainable without knowledge. The end of the virtuous life is the ideal of complete self-sufficiency and self-mastery of the individual living according to the harmonies of his or her inner rational nature and the corresponding universal rational necessity existing in the cosmos.

virtues, cardinal the highest ideals or forms of conduct in a given culture. All others are of secondary importance to them and are derived from them and/or depend upon them for their existence. Greek culture stressed four basic (cardinal) virtues: WISDOM or PRUDENCE, COURAGE or fortitude, JUSTICE or righteousness, and moderation or temperance (see SŌPHROSYNĒ). Christian teaching added the virtues of FAITH, hope, and charity or love (I Cor. 13:13).

virtues, dianoetic (Aristotle) also called *intellectual virtues* (*dianoetic,* from Greek, *dianoētikós*; from *diánoia,* the intellect) **1.** the intellectual (rationally thought-out) virtues or values. **2.** in Aristotle the phrase *aretai dianoētikai* refers to the values inherent in the awareness (and acceptance) of the rational principles which guide moral conduct. This is contrasted with the moral virtues (see VIRTUES, MORAL [ARISTOTLE]), which have to do with the everyday reasoned control of our sensitive and appetitive life. According to Aristotle, the rational part of the soul has two parts: (a) that which contemplates the unchangeable, universal, eternal principle of things; and (b) that which contemplates objects that are subject to change. The ARETĒ (functioning excellence) of the first is the intellectual virtue of SOPHIA, abstract wisdom (theoretical intelligence); the *aretē* of the second is PHRONĒSIS, practical wisdom (prudence, thoughtfulness, ability, and intention to do the right thing). See DIANOIA.

virtues, moral (Aristotle) those functioning excellences (*aretai*) of human conduct that are controlled by the rational part of humans. See ARETĒ. Some of the main points in Aristotle's ethical philosophy: **1.** moral virtues are achieved by means of a consistent practice that creates a habit of action. **2.** the principal ingredient in this process is the following of the mean between extremes. See MEAN, THE (ARISTOTLE). Extremes are to be regarded as vices. For example, the moral virtue of courage is the mean between two extremes: that of foolhardiness (rashness, stupidity) and that of cowardice (being overwhelmed by fear). **3.** an action is not in itself a virtuous action merely because it follows the mean. An action is a morally virtuous action because it conforms with, or is controlled by, reason. Insofar as that action conforms with or is controlled by reason, it will automatically involve a mean between extremes.

vital force sometimes called *vital impetus* or *vital principle*, a form of energy, regarded as unique and distinct from others (such as mechanical, chemical, or molecular) that is manifested in living phenomena and is the cause of life. Usually regarded as nonphysical. See ÉLAN VITAL.

vitalism in general, the belief that the activities of living organisms are due to a VITAL FORCE or vital principle that is different from other physical forces in the universe. Other names that have been used for this living force or principle are DEMIURGE; ÉLAN VITAL, ENTELECHY, NOÛS (PLATO), PSYCHĒ (ARISTOTLE). Vitalism has many things in common with HOLISM and organismic biology. All three contend that there is an ultimate, radical, and real dichotomy between living (organic) and nonliving (inorganic) phenomena. Some of the main beliefs of vitalism: **1.** the functions of a living thing are manifestations of a force (entity, substance, energy, impulse, impetus, *élan vital,* agent) that is within it. **2.** usually, this force is regarded as being nonphysical, invisible, and intangible, and as exemplified in the activities of living things. Some examples are striving to attain a goal, replication, self-regulation, self-repair, and consciousness. Such behavior, according to vitalists, cannot be explained in a purely mechanistic or materialistic way. **3.** living things cannot be reduced to a complex of inorganic substances. **4.** the vital force gives to living things special characteristics that are not found in nonliving things. **5.** most vitalists regard the force as possessing a unity of its own that can exist independently of the physical bodies to which it gives life. See EVOLUTION, EMERGENT.

void (atomists) the atomists (see ATOMISM, GREEK) accepted the notion of a void, an empty space or vacuum, and called it a *not-being* (a nothing) as opposed to a *being* (the self-moving, eternal, material atoms). The void possesses no qualities whatever, no powers, no potentiality, no existence in any way. It is regarded as pure empty space, in which or at which there is absolutely nothing present. The void is the place that atoms occupied before they moved to another place and the place that would be occupied by other atoms shortly. The atomists defended the void with arguments such as the following: Objects and the atoms of which they are composed could not move unless a void existed between the atoms. That a void exists in things is evidenced in that some objects can be compressed and some absorb liquids. In compression the atoms are pressed into the void existing between them. In absorption the atoms of a liquid enter into the empty interstices between the atoms of the object and occupy that void. It also is in reference to a void that things can be distinguished, separated, and classified.

Philosophers including Parmenides, Aristotle, the Stoics, Descartes, Leibniz, and Kant rejected the notion of a void.

volition 1. the act of willing. **2.** the power of willing. **3.** the use of the faculty or power of will. Sometimes used synonymously with *choice*, *determination*, and *preference*. See entries under WILL.

Voltaire, François Marie Arouet de (1694–1778) French writer, poet, playwright, philosopher, historian, moralist, free-thinker, polemicist, encyclopedist; born in Paris; educated in the classics and law at the *Collège Louis-le-Grand*. He spent the period 1726 to 1729 in England, where he read Shakespeare and most of the rest of the best in English literature; he also developed an intense admiration for Isaac Newton. His published *Letters on the English*, which appeared in 1733, after his return to France, express his admiration for the freedom of thought he had found in England and the rights of men of literature against the power of religious authority, the king, and nobles.

Voltaire's works are too numerous for more than a brief recounting here. Of his novels, *Candide* (1759) is known best. He contributed extensive articles to the *Encyclopédie*, which had been founded by his friends Diderot and Jean Le Rond d'Alembert. In 1764, Voltaire published the *Dictionnaire Philosophique*.

voluntarism (ethics) the belief that: **1.** the human will is the fundamental and ultimate ground in the making of moral decisions and in arriving at moral values. **2.** the human will is superior to, and must govern the other criteria for sources of moral worth such as conscience, the rational faculty, intuition, tradition, and the feelings.

voluntarism (metaphysics) the belief that: **1.** the will is the primary and dominant factor in all human experience and in all the processes of the universe. **2.** the will thought of as a force (primarily as analogous to the human will) is the cause of change everywhere. **3.** this will (in most cases) is a nondirectional, nonpurposive, spontaneous, and blind impulse inescapably immanent in all things and the root cause of their behavior.

voluntary action some of the characteristics included in the concept of voluntary action: **1.** a voluntary action is one that is caused by an inner mental event, such as willing (VOLITION), a drive, a desire, an interest, a motive, or a demand to choose. **2.** it is not done because of external compulsion but due to an inner compulsion. (In general an INVOLUNTARY ACT is caused by some event external to the agent.) **3.** a voluntary action is done out of intent and deliberation, and hence is a self-determining act. See ACT/ACTION; CHOOSING.

voluntary-involuntary actions actions that are caused by the agent himself or herself, by a self-determined inner COMPULSION to act (voluntary), but which are externally compelled (involuntary) against the true wishes of the agent and contrary to what the agent would do on his or her own. Example: obeying a captor's commands.

vortex theory (Descartes) also called *theory of vortices,* a theory shared by Cartesians and by occasionalists. Many of these ideas had their source in Greek philosophy. The main points: **1.** empty spaces or vacuums do not exist. A subtle matter (later called *ether*) fills the empty space erroneously supposed to exist, as in vacuums produced by pumps. See MATTER (DESCARTES). All space is occupied by something. No space can be unoccupied. Unoccupied space is a false appearance, an illusion, and a logical self-contradiction. **2.** the universe moves like a whirlpool (vortex), and the planets are like the objects carried by the movements of the whirl. **3.** by means of geometry and mathematical analysis (such as analytic geometry, which Descartes invented), explanations in accordance with the universe's whirl can be given for the coming into existence, the maintenance in existence, and the passing out of existence of all things in the universe. **4.** all action occurs by physical contact. Bodies are moved by other bodies by physical pressure, impact, and crowding. There is no such thing as action at a distance. **5.** the essence of matter is extension, to be inert (to be at rest), and to receive motion imparted to matter by God. **6.** matter of itself does not have the power to move. **7.** matter of itself does not have the power to remain in motion (even when once set in motion). **8.** matter of itself does not have the potential to move another body. **9.** God was the cause of all the motion in the universe at the moment of God's creation of the material universe. **10.** the quantity of motion (and matter) in the universe remains the same as that quantity that God imparted at Creation. **11.** had God not given matter (the universe) this motion, it would not of its own possess it, and matter (the universe) would be motionless. **12.** this motion is circular (vortical), geometrical, causally determined, and without final purposes of its own. See CARTESIANISM and OCCASIONALISM (MIND/BODY THEORY).

W

warranted assertibility sometimes called *warranted assertion*, refers to truth regarded as abstract knowledge secured by strict use of the methods of logical and scientific inquiry whereby a state of affairs that is somewhat confused and unarticulated becomes ordered and unified in our experience. The phrase is associated with the experimentalism and INSTRUMENTALISM of John Dewey.

ways, the five (Aquinas) see FIVE WAYS, THE (AQUINAS).

Weltanschauung (German, a world view) a comprehension of reality as a whole; the overview of a cosmology; a person's all-inclusive conception or perspective of things and life; sometimes given as *Weltansicht*. Examples: The hippie *Weltanschauung*, the socialist *Weltanschauung*. See WORLD VIEW.

Weltschmerz (German, world sorrow) a sentimental pessimism.

whatness see QUIDDITY.

Whitehead, Alfred North (1861–1947) British mathematician, logician, philosopher born on the Isle of Thenet, off East Kent, and educated at Cambridge, where he became, in 1884, a Fellow of Trinity College. He and his student Bertrand Russell collaborated on the 3-volume *Principia Mathematica* (1910–1913). He later taught briefly at the University of London and for many years at Harvard.

His major works, in addition to *Principia Mathematica*, are *A Treatise on Universal Algebra* (1898); *An Introduction to Mathematics* (1911); *An Enquiry Concerning the Principles of Natural Knowledge* (1919); *The Concept of Nature* (1920); *The Principle of Relativity* (1922); *Science and the Modern World* (1925); *Religion in the Making* (1926); *Symbolism, Its Meaning and Effect* (1927); *Process and Reality* (1929); *The Function of Reason* (1929); *The Aims of Education and Other Essays* (1929); *Adventures of Ideas* (1933); *Nature and Life* (1934); *Modes of Thought* (1938); and *Essays in Science and Philosophy* (1947).

whole 1. total and complete; refers to something that has parts and has no parts lacking. *Total* implies that all the parts of a whole are present as an aggregate. **2.** a unity or system, as in *an organic whole*. See GESTALT.

whole-part, principle of its main points: **1.** the explanation of a *whole* is not complete when only its constituent parts have been explicated or analyzed. A full explanation must take into consideration the interrelationships on many levels of the parts integrally interacting with each other and producing functions or activities unexplainable in terms only of the enumeration of its parts. **2.** a whole in itself has properties (characteristics, qualities) that are distinct from any of the properties that can be found in its parts and/or that cannot be found in any of its parts. In this sense the *whole* is regarded as being greater than the totality of its parts. **3.** the parts of a whole are so interdependent that a change in any one of them will bring about a change (a) in all (or some) of the other parts and (b) in the properties or functions of the whole. Compare with HOLISTIC EXPLANATION.

wholism see HOLISM.

will the power to control and determine our actions in the context of our desires and intentions. See CHOOSING; VOLITION; and entries under VOLUNTARY.

will, autonomy of the (Kant) the condition of the (pure, rational) will in which the will is guided (governed, directed, motivated) to choose *unaffected* by such things as consequences, results, ulterior ends, compulsion, fame, happiness, and pleasure for oneself or for others, but *affected* only by an obligation to the rational and universal principles (laws, duties) of morality. Opposite to ENDS, HETERONOMY OF (KANT). See ETHICS (KANT).

will, faculty theory of the the theory that the will is a FACULTY or a power of the mind that is able to cause itself to act in accordance with what has been chosen as the best way to act.

will, free elective (Kant) the will is not affected by feeling or emotion at the time of its action; feeling later gives support to the free elective will. See ETHICS (KANT).

will, the general 1. refers to an autonomous and sovereign personality (self, ego, will) regarded as possessed by society or the state that initiates and decides courses of action to be taken by its individual members or by a collection of them. Ideally, a conformity (harmony) should exist without coercion between the general will and the will of each individual (or the will of the collection of individuals, such as found in institutions). In this situation obeying the general will would in effect be obeying one's own will, and vice versa. **2.** the expression of the will of all; the unanimity of people about ethical, political, social, and economic values and goals. **3.** the general and objectively real public consensus that is (should be) the ground for making political and ethical decisions, without which consensus a society cannot function properly.

The general will is associated with the philosophy of Rousseau, who thought of it as the collective voice of the people to be respected and obeyed above all other authority.

will, the good (Kant) see ETHICS (KANT).

will and the understanding (Descartes) will is the assenting or the dissenting to some choice, desire, or truth; the faculty of willing is related to the faculty of understanding in that the understanding enables one to perceive the alternatives from which one can choose but itself cannot accept or reject, affirm or deny, a possible choice.

will and the understanding (Spinoza) Spinoza made no distinction between the understanding and the will. In his view, once the understanding has a clear and distinct idea, it is then impossible for the will not to accept it. For Spinoza the perception of truth is identical with having knowledge of that perception and with accepting it.

will to believe (James) the central points: **1.** belief in things for which there is no clear or conclusive evidence, or for which the evidence is not complete, is a human right and is necessary for intellectual and emotional adaptation to the exigencies of life. **2.** the will to believe in the absence of evidence is a reasonable and creative aspect of the mind, enabling decisions to be made and opening possibilities for discovery and commitment.

will to power (Nietzsche) the view that all human action is ultimately motivated by power and aims at control and/or superiority over others maintained and supported by power. The means and values used in this process are (should be) determined by the individual wishes and creative standards of the superman.

wisdom 1. prudent judgment as to how to use knowledge in the everyday affairs of life. **2.** the correct perception of the best ends in life, the best means to their attainment, and the practical intelligence in successfully applying those means. See VIRTUES, CARDINAL.

Wisdom, John (1904–1940) English philosopher; educated at Cambridge, where he later held the Wittgenstein chair in philosophy. In the tradition of analytic philosophy, Wisdom had the primary aim of redefining and redirecting the nature and purpose of philosophy. He believed, in so doing, that the usual problems and areas of philosophy would disappear, and philosophy would be seen as an analytic-linguistic tool for use in understanding such things as the ultimate source and structure of concepts and what we call *facts*. Wisdom's two important works are *Interpretation and Analysis* (1931) and *Problems of Mind and Matter* (1934).

Wittgenstein, Ludwig Josef Johann (1889–1951) Austrian engineer, mathematician, logician, philosopher born in Vienna and educated at the Technische Hochschule, in Germany, and the University of Manchester, in England. His engineering research concerned designing aircraft propellers and a jet engine. Intrigued by Bertrand Russell and Alfred North White-head's *Principia Mathematica* and by other philosophic work being done at Cambridge in the philosophic foundations of mathematics, Wittgenstein enrolled at Cambridge to study under Russell.

While Wittgenstein was a soldier in the Austrian Army, he finished a rough manuscript he had been working on for several years, his *Logisch-philosophische Abhandlung*, which was later included in the *Tractatus Logico-philosophicus* (1922). In 1929, he returned to Cambridge and was awarded a Ph.D. on the basis of his *Tractatus*. His oral examiners were Russell and G.E. Moore. (In 1937, he filled Moore's vacated professorship.) He lectured at Trinity College, Cambridge, from 1830 to 1936, when he took a year off to write his *Philosophical Investigations*, and from 1944 to 1947.

Wittgenstein's main works were compiled and published after his death from his notes and from lecture notes taken by students: *Tractatus Logico-philosophicus* (1922); *Philosophical Investigations* (1953); *Remarks on the Foundations of Mathematics* (1956); *The Blue and Brown Books: Preliminary Studies for the Philosophical Investigations* (1958); and *Notebooks 1914–1916* (1961).

Woodbridge, Frederick James Eugene (1867–1940) American philosopher of the naturalistic school of thought; modern Aristotelian realist; born in Windsor, Ontario, and came to the United States in childhood. He was educated at Amherst College, Union Theological Seminary, and at the University of Berlin. He taught philosophy at the University of Minnesota and at Columbia University, where he later served as a dean. His main works are *The Purpose of History* (1916); *The Realm of Mind* (1926); *The Son of Apollo: Themes of Plato* (1929); *An Essay on Nature* (1940); and *Aristotle's Vision of Nature* (1965; compiled and edited by John Herman Randall, Jr.).

word 1. a structuring of marks and/or sounds that retain their general form and the same or similar meanings at different times in the process of communication. **2.** an intelligible mark and/or an articulate sound that (a) symbolizes a meaning, (b) is regarded as an ultimate and independent unit of communication, and (c) is essential to the formation of a sentence. A word may have more than one meaning. A word may be syntactically classified in a number of ways such as noun, verb, adverb, adjective, preposition, or conjunction.

world soul sometimes called *world mind, world spirit* (all terms frequently given initial capital letters), the all-pervading immanent cause of order, life, and intelligence in all existing things, usually thought of on the analogy of the soul and its controlling and integrating influence on the body. The main argument for a *world soul*: The soul is the cause of order, life, and intelligence. Nothing that does not possess order, life, and intelligence can create something that has order, life, and intelligence, since *like* can only create *like*. Things in the universe possess order, life, and intelligence. Therefore, there must be a world order, a world life, a world intelligence—in short, a world soul—that is their source. See *LÓGOS*.

world view sometimes referred to by the German term *WELTANSCHAUUNG* **1.** the collection of beliefs (ideas, images, attitudes, values) that an individual or a group holds about things such as the universe, humankind, God, and the future. **2.** a comprehensive outlook about life and the universe from which one explains and/or structures relationships and activities.

A *world view* may be deliberately formulated or adopted, or it may be the result of an unconscious assimilation or conditioning process. It is the general perspective from which one sees and interprets the world.

X

Xenophanes (c.570–c.480 BC) Greek philosopher, born in Colophon, Ionia. He was a disciple of Anaximander and is sometimes claimed to be the founder, rather than Parmenides, of the Eleatic School of philosophy. He is best known for his criticism of the gods as having human qualities and form.

Z

Zeitgeist (German, the spirit of the time) the spirit of the age.

Zeno (of Citium) (335–263 BC) Greek philosopher, born in Citium, Cyprus; went to Athens in 313 BC to study philosophy. He soon founded the Stoic school of philosophy, so called for the *Stoa Poikile*, or painted porch, where he taught. Zeno was an eclectic and synthesizer, much influenced by the ideas of Socrates, Heraclitus, the Cynics, and the Megarians. His book *Politeia*, a *Republic*, outlined an ideal state that encompassed all humankind in brotherhood, tolerance, love of humanity, and acceptance of the rational laws of the universe predetermining all things toward a *good*.

Zeno (of Elea) (c.490 BC–?) Greek philosopher, mathematician, logician, linguistic analyst; birthplace unknown. He was a student and friend of Parmenides and known as a member of the Eleatic School—another famous member was Melissus. In Zeno's 40th year, during the early youth of Socrates, Zeno was in Athens, where he lived for many years, as suggested in Plato's dialogue *Parmenides*.

Zeno developed what are called Zeno's Paradoxes. Parmenides believed that the *one* was the only real existence; all else was illusory. The *one* was eternal, timeless, motionless, unchanging, immutable, indivisible, all-encompassing—all that there is, or was, or ever will be. Philosophers considered Parmenides' position about the *one* to be inconsistent. Zeno, by means of his paradoxes, attempted to show that the opposite position—that existence is composed of the motion and plurality of things in space and time—has inconsistencies far more difficult to resolve than Parmenides' philosophy of the *one*.

Zeno's paradoxes Zeno of Elea, a disciple of Parmenides, attempted in a series of arguments to disprove positions contrary to Parmenides' philosophy that only the unchanging *one* exists and hence nothing in reality can move. Zeno's arguments proposed to show that the concepts of *many* (plurality), *motion* (change), and *place* (space) were inherently contradictory, led to absurdities, and therefore could not be used to explain the universe and its phenomena.

The most famous of the paradoxes is the Achilles and the Tortoise Paradox, used to deny the existence of motion: If there is motion, then the slower (the tortoise) beginning first in a race will never be overtaken by the faster (Achilles). Achilles must reach the point to which the tortoise has already advanced. But during the time it takes Achilles to get to that point, the tortoise has advanced to another point. The tortoise may cover less ground; nevertheless, it is still advancing since it is not at rest. The distances between Achilles and the tortoise are successively less but without limit (on the assumption of the principle of the infinite divisibility of magnitudes that there are an infinite number of points between any two points). The tortoise will always have a lead regardless of how close Achilles gets to the tortoise. Achilles, though he is the faster, will never overtake the tortoise. This is an absurd conclusion, so the statement "Motion exists," from which it is derived is also absurd. See *REDUCTIO AD ABSURDUM*.

zetetic (from Greek, *zētēsis,* an inquiry, an investigation, a search for something) referring to the inquisitive (inquiring) quality of (a) the investigator seeking truth, and/or (b) the method of questioning used by the investigator. *Zetetic* is usually used in the context of a common search for an unknown truth. See DIALECTIC.

ABOUT THE AUTHOR

Peter A. Angeles received his B.A, M.A., and PhD. degrees from Columbia University, New York. He has taught philosophy at the University of Western Ontario, London, Ontario, Canada; Albert Schweitzer College, Switzerland; the University of California at Santa Barbara; and is presently teaching at Yavapai College, Arizona. He is Professor Emeritus of Philosophy at Santa Barbara City College, where he taught and was Chairperson of the Department of Philosophy from 1970 to his early retirement in 1990. He is the author of *An Introduction to Sentential Logic*; *The Possible Dream: Toward Understanding the Black Experience*; *The Problem of God and Critiques of God* (Ed.); *Dictionary of Christian Theology*; *When Blind Eyes Pierce the Darkness*; and numerous articles in scholarly journals.

He is currently living in Sedona, Arizona, and writing a *Dictionary of World Religions* and another series of 52 half-hour weekly children's stories for his radio show *Children's Story Time*; and is producing more of his one-act plays.